# In the
# Nature of
# Things

# In the
# Nature of
# Things

Language, Politics, and the Environment

Jane Bennett and William Chaloupka, editors

University of Minnesota Press
Minneapolis   1993
London

We gratefully acknowledge the following permissions: "Voices from the Whirlwind" by William E. Connolly was first published in *The Augustinian Imperative: A Reflection on the Politics of Morality* by William E. Connolly, copyright 1993 by Sage Publications, Inc., reprinted by permission. An earlier version of Shane Phelan, "Intimate Distance: The Dislocation of Nature in Modernity," was published in *Western Political Quarterly* 45:2 (June 1992): 385-402, reprinted by permission of the University of Utah, copyright holder. "Building Wilderness" by Wade Sikorski is drawn from material included by permission of the University of Alabama Press, from *Modernity and Technology: Harnessing the Earth to the Slavery of Man*, by Wade Sikorski, © 1993 the University of Alabama Press.

Published by the University of Minnesota Press
2037 University Avenue Southeast, Minneapolis, MN 55455-3092
♻ Printed on recycled paper (50% recycled/10% post-consumer)

**Library of Congress Cataloging-in-Publication Data**

In the nature of things : language, politics, and the environment /
Jane Bennett and William Chaloupka, editors.
    p.  cm.
    Includes bibliographical references and index.
    ISBN 0-8166-2307-4 (alk. paper). — ISBN 0-8166-2308-2 (pbk. :
alk. paper)
    1. Human ecology—Philosophy.  2. Philosophy of nature.  3. Human
ecology—Moral and ethical aspects.  4. Environmental protection—Moral and
ethical aspects.  I. Bennett, Jane, 1957-      II. Chaloupka, William, 1948-
GF21.I53  1993
304.2'01—dc20                                         92-47101
                                                        CIP

# CONTENTS

Introduction

# TV Dinners and the Organic Brunch

There has grown up in the United States in the late twentieth century a profuse and polyglot discourse about "nature." Profuse because the category "nature" encompasses so much—the geological, biological, and meteorological "environment"; animals and plants; human bodies; and the inherent character or moral essence we seek to discern in all of the above. Polyglot for the same reason.

Despite the diffuseness of its object, however, this nature discourse has a kind of structure. It has tended to revolve, at least until quite recently, around two poles, two sets of assumptions, priorities, dreams, and convictions. The first is displayed in a scene from Jim Jarmusch's 1985 film, *Stranger than Paradise*. In it, a young woman who has just emigrated from Hungary to New York sits in the 1950s-style apartment of her American cousin, a sleazy, small-time operator who is not particularly pleased to see her. Both are sullen.

> He: You sure you don't want a TV dinner?
> She: Yes, I'm not hungry. (pause) Why is it called a TV dinner?
> He: Uh. Spose to eat it while you watch TV. (pause) Television.
> She: I know what a TV is. (pause) Where does that meat come
>     from?

He: Whattaya mean?
She: What does that meat come from?
He: I guess it comes from a cow.
She: From a cow? It doesn't even look like meat.
He: (sigh) Eva, stop bugging me, will you? You know, this is the
    way we eat in America. I got my meat, I got my potatoes,
    my vegetables, I got my dessert and I even don't have to
    wash the dishes.

What *does* it mean that our meat bears no sign of once being something animate? That we call it by names different from the animal it used to be? Why would the sight of a whole dead animal on the table—a sight that was, up until the seventeenth century, appetizing to Europeans—now disgust and disturb us? Perhaps we mask the animal status of our food in order to mask our own link to the animal world: to forget that we, like other animals, die, decay, and eventually become food. Perhaps the sight of a whole dead animal on the table repels because it disrupts our self-image as the beings who transcend the merely natural, because it interferes with our attempt to define ourselves in contradistinction to the merely mortal.

You see, you got your humans and then you got your animals and plants. We construct a social world; they are sunk in a natural one. We exist in the realm of freedom; they in the realm of necessity. Humans are intrinsically valuable subjects; nature is a set of resources, raw material for culture.

But if this construction was convenient and even efficient, it also has proven to be unstable. The human body, for example, poses a problem for this set of definitions. Like a dead animal on the dinner table, the body is a beastly reminder. And so the body's affinity to meat must be disguised, its status as flesh concealed. Olfactory and visual evidence of digestion, sweat, defecation, arousal must be prevented or masked.[1]

Humans have long understood themselves in contrast to (and in the context of) the natural, the base, the animal-like. The play of disguises, of hide-and-seek, is an enduring cultural theme. But, even so, we find evidence (here and there, at the margins of the social scene) that the construction has developed and mutated. Consider the following recommendations, made in a seventeenth-century European book of manners:

It is not a refined habit, when coming across something disgusting in the street ... , to turn at once to one's companion ... and hold out the stinking thing for the other to smell, as some are wont, who even urge the other to do so, lifting the foul-smelling thing to his nostrils and saying, "I should like to know how much that stinks."

Or this fifteenth-century admonition:

> Before you sit down, make sure your seat has not been fouled.[2]

The premodern self needed these rules; we no longer do. We are more *civilized*; we have, that is, established more space between the human and the animal. Our threshold of repugnance for the animal-like has advanced—the body, like the physical environment, is to be subdued through science and technology, reshaped according to a conscious, rational design.

But to describe the contemporary orientation to internal and external nature in terms of repugnance and mastery is not to tell the whole story. There is more to this grid of stabilities and instabilities. As an external that we approach and avoid, "the natural" has also been constructed as a source of meaning and truth: something to be valued, cherished.

Sometimes these elements—body and other, meaning and instability—come together, visible to the astute observer. Consider, for example, Michel Foucault's reading of the commonsense notion that truth is lodged in one's gut:

> Part of the modern technology of the self consists in using bodily desire to measure whether or not a person is being truthful. "Do you really mean it?" "Are you being honest with yourself?" These are questions people have come to answer through trying to chart what the body desires: if your body doesn't desire it, then you aren't being honest with yourself. Subjectivity has become yoked to sexuality: the truth of subjective self-consciousness is conceived in terms of measured bodily stimulation.[3]

Consider, in this same vein, the appeal of holistic medicine, the belief that organic vitamins, fabrics, and foods are somehow superior to synthetic counterparts, and the condemnatory power of the claim that a practice or belief is "unnatural." Consider, in short, the presumption that what is natural is really real and even normal, that the structure of nature has existential and moral significance.

A more complete story of the contemporary orientation to nature, then, would say that although we try to master the environment and efface traces of nature in the body, we also regard them as indices of authenticity, as guides to the good. Another way to make this point is to say that "nature" has performed an identity function allied to an ontological one. Nature is the other against which the human is defined, the raw to the culturally cooked. But nature is also the original, the given versus the made, and as such it provides the comfort of an existential foundation. Nature in contemporary environmental discourse, then, is not only the realm of beasts but also of God, of what lies beyond or behind the precarious web of semiotic constructions. This prediscursive reality is assumed to be intelligible—how else could we distinguish between the authentic and the synthetic? And would not such a morally privileged complex of rankings, divisions, affinities, and antinomies offer profound guidance for a social and political order?

These two positions, symbolized on the one hand by the TV dinner and on the other by the organic food store, have structured contemporary nature discourse. The dominance of this pair is perhaps most apparent in the environmentalist sector of nature discourse, that is, in the debates regarding pollution, hazardous waste, acid rain, global warming, species depletion, and so on.

There are a great many environmentalists who adopt a modernist or TV dinner approach. The variety of policies they endorse—tax incentives for pollution reduction, user-fee schemes, government regulation—all display a faith that some rational plan, combined with new technical devices, will enable us to continue an aggressive, high-consumption course. For them, nature is a deposit of useful resources—or at least potentially one, for often nature must be reorganized before it becomes docile matter standing in reserve for human use.[4] Mountains must be mined, swamps drained, soils debugged, fruits irradiated. Sometimes this reorganization has undesirable side effects: pollution, unsightliness, health hazards. That is why the "standing reserve" must be used in accord with a good resource management plan.

Much that has been written about the environment by economists and political scientists falls into this category of "resource management." It presupposes a view of nature as morally insignificant matter to be mastered by technologically proficient humans. This view is, of course, hotly contested. For those environmentalists working within the holist tradition of deep ecology, nature is the original source of value, and only if we learn to attune ourselves to this morally significant order can we overcome the drive for mastery underlying our environmental problems.

Lately, however, new voices have entered the environmentalist debate, and nature discourse in general. They find the boundary between nature and culture—a distinction at the very heart of both the management and holist orientations—increasingly difficult to police. On the one hand, technology, a human creation, is more and more out of human control; on the other hand, nature is becoming more and more humanized. Artifice betrays the intentions of its designers, and the given buckles under the weight of the made. Langdon Winner makes the first point in his *Autonomous Technology*; Bill McKibben makes the second in *The End of Nature*.[5]

For McKibben, the idea of nature as independent, as not-us, "will not survive the new global pollution—the carbon dioxide and the CFC's and the like. ... By changing the weather, we make every spot on earth man-made and artificial."[6] McKibben laments this, for the very thing that could stop us from continuing to destroy the planet—a sense of the awesome autonomy of nature—is no longer possible. We find ourselves and our products everywhere we go: in the fire management strategies of the wilderness, in the recreation area rules for Walden Pond, in the mild temperatures of November.

Donna Haraway, who describes her writing as the attempt to "stage conversations on the fate of the riven categories of 'the human,' 'the natural,' and 'the artifactual,' " agrees that these distinctions have less and less purchase.[7] "Nothing really convincingly settles the separation of human and animal," she writes. All the tokens of human uniqueness—language, tool use, social behavior, mental events—are now currency for apes and dolphins and house pets. "Organic" sense perception is thoroughly enmeshed with "sonography systems, magnetic resonance imaging, artificial intelligence-linked graphic manipulation systems, scanning electron microscopes," to name just a few.[8] Moreover, because "our best machines are made of sunshine, ... nothing but signals, electromagnetic waves, a section of spectrum," there is less and less utility to the physical/nonphysical distinction.[9]

Haraway, however, repudiates the holist longing evident in McKibben's grief for the nature we have killed. McKibben is alert to the ways in which nature has now become cultural artifact; Haraway suspects that this has always been the case, that even preindustrial nature took shape by virtue of its location in a cultural project, in, for example, the myth of the Garden. In opposition to McKibben, Haraway affirms the late-modern experience of blurred boundaries between nature and culture; she identifies positive ecological and feminist potential there.

The essays in this volume arise in response to fears typified by McKibben and hopes typified by Haraway. They are skeptical of both the resource management orientation and its holistic alternative. They share Nietzsche's wariness "of attributing to [the universe] heartlessness and unreason or their opposites: it is neither— ... nor does it wish to become any of those things; it does not by any means strive to imitate man."[10] This book does not systematically review the established positions in nature discourse, but continually returns to the idea that these positions rest upon an appeal to nature either as ethical model or as pliable field of human action. The essays here explore the environmentalist implications of recent work that has thrown the very idea of nature as a founding center into doubt. They arise in the wake of an intellectual movement that has been called, variously, *poststructuralism*, *postmodernism*, *deconstruction*, but is probably better described by its interest in *rhetoric*—the ways language captures and constructs events, rather than merely "refers" to them.

Writers who take rhetoric as their first political question have made it difficult to ignore or deny the discursive character of nature claims, even as they insist upon the recalcitrant remainder or "wildness" in even the most human of creations, language. This insistence is often ignored by critics who ridicule the claim that "nature" is a discursive object—"Run yourself head first into that tree," they say, "and see if it's real or if it's a text." It is worth repeating, then, that the discursive position is in no way "idealist." That is to say, it does not deny the reality of physical, objective events in favor of some otherworldly ideal. Quite the contrary, the whole point is to make problematic transcendental appeals of social theory in order to ac- knowledge the inevitability of the resistances posed by "the world" to hu- man projects and projections. In the typically European terminology of this movement, the target is "metaphysics," the confidence that we will assem- ble a social theory that finally clarifies the meaning of human nature, nat- ural resources, and social relations, and thus renders them fully suscep- tible to control.

This third approach to nature discourse takes language very seriously, and finds it ever-intrusive upon our ability to talk or write transparently about the natural world's impact on the social and political one. Within this approach, social theory is seen to have had an underlying theme uniting liberals, conservatives, and radicals alike. That theme was the "logic" of na- ture. Instead of that dubious logic, our authors might substitute "rhetoric" or, more precisely, "rhetorics." Once one begins to see "rhetoric" where Western social theory had claimed "logic," the privileged form of nature discourse becomes interpretation, reading, disclosure of rhetoric-hiding- as-scientific-fact.

The "third way" we believe these essays begin to evoke is, thus, more eclectic than, say, the "deep ecology" approach. Some of the essays are more affirmative of the rhetoric focus than others, but all are informed by it. We celebrate the mix of modernist and postmodernist insights that the essays contain. We have in this volume tried to show that these two tradi- tions truly can speak to one another. Readers will find a range of takes on the increasingly important issue of alterity—on nature-as-other. Some of the authors take modernist approaches as their target; others blend mod- ernist and rhetorical concerns. Some are closer to Heideggerian analysis, feminist theory, theology, critical theory, or even botany. Some take classi- cal political theory texts as their starting point; others start from literary works, movies, or political and social practices, events, or strategies. What these authors have in common is that the phrase "nature discourse" catches them up, leading them to wonder how each term captures the other, and what that relationship means for political and social analysis—and for politics.

## Wildness, Artifice, Talk, and Ethics

The essays in the first section of the book explore the idea that nature is a place, a geographical site, and look at how notions of the "wild" or "wilderness" function in a variety of existential and political agendas. Each provides evidence that wilderness retains a privileged place in the metaphor and identity repertoires of even those Americans who construe themselves as *masters* of it. William Chaloupka and McGreggor Cawley study the role of site and space in the debate over wilderness preservation. Using this corner of environmental politics as a way to raise the issue of utopian political thought, they then suggest that the role of language has already been incorporated into this political question, even if in unrecognized ways. They find in Foucault's notion of heterotopia a basis for ongoing oppositional politics, even after the more utopian nature claims have lost their authority. Wade Sikorski offers a Heideggarian reading of the link between "wildness" and "dwelling," articulating an orientation to the world that lets one live a "gentle life, without invoking a metaphysics of principles, condemning judgments, or universal morals," which is to say, without some of the staples of environmentalist terminology usually used to endorse such gentle living. Shane Phelan examines the orientation to nature bequeathed to us from Rousseau and other state-of-nature theorists, compares it to a Nietzschean alternative, and then formulates a third ethic of "intimate distance."

We entitle the second section "Animal and Artifice" to mark the fact that these essays focus less upon nature as "environment" and more upon human and animal nature. Of course, this distinction between "inanimate" and "animate" is quite fungible, and the essays in this group are better described as exploring the problematic character of such boundaries. Michael Shapiro accomplishes this through a reading of the complex pattern of identity relations among humans, animals, and androids in *Blade Runner*, the film version of Philip Dick's science fiction novel *Do Androids Dream of Electric Sheep?* "When humans try to distinguish themselves from animals," Shapiro writes, "the primary strategy has been to locate humans in a meaning frame in which they have a capacity that transcends the merely physical. . . . However, in the confrontation with the cyborg, the strategy has been, in part, reversed, for cyborgs, it would seem, are machines; they have been made in contrast to humans, who are 'physical.' " Valerie Hartouni explores the natural/artificial distinction central to the debate about biotechnology. She exposes the recurrent influence of Aldous Huxley's *Brave New World* and shows how the fear that genetic engineering will make artificial selves obscures the extent to which we are already power-laden and "unnatural" beings. The artifice in the Shapiro and Hartouni essays is technology, science, and machine; for Jan Dizard it is law, regulation, and rights. Dizard's essay on deer overpopulation in the Quabbin reserve closes the section with an analysis of animal rights, hunting, and resource management discourses, and of the different boundary each draws between the given and the made.

The essays in the third section, "Environmentalist Talk," provide textual analyses of environmentalist discourse and look at the political economy of its structure. John Rodman examines the discourse of coastal dune restoration, raising questions about how we think and what we presuppose when we use the categories "native" and "exotic." Tim Luke presents a critique of "green consumerism" and the focus on recycling, arguing for an environmental ethic that does not focus exclusively on individual consumption but also locates responsibility in the social and economic structures that require high-consumption and ecologically irrational life-styles. Cheri Lucas Jennings and Bruce Jennings read the controversies surrounding organic produce and agriculture as a map of environmentalism's relations to race, imperialism, science, regulatory politics, and consumer practices. For them, the signs posted in supermarkets describing chemicals used on fruits and vegetables are "signs" of a larger order that includes some concerns and excludes others.

The essays in the last section, "The Order(ing) of Nature," again focus on the entwined fates of humans and nature, this time considering the ethical implications of a particular construal of nature. William Connolly juxtaposes two nature stories, the biblical tale of Job and the nineteenth-century memoir of the hermaphrodite Herculine Barbin. Connolly shows how the persistent assumption of a moral order in nature is part of a "politics of existential suffering" and how this demand for an intrinsic moral order fosters deniable cruelty in life. He articulates an alternative ethic where "the uncanniness and contingency of nature begin to sink into the presumptions of established practices." Rom Coles, drawing upon Theodor Adorno and Barry Lopez, offers a theory of ecological judgment, an "alternative way of inhabiting our terrains, in which self and what lies beyond are seen to belong together most profoundly," not because they form a harmonious system, but because their agonistic intermingling "is the wellspring of what intelligence, freedom, and fertility we can live and impart to the living earth around us from our bizarre position of awesome potential power." We end the volume with Jane Bennett's exploration of the political potential of one kind of "rhetorical" approach to environmentalism. Bennett focuses on Donna Haraway's nature tale and contrasts it with that of Thoreau. She argues that "the zeal to expose false harmonies and to denaturalize identifications also entails a risk—the risk of becoming prosaic, of forfeiting politically indispensable identifications and the ethical imagination inspired by wonder."

As diverse as this collection is, some elements are surely not treated as seriously as they could have been. The theoretical focus of the volume is Western, and its topics are mostly North American. The Western and American debate about nature is a complex and disharmonious one, and the essays included here challenge dominant Western conceptions by drawing upon resources within the Western tradition. Environmentalist politics now suggests a huge range of political practices and potential issues. The list included here—from wilderness preservation to reservoir management to biotechnology to recycling—only indicates that breadth; it does not attempt to catalog it. Although several of the essays—those by Hartouni, Connolly, Phelan, and Shapiro—address the intertwining of gender and nature discourses, and Lucas Jennings and Jennings focus on the interaction of race and environmental politics, much more could be said (and has been said well in other places) about the connections among gender, "race," imperialism, and nature discourse. In short, as much as we have included, much more is yet implied.

## Energizing Ecology

Among the groups in this country that have most enthusiastically embraced environmentalism, intellectuals and academics have been particularly visible. College towns abound in recycling programs, alternative energy experiments, bicycles, and health food stores. Courses in environmental studies have sprung up in a wide variety of disciplinary settings, including biology, chemistry, political science, sociology, and economics. To be sure, environmental issues abound in other settings, perhaps more vigorously. Native Americans argue about toxic dumps on their tribal lands. Residents of poor neighborhoods adopt environmentalist claims as a mark of community pride and as a defense against industrial practices allowed where they live, but not in wealthier parts of town. But the *words* of U.S. environmentalism—its terms and theoretical style—have generally been intellectual and scientific, so much so that the most enduring criticism of the movement involves the social status of its proponents.

At the same time, down the hall from the departmental recycling bins, another intellectual movement has been gathering momentum. Its locus has been the humanities. It attacks essentialist and foundational claims, exposing the exclusions and impositions they engender. And it exempts no such claims, even if they ground an otherwise politically attractive agenda, such as ecology. This critical movement throws the idea of nature and its alleged lessons into doubt more thoroughly and relentlessly than any positivism or skepticism before it ever did.

What happens to environmentalist concerns when the object of those concerns, the thing for the sake of which one speaks—nature, wild lands, animals—begins to lose its status as an object, a given, already set thing to which we can refer as if we were not involved in its construction? The essays in this volume offer a variety of responses to this question. We hope that serious readers from many backgrounds and orientations will find accessible and provocative grounds here for what promises to be a continuing inquiry into the human relationship to nature.

This collection received considerable help, beyond the diligent efforts and good humor of the contributors. We would like to thank Kathy Ferguson, William Corlett, and an anonymous reviewer, whose detailed and caring comments helped push the book toward its current form. We are also grateful for the help of the book's editor, Lisa Freeman.

Jane Bennett and William Chaloupka

## Notes

1. See Brian Key Wilson, *Media Sexploitation* (New York: Signet, 1976), chap. 5–6.

2. Norbert Elias, *The History of Manners: The Civilizing Process*, vol. 1, trans. E. Jephcott (New York: Pantheon, 1978), 131, 129.

3. Michel Foucault and Richard Sennett, "Sexuality and Solitude," *New York Review of Books*, May 21–June 3, 1981.

4. For a profound critique of the environmental management orientation, see Martin Heidegger, *Age of the World Picture* and *The Question Concerning Technology*, trans. William Lovitt (New York: Harper, 1977).

5. Langdon Winner, *Autonomous Technology: Technics Out-of-Control as a Theme in Political Thought* (Cambridge: MIT Press, 1977); Bill McKibben, *The End of Nature* (Garden City, N.Y.: Anchor, 1989).

6. McKibben, *The End of Nature*, 58.

7. Donna Haraway, "The Actors Are Cyborg, Nature Is Coyote, and the Geography Is Elsewhere: Postscript to 'Cyborgs at Large,' " in *Technoculture*, ed. Constance Penley and Andrew Ross (Minneapolis: University of Minnesota Press, 1991), 25.

8. Donna Haraway, "Situated Knowledges: The Science Question in Feminism and the Privilege of Partial Perspective," *Feminist Studies* 14 (1988): 581.

9. Donna Haraway, "A Manifesto for Cyborgs: Science, Technology, and Socialist Feminism in the 1980s," *Socialist Review* 15, no. 2 (1985): 70.

10. Friedrich Nietzsche, *The Gay Science* (New York: Vintage, 1974), #109.

# Part I

The Call of the Wild

Chapter 1

# The Great Wild Hope:
# Nature, Environmentalism, and the Open Secret

William Chaloupka and R. McGreggor Cawley

*We simply need that wild country available to us, even if we never do
more than drive to its edge and look in. For it can be a means of
reassuring ourselves of our sanity as creatures, a part of the geography of
hope.*

Wallace Stegner[1]

*But, I don't know, maybe somewhere I have some, not hope, but some
opening to the void. Maybe there will appear, out of the absence of
representations, some new events, even more fascinating than past events.
But we cannot create them out of our own will or representations. That is
sure.*

Jean Baudrillard[2]

## Nature and Discourse

In 1985, a dormant volcano erupted in Colombia, South America, leaving
more than 20,000 people dead. An earthquake rocked China in 1976, killing 250,000 people; another hit Armenia in 1988, killing 45,000 people; yet
another shook Iran in 1990, killing 29,000 people. In the United States,
Mount St. Helens and San Francisco serve as reminders that these occur-
rences are not as distant as they seem. What kind of twist in contemporary
sensibilities would be required for us to acknowledge a "need" for these
things, to find them "reassuring," to recognize our "sanity" in them? What
political maneuvers have wilderness advocates made, capturing this unruly
ground, claiming it with the unlikely (and colonial-sounding) name Stegner gives it—a "geography of hope"?

One response might impose categories: some natural events embody
"wilderness"; others denote "natural disasters." But this answer is more
treacherous than it seems. Wilderness, volcanos, and earthquakes are obviously different faces of the "natural world," a supposedly unified phenomenon praised as teacher, challenger, and exemplar by a long-standing
environmental movement throughout the world. In fact, hurricanes,

storms, floods, droughts, avalanches, and other "natural disasters" offer graphic examples of just how "wild" nature can be.

In contemporary discussions, wilderness becomes home to the vulnerable side of nature, the sites that need protection from human intrusion. The immodestly named National Wilderness Preservation System follows directly from that shift, bringing with it an extensive set of special management procedures. Conversely, more violent natural events are coded as "natural disasters" from which we must protect *ourselves*—a project typified by the (also immodestly named) Federal Emergency Management Administration's grants for "earthquake response plans." In California, state government helps underwrite insurance against earthquakes; it would not make quite the same sense to insure against wilderness.

Sometimes events challenge our ability to sustain these categories. Consider, for example, Yellowstone in 1988. Confronted with the worst fires in 300 years, since before European intervention, public officials quickly discovered how unstable these categories were. The ensuing policy debate, which was nearly as heated as the fires themselves, centered on the question of which category—wilderness or natural disaster—should be invoked. If the former, then fire appeared as a natural process needing "preservation" (i.e., unencumbered burns). If the latter, then fire presented a threat requiring an appropriate response plan. The Park Service's attempt to resolve the question by drawing a distinction between "natural" fires (i.e., lightening-caused) and "human-caused" fires only fueled the policy conflagration. As some critics were quick to note, in a sense all fires in Yellowstone are human caused; all are consequences of the large, mostly roadless, forest's having been carefully maintained in a fireless condition for decades. The debate over the Yellowstone burn policy amounted to a very public, visible allocation process that took years to settle.

The Yellowstone debate—and other aspects of the puzzling "politics of nature"—might begin to make sense if we focus on the categorization process itself, rather than on the supposedly unified and "natural" processes we submit to those categories. Although certainly "real" phenomena in the sense of a physical presence, wilderness, volcano, and earthquake are also *products* of the categorization process—of language and, therefore, of cultural practice. Rather than names for natural phenomena, "wilderness" and "natural disaster" offer codes for human relationships with nature.[3] These terms reference nature, but their aim turns toward society and meaning; in Baudrillard's terms, they are our attempt to create, out of our own will or representations, the Other we choose to encounter. In turn, the "politics of the environment" frequently involves an allocation of events into discursive categories (e.g., narrative genres). Europeans, for example, first encountered the Northern Rockies as obstacle. The trajectory of the

Rockies—first obstruction, then locus of (military, mining, and recreational) adventure, now evidently part of a geography of hope—is no simple advancement of sensitivities or development of knowledge about the natural world.

Embedded within the politics of nature there lies a way of speaking—a discourse—that precedes and preempts political responses to nature or calls to action on nature's behalf. This discourse privileges a view of nature's activism and agency. These presumptions extend back to the earliest moments of the emergence of modern political order, forming the basis for that emergence. A transaction with an activist nature has been necessary for democratic life ever since Hobbes first postulated a civic encounter with the wild sea monster, Leviathan. Throughout the history of Western political thought, nature has held promise for clarifying almost every aspect of human life.

More specifically, nature has continually been the preferred sign (symbol, code) for the justification of authority. This is a pattern established for modernity by Hobbes—the nature of the human organism, properly understood, justified coercive political authority. Descartes and his followers then completed the picture, implementing a modernist conviction that nature could be a passive, external target for an emerging rationalist and scientific gaze.[4] Once the pattern argued by Hobbes and Descartes was established, variations on it soon became a central basis for developments in Western political thought. When the link between the terms of nature and knowledge and the justification of authority became evident, nature quickly and effortlessly entered authoritative political discourse. To put it another way, it is remarkably post hoc to ask, Should trees have standing? Elements of nature, including trees, have occupied a privileged position for nearly as long as there have been people around to observe them, to appeal to them as a source of authority in political discourse, to speculate about hearing them fall in the forest.

Yet nature, like everything else we talk about, is first and foremost an artifact of language. As recent developments in literary criticism have made abundantly clear, language is not dependable. Trying to refer to things, language produces referents that tend to slip and disappear. As such, nature brought into political life, into language, can hardly remain "natural."[5] Therefore, any attempt to invoke the name of nature—whether apologetic or confrontational in relation to authority—must now be either naive or ironic. It can be anything but direct and literal.

The language of nature and Other implies inevitability at the same time that it covers our efforts to manage relations with an Other—something outside ourselves, something to confront or avoid or learn from or redefine. Calling wilderness a site for the Other—wildness, beyond culture—

has the simultaneous effect of diminishing other Others: most important, the Indian inhabitants whose claim to that natural land is so much stronger than that of the Europeans whose language this discourse adopts. Theories of the wilderness Other, including Stegner's geography of hope, repeat a pattern that is, as Tzvetan Todorov notes, precisely as old as the European presence in this hemisphere. Todorov's Columbus was intensely interested in Otherness, but it was primarily a feature of the land; "Columbus does not succeed in his human communications because he is not interested in them." Todorov cites Columbus's journals to document the explorer's posture in these "new" lands, his "summary perception of the Indians, a mixture of authoritarianism and condescension; the incomprehension of their language and of their signs; the readiness with which he alienates the other's goodwill with a view to a better knowledge of the islands he is discovering; *the preference for land over men*. In Columbus's hermeneutics human beings have no particular place." [6]

In this essay, we will investigate one of the key intersections where interpretations of nature, place, and U.S. politics convene: the political discourse of American environmentalism and, especially, wilderness advocacy. Contemporary literature on the environment and wilderness continually portrays nature as a "place" beyond the boundaries of human society, if still susceptible to the consequences of human activity. In pursuing that portrayal as something like a first principle, however, environmentalists frequently encounter ironies and ambiguities. Our argument begins with the claim that some of the confusion and frustration that result might be resolved by incorporating an alternate definition of "place"—a version of the relations among site, nature, and discourse informed by Michel Foucault's concept of "heterotopia."

## Heterotopia

The social sciences generally have little to say about "special places." These are "examples" or, even worse, merely "cases." Whether a set of behavioral laws or organizational patterns or institutional structures, there must be an explanatory principle under which each site fits—something must be exemplified at a site. Critics of social science deny that such principles operate uniformly, with few problematics arising in challenge. Poststructuralists, in particular, claim that these principles reflect a faith in (or a hope for) totality or even metaphysics as the basis for social scientific inquiry. At the same time, the rhetoric of social science, the terms in which social scientific pursuits of knowledge are phrased, has covertly abetted the operations of power.

Michel Foucault launched a particularized version of this attack on the social sciences, and one of his approaches relates to this question of "special places." Place (or space and propinquity) is crucial in our era, he argues, surpassing such organizing principles as time, force, and dynamics. "The problem of the human site or living space is . . . that of knowing what relations of propinquity, what type of storage, circulation, marking, and classification of human elements should be adopted in a given situation in order to achieve a given end. Our epoch is one in which space takes for us the form of relations among sites." [7]

Particularization—attachment to special sites and relations among sites—is an important poststructuralist strategy in the struggle against unproblematic, totalizing formulations of what knowledge might be. Foucault understood that utopia had long served as a characteristic treatment of *place* in post-Enlightenment knowledge. Utopia is a hypothetical place we evoke to produce critique or confirmation of some existing condition or institution. "Utopias are sites with no real place. They are sites that have a general relation of direct or inverted analogy with the real space of Society. They present society itself in a perfected form, or else society turned upside down, but in any case these utopias are fundamentally spaces." [8] Utopia, then, confirms (even if in the act of critique) the trope of analogy, and the confidence that goes with it; society can be represented in abstraction, and this is a credible form of social commentary.

Against this totalizing treatment of place, Foucault poses an alternate conceptualization, the heterotopia:

> There are also . . . real places—places that do exist and that are formed in the very founding of society—which are something like counter-sites, a kind of effectively enacted utopia in which the real sites, all the other real sites that can be found within the culture, are simultaneously represented, contested, and inverted. Places of this kind are outside of all places, even though it may be possible to indicate their location in reality. Because these places are absolutely different from all the sites that they reflect and speak about, I shall call them, by way of contrast to utopias, heterotopias. [9]

The heterotopia is not mutually exclusive in relationship to utopia; Foucault gives the example of the mirror as something that functions as both. What the idea of the heterotopia does is to express the importance for knowledge of special, particularized places—a move of notable importance for the poststructuralist response to social science and to society in general.

Foucault thought that heterotopias had long been established, in every culture. But the contemporary period privileges what he calls "heterotopias of deviation" where "individuals whose behavior is deviant in relation to the required mean or norm are placed," including the prisons and psychiatric hospitals Foucault analyzed so forcefully. Other kinds of heterotopias are disappearing from contemporary society, including "crisis heterotopias," which are "privileged or sacred or forbidden places, reserved for individuals who are, in relation to society . . . in a state of crisis." (Much of Foucault's work through the 1970s investigated the remnants of such crisis heterotopias, including the nineteenth-century boarding school.)[10] Heterotopia thus presents the spatial sortings and movements societies perform as an important part of politics. Places are created and identified, at tension with everyday space. Theorizing about utopia is only an abstracted, idealistic (hence simplified and unidimensional) version of a much richer, contradictory, political activity.[11]

By situating his studies of institutions in a spatial framework, Foucault implies that cartography might even be an appropriate model for social science. He reviews the cemetery as a heterotopia that has undergone a transformation, locating a change in social environment. But, in a spatial analysis, change also could be modeled by juxtaposition; the diversity of spatial relations necessarily implies that a heterotopia can be connecting "sites that are in themselves incompatible." "The theater brings onto the rectangle of the stage, one after the other, a whole series of places that are foreign to one another. . . . the cinema is a very odd rectangular room, at the end of which, on a two-dimensional screen, one sees the projection of a three-dimensional space." Another contradictory site is the garden, which "is the smallest parcel of the world and then it is the totality of the world. The garden has been a sort of happy, universalizing heterotopia since the beginnings of antiquity." Furthermore, "indefinitely accumulating time" can be the juxtaposition (of incompatibles) functioning as a heterotopia, in the example of the museum or library in Western culture.[12]

Heterotopias are not simply public space; they "always presuppose a system of opening and closing," some rules of inclusion and exclusion (even if that means compulsory attendance or seeming openness, in which cases the exclusion or inclusion operates covertly). Although Foucault elaborates little on this point, this rule-laden aspect of heterotopias no doubt emerges simply because of what they are (e.g., both spatial and special). This is another hint of the constitutive character of the relationship between heterotopias and human activity, in keeping with Foucault's view of the operations of power.

As is always the case in reading Foucault, we must guard against equating his (continually multivalent) talk of rules and functions with any simple determinism:

> Heterotopias . . . have a function in relation to all the space that remains. This function unfolds between two extreme poles. Either their role is to create a space of illusion that exposes every real space, all the sites inside of which human life is partitioned, as still more illusory. . . . Or else, on the contrary, their role is to create a space that is other, another real space, as perfect, as meticulous, as well arranged as ours is messy, ill constructed, and jumbled. This latter would be the heterotopia, not of illusion, but of compensation.[13]

Utopia, then, is only a pale version of an activity that actually happens in societies; for example, the spatial movement of people and rituals. The compensatory impulse (which hides, suppresses, renders invisible) reverses into its opposite polarity, an impulse to expose (to reveal and problematize). Political activity repeatedly displays an oscillation between these poles, and it quite often assumes this geographical (or architectural) basis; the utopian generalizations of nature, ideology, and the like come along after the politics of space have already happened. Utopia recalls this more generalized activity; heterotopia emerges from the specific, political activity of establishing sites and practices. Such special sites often bring together opposites in ways that allow us to work on those oppositions, and on ourselves. Brought together—either physically or as categories—diverse phenomena become discursive, practices are elaborated, and the special play of language, space, and context commences in an open, visible way. We could even say that, at the margins, these places *make* us; the relationships gathered there are our alternate "constitution." [14]

## Wilder-ness

We have summarized Foucault's treatment of heterotopia at length here because the politics of space seems to intersect with the environmental discourse at nearly every turn. A sense of place, as Samuel Hays argues, allowed environmental social theory to incorporate seemingly diverse concerns:

> It was this sense of place that undergirded not only the defense of home and community, on the one hand, and a pleasant and healthy workplace, on the other, but also the protection of natural environments at some distance from home and work that were thought of as integral to one's quality of life.[15]

Nowhere in the environmental discourse is attention to place more urgent than in the curious dialogue over wilderness.

Wilderness advocates presuppose that, at certain sites, the possibility of the Other can at least be imagined. However, these sites have to be preserved with a specific dynamic intact. They need to be countersites that enable the Other; at the same time, that Other must be incorrigible—it must be wild, dangerous, and fundamentally unpredictable. In short, wilderness is posited as an "other place" for use against a normal, everyday space from which one wishes to stand apart, to criticize.

Understanding these claims, critics of wilderness also frame their complaints in the language of place. Affecting the confessional style that has become a familiar genre in the wilderness dialogue, William Tucker explains:

> For a while I adhered to a rule of waiting to make important decisions until I could do it in a setting of hills and trees, completely isolated from everyday concerns. I finally gave it up when I realized that I was inevitably coming to the wrong decisions. Ideas that seemed crystal-clear in isolation always became muddled and complicated when put in a human context.[16]

Tucker's challenge here is not "against wild things, scenic beauty, pristine landscapes, and natural preservation." Instead, he takes exception to the allegation that "society itself is a 'cage' and that social relations are imprisoning. But wilderness still offers us a vista of hope."[17] In dispute, then, is not that wilderness offers sites beyond society, but whether or not those sites actually offer the promise of escape.

There are other, even more intriguing, twists in the wilderness dialogue. For example, Roderick Nash begins his famous history of wilderness preservation by noting the discursive character of wilderness:

> "Wilderness" has a deceptive concreteness at first glance. The difficulty is that while the word is a noun it acts like an adjective. There is no specific material object that is wilderness. The term designates a quality (as the "-ness" suggests) that produces a certain mood or feeling in a given individual and, as a consequence, may be assigned by that person to a specific place.[18]

Yet Nash goes on to warn that the "greatest long-term threat to the interests of people who covet the wild may reside in the *garden scenario*. It . . . ends wilderness, [even if] beneficially rather than destructively."[19]

It may not be surprising that wilderness advocates have strenuously opposed the idea of the garden. After all, the garden has heavily Christian overtones, implying that humans were given the gift of sovereignty over nature, and that we bungled that stewardship in a way redeemable only by faith—by submission rather than, say, politics.[20] Moreover, if we begin to see wilderness as a garden, we have already admitted that design can utterly encompass "nature," thereby exhausting the possibility of an "other" space—of a refuge from discipline.

However, there is also a sense in which Nash simply wants it both ways, and is willing to use any argument available to protect the wilds. At some points, wilderness has only to do with wildness; but at other points, management of very specific trees and mountains is at stake. Indeed, Nash even suggests that the *absence* of danger is what makes wilderness possible; activists had shown "that wilderness deserved a place within the totality of American civilization as one of its distinguishing and valuable assets. The wild no longer posed a threat to civilization in the United States."[21] All of this shifting could be read as a mature complexity of wilderness theory— Nash's reading—or, less charitably, as indication that good intentions provide cover for a variety of errors in that corner of American theory. Our reading takes a somewhat different path; the dichotomies and contradictions of wilderness theory are notable precisely for their reluctance to cohere, their pattern of resistances.

Here in the wilderness-garden we first glimpse a recurring theme of wilderness politics—the open secret. The problem with the garden is that it has been designed, and design is anathema at a site where the Other is supposed to be present. Wilderness is supposed to be the place where we escape from design, while still preserving the notion of a lesson (and its constant companion, the lesson *plan*). We know wilderness cannot be both Other and intelligible plan. To advocate wilderness policies and plans (a necessary form of advocacy in the contemporary political world) is to commit oneself to an open secret.[22] Advocates accept such plans as a sort of fiction, but they also insist that the plan's source is an Other available only at a specified, wild, site.

The open secret is not necessarily a weakness of the wilderness advocates, as long as it holds. It must remain open—available to every advocate, well enough known that the role of teacher is allocated to the wilderness countersite in political discourse. But that message must also remain secret—unspoken in any direct way—because it introduces a dangerous contradiction to that political message. This helps explain why a fairly arcane episode such as the debate over how to fight the Yellowstone fires was so controversial; it threatened to give away the open secret. To discuss the fires fully was to place issues of origin and agency in too visible a context, encouraging everyone to ask how so much authority could have been assembled in the name of a force—untouched nature—that was so problematic, given that this land had been so thoroughly managed for such a long time. The other side of the open secret is important, too; justifications cooked up by oil companies, timber barons, and even New Age church settlements for their claims on wild lands are frequently so silly that "wilderness theory" simply recedes as a point of contention.

Foucault notes that the garden has been "a sort of happy, universal heterotopia since the beginnings of antiquity," but it has also been a contradiction—smallest site and totality of the world. Holding these contradictions (happily) together is no small problem; it mandates a project enormously discursive and thoroughly artistic—conducted under the sign of the Other, but also in its absence. No doubt, Foucault is making a little joke in that formulation; the idea of a happy universalism is quaint or nostalgic, given the theoretical concerns of intellectual life after modernism's demise. As long as representation was a generally viable mode of political discourse, such little jokes were precisely that—small, and not particularly dangerous. Now, however, each such little joke opens onto issues of power and knowledge. The basis of wild country shifts and changes. The entire area of discussion becomes an open secret; wilderness is the site where we assemble in opposition, constituting ourselves apart, simply by our presence in the woods, apart from the city.

Remembering Foucault's rebuttal of utopia, we can do more with these issues of the Other, wilderness, and heterotopia. It should come as no surprise that Foucault is trading on the Nietzschean question of the Other; utopia stands for an ability to imagine a "no place" from which we could (imagine that we) stand apart, at a removed and critical distance.[23] Foucault's heterotopia argument shows how opposition and analysis persist, even if we abandon the ideal of utopia. This is an important conclusion, given the nearly constant complaint that poststructuralism plays fast and loose with a necessary basis of social criticism—that Enlightenment ability to stand apart (or its slightly different romantic variant). Armed with the analytic category of the heterotopia, all sorts of problematizing analyses remain possible: for example, we can trace genealogical transformations in particular kinds of places (as Foucault does with cemeteries); we can locate the emergence of new heterotopias (his prisons and hospitals) and the demise of others (sacred sites); we can discuss the political ramifications of the aesthetic (as in theaters, museums, cinema, and television).

With the heterotopia at hand, the romantic idea of wilderness (wilderness-as-utopia) begins to unravel. As utopia, wilderness must *stand for* an ideal, a transcendent category only *represented* in this or that location. In other words, wilderness must be the sign of nature, the wild, the Other—"out there," beyond design. Yet, wilderness itself—in its geographic specificity—cannot very well be this ideal. To ask a place to be both "no place" and sacred site is to ask a bit much, especially if the point of the exercise is to evoke what is natural.

Wilderness advocates try to escape this problem by narrowing and mystifying the core of "the wilderness experience." Thus, what is at stake is not a preserve or a garden where nature (and our control of it) can be reenacted; instead, the issue becomes the relationship with the wild. The actual wilderness utopia ceases to be the patch of land inside "wilderness boundaries," and becomes instead the *experience*: Nash's "mood or feeling," or Stegner's "means of reassuring ourselves of our sanity." Even if wilderness is a place—geographic, all too geographic, to paraphrase Nietzsche— "experience" could be utopian, especially if we devalue the narratives that actually bring that experience back to the city.

Yet, this romantic protest becomes more and more abstract—more hilarious, really—amidst the political scene that gathers around wilderness. Rather than providing opportunities to distinguish among wilderness, parks, and gardens, the activities of "wilderness managers" continually confuse the boundaries. In a society that designs, incorporates, and bureaucratizes as well as this one does, wilderness "parks" will be established, some with visitors' centers and rangers. This allocation carries some larger, cultural significance, in Nash's (urgent) judgment. Exactly where the garden ends and the nongarden (or antigarden, or the nature that the garden incorporates) begins becomes a matter for continuing negotiation. With each congressional hearing, however, any faith in the possibility that "the wild" is at stake becomes increasingly remote. Larger and larger issues are debated in euphemistic terms implicating smaller and smaller animals. Take the spotted owl. *Please*. Indeed, one hopes for dark humor here, because the alternative would seem to be that the whole discussion has become merely pathetic. There are other possibilities, however.

## Resistance

If there has been an interesting oppositional politics around the politics of wilderness—and it seems to us that this has been the case, at least intermittently—it may be that this politics makes more sense if taken out of the romantic or utopian mode. In other words, wilderness activists may have been doing something different from what they say (and think) they are doing. In fact, some of environmentalism's best actions have been heterotopic, self-consciously creating juxtapositions and alternate loci for withdrawal and opposition. Surely, this is the meaning of the enduring localism of the wilderness movement; each defense of each wilderness cites the virtues of that location, inviting people to visit, for example. These are not defenses of nature's signs, but attempts to preserve and heighten the power of each chosen site as a counterplace to contemporary society.

Nash admits as much by noting the connection between wilderness and the rise of the "counterculture" during the 1960s: "The counterculture inevitably found value in wilderness which was, after all, diametrically opposed to a civilization many had come to distrust and resent. . . . It followed that defending wilderness was a way of resisting the so-called establishment." A more precise intersection between these forces, Nash argues, came from Gary Snyder, who "associated the counterculture symbol of long hair with wilderness. The establishment, he felt, preferred trimmed, shaved, controlled hair just as it liked an environment ordered in the interests of man." Moving beyond the "passive escapists," Nash takes note of Edward Abbey, who characterized wilderness as a "refuge from authoritarian government, from political oppression [and] a base for resistance to centralized domination." [24] And in *The Monkey Wrench Gang*, Abbey offers a fictionalized account of what he means by a "base for resistance."

Building on Abbey's plot, another famous image is Earth First!'s filming of its members draping an image of a crack over the hated Glen Canyon Dam in Arizona. That act problematized the dam, fictionalizing it and literally marking it as a site of contention. Another famous image is Gerry Mander's magazine advertisement against dams that would flood the Grand Canyon, downstream a few miles from the Glen Canyon Dam. The ad asked whether readers would mind if someone flooded the Louvre. Comparing the Grand Canyon to a museum, Mander inaugurated a successful effort to preserve it as an oppositional site, or at least to problematize it. Each of these oppositional activities constitutes an alternate site as a strategy, and the goal of each strategy is to form a culture of opposition, drawing upon persons who now would question their old economies of habit, discipline, and obedience.

As heterotopia, wilderness may even begin to make sense. This is a real site, as contradictory as any real site will be, but with tensions exploited in a political culture hoping to preserve some remnant of sacred space, accessible only after arduous effort. Many of the best wilderness politicizations play with the ambitions of design by setting design against itself. Visited as heterotopia, wilderness is political, often a trickster's space: not actually natural (in the sense that any heterotopia is necessarily a cultural practice, even if located at a real space), but at tension with the modernist city anyway—the deliberately overgrown garden. Wilderness becomes a "space of illusion that exposes every real space," a ceremonial position taken willfully, at tension with modernity but also at tension with any romantic conception of the "natural." This is a remnant of Foucault's "crisis heterotopia," a reenactment of the Blackfeet sweat lodge or Nez Perce buf-

falo expedition that places itself outside—at tension with—the heterotopias of deviation that have long since captured or created discourses of
treatment, healing, and "wellness."

Taking this impulse to politicize space seriously, poststructuralists have
offered more spectacular claims, undermining the policy analyst's characteristic hope that this is merely a clash of goals, a matter for ongoing waves
of policy dispute and resolution. Jean Baudrillard has suggested that design, rather than nature, is the organizing principle of contemporary society. If that is the case, it would follow that "nothing escapes design":

> Everything belongs to design, everything springs from it. . . . the
> body is designed, sexuality is designed, political, social, human
> relations are designed, just as are needs and aspirations, etc. This
> "designed" universe is what properly constitutes the
> environment.[25]

In Baudrillard's view, there is no "nature" out there. Instead, the wild (especially when phrased as "environment" in this century) is a network of
messages and signs. Hence, "design and the environmental disciplines can
be considered as one of the branches of mass communication, a gigantic
ramification of human and social engineering. From this moment on, our
true environment is the universe of communication." [26] Of course, Baudrillard is speaking of "environment" in very broad terms, perhaps distinct
from, but no less broad than, the ways environmentalists would define it.

Narrowing that focus, we could ask, What would it mean, for wilderness,
if "our true environment is the universe of communication"? Carrying our
communicating, disciplined selves out to a wilderness escape, we find
functions and roles, even there. We find assignments, too; we are there to
relax, to recuperate, to report back that nature still exists, that it still
teaches lessons. All of these are functions of selves in a disciplined, controlled context, leading us to incorporate disciplinary practices as thoroughly our own. Baudrillard understands this, and rewrites it as a partici-
patory urge for wilderness, as one of his examples of "objective irony":

> Nature (which seems to become hostile, wishing by pollution to
> avenge its exploitation) must be made to participate. With nature,
> at the same time as with the urban world, it is necessary to
> recreate communication by means of a multitude of signs (as it
> must be recreated between employers and employees, between
> the governing and the governed, by the strength of media and of
> planning). In short, it must be offered an industrial contract:
> protection and security—incorporating its natural energies, which
> become dangerous, in order to regulate them better.[27]

The most fearsome possibility, then, may be the reverse of the one we had been worrying about. Having "preserved" wilderness in order to ensure that there would be an escape, "to nature," wilderness activists carefully neglected the possibility that there is no such thing as nature, at least in the sense that the liberal tradition of political theory has presumed. Reversing that error, Baudrillard can locate his "opening to the void," and can, as a result, write about the deserts of the American Southwest as eloquently as anyone since Edward Abbey.[28]

Indeed, at the very roots of the modern wilderness dialogue are indications that exhibit the falseness Baudrillard evokes. Writing in 1898, Sierra Club founder John Muir observed:

> The tendency nowadays to wander in wilderness is delightful to
> see. Thousands of tired, nerve-shaken, over-civilized people are
> beginning to find out that going to the mountains is going home;
> that wildness is a necessity. . . . Awakening from the stupefying
> effects of the vice of over-industry and the deadly apathy of luxury,
> they are trying as best they can to mix and enrich their own little
> ongoings with those of nature, and to get rid of rust and disease.[29]

Thus, even for Muir there is no native Other out there—no Native American, no alternate world, no confirmation or rejection of liberal social nature. What is "out there" is design, an unmistakable reminder that the world of communication, production, and work maintains its hegemony. In this case, then, Baudrillard's point coincides with Foucault's, but Baudrillard (as usual) is arguing from the "position" of an ecstatic, headlong rush against the utopian model of politics. Imagining a point apart would make little sense if that imaginary point had already been colonized, long since made a part of what the critic would like to oppose.

Having gambled a large stake on the liberating qualities of "nature" and "wildness," wilderness advocates face a disquieting possibility. Their "escape" might already have been domesticated, a disciplined locus for therapeutic treatment of "rust and disease." As James Bernauer explains, this encounter with limits that have proliferated the false sign of freedom is Foucault's central project, best realized in his attack on humanism, "the modern age's most subtle incarceration":

> Humanism represented the incarceration of human beings within
> a specifically modern system of thought and practice that had
> become so intimately a part of them that it was no longer
> experienced as a series of confinements but was embraced as the
> very substance of being human. The prison that becomes the
> special target of Foucault's criticism is none other than the
> modern identity of man himself. This identity is the center of that

humanism that is both a particular understanding of human reality and a technology for human development: a truth that is power and a power that exhibits itself as truth.[30]

Foucault's position suggests how we might elude such a trap, allowing room for analysis of a much broader range of political events. This preserves the possibility for that ecstatic contradiction to imprisoning power, which Bernauer argues is also a coherent, central part of Foucault's work. Heterotopia locates specific political activity; such a place may function as an escape or retreat, but it is not a free zone, sanctified by some metaphysical system that renders controversy moot.[31] It is not utopia; the relations brought together by societies when they create or transform heterotopias are diverse, even contradictory. Although one might issue authoritative moral edicts from a heterotopia, the interesting political move has already happened in constituting that space.

In other words, heterotopia could not be critical theorist Jürgen Habermas's place, for example. The heterotopia's diversity (as a real place) necessarily guarantees conflict and tension more thoroughly than even the most dialectical (if still Hegelian) social science ever could. Blocking each escape to an ideal space somehow beyond the space in which we live, the point is to focus on struggles that *can* be attempted. Foucault was neither liberator-at-large nor removed critic; he was not playing the role of the romantic—but neither was he submitting to imprisonment and despair.

Critics of wilderness protests such as Tucker object to the notion that "wilderness is a value against which every other human activity must be judged," but he would only find his judicial values elsewhere, in *human* nature. To be sure, the apologists deny any escape; what is less easily understood is that Foucault is not at Tucker's side. Despite the oft-repeated criticism that he offers "no escape," Foucault is actually displacing escape into its more particularistic form, problematization. The poststructuralist would not argue that the romantic (the hiker, say) is the *same* as the apologist (the miner, perhaps). But he would find them both held within a grid that makes their appeals to freedom, nature, and wildness ring false.

Wilderness heterotopia is an intervention into that grid—the spatial arrangement of sites of escape, as well as other reenactments. If wild places are sites where we (convince ourselves that we) might yet be undisciplined, free persons, the rapacious miner and the romantic hiker meet at that site, with the same hopes, on common ground. They take the message back to the city that we are all still free (having had a recreational escape, in one case; in the other, having provided for the material needs of free people). Both believe they have dealt with "nature," that they have expanded human limits, at least temporarily. By their commitments and practices, both sides of the wilderness debate routinely imply that the frontier can be reenacted continuously, that its closing can be overcome repeatedly, perhaps forever.

What has been framed as an experience with wildness, of crossing boundaries, turns out to have been a very civilized encounter, one that either creates "civilized" selves in the contemporary sense or searches for ways to oppose that activity. Rather than fleeing society, we may have fled to its mirror (in the sense that it is a recognizable but reversed image), to a microcosm site. Wilderness could be such a site, a place where visitors re-enact a familiar and special pattern. It is a pattern that recurs throughout our politics; the romantic (the escape, the natural) teases the conventional (the settled, the already agreed upon). As it turns out, the romantic, having already entered into discussion with the conventional, is no longer wild. The romantic ceases to be Other, at least in any recognizable form, and begins to offer testimony on how thoroughly Other can be incorporated. We signal such testimony when we try to talk about wilderness in terms of preservation, ethics, or legal status, thus diminishing the wildness that (supposedly) is its subject.[32]

At the heart of this pattern is an unavoidable conclusion: both "nonwilderness" and "wilderness" have been constituted. They make a system that promises coherence so convincingly that a national debate can sustain those categories, as is attested to by the arguments between James Watt and environmentalists.[33] Upon reflection, however, the categories collapse, and are seen to share a project; possible arenas for the exercise of power have been created, a site has been established where we can reenact "nature."[34]

Yet this reenactment is always confusing, constantly denying the confidence it seems to promise. More than a pure museum of hope, wilderness is a device by which hopes are made impossible, no matter what "choice" we think we are making. Rather than situating choice between large value systems, each symbolized by one or another stance toward nature, wilderness is a place where these "opposites" come together, each relying on the other. Wilderness can be a base for resistance (Abbey's hope) precisely because it muddles human relations (Tucker's complaint). At the same time, Tucker's complaint—which on its face is an apology for extractive industries—also refutes his utopian targets; as a discursive category wilderness cannot be an escape from the relations that delineate nonwilderness. Instead, as we have argued, the real wilderness story has revolved around an entirely distinct plot; in wilderness, as in a few other special sites, we have been learning to make selves.

## Conclusion

It is one of Foucault's most recognized accomplishments to have found compelling ways to bring attention to the processes by which the habits of self-disciplined individuals have been built. By working out the patterns we would use to talk about ourselves as disciplined, reflective, responsible, and hence "self-controlled" individuals, the discourse (e.g., about prisons) formed us, or rather produced the arena in which (and the rules by which) we could form ourselves. The mechanisms of this production were discursive (having to do with ways of speaking, with discourses) as well as institutional. The poststructuralist concern for the making of self is more than a psychology of habit. When one alters the notion of the constituent individual, the very roots of the state are at issue.

There is one last sense, then, in which the wilderness is importantly heterotopic; it is the place seemingly without institution or movement. Unlike the ship (which Foucault saw as a heterotopia of motion), the wilderness stays there, settled in as much as any sociological fact or social science or metaphysics could ever be. But the wilderness is supposedly beyond institutions. Government structures surround and envelope it, but they are presumably dedicated to keeping wilderness wild, available for a diversity of escapes.

To the extent that wilderness advocates have eluded the discourse of rationalism (in which one searches nature for solutions), they have done so as heterotopians, not as nature utopians. The liberal discourse—in which one looks for values to resolve differences—is also made problematic in the same move. The shape of the discussion—its rules and patterns—is altered, in a way that is radical. This is a necessary shift. Understood as Other in the contemporary debate, wilderness is too easily resolved into another obstacle, another problem for rationalism to resolve. As decades of environmental impact statements now attest, such "problems" quite easily transform environmentalists into mirror-image rationalists whose discourse is shaped by a search for mastery.

Wilderness-as-heterotopia, in short, highlights some problematic aspects of the ways environmentalists constitute themselves as political persons. Utopia and its negative twin, dystopia, are constructs of exteriority; under their sign, we are supposed to move ourselves by imagining external possibilities. Heterotopia reminds us of our role in assembling such externalities. Accordingly, such analysis destabilizes environmentalist self-identifications; by elevating "the land," the effect has been to diminish several other histories, most notably histories in which naturalistic terms conspire with hegemonic power to deflate the hopes of women, blacks,

Indians, and every group marginalized as the human Other. Further work on this heterotopic perspective would surely involve mapping such complicit self-constructions, which could be made more visibly self-protection schemes for hegemons-in-crisis.

Even though wilderness politicizers (on both sides, from James Watt to Muir's Sierra Club descendants) have often sought merely to rehabilitate utopian or romantic possibilities, there are other ways to politicize the environment. At the same time, the notion of a postmodernist environmentalism seems improbable. A preconception about the poststructuralists seems to stand in the way of any serious consideration of them by wilderness and ecology theorists; Foucault's political theory has been widely criticized as disconnected or duplicitous, for his refusal to argue a "basis" for the political critique he clearly does make. This complaint about Foucault is a variant on a critique made against poststructuralist politics in general.

The wilderness debate serves as a sort of singular example, grounds on which several theoretical issues can be more usefully addressed. Foucault's insistence on situating discourse in places—heterotopias, in the case examined in this essay—is a reminder of the specificity of all political debate. It is no evasion to argue that politics has long tended toward the particular, addressing a specific site and a localized nexus of authority and knowledge. When Foucault identified heterotopias, he reminded us of the places and grounds people have long chosen on which to contest power (or the fates, or whatever). With or without a metaphysics to govern every action, we still can (and do) choose such sites. The attachment of wilderness activists to specific sites carries some similarity to Foucault's move; their specificity is at least in tension with grand statements made on behalf of their cause.

Foucault's cartographic social criticism reminds us how futile it would be to choose no place. The flight from an ideologically sanctioned "critical distance" could hardly change that; politics happens from places and sites—constructed and privileged or deemphasized and repressed. A denial of critical distance is still issued from some place, and the privilege of that place may well be established by society, tradition, or some other source. To put this another way, it is obviously always possible for a cartographic political theory to stand apart, at a site removed. What would be odd would be a claim to escape place. But, just as obviously, such distance earns no privilege, other than what it can convincingly claim on the basis of what it finds at that site (or perhaps the arduousness of the journey to get there).

Moral and political choice can generate critique—perhaps an exposing of power, or of knowledge—from such places. The complaint that postmodern political thought cannot speak from such a place is, finally, coy and empty. What postmodernism abandons is a special claim of privilege to speak beyond a particular context, in the style now well established as modernist and ideological. The problem for wilderness advocates is almost precisely the opposite of the one that bothers postmodernists. Wilderness advocates have made too much of their sites (but only a little too much). Hoping to find nature's commands, they have sometimes missed the definitive struggle taking place *around nature*. Diminishing the hegemony of utopia, establishing the pervasiveness of site and locus as what continues in the political scene, Foucault had already, some time ago, completed the deconstruction of critical distance—not by abolishing distance (how could he have?), but by situating the critique where it has long occurred, even where it "belongs."

## Notes

1. Wallace Stegner, *The Sound of Mountain Water* (Garden City, N.Y.: Doubleday, 1969), 153.

2. Quoted in Eric Johnson, ed., "Baudrillard Shrugs: A Seminar on Terrorism and the Media, with Sylvere Lotringer and Jean Baudrillard," in *Jean Baudrillard: The Disappearance of Art and Politics* ed. William Stearns and William Chaloupka (New York: St. Martin's, 1991), 302.

3. To cite another example, earthquake scientists have long downplayed such objective measures as the Richter scale; the "severity" of an earthquake has much more to do with zoning, wealth, and time of day (during work, transit, or sleep times, for example). In that sense, earthquakes are thoroughly discursive and political; they arise as a consequence of how societies are structured. The much anticipated and feared New Madrid fault in the Midwest is important not for geophysical reasons—it would produce a small earthquake, in all likelihood—but precisely because people have not talked seriously enough about it.

4. Our thanks to Kathy Ferguson for reminding us of this connection.

5. Elizabeth Ann R. Bird raises a related concern in "The Social Construction of Nature: Theoretical Approaches to the History of Environmental Problems," *Environmental Review* 11 (Winter 1987): 255–64.

6. Tzvetan Todorov, *The Conquest of America*, trans. Richard Howard (New York: Harper Colophon, 1984), 33, emphasis added. The exclusion of the human Other is occasionally an issue among wilderness advocates. There are several current examples, including the ongoing collaboration between white environmentalists and some Blackfeet in a fight over the future of tribal lands near Glacier Park in Montana.

7. Michel Foucault, "Of Other Spaces," *Diacritics* 16 (Spring 1986): 22. Given recent interest in distinguishing the "stages" of Foucault's work, the editor's note to this essay may be of some interest: "This text, entitled 'Des Espaces Autres,' and published by the French journal *Architecture-Mouvement-Continuité* in October, 1984, was the basis of a lecture given by Michel Foucault in March 1967. Although not reviewed for publication by the author and thus not part of the official corpus of his work, the manuscript was released into the public domain for an exhibition in Berlin shortly before Michel Foucault's death (22n)."

8. Ibid., 24.

9. Ibid.

10. Ibid., 24–25.

11. We should mention that, although we are discussing Foucault's notion of heterotopia,

the themes and patterns of this discussion recur throughout his work. Specifically, the practice of critical theory from a position not validated by an ideal realm (either explicitly utopian or covertly so, in the form of rationalism) is a goal throughout Foucault's work. James Bernauer calls this practice "thinking from without," and elaborates it as the culmination of Foucault's intellectual journey. That such thought "must necessarily find itself in a realm of exteriority is, first of all, a recognition of the sovereign place occupied by language. Since it inhabits a world that is linguistic, human reality is rooted in an 'I speak' rather than in an 'I think.' The transition from one to the other reflects a displacement of reality from an interiority that had been considered sovereign for the experience of thought to an exterior realm of language within which man and his thought are now dispersed. This realm of exteriority represents the necessity for thought to operate outside of a strictly Kantian framework." James W. Bernauer, *Michel Foucault's Force of Flight: Toward an Ethics for Thought* (Atlantic Highlands, N.J.: Humanities, 1990), 58.

12. Foucault, "Of Other Spaces," 25–26.

13. Ibid., 27.

14. This play on *constituting* and *constitution* was suggested, in a different context, by Thomas L. Dumm, *Democracy and Punishment: Disciplinary Origins of the United States* (Madison: University of Wisconsin Press, 1987), 6, 10.

15. Samuel P. Hays, *Beauty, Health, and Permanence: Environmental Politics in the United States, 1955–1985* (Cambridge: Cambridge University Press, 1987), 529.

16. William Tucker, *Progress and Privilege* (Garden City, N.Y.: Anchor/Doubleday, 1982), 136.

17. Ibid., 134–35.

18. Roderick Nash, *Wilderness and the American Mind*, 3rd ed. (New Haven, Conn.: Yale University Press, 1982), 1.

19. Ibid., 380.

20. At the same time, wilderness advocates have long appropriated other aspects of Christian mythology, especially the notion of the vision quest into the desert, into wilderness. But that is another tension, another story.

21. Nash, *Wilderness and the American Mind*, 248. It is also useful to recall Thomas Dumm's discussion of danger in *Democracy and Punishment*: "In the modern era, danger has been internalized as a behavioral imperative" (p. 8). Perhaps the best of contemporary wilderness advocates have transposed the idea of the wild and dangerous, recognizing that whatever happens in the woods could hardly match the horror awaiting back on the job. "Fear, a disabling, incapacitating, paralyzing reaction to danger, constitutes a breaking point, a breaking off of the modern regime of truth" (p. 153).

22. Jane Bennett's version of Thoreau's "as-if stance" and Donna Haraway's postmodern version evoke a similar strategic encounter with nature. See Bennett's essay in this volume.

23. On this question of Nietzsche and other, see Peter Sloterdijk, *Thinker on Stage: Nietzsche's Materialism*, trans. Jamie Owen Daniel (Minneapolis: University of Minnesota Press, 1989).

24. Nash, *Wilderness and the American Mind*, 248, 252, 263.

25. Jean Baudrillard, *For a Critique of the Political Economy of the Sign* (St. Louis, Mo.: Telos, 1981), 198, 200–201.

26. Ibid., 200.

27. Ibid., 201.

28. Compare, for example, Jean Baudrillard, *America* (London: Verso, 1989) and Edward Abbey, *Desert Solitaire* (New York: McGraw-Hill, 1968).

29. John Muir, *Our National Parks* (Madison: University of Wisconsin Press, 1981), 1.

30. Bernauer, *Michel Foucault's Force of Flight*, 9.

31. Surely this informs Foucault's inclusion of pre-Enlightenment societies; not only the metaphysics of the Enlightenment but Christian ones also are problematized by this spatial politics.

32. Murray Edelman's discussion of the functioning of antidiscrimination laws could be applied to the effort to protect wilderness, as well: "The study of antidiscrimination laws furnishes an explanation of the counterproductive effects of many efforts to solve social problems. Legislation declaring it illegal to discriminate against people because of their race or their sex may deter some offenses, and there are occasional prosecutions; but it is hard to say whether such laws have had a significant impact upon discrimination, even in the rare cases in which they have been enforced resolutely. Sophisticated research on this issue concludes that regardless of the formal actions it occasionally generates, this form of legislation reaffirms the very differences in dignity and treatment it is intended to eradicate. The law defines the people it ostensibly helps as victims in need of protection. This sign of their debased status legitimizes the view that is already widespread, adding to the ideological pressures against effective enforcement of the laws. More important, it contributes to a low sense of self-worth in victims of discrimination and to the public impression of them as inferior." Murray Edelman, *Constructing the Political Spectacle* (Chicago: University of Chicago Press, 1988), 26.

33. R. McGreggor Cawley and William Chaloupka, "Federal Land Policy: The Conservative Challenge and Environmentalist Response," in *Federal Lands Policy*, ed. Phillip O. Foss (Westport, Conn.: Greenwood, 1987), and "James Watt and the Environmentalists: A Clash of Ideologies," *Policy Studies Journal* 14 (December 1985).

34. This site is not unlike another heterotopia mentioned by Foucault: "Quite recently, a new kind of temporal heterotopia has been invented: vacation villages, such as those Polynesian villages that offer a compact three weeks of primitive and eternal nudity to the inhabitants of cities. . . . the rediscovery of Polynesian life abolishes time; yet the experience is just as much the rediscovery of time, it is as if the entire history of humanity reaching back to its origin were accessible in a sort of immediate knowledge." Foucault, "Of Other Spaces," 26.

Chapter 2

# Building Wilderness

Wade Sikorski

*Mortals dwell in leaving to the sun and moon their journey, the stars
their courses, to the seasons their blessing and their inclemency, they do
not turn night into day nor day into a harassed unrest. Mortals dwell in
that they await the divinities as divinities. In hope they hold up to the
divinities what is unhoped for. They wait for intimations of their coming
and do not mistake the signs of their absence. They do not make their
gods for themselves and do not worship idols. In the very depth of
misfortune they wait for the weal that has been withdrawn.*

Martin Heidegger[1]

This quotation from Heidegger tells how dwelling lets the wildness of
things be, how it leaves to the sun and the moon their journey, the stars
their courses, the seasons their differences, and the gods their absence.
Leaving things alone, dwelling does not impose any truth on the thing that
is not its own, but lets the wild-erness of Being be. And it does this while it
builds a world, while mortals, man and woman, draw things near to their
life, handling them, dwelling amid them. Situated in time, life, and culture,
dwelling *builds* wild-erness, an anarchic, centerless, and nonmetaphysical
interpretation of the thing's thinging. Forgetting the authority of origins
and the morality of transcendent and universal truth, dwelling cultivates
difference, includes alterity, nurtures diversity, protects ambiguity, spares
multiplicity, frees irony, and makes it possible to understand it all as the
world's worlding.

In the pasture behind my home there are still traces of how an earlier
family tried to conquer the prairie, tame it, make it useful, and of the consequences they met when they failed. Just a ways down a creek full of cat-
tails and reeds, an old farmhouse, faded gray and falling down, stands near
a small pond and a dying tree. Beside it, barely visible through the growing
grass, are the foundations of other buildings, a granary, a blacksmith's
shed, a woodshed, and perhaps a barn. Further away, a line of rhubarb

plants still struggles against the prairie grass, probably near what used to be a garden. Further away still there is a shelter belt of aged and slowly dying cottonwood trees, maybe sixty feet tall.

People used to live here, now the cattle have pushed into their old home, seeking shelter from the winter storms. They have stomped the floorboards into the ground and rubbed against the supporting braces, knocking down walls and leaving strands of their hair on the nails that stick out. The brick chimney has collapsed, leaving a hole in the roof for the rain, the snow, and the wind to come in. Soon, the entire building will fall to the ground, leaving the cattle without a shelter.

The soil around this old farm is sandy. In the 1930s, when the drought and the grasshoppers came, it blew. Badly. Where there was once wild and lush prairie, a home to buffalo, prairie dogs, coyotes, and Indians, shifting sand dunes grew, rolling and crashing like a storm-tossed sea behind the plow used to turn under the prairie. Now, the grass grows only in clumps almost a foot apart, so fragile that you can reach down and pull them up by the roots with one easy jerk. The thick, rich sod of the prairie has been replaced by scattered desert plants, cactus and yucca. Only in the past few years have some of the worst blowouts grassed over enough to stop the blowing. Now, depleted, exhausted, this old farm is a winter pasture for our cattle; the people who lived here have left, probably for the city.

There are many old farms like this on my family's ranch in southeastern Montana. We remember them by the names we call places—the Chapman place, the Morton place, the Pepper place, the Blazer place, the Sawyer place, the Harris place, the Jones place, the Hough place, the Frankie place, and the home place. And perhaps there are a few places whose names we have forgotten. All of them were farms and homes that my family took over when the land would no longer support them. When I was a little boy, we had one of the largest ranches in Fallon County. Now, though we have sold none of our land and have even bought some, most of our neighbors are bigger than we are. Perhaps one day, following this "natural" progression, it all will simply become the Sikorski place, and the names of all the places we remember will be forgotten, like the names of all the places the Indians remembered.[2]

The Reagan administration, and now the Bush administration, following the truth of our time, calls this displacement progress. The inefficient and nonproductive are swallowed up and dis-placed by the more efficient and more productive, and the whole economy is made more rational as a result. Resources—human as well as nature's—are recentered, distributed, and used in a way that maximizes their utility for a global economy. Large scale is more efficient and more productive, more capable of rendering up nature as a resource for the economy, and so it is more rational. Who but a poet can be so sentimental as to doubt this truth?

Before writing my dissertation, I returned home from my graduate studies at the University of Massachusetts to my family's ranch in Montana and built an underground house on the south side of a hilltop near this old farm. I guess I was homesick. I suppose, being indebted to both Nietzsche and Derrida, that I should be suspicious of this feeling, but I could not avoid it. I wanted something to stay near, to be at home with—to stop the world from shaking. (Shall I confess now to an ambiguous relation to Derrida? I love the wild an-archy of his writings, but I also feel threatened by them. Where is there a place to live in his world, to build and dwell? To stay put? It seems to me that Derrida's wanderings duplicate the endlessly displaced revealing of Enframing [Heidegger's name for modernity].[3] For all his subversion of reason, hierarchy, and all centers of certainty, Derrida has not overthrown technology; he has fulfilled it. Endlessly displacing meanings, he has left us all homeless. And so there is a great and ironic truth in Derrida's writings.)

Accepting the postmodern summons for anarchy and difference, but also wanting to situate it, find a place for it, the examples that guided my building were the Arks that the New Alchemists had built—greenhouses that nurtured and supported a wide diversity of life, whose boundaries between "inside" and "outside," "wild" and "cultivated," were thoroughly transgressed. Inside, the Arks duplicated, by means of cultivation, the wilderness the outside represented, but lacked.[4] Seeking to live a life that was my own, free of the demands of reason and economy that had ruined so much of the land I was raised on, wanting a home that would not be displaced by something far removed from it, I turned to Martin Heidegger and Henry David Thoreau to guide my thinking. Looking for a home when the whole world seemed lost and homeless, I built to keep my life, my home, and my thought from being displaced by the logic and imperatives of Enframing.

By putting together what Enframing had torn apart, by re-placing building and thinking and dwelling, by situating my thought in my life and my place, I hoped to recover from my homesickness. Perhaps Thoreau thought it all for me when he went, as he called it, home to the wilderness around Walden Pond to sort the irrupting, anarchic, and possibly mean experience of life out from the distant demands modernity has imprisoned it in and let it be:

> I went to the woods because I wished to live deliberately, to front only the essential facts of life, and see if I could not learn what it had to teach, and not, when I came to die, discover that I had not

lived. I did not wish to live what was not life, living so dear, nor did I wish to practice resignation, unless it was quite necessary. I wanted to live deep and suck out all the marrow of life, to live so sturdily and Spartan-like as to put to rout all that was not life, to cut a broad swath and shave close to drive life into a corner, and reduce it to its lowest terms, and if it proved too mean, why then to get the whole and genuine meanness of it, and publish its meanness to the world; or if it were sublime, to know it by experience, and be able to give a true account of it in my next excursion.[5]

Building somewhat more luxuriously than Thoreau because I wanted to build more permanently, the earth-sheltered house that I built cost only about $6,000 for materials. With a little help from my family, I did most of the work myself, from designing it, digging out the hillside, mixing and pouring the concrete, and erecting the walls to doing the wiring and the plumbing and the finishing. When I was through a year later I had a family-sized house and greenhouse that, using only passive solar heat, seldom went below 60 degrees on even the coldest and windiest of Montana's winter days.[6] Unlike Thoreau, I have had less luck feeding myself with the food that I grow in my garden, because a series of exceptionally severe droughts produced a plague of grasshoppers that have stripped my garden to bare ground several years in a row. Someday I hope to build wind-powered electrical and water systems to make my house completely independent of the utilities.

In this age when our planet's doom seems almost assured, when the world's industrial economies threaten the entire biosphere with the twin perils of the greenhouse effect and the depletion of the ozone layer, when the ecologically essential forests of the Amazon are being mowed down to provide profits for the fast-food industry, when the topsoil of almost every country in the world is eroding many times faster than it is being rebuilt, when the number of species becoming extinct is comparable only to the Great Extinction that ended the age of the dinosaurs, it seems like a pitifully small thing to build a house that does not need utility heat. And perhaps it is. Perhaps I should instead be engaged in a desperate politics of reform and protest, maybe even revolution. Time is so short. And there is no promise that the Turning will come in time to spare the earth or humanity.[7]

And maybe, too, Derrida is right. You can't go home because home is always already different from itself, from the way it was supposed to be. (And I must admit, from personal experience, that home is an elusive place, always beckoning, promising—and never what it is supposed to be.) I still don't know if home, a place where things are safe, is ever possible.

But I do know that its promise of safety calls out to me, has a pull on me I cannot refuse. There must be some way to build home, to situate life, and live in peace by saying, at least for here and now, that this thing is so and that thing isn't. Home is the only place where that can be said, I think. Donna Haraway agrees with me, at least to some extent.[8] Only partial vision, limited voice, and situated knowledge do anything that matters. Disembodied knowledge, unlived truth, and genderless science reveal nothing because they are *connected* to nothing. They are not alive. To act in the world and make it better you have to be someone, be somewhere, tied to institutions, related to people. And be limited by that body, place, and time. You have to have a place, a home.

Even though there is desperate need for worldwide change, limited by the knowledge my place makes possible, I hesitate to legislate the law of other places. To provide, at last, a solution to our problems. Maybe that, after all, is *the* problem—trying to control things by displacing ourselves from them, by invoking universal and timeless dualities, this one good/that one bad, and subjecting ourselves to their dis-placement. That is the prison our metaphysical archy-itecture of science, reason, principles, and morals has trapped us in. It has made us homeless by dis-placing the truth of our body, our place, our culture, our hopes and dreams, our frustrations and despairs. They are merely "subjective," which is to say, irrelevant and meaningless. Untrue. Instead of a situated knowledge, we must offer universal and objective critiques, judgments, condemnations, and promises of salvation,[9] even when the philosophies underlying them are purely materialistic, as in Marxism or Freudianism.

Seeking universal foundations for action by separating the knower from the known, then building a discursive archy-itecture that supports itself with rejection, marginalization, exclusion, and control, modern critique conventionally leads us to separate our life from ourselves and our place on the earth and put everything under the governance of a politics of cold distance—of rules, systems, laws, principles. Things have to be the same for everyone, everywhere. That is what meta-physics is, after all, the submission of the *physis*—Greek for nature or earth—to something above it, beyond it, to something it is not—usually reason, logic, or principle. Building the archy-itecture of universal reason, eternal truth, and unqualified technology, we reject the an-archy of our place, our home, our life, the earth itself, and put ourselves beyond them. And our lives become governed by things far removed from our own home—our cares, fears, loves, and needs. Caught in the discursive archy-itecture of Enframing, we become homeless.

When time is short and the earth is dying it seems like we should do something—a dictatorship of ecologists maybe? Tempting, too tempting.

But perhaps it is especially when time grows short that there is need of careful thought—thought that is freed from the archy-itecture that has built the systems that, having removed themselves from it, endanger the whole earth. Acting, I suspect, without turning away from Enframing's reason and technology and ceasing to live and think it will only assure that everything will be rebuilt once again as it was, even under a dictatorship of ecologists. If it survives the archy-itecture of Enframing, humanity will build and live differently, will think first of home and act first locally. It will learn to respond with care to the earth, the sky, the sacred, and the death of all mortals, instead of a reason that is far removed from the earth. The thoughts of Enframing must be deconstructed where they are the most secure, in the lives of we mortal humans who build and dwell, in our dependence on the institutions and systems that trap us in Enframing's networks of technopower, its bipolar hierarchies, and the reign of monstrous others it produces that displace us from our lives. Until this turning is freely done in each of our lives, until thinking is free of Man's[10] reason, nothing, I suspect, will change, no matter how much we will it.

Freedom does not come by making the world conform to our prescriptions, demands, and chosen imperatives, but only with a gentle release toward Being, with a meditative listening to the whisper of the world worlding as it happens at home. Then, as an-archists repudiating the archy-itecture of reason, ideology, technology, methodology, and principle, we build and dwell in a way that does not destroy the earth. An-archy is the way of Being following the Turn, the way in which the thinker lets the wilderness of things be. The way we come home.

The wilderness, or anarchy, of Being is not the opposite of civilization, as it has long been characterized in the Western tradition, virginal, unhandled, inhuman, untouched, but rather a building that we dwell in, that we have built because of what we, as earthly and mortal beings, are. In Being's wilderness we do not strip away our earthly connections, our belonging with human and nonhuman others in biotic communities, becoming a lonely outcast in the world's vastness, at last free of ourselves, but rather we find a place where we learn of our life's connections with our earthly situation, with the others and shadows we think we are not, resituating ourselves in the community of life we humans have long tried to escape.

In going into the wilderness, which is as easily found in the city as the vast rain forest, we are going home because wilderness is the place where we recover the things that are most ourselves, but that we have denied, repressed, forgotten. Building wilderness is a lot like interpreting dreams. In doing it, we encounter the surprise of contingency, an otherness that is not really so other because it is our own Being. A returning of the other, it is a place in our life that reminds us of our ties to the earth and our place on it. As such, it is a life governed by the situated ways of thinking and love, not by the distant summons of morals, principles, or reason. To dwell is to build a place to think of love, care, and peace—and, unavoidably, their others too, for they too are needed to build a world.

Surprisingly, the Old English and the High German word for building, *baun*, means to dwell, to remain, to stay in a place, according to Heidegger.[11] The original meaning of the verb *bauen*, namely, to dwell, has been more or less lost to us. But in the word *neighbor*, in Old English *neahgebur*, a trace of it remains. *Neah* means near and *gebur* means dweller—near-dweller. Not only does the old word *baun* tell us that to build is really to dwell, it also suggests what dwelling brings forth—Being. In German, the old word *bauen* is also related to the words *bin* and *bist*. Thus, *ich bin*, I am, and *du bist*, you are, mean not only that we are, but that I dwell, you dwell. We live; we have a place that we live at, the world worlds because we are there. The way in which you are and I am, the way in which we, as mortal Beings, are upon the earth, is as dwellers. To be a mortal is to be a dweller, a Being whose life is built amid a place on earth. Living, we build a world for ourselves, tend for it, care for the people and things that share it with us. Even such things as "nature," "the gods," "humanity," and "death" are buildings, names for the thoughts that we dwell amid, construct our world with. The world worlds when we build, dwell, and think.

Building also means, though less commonly now, to cherish and protect, to bring forth as a preserving and caring, and especially as a cultivating and nurturing of the earth. For example, after many years of careful work, after a farmer has cultivated a rich layer of humus in his soil, he says that his soil is built. As cultivating and nurturing of the abyss, building is an open and responsive caring that brings forth the gods. Making possible any interpretation of the world's worlding, it takes place before them and seeks their blessing and their gifts in a bountiful harvest. To practice the art of agriculture, as the past of the word suggests, is to cult-ivate the favor of the gods, to bring their message forth, to attend to the earth that conceals it, and to abide with the truth brought forth.[12]

But not all building is tending to the soil, since ships and temples are also built. This distinction does not, however, mean that building as cultivation and building as construction are two different things, contraries that must oppose each other. As ways of making things, both modes of building bring forth, cultivate and care for, the sacred ones that govern dwelling.[13] All thoughts, names, words, or things are buildings, care-ful constructs made for the purpose of dwelling. Building is always world building, and, whatever is built, it is done in poetry, prayer, and song.

Even in these, the darkest of times, when the gods have fled, poetry is an embarrassment, prayer a superstition, and song an industry. When Enframing darkens the world, building as artful cultivation is eclipsed and building as willful fabrication guided by the universal imperatives of technological efficiency comes to the foreground, concealing any way of knowing mystery and beauty. "The earth and its atmosphere become raw material. Man becomes human material, which is disposed of with a view to proposed goals."[14]

This is a decisive occurrence: dwelling is no longer experienced as humanity's Being, a way of living in the world.[15] Instead, harnessing the whole world to its cold and de-secrating logic, it becomes a slave to Man's distant economies and imperatives, and all possibilities for the wild anarchy of the world's worlding are concealed. Even so, this silence that conceals the poetic and sacred character of dwelling can yet be listened to, heard beneath the distracting noise of modernity's archy-itecture of definitions that it builds in the service of Man's reason.

If we cultivate this silence, this flight of the gods, Heidegger says, we can still hear the calling amid our life's cares that calls us to think building as dwelling, to spare, venerate, and free the wildness in our being on earth, and to understand building as a cultivating of the abyss. Without foundation, essence, or universal reality, the abyss is the true ground, the earth on which our world is built. It is necessary to acknowledge this in our thinking before our building is free:

> The word for abyss—Abgrund—originally means the soil and
> ground toward which, because it is undermost, a thing tends
> toward. But in what follows we shall think of the Ab- as the
> complete absence of ground. The ground is the soil in which to
> strike root and to stand. The age for which the ground fails to
> come, hangs in the abyss. ... In the age of the world's night, the
> abyss of the world must be experienced and endured. But for this
> it is necessary that there be those who reach into the abyss.[16]

If we reach into the abyss that now conceals the poetry in building, we come to understand that we dwell not because we have built, have erected houses, bridges, and roads, but we build and have built because we dwell, because we cultivate the (absent) gods in our thinking, because we are, as living mortals, possessed by the summons of poetry and prayer as they rise up singing from the abyss.[17] Just as we cannot speak language, master all its ambiguities, and subject it to our will, but must yield to its appropriation of our being, allowing it to speak us as the void we are, so too we build only because we dwell, only because the song of poetry has already gathered us into the absence that governs the thinging of the thing.

"But in what," Heidegger continues, "does the nature of dwelling consist?" [18] To answer we must again follow language back into its home. According to Heidegger, the German word for dwelling, *wohnen*, has its roots in the Old Saxon word *wuon*, and the Gothic word *wunian*, which both, like the old word *bauen*, mean to remain, to stay in place. But, unlike the word for dwelling that later developed into the English word for dwelling, the Gothic word is more descriptive of how this dwelling is experienced. *Wunian* used to say to be at peace, to be brought to peace, to remain in peace. As Old English did once too, the German language said peace with the word *friede*, now meaning the free. Long ago, the word *free* was associated with what was loved and called for protection from harm and danger, safeguarded in its nature. To free means to spare, to love, befriend, and care for; to spare not only in the negative sense of not harming what we love, to not set upon it as a means, a tool, a way to will the will, but also, and more important, in the positive sense of leaving something beforehand to its own ways, actively, thoughtfully, lovingly, preserving it in its peace, keeping it safe in its serenity or tranquility. Leaving their being wild, in other words, free of any archy-itecture that would deny them their place, their home.

To dwell, then, in its most profound sense, is to preserve things in their peace, to spare them actively from anything that might disturb them, make them different from what they are, as a lover would a beloved, a mother her child. As dwellers, our calling, as Heidegger has described it from time to time, is to be the "Guardians of Being," the friends of the world's worlding, the lovers of the earth's wilderness. The fundamental way of dwelling, even in this destitute time of the world's night, is this nurtural sparing and preserving that accepts things as they are—despite their wildness, their difference, their contrary nature, and allows them to become what they will.

Gently unassuming, dwelling builds no centers that demand the submission of everything in the world to principle, ethic, or law. And so it is not anthropocentric, or even biocentric or ecocentric. The haunting wail of the coyote, the timid wanderings of the rabbit, the predatory hunger of the wolf and the bear, the graceful leap of the deer, the awesome complexity of the whale's song, the formidable hiss of the mountain lion, the soaring arch of the eagle—all of these are buildings that house the world's differences.

And because the world is built of them, the thinker loves all of them as they are, without judgment, evaluation, or reservation. And she will in turn build a way to dwell in peace with them. Throughout its whole sundering breadth, the acceptance of the friend, the foresight of the wise, the care of the lover, and the courage of the hero pervade dwelling, determining its whole way of Being, which is the stay of mortals on the earth, under the sky, before the gods. To dwell, Heidegger argues, is to gather things together—the earth, the sky, the gods, and the life together of mortals—and accept each, however different, however other, as a part of the dwelling place, keeping safe the peace of the world.

The earth, the sky, the gods, and the mortals are the different aspects of the world's worlding. Worlded by the world's worlding, mortals dwell by sparing and keeping safe the oneness of and the alterity of things, earth and sky, gods and mortals, that happens in the fourfold occurrence of things. As Heidegger says: "Thinging, the thing stays the united four, earth and sky, divinities and mortals, in the simple onefold of their self-united fourfold." [19]

As the fruitful womb of all that rises forth as plant and animal, that irrupts with rock and water, and yet takes it all back again in death, decay, and time, the earth is the wild and concealing darkness, the fertile mystery hiding the truth of things in dark obscurity.[20] Says Heidegger, "Earth is the building bearer, nourishing with its fruits, tending water and rock, plant and animal." [21]

Earth is what the early Greeks thought as chaos. Chaos, according to Vycinas, was not the mindless disorder that we think now under the reign of reason's archy-itecture, but the open abyss, the wild nothingness, the groundless ground, the womb from which things rise up and appear of their own mysterious unknowable nature.[22] Physis, as the mystery and power of the earth that brings things forth, brings them forth from the earth's concealment.[23] For Heidegger the earth, as physis, is not an object of utility, a universal truth, or a timeless foundation, but a *way* of Being, the way it is when it is concealed when a world worlds. Despite its unfathomable anarchy, despite the innumerable ways it can be, it, like the other parts of the fourfold, is a building, a construct of dwelling and thinking brought forth by a world's worlding. The source of the wilderness of Being, the earth keeps and safeguards the seeds of things that, in their own way and time, rise up into the sky to be greeted by the gaze of mortals and drawn near to the bounds of the holy.[24]

The sky, as the horizon surrounding the places of mortals in their life upon the earth, reveals things as they present themselves in the different worlds of mortality. "The sky is the sun's path, the course of the moon, the glitter of the stars, the year's seasons, the light and dusk of day, the gloom and glow of night, the clemency and inclemency of the weather, the drifting clouds and the blue depth of the ether." [25] All these things that appear under the sky appear in the nearness of mortals. The world worlds the nearness of their life, travails, movements, and gods they pray to. Gathered beforehand into the world's worlding, the horizon changes with their wanderings, and things rise up in their presence and fade into obscurity with their passing.[26]

According to Heidegger, "Mortals dwell in that they receive the sky as sky. They leave to the sun and the moon their journey, to the stars their courses, to the seasons their blessing and their inclemency; they do not turn night into day nor day into a harassed unrest."[27] The way the world worlds when it is unconcealed, the sky is sky only because it stands in contrast to the earth, its other. What the earth brings forth, the sky reveals. The alterity between earth and sky is the contrast between Being as the abyss and Being as presence, between concealment and unconcealment. Dwelling is letting this otherness, this difference be in whatever way it is worlded.

The Gods are the buildings, the truths, that gather mortals into their care, the messengers bearing myths that surround and govern the life of mortals with the reality of their dwelling. They are the bearers of the holy, the truth, which bounds the comportment of mortals to the things that appear under the sky, on the earth. Says Heidegger, "The divinities are the beckoning messengers of the godhead. Out of the hidden sway of the divinities the god emerges as what he is, which removes him from any comparison with beings that are present."[28] Even in a destitute world, a time marked by the flight of the gods, the absent gods still, by being the other to mortality, provide the limits and truth of mortal relations to things. How they bring them forth, how they use them; even what they are, how they are known. The flight of the gods means that mortals cannot have a free or peaceful relation to things, but yet things still are and that means that the absent gods still govern the way that we cultivate things, build worlds, if only in their absence.[29]

According to Vycinas, a god for Heidegger is not as we Christians know them, a supernatural entity that reveals its presence in a miraculous or unnatural intervention, but is instead more like the early Greeks knew them, as truths that are revealed in the ordinary way of things, never against them. For the Greeks, a god does not have to disturb or distort nature to be known, but rather is known as the truth of nature. A god is not above nature, outside it, or apart from it, but is in it and finds its way through it. As a result, Greek thinking (before Plato) did not de-secrate nature as Christianity has since Augustine, withdrawing the holy from it, but rather it revealed the holy through it.

A god is a world, a building that gathers things into it, providing them their place and interpretation, even when they present themselves in sundering dispersion. Because the Greeks knew many gods, they knew many worlds or ways of Being, and were present in them all simultaneously—ambiguously, tragically, ironically. Because the truth, the way of Being, or interpretation, surrounding it is different, the thing is different in each world because it houses a different god.

Night, for example, in the world of Artemis and night in the world of Hermes are different buildings because they disclose different truths. Since Artemis is the goddess of wild and unexplored nature, her nights are frightful and mysterious,[30] and since Hermes is the god of luck, thieves, and gamblers, his night is an advantageous or disadvantageous cover for one's pursuits.[31] Similarly, love, as a truth of Hermes, is a matter of luck or opportunity, a pleasant occurrence because it brings nothing with it but itself, while as a truth of Aphrodite it is a blissful unification, breaking all bounds and inviting sudden tragedy because it overwhelms conventions, ethics, and responsibilities, bringing with it scandal and disgrace.[32] Gods do not specialize in a portion of nature—Apollo the sun, Aphrodite sex—as we Christians think; they house all things in the world and they reveal their mystery through them all.

A god for Heidegger is the gathering, the building or the circling boundary, that holds things in their place, making possible an interpretation of them. A thing is because it houses a god; it is what it is because it houses a particular god, even though its nature may be something entirely different if a different god is invoked. "Nature" was never a fixed essence or foundation for knowing things, but a building that was continually remade as the god housing it changed. As a result, the reality of a god never, for the Greeks, hinged on their power as causes because they were known not as nature's puppet master but as strife-torn truths bringing forth the realities of things. The gods were nature—in all its ambivalent modes.

While the gods are the truths of all things, mortals are the measure of all things, their death the possibility governing the building of all things—even the gods and nature. Their mortality, their death—which, as a terminal nothingness, beckons to them all their life long—brings them into the world, forcing on them a need for building that moves them near to the earth, and makes them responsive to its irrupting wilderness. The prospect of death calls us to our home, our earthly Being, concealing the difference between humanity and earth while revealing it. Says Heidegger, "The mortals are the human beings. They are called mortals because they can die. To die means to be capable of death *as* death. Only man dies, and indeed continually, as long as he remains on earth, under the sky, before the divinities." [33] Summoning them to their lives made of earthly belonging in anxiety and dread, death gathers mortals up into the world, situating them, limiting them, compelling their attention, making their life whole, holy, complete, meaningful by making them accept their calling as the Guardians of Being.

For mortals, death is the shrine of nothing, an empty void that nevertheless is, that, in its nullity, in the care it imposes and demands in our life as dwellers, governs the presencing of things. As something radically other to it, it presents the mystery of Being itself, the astonishing presence of the thing, and it is the measure of every mortal life, the conclusion that calls us to our truth, to accept the earthly summons of dwelling and thinking. Death governs our building, situating us in our limits, and setting us to our work.

But even while we are building, living our earthly life, says Heidegger, "man is allowed to look up, out of it, through it, toward the divinities. The upward glance passes aloft toward the sky, and yet it remains below on the earth. The upward glance spans the between of sky and earth. This between is measured out for the dwelling of man." [34] The world and every thing that comes from the earth is as it is because as mortals build things they anticipate the nothingness of death, and against it ground the earthly presence of the thing as a reality in their life. The earth's irrupting finality, death, governs all humans, confining them to the sky's horizon, under which things rise up from the earth, bounded by the sway of the gods. Death calls on humanity to dwell upon the earth, under the sky, before the gods.

Anticipating their death, caring for their life, building the world, mortals dwell in saving the earth, setting it free. They do not seek to master it, to subjugate it, to tame its wild ways, in order to make it a slave to their thoughtless whims. Mortals dwell in receiving the sky as sky, and they dwell when they let the earth bring things forth in its own way. Mortals dwell in acknowledging their situation and their limits, and accepting death as their fate and living life in the face of death.[35] Mortals dwell in seeking a good death, a life that matters. But they do not darken their days with gloomy meditations on their end, nor do they make death their goal, argues Heidegger. The prospective moment when the earth possesses all mortals body and soul, death is the guide of mortal life, the place where the earth irrupts and asserts its sway, determining how things will present themselves. Connecting mortals to the earth, it is the guiding concern that determines how a thing is to be done, whether it is to be done or left undone. Death is the shrine of Being, and mortals dwell through acknowledging its presence in their lives, through accepting the cares it imposes.

Dwelling occurs in saving the earth, in receiving the sky, in awaiting the divinities, in initiating the mortals. In building a home. It is the fourfold preservation and sparing of the fourfold, the setting free of the thing into its own differences. Dwelling preserves the thing as it rises from the earth, and mortals dwell in letting things be in their presencing. Mortals do this by nursing and nurturing the things that grow and carefully constructing the things that do not grow. Seeking to secure the fourfold in things, to let their earth be itself, mortals build, bringing forth in their cultivating and constructing their dwelling place.

In the second part of "Building Dwelling Thinking," Heidegger gives some examples of what the relationship between building and dwelling is. The first is of bridges, which are buildings that gather a whole world together—the economies of life, the beauty of the sky, the changes in the weather, the connections between places. A bridge is a building that unites the fourfold. He says:

> Always and ever differently the bridge escorts the lingering and
> hastening ways of men to and fro, so that they may get to other
> banks and in the end, as mortals, to the other side. Now in a high
> arch, now in a low, the bridge vaults over glen and stream—
> whether mortals keep in mind this vaulting of the bridge's course
> or forget that they, always themselves on the way to the last
> bridge, are actually striving to surmount all that is common and
> unsound in them in order to bring themselves before the haleness
> of the divinities.[36]

A crossing linking earth and sky, the divinities and the mortals, the bridge is a thing; it gathers the fourfold, and in doing so it allows a site for the fourfold, a place for it to come to presence. A river has many points that can be crossed by a bridge, but until a bridge is built, none of them are places, spaces within which something has been made room for. A place is something that has been cleared and set free, something built, bounded by a boundary. But for the Greeks, and for us seeking to find the way all things are built, a boundary is not the geometric point where something ends, but the beginning where something begins its presencing, not an encircling mark imposed by the will, but a horizon for revealing the thing.

Space is space because mortals dwell in it, handle it with their hands and their tools, bringing forth the god that houses it. Space is space because it is also a home. Thus, spaces receive their being from their locations, which are locations because of their place in the lives of mortals, not from geometric space itself, an abstraction beyond the earthly life of humanity.[37] Even spaces preserved from the direct hand of Man are opened up as spaces by their proximity to mortal life—the Custer Battlefield, the Medicine Rocks State Park, the Custer National Forest. Spared from industrial development, these spaces of wilderness receive their location, their boundary, from the existence of Man. Wilderness, for Enframing, is merely something Man is not, something he has not imposed his will on. Yet even here, wilderness is something built because Man designates it as his other, thereby bringing it into being. Despite Man's depravity, his boundless will to define everything as his utility (if only by exclusion), something sacred, something beautiful, something magical still speaks from these locations and protects these things from the hand of the developer, the strip miner, and the businessman.

The nature of building is letting dwell, accepting life on the earth under the sky and responding thoughtfully and carefully to their summons. Heidegger gives an example of this in an old farmhouse in the Black Forest, built 200 years ago.[38] In this house the self-sufficient power of dwelling let earth and sky, divinities and mortals enter into simple oneness and ordered the house into Being:

> It placed the farm on the wind-sheltered mountain slope looking south, among the meadows close to the spring. It gave it the wide overhanging shingle roof whose proper slope bears up under the burden of the snow, and which, reaching deep down, shields the chambers against the storms of long winter nights. It did not forget the altar corner behind the community table; it made room in the chamber for the hallowed places of childbed and the "tree of the dead"—for that is what they call a coffin there ... and in this way it designed for the different generations under one roof the character of their journey through time.[39]

The farmhouse was built only because the craftsmen who built it already dwelled, respecting the weather in its changes, knowing both birth and death, and responding to the needs of life.

The housing crisis, the homelessness that we face today comes not from any lack of housing, though there is that in tragic plenty, but from modernity's rootlessness, aimlessness, and nihilism—from our life being rooted not in the earth, but in some cold distance. The homeless that fill our streets, dirty, unkempt, cruelly tousled by a society of affluence, are only a symptom of a deeper homelessness that we all share with them and makes us indifferent to their life of despair and pain, a deeper failure to spare the earth. Subject to the utility of a global economy, people cannot dwell in trailerhouses, awaiting their next job a hundred miles away. Cut off from the earth that sustains them and the family that gave them birth by a god that has no earthly place, they cannot have a care for the earth they live upon, nor can they offer a thoughtful interpretation of what anything is for; they can only drain it for what they can use and move on when the smell becomes too strong and the poison too deadly. Denied initiation to their nature as mortals, subjected to their utility as instruments of the modern economy, they cannot accept their ties to the earth, and thus come to care for it, set it free.

Before anything can be spared, mortals will turn from its way and build not by the standards of Man's reason, which closes itself off from the earth and builds according to the homeless archy-itecture of Man's will, and begin to think, opening themselves up to the earth and responding to the world's worlding. Handmade, near to the life of mortals, building as thinking responds to the dwelling place, its climate, its soil, its people, and its gods. Accepting its situation, it builds as a response to the world that world's there and leaves the things present themselves there as things deserving the care of thinking. Celebrating the care of friendship, the nurturing concern of the lover, it does not reduce the wilderness of Being to Man's utility and it does not subject it to necessities of distant and thoughtless metaimperatives.

A discursive prison that has locked all the earth up in its archy-itecture and made it available as Man's utility, Enframing builds homogeneity over vast areas, callously leveling everything, bounding it, and organizing it according to an indifferent plan, a distant and calculating will. To secure Man's willing it makes everything into a transparent re-presentation of Man's utility, controlled, secured, defined. The disorder, dispersion, dirt, noise, irrationality, ambiguity, and slack that are the shadow of Man's building the world as his utility are rigorously excluded because, being wild and uncontrolled, they are not Man's will and threaten the security of his intentions. Such wilderness is dangerous and must be bounded, isolated, separated, and distinguished from Man's civilization. And if it is there "protected," as in parks, it is only to make it safe by distinguishing it. This is not Man's domain.

Thinking, on the other hand, responding to the builder's time and place and not to a distant summons of an inappropriate technology or a global economy, builds to protect heterogeneity, difference, diversity, and dispersion—to protect the wild-erness of the dwelling place. For thinking does not seek to bound wilderness up as something uncontrolled and distinguish it from Man, because it does not know that difference.

In diversity, anarchy, and in the openness to it, the mystery of the earth and the holiness of the world's worlding are revealed. Thinking builds to spare the wild-erness of things not because it is useful to do so, but because in its sparing it is opening itself up to the happening of truth. Thinking knows that truth is not Man's truth, an ordering that is projected over things by Man's will, but is the world's worlding, the happening of the thing at a particular dwelling place. Thinking is directed toward the thing in all its wildness, and because it is, it does not seek to fabricate Man-made simplicity by positing a boundary of control, imposing operational definitions within it, and using analytic methods to extract Man's truth from it. Thinking can know its truth and build according to it only when things are left alone, left wild, when they are not made into objects of Man's will, but are accepted and allowed to go their own way. It is then, and only then, that the whisper of the world's worlding can be heard. Seeking truth, the thinker must silence her willing, and in that silence let the earth come forward.

Despite thinking being a response to something local, it is possible to hint at some things thinking would tend to build and the way it would proceed. Since thinking does not seek control over vast extents—and indeed cannot because human control over a thing's presencing conceals its earthly truth—it will not build vast energy grids, but will instead build local, small-scale, and simple energy systems because they will be responsive to the nature of local needs and the handmade cares of the household.

Instead of relying on distant economies to supply it with food, housing, energy, and many tools, the thoughtful household would attempt to make most of the things it needs itself. And instead of depending on a global economy to supply it with things it cannot build itself, it would rely on barter and community work.

Perhaps in this time of gathering storm clouds the buildings that thinkers would build most often are Arks, secure places that protect the wilderness of things from the callousness of Man's utility. In biblical times, Noah built an Ark to give protection to two of every kind of creature, one male, the other female, sparing them from the rage of God's judgment against humanity's corruption.

Whatever it is in the biblical tradition, thinkers responding to the signs of the gathering storm might find that the Ark can be used as an instrument for protecting an-archy, for preserving difference, for freeing the thing to thing. For building wilderness. A strong place made to keep things safe, it does not seek to subject the things within its protection to command, control, or an archy-itecture of any sort, but to spare them from the tempest that rages outside it, keeping them safe for a day when they can leave its confines and freely go their way. Since the time of Noah, the Ark has been a holy instrument, a sacred instrument because it protects the whole dispersion of things and keeps their integrity safe. It was in an Ark, an Ark of an entirely different construction, we should be reminded, that the holy objects of the Jews were kept safe from the trials of time and use.

Noah's Ark was built to protect the creatures of the earth from the flood God judged the world with, but ours will be built to protect the sacredness, integrity, and an-archical dispersion of the creatures of the earth from the careless and indifferent judgments of Enframing. Man's utility has covered the earth with a monoculture of plants that he has judged the most productive for his economies, pushing all others to a shrinking margin, specially designated "wilderness" areas, where they are endangered because the ecosystems that nurtured them are falling apart in the too limited space left to them. Following the broad diversity of the earth's plants to the margins of Man's utility, many species of animals, such as the wolf, the bear, the whale, and the mountain lion, are similarly endangered. Amid the vast fields of Man's monoculture, many insects become pests and are treated with heavy doses of poison, further disrupting the cycles that renew and protect the earth.

As a result, the task of modern Ark builders, responding to the looming storm clouds of the world they dwell in, will be to find ways to spare the an-archy of these dispersed beings from the tempest of Man's will. The seeds of endangered plants will be gathered and planted, animals endangered by a collapsing ecosystem will be gathered up and placed in zoos that nearly as possible duplicate their usual habitats, protected for a day when they can again resume their way. In addition, libraries, sanctuaries, institutions, and communities will be built to protect and nurture dissident ideas, places where poets and thinkers can renew themselves, attending to the wilderness within themselves that alone makes possible a renewal of the earth.[40]

As in Noah's time, Ark building does not begin with large numbers of people, political action, tight organization, or extensive plans, but with a thoughtful and personal response to the perils of the time. While nothing can be done by reason unless everyone does it together, thinking begins in a small way with the individual opening herself up to the whisper of the world worlding at her place, and it proceeds with the responses she makes in her building and dwelling. Since it builds small, and comes to its truth through the things near to it, thinking can, as it always must, start with one thinker dwelling amid the cares of her own life, quietly meditating on the wilderness of things most near to it. By cultivating friendship, protecting difference, nurturing growth, and accepting challenge in her own life, the thinker builds a wilderness, and once this world is built it can be shared with others. Perhaps by living this gentle life, without invoking a metaphysics of principles, condemning judgments, or universal morals, she can open up ways for others to live their lives in a better, more poetic and beautiful, way.

## Notes

1. Martin Heidegger, "Building Dwelling Thinking," in *Poetry, Language, Thought* (New York: Harper Colophon, 1971), 150.

2. For an excellent description of a farm community under stress, see Jeff Pearson and Jessica Pearson, *No Time but Place: A Prairie Pastoral* (New York: McGraw-Hill, 1980), 258. The way the Indians were pushed from their home, the land, is one of the ugliest pages in American history. See Dee Brown, *Bury My Heart at Wounded Knee* (New York: Pocket Books,

1959).

3. *Enframing* is the name Martin Heidegger gives to modernity. It describes the way things are present to us in the modern world—caught in a frame, enchained. They are as objects for Man's utility and technology, held in reserve for his unbounded willing and control. Within its archy-itecture, everything becomes a means for something else, a tool for Man's willing—God, nature, conventions. Revealed as Man's utility, everything is displaced, moved far from itself, made homeless by being made into something it is not. And wilderness, which is bounded up and controlled as something uncontrolled, is built as the other of Man's ambition.

4. I got the idea of the Ark from Nancy J. Todd, ed., *The Journal of the New Alchemists, No. 7* (Brattleboro, Vt.: Stephen Greene, 1981).

5. Henry David Thoreau, *Walden and Other Writings* (New York: Bantam, 1962), 172.

6. Anyone wanting advice on building their own house, feel free to contact me at home, Box 202, Willard, MT 59354, telephone (406) 775-6378. Some do-it-yourself books that I used and can recommend: Mario Salvadori, *Why Buildings Stand Up: The Strength of Architecture* (New York: W. W. Norton, 1980); Bill Keisling, *Solar Water Heating Systems* (Emmaus, Pa.: Rodale, 1983); Edward Mazria, *The Passive Solar Energy Book* (Emmaus, Pa.: Rodale, 1979); Robert L. Roy, *Underground Houses* (New York: Sterling, 1982); David Martindale, *Earth Shelters* (New York: E. P. Dutton, 1981); Underground Space Center, University of Minnesota, *Earth Sheltered Housing Design: Guidelines, Examples, and References* (New York: Van Nostrand Reinhold, 1978); Alex Wade and Neal Ewenstein, *30 Energy-Efficient Houses You Can Build* (Emmaus, Pa.: Rodale, 1977).

7. The Turning is another concept of Heidegger's. It describes the return of Being. It is a way of being in which we let the world world, the thing thing, and our thought be. We do this instead of subjecting things to Man's will, reason, and technology. Being will be as an-archy, as something not governed by the meta-physical (supra-natural) archy-itecture of reason, morals, principles, or other eternal universals. Man will not oppose himself to Nature, define it as his other, something to be bounded, controlled, isolated, subjugated, but will accept the earth as his own being.

8. Donna Haraway, *Simians, Cyborgs, and Women: The Reinvention of Nature* (New York: Routledge, 1991), 196.

9. Reiner Schurmann, *Heidegger on Being and Acting: From Principles to Anarchy* (Bloomington: Indiana University Press, 1987), 97.

10. Man, capital M man, is the archy-itecture of modernity, the commanding source and origin governing the presencing of all things. In the age of Enframing everything is as a means for Man to will his will. Man, as Foucault also argues, is a historical fabrication, born with the modern age, destined to pass away with it. Mortals have always existed, but Man has not, and will not last long.

11. Heidegger, "Building Dwelling Thinking," 147.

12. Wendell Berry, *The Unsettling of America* (San Francisco: Sierra Club Books, 1978), 87.

13. Heidegger, "Building Dwelling Thinking," 147.

14. Martin Heidegger, "What Are Poets For?" in *Poetry, Language, Thought* (New York: Harper Colophon, 1971), 111.

15. Heidegger, "Building Dwelling Thinking," 148.

16. Heidegger, "What Are Poets For?" 92.

17. Heidegger, "Building Dwelling Thinking," 148.

18. Ibid., 149.

19. Martin Heidegger, "The Thing," in *Poetry, Language, Thought* (New York: Harper Colophon, 1971), 178.

20. Heidegger, "Building Dwelling Thinking," 149.

21. Heidegger, "The Thing," 178.

22. Vincent Vycinas, *Earth and Gods: An Introduction to the Philosophy of Martin Heidegger* (The Hague: Nijhoff, 1961).

23. Schurmann, *Heidegger on Being and Acting*, 171.

24. Heidegger, "Building Dwelling Thinking," 149.

25. Heidegger, "The Thing," 178.

26. Heidegger, "Building Dwelling Thinking," 150.

27. Ibid.

28. Heidegger, "The Thing," 178.

29. Martin Heidegger, "Poetically Man Dwells," *Poetry, Language, Thought* (New York: Harper Colophon, 1971), 220.

30. Jean Shinoda Bolen, M.D., *Goddesses in Everywoman: A New Psychology of Women* (New York: Harper Colophon, 1984), 46.

31. Jean Shinoda Bolen, M.D., *Gods in Everyman: A New Psychology of Men's Lives and Loves* (New York: Harper & Row, 1989), 162.

32. Bolen, *Goddesses in Everywoman*, 233.

33. Heidegger, "Building Dwelling Thinking," 150.

34. Heidegger, "Poetically Man Dwells," 220.

35. Heidegger, "Building Dwelling Thinking," 151.

36. Ibid., 152.

37. Ibid., 154.

38. Ibid., 160.

39. Ibid.

40. One example of this kind of Ark building is William Connolly's pursuit of an "agonistic ethic of care for otherness." Resisting the effort to build the world of evil others, Connolly suggests that we cultivate an ethic of care for the ambiguities involved in any affirmation of identity or difference. See William Connolly, *Identity\Difference: Democratic Negotiations of Political Paradox* (Ithaca, N.Y.: Cornell University Press, 1991), 14.

Chapter 3

# Intimate Distance: The Dislocation of Nature in Modernity

Shane Phelan

Contemporary political theory has moved increasingly to adopt the methods of literary analysis in an effort to understand both canonical texts and current sociopolitical events. This analysis focuses less on the meaning of terms than on the role they play; it involves a "shift from historical definition to the problematics of reading." [1] This new theory is especially helpful in discussing some of the central, and essentially contested, concepts in political theory. It helps us to understand these terms, not as unified markers, but in terms of the role they play in a given writer's thought or in the dynamics of a political culture.

One of these key terms is *nature*. Nature has had many meanings in political theory, and the unity and stability of those meanings has varied over time. A central feature of modernity is the shifting, problematic relation between nature and culture. In Ernesto Laclau's terms, nature has been "dislocated" insofar as its identity or meaning "depends on an outside which both denies that identity and provides its condition of possibility at the same time." [2] Dislocation describes a situation of inescapable ambiguity. The opposition to "culture" provides the bedrock meaning of "nature" in the West, but this opposition has become fraught with tension. Since the eighteenth century, the "outside" of culture has given meaning to nature, but it has also increasingly been used to deny the identity of nature as something distinct from culture. The consolidation by the eighteenth century of a mechanistic view of nature gave rise to the "return of the repressed," the elements of animism and vitalism that had previously been included within nature. The modern form of these elements is social constructionism in its many varieties.

This dislocation of nature is directly relevant to arguments about and within current social movements. They are relevant because nature underlies several crucial nodes of political argument: ideas of justice, of the desirability of change, of freedom and the limits of human action, of the source and possibility of knowledge, all involve differing senses and aspects of nature. The destabilization of nature is the opening into a new politics and a new common life, but only if its many dimensions are explored.

This chapter will explicate the dilemmas of modern nature. After a brief description of some of the definitions and uses of the category of "nature," I will examine the work of Rousseau and Nietzsche as paradigmatic of the dislocation of nature in modernity. I will then return to nature as a category and argue that we can deconstruct, but not eliminate, this vital and inherently ambiguous idea. I will urge instead the notion of nature as "intimate distance," exploring the implications for theory of such an idea.

## Nature

Nature has several meanings in political theory. As the origin, nature is both the source of authenticity, the precultural "reality," and the archaic, the primitive, the incomplete. As the real or authentic, nature serves to call us home, to remind us of what we "really" are, and to critique culture. In the second usage of nature as origin, nature is a ground that requires supplementation; it is a lack. The "merely natural" has served to privilege human culture over other animal life, to justify racial oppression in the name of civilization, and to provide a rationale for male domination of women.[3] It has been impossible for women and colonized people to use nature as origin, as authenticity, in their favor without having the corresponding use of origin as lack brought to bear against them.

A related, but distinct, usage calls on nature as limit. In this role, nature has served as a barrier to social and political change. Within liberal theory, the claim that a given feature is natural is a way of refusing to consider the possibility of different ways of doing, thinking, or being.[4] In this view, nature can be identified with the given world. Conservatives have used nature in this way to endorse existing arrangements and to argue against such imagination, and even those we might not simply call "conservative" rely on nature as limit at the points in their arguments when they wish to shut the doors of possibility. For example, Jane Flax describes this use of nature when she writes of Freud that "he displaces conflicts within culture onto conflicts between 'nature' and culture; hence he renders their social sources, especially in gender relations and discourse dependence, opaque and inaccessible." [5]

This use of nature is not the property of any one ideological orientation, however. It is a buttress for liberal thought, prevalent among both those who seek to counter teleological or other condemnations of unpopular acts or identities and those who condemn them. For example, many lesbian and gay rights activists counter conservative objections with the argument that existence proves nature, while their opponents appeal to the prevalence of heterosexuality for refutation.[6] Both sides tend to use numbers for support; while gay/lesbian activists argue that 10 percent of the population "is" gay, and that this is too large a proportion to be considered deviant, their opponents challenge the 10 percent figure (thereby implicitly acceding to the hypothetical argument) and point to 90 percent heterosexuals as proof of the intent of nature.

Related to, but not the same as, nature as origin is nature as lawgiver and orderer, the source of natural right. The tradition of natural right relies on nature as rational order, as something to be known through philosophy. In speaking of these connections, Leo Strauss writes that "the idea of natural right must be unknown as long as the idea of nature is unknown," and that "the discovery of nature is the work of philosophy." [7] This tradition resists the equation of the empirical with the natural, "for the discovery of nature consists precisely in the splitting-up of that totality into phenomena which are natural and phenomena which are not natural: 'nature' is a term of distinction." [8] Here, nature is not an origin so much as a goal, a telos to which things aspire.

Returning to my earlier example, we see that nature as order is also a mainstay of antifeminist and antigay argument. Indeed, the "90 percent" argument has as much to do with this sense of nature as it does with nature as limit. Sexuality may not in fact be limited to heterosexual desire, but nature would have it so. Women may contest familial patriarchy and male domination, but in so doing they become monsters. This use of nature is much less ambiguous than nature as the given, however, and it does not generally appear in feminist or gay/lesbian literature. While Strauss's remarks may be taken to suggest that the existence of male domination does not endorse it as "natural," in fact nature as order has a rhetorical history in conservative discourse that is lacking among liberals or radicals.[9]

All of these uses of nature share the quest for clarity, for certainty, that dogs Western thought. Their coexistence is evidence of the foundational status for political theory of the category of nature; contradictory projects and perspectives seek to use the same icon in their service. Rather than

abandon nature, the competing parties continually challenge one another's uses of it.

Since the eighteenth century, we have seen the growth of another idea
of nature. In this view, nature and history do not clearly divide. The idea of
a "second nature" enters here, where nature becomes affiliated with habit.
We find an increasing awareness that nature is not a thing that can be evaluated separately from human creation, and especially that human nature is
inseparable from human activity. Nature shifts from a thing to a process,
but never completely. This dislocation and fluctuation is demonstrated in
Rousseau and Nietzsche, but it is not limited to them. It is to this demonstration that I now turn.

## Rousseau

The popular caricature of Rousseau is as a "nature boy," confident in the
"innocence of nature" [10] and the possibility of virtue in accordance with
nature. However, as Jean Ehrard has shown, the idea of "idyllic naturalism"
is not that of Rousseau so much as it is that of his predecessors.[11] Rousseau's project is not to return us to nature, but to "denature" us in order to
fulfill the human promise of civil and moral liberty.[12] As Asher Horowitz
describes it, Rousseau provides the bridge from the Enlightenment to the
nineteenth century through his "thoroughgoing historicization of human
nature and a naturalization of history." [13] This dual move is not a demoli-
tion of the categories or oppositions between nature and culture, but it is
a dislocation precisely in Laclau's sense.

In *The Discourse on Inequality*, Rousseau describes our progress from
nature to present society. He makes the condition of nature sound free of
trial and tribulation; however, he does not make it sound human. While he
tells us that we might wish to go back, he believes that "peace and innocence have escaped us forever." "When men could have enjoyed it they
were unaware of it; and when they could have understood it they had already lost it." [14] His concern is with the present, and history, both actual
and hypothetical, serves as a guide for understanding and evaluation of the
present. His concern in the *Second Discourse* is "to mark, in the progress
of things, the moment at which right took the place of violence and nature
became subject to law, and to explain by what sequence of miracles the
strong came to submit to serve the weak, and the people to purchase imaginary repose at the expense of real felicity." [15]

The question for Rousseau, then, is how the naturally strong come to
subordinate themselves to the naturally weak, inverting the natural scale of
value. The *Second Discourse* gives us the answer. We are introduced to the
original human, still for Rousseau really an animal, and are told that its life

is straightforward, independent, with no great concern for others beyond the dictates of innate compassion. Compassion, the natural distress we feel at another's pain, "in nature supplies the place of laws, morals, and virtues." [16] In this passage, Rousseau describes the voice of this natural feeling as one that "none are tempted to disobey." It is perfect and complete within itself. And yet, it is not; if it were so, we would not need laws, morals, and virtues.

The development of society and the increasing dependence and interdependence that resulted led to the need to convince others of one's value. At this point, precisely those traits valued in nature—compassion, honesty, and so on—became liabilities in the quest for status. The winners are the hypocrites, those who respect themselves so little that they will do anything for worldly gain. Thus we see the strong, "honest poor" held down by the weak, scheming rich.

It is revealing that Rousseau identifies the process of inversion with that whereby "right took the place of violence and nature became subject to law." [17] With this conjunction, he expresses a fundamental ambivalence toward society and nature. If we heard of right replacing violence outside of the context of this sentence, we would be sure that a progressive step was being described. Here, however, we must be cautious. What seems to be happening here is a denial of natural right, and an awareness that law is not natural but social. Rousseau knows that the Enlightenment's "right" is an abstract notion that blinds people to the facts of inequality, and the simultaneous move from nature to law, from violence to right, is an expression of that awareness. His description of the founding of society is a parody of earlier contract theory; in his story, the contract is a sham. Similarly, the imposition of law upon nature implies a view of nature that lacks its own law. This nature, this flux, is contrasted to the law, which is solid and fixed. What is fixed in the *Second Discourse*, however, is injustice.

Thus we find a deep ambiguity in Rousseau concerning the idea of nature. On the one hand, nature is the voice of reason and order, origin as authenticity. As William Connolly describes this side of Rousseau, "the natural condition must be a condition of simplicity, innocence and perfection. And its perfection must degenerate only through action in which human beings themselves are implicated." [18] In this natural state, we are social beings only minimally; while possessing compassion, we are fundamentally disinterested in others and independent of them. And this, indeed, is one sort of ideal for Rousseau.

On the other hand, we find that nature is too simple really to fulfill the complex nature of humans. Humans are unique in their capacity for consciousness and transformation, their ability to act beyond instinct. Because of this, the state of nature is not only irretrievable, it is undesirable, for at that stage we are not fully human. Human destiny lies in society and the development of institutions that will leave us as free as we were in the state of nature, but not free in the same way. Civil liberty is the liberty of a reflective subject who endorses the rules of the human order within which he lives. His view that the general will is indestructible suggests that we are by nature meant to live in common with others and to will the common good, thinking of what we share.[19]

Is virtue then "natural" for Rousseau? Or is it a product of civilization, which in turn is threatened by culture? While we might say that Rousseau has a certain vision of "natural virtue," this virtue is not easily translatable into Christian morality. Our natural virtue consists simply in the lack of "active egotism"; naturally, we are indifferent to others. Thus we do not "naturally" lust after domination or violation of others; we are concerned only with self-preservation, and as such are neither good nor bad. The only other motivating force is compassion, which serves to limit the aggression of otherwise asocial, amoral beings.

This ambiguity is not evident merely in the "political" works. The *Emile* provides a closer treatment of nature. While Rousseau opens by saying, "Everything is good as it leaves the hands of the Author of things; everything degenerates in the hands of man,"[20] he proceeds from there to tell us how to transform the natural man into a citizen. Proper training has the effect of bringing us into line with the education nature has in mind for us. Doing this requires, first of all, that we become immune to our social context. Our social existence is profoundly unnatural. He argues that "good social institutions are those that best know how to denature man." "Nature" is not nearly reliable enough to make good social beings; it must be aided, shaped, overcome by human design. Here, nature as origin is both the authentic and the incomplete. The best education unites nature and society, body and mind and will. The goal of education is "the very same as that of nature."[21]

Laws, morals, and virtue supplement nature in a dual sense. In one sense, they are simple substitutes for nature, doing the same job, saying the same things. In another, they arise through the inadequacies of nature. The substitution of natural liberty for moral or political liberty is an advance; nature is good as far as it goes, but it does not go nearly far enough. Humans, it seems, are both natural and nonnatural (or potentially so); *perfectibilité*, even when it improves us, also removes us from nature—but not absolutely. The line between nature and not-nature has been thoroughly problematized by Rousseau.

Ehrard suggests that this new thought, and the problems raised by it, is not Rousseau's alone, but is shared by the whole range of Enlightenment thinkers.[22] It is, as a central idea, not one simply to be defined or analyzed;

clarification and analysis will inevitably fail to do justice to its complexity. This is not an admonition to cease study, but a warning that attempts finally to say, "Here is the meaning of nature in Rousseau's thought" will always fail.

However, we may try to locate the *place* of nature. In Paul de Man's reading, "nature" does not denote "a homogeneous mode of being" in Rousseau's thought, but rather "connotes a process of deconstruction." [23] "Nature" is the name given to "any stage of relational integration that precedes in degree the stage presently under consideration"; this appellation "conceals the fact that it is itself one system of relations among others," [24] subject to history and variety as much as the present. Far from being an element in a theory of history, "nature" has embedded within it that very theory. Nature does not "refer" to a time/place/mode so much as it *constitutes* a conceptual opposition between nature/culture, private/public, female/male, particular/general. At the same time, the category of nature is "self-deconstructive" in that it "engenders endless other 'natures' " by which to measure the succeeding period. There is no point at which nature is reached, and no time when denaturation is complete. [25]

Similarly, Ehrard explores the "duality of points of view" from which Rousseau uses nature. He distinguishes the sense of nature as thing or state from nature as process or becoming, and argues that Rousseau uses both, not from sloppiness, but as a result of conflicting aims. When the aim is social criticism, he uses "the fiction of natural man"; when he is discussing philosophic method, he returns to the notion of a socially, historically created human nature. For Rousseau, nature is "at the same time a historical phenomenon and a transcendental reality"; [26] which sense is used depends on the point of his argument. Rousseau does not, then, simply rely on nature as a standard for evaluation of societies, but constructs "natures" as part of his political judgment.

Rousseau's construction of nature, then, is part of what Michel Foucault labels the "empirico-transcendental doublet" of "man" that is created in the late eighteenth and early nineteenth centuries. The new questioning of human nature, that is, the process of inquiry into "a being whose nature (that which determines it, contains it, and has traversed it from the beginning of time) is to know nature, and itself, in consequence, as a natural being," necessarily involves the dislocation of nature as a larger category. [27] The ambiguity in Rousseau is not unique to him, but is shared by philosophers of all political persuasions, reflecting a general uncertainty over the place of nature.

## Nietzsche

Asserting that "man has become more natural in the nineteenth century,"

Nietzsche argues that this is not a return, but a new point reached only after struggle. By "natural," Nietzsche means that Europeans in the nineteenth century are "coarser, more direct, full of irony against generous feelings even when we succumb to them." [28] He explicitly contrasts the nineteenth century view with that of the eighteenth, the age of Rousseau, of nature as beauty and order and harmony. He sees this view of nature as bound to the "slave morality" of Christianity, a morality that denies conflict and struggle. Slave morality severs us from nature by imposing a whole metaphysical schema on existence. Thus, being "natural" here means to be pre- or nonmoral, not to be anti- or immoral. Being natural requires rejecting moralities that restrain and deform our instincts.

Nietzsche does not reject all morality, however. He finds morality to be "a system of evaluations that partially coincides with the conditions of a creature's life." [29] The key word here is "partially." What of the noncoincident part? Does he mean that morality supplements and supports life to a certain point at which it becomes irrelevant, or does he mean that at that point it becomes antagonistic toward life? Or does he perhaps mean that morality fosters certain forms of life, certain forms of will to power, but not others? Whichever of these we choose, we must acknowledge that morality is not simply opposed to nature, nor can we speak of the natural self as something distinct from the cultural self. The question is not whether to endorse morality or not, but which morality.

More fundamentally, however, Nietzsche rejects any notions of a stable human nature. We are constantly mutating, as it were:

> As we are merely the resultant of previous generations, we are
> also the resultant of their errors, passions, and crimes; it is
> impossible to shake off this chain. Though we condemn the errors
> and think we have escaped them, we cannot escape the fact that
> we spring from them.[30]

Nietzsche sees what Rousseau saw; nostalgia must not be confused with the belief in the possibility of regression. We may sigh for the past, but it cannot guide us. For Nietzsche, the "return" to nature is "really not a going back but an *ascent*—up into the high, free, even terrible nature and naturalness where great tasks are something one plays with, one *may* play with." [31] Nature is not something to return to, but something to work toward. Nietzsche argues that we inevitably "plant a new way of life, a new instinct, a second nature, that withers the first." [32] Nature is not opposed to culture for Nietzsche, but is its product; culture and history are part of our nature, forming it, while our nature in turn produces our culture.[33] Thus Nietzsche tries to eliminate the ambiguity in nature by assimilating it into culture.

This transformation is harder than it seems. What would working toward nature mean? If nature is the product of culture, what might distinguish "natural" outcomes from "unnatural" ones? Surely, Nietzsche does not endorse as natural any historical outcome; most notably, European Christian civilization is unnatural. Further, as a goal, nature is not simply the existing state at any time; nature may be the product of culture, but it is not any culture at any given time. Some cultures are more natural than others, and a given culture may become more or less natural over time.

Nietzsche in fact moves on two tracks. In the first, perhaps more careful thought, he resists the idea of nature as anything more than a ground for action, as something with "order, arrangements, form, beauty, wisdom." Here, morality removes us from nature by imposing purpose, order, and the like on chaos. This is the sense in which morality coincides with life; we cannot live in chaos, so we build an ordered, orderly world. The "return to nature" of the nineteenth century amounts to our recognition that this is the case; it is the "de-deification of nature" in favor of recognition of history and human agency.[34]

The second thought represents Nietzsche's own inability to live without these notions, this order. We find that this postmoral self is validated in his discourse by its connection to nature. He asks: "When may we begin to '*naturalize*' humanity in terms of a pure, newly discovered, newly redeemed nature?"[35] Lurking in this question is a telic nature; the nature that we work to create is simultaneously waiting to be discovered. Nietzsche has not eliminated the ambiguity, but continues to move within it.

Nietzsche has actually taken aim at two targets. The first is that of "nature" as material entity, as "neutral" reference; this must be challenged on epistemological grounds. The second is that of nature as an order that corresponds to moral notions. This is less dispensable for Nietzsche, but still not unambiguous. He is, in fact, moving within the same duality as that which governed Rousseau. While he develops a sophisticated, historical nature for ontological and epistemological purposes, his moral and political discourse relies on a more settled nature. This more traditional nature is directly linked to the political anachronism that rests so poorly with his radical metaphysics.[36] When Nietzsche tells us that domination and exploitation are natural, he is instructing us to accept, even celebrate, these without the genealogical inquiry that he applies to other values and concepts.

A more visible gap between Nietzsche and Rousseau revolves around the issue of compassion or pity. When Nietzsche states that pity is a dangerous force that enhances suffering, he is in apparent conflict with Rousseau, who sees our natural compassion for others as the balance to our basic love of self. This conflict is the basis for Nietzsche's scorn, his charge that Rousseau points toward the "softening, weakening, moralization of man." [37] However, we find that Nietzsche in fact agrees with Rousseau that there is such a thing; while "empathy with the souls of others is originally nothing moral, but a physiological susceptibility to suggestion," [38] this does not dispute Rousseau's point. The two thinkers agree that "before culture" we have an innate impulse toward compassion.

The two thinkers differ in their view of the relation between natural empathy and social emotions such as pity. Where Rousseau seems to equate the two, Nietzsche sharply distinguishes between "physiological susceptibility to suggestion" and pity, which is a form of will to power indulged in by the weak. [39] Pity is a celebration of another's weakness, rather than an ennobling sentiment. The spread of pity, in Nietzsche's view, is a direct indication of passive nihilism in a society. [40] Thus, while for Rousseau the erosion of pity is a degradation, a problem, it is for Nietzsche a sign of health and strength.

Both thinkers agree that at some point the physiological order is turned upside down. For Nietzsche, the consequence of the slave revolt in morals is the creation of a new elite that is always conscious of its own relative position, always weighing itself against others; it is unhealthy precisely because it is self-conscious, reactive rather than active. Rousseau would agree with this portrait, and this evaluation of the situation; the transition from *amour-de-soi* to *amour-propre* is a transition from active to reactive love of self. However, the *Genealogy* describes a nonreflective natural elite based on strength. This elite is indifferent to others, but this indifference extends to the absence of compassion for the weak. Thus the elite see no problem with rape and pillage, for they do not see those attacked as equal to themselves, as "like" themselves; they do not aim at domination, but they do not refrain from violation. While Nietzsche argues that empathy may be physiological in its origin, his early strong people in the *Genealogy of Morals* have already lost, or contained, that empathy. The strong lack compassion for the weak, and it is this lack that partly defines their strength.

Rousseau is seen by Nietzsche as the champion of equality, the desire for which rests on *ressentiment*. Nonetheless, the ends toward which these two thinkers aim are curiously similar. Rousseau's ideal is not the loss of self-reflective awareness, for he knows that we cannot go back; it is the development of a strong, simple people who do not live in envy and *amour-propre*. Nietzsche also values self-consciousness, as an ambiguous achievement of culture; for him, too, the progress toward which Europeans are moving does not consist in regaining an earlier morality, but in living "without becoming embittered," in overcoming the distinction between the ideal and the actual that frustrates everyone who takes it seriously. [41]

Nietzsche can no longer deny the tension implicit in Rousseau between acceptance and rejection of the existing order. Because Rousseau could not in the end accept or reject the moral values of a Christian society, he was forced to insist on "the preservation of existing institutions, maintaining that their destruction would leave the vices in existence and remove only the means to their cure." [42] Nietzsche's attempt to move beyond good and evil invites us to reformulate the issue, though we must struggle for the words to do so. His failure to extricate himself completely from the matrix of nature demonstrates the immense difficulty, and the extreme importance, of the task.

In fact, Nietzsche is at least one of the many descendants of Rousseau. Both thinkers hold together the knowledge of our inevitable historicity with the sense that things were better when we had less history behind us. They share the belief that freedom is never a condition in which we find ourselves, but consists in struggle; freedom does not consist in simply having overcome nature, but in the continual transformation of nature without ever "leaving" nature itself.

The link between these two is not that they say the same things, but that Rousseau's insights into and ambivalence toward the Enlightenment are shared and developed by Nietzsche in the light of the nineteenth-century development of history and disappointment with human nature. Before the French Revolution, Rousseau could still turn from these problems to envision a free and ordered society, ignoring his own machinations into Emile's construction and thus the antidemocratic, antilibertarian element in his thought. The force of the Revolution, and of Kant, worked against any such denial or tensions in thought. Nietzsche's more extensive dislocation of nature is rooted in the simultaneous historicization of human life and disappointment with the fruits of that history. After the Revolution, Nietzsche could have no patience with someone who seemed to call for autonomy and yet endorsed coercive education; the loss of telos led also to the loss of legitimacy for such projects.

## Intimate Distance

Much of the annoying energy of "postmodern" analyses resides in the persistent transgression of seemingly obvious and "natural" categories, such as nature. Dislocation reaches its limit when we finally abandon the attempts to limit and fix nature, when we use nature as a foundation only with a strong sense of irony arising from knowledge of its ambiguities. Postmodern theories have enabled us to recognize that nothing ever simply "is" or "is not" natural, that nature never "is," in fact, anything determinate at all, but that nevertheless nature is ever present, that which is about us always. [43]

Can we then say anything about nature? Is there any way to describe a thing/process that insistently oscillates from one pole to the other? I will argue for the formulation of nature as "intimate distance" as a way to move in this direction. Postmodernism signals not the death of nature, but the return of nature as intimate distance.

In *Spurs*, Jacques Derrida's essay on Nietzsche, he describes the position of woman in terms that are strongly reminiscent of the treatment of "nature":

> Perhaps woman is not some thing which announces itself from a distance, at a distance from some other thing. In that case it would not be a matter of retreat and approach. Perhaps woman—a non-identity, and non-figure, a simulacrum—is distance's very chasm, the out-distancing of distance, the interval's cadence, distance itself, if we could say such a thing, distance *itself*.[44]

Whether or not we endorse such a description of "woman," the identification of women and nature in the West makes this a revealing and useful passage. Certainly Derrida's treatment of Rousseau develops this line of thought. In language strikingly similar to that used above, he argues that for Rousseau, the question is not that of "departing from nature, or of rejoining it, but of reducing its 'distance.' " [45] His analysis draws on the idea of nature as supplement.[46] *Supplement* is a term that embodies the ambiguity of Rousseau's understanding of nature. In the first usage, the supplement is that which is added to a full, self-sufficient unit. However, the second usage of *supplement* is that of fulfilling a lack.[47] Derrida uses this notion of supplement as addition/completion to analyze Rousseau's thoughts on nature and politics. Nature is always here, always itself, and yet it is not sufficient.

Returning to the above quote, we can see some of the issues that have plagued thought about nature. Perhaps, as Derrida says, it is "not a matter of retreat and approach," of nearer or closer to nature, for we are always in nature, we are always nature, but yet we are not natural. We cannot simply return to nature, but we abandon it only at our peril.

Perhaps nature, always with us, never directly accessible, is distance itself. Perhaps we return to the idea of nature in order to describe the not-quite-thought, the not-quite-manifest and yet surely here. It limits, it guides, but it never simply and plainly commands us. That which enables us to "leave" nature, to distance ourselves from it, is itself natural in the sense of the given, the existing, but it is profoundly unnatural in any simple teleology. "Intimate distance" captures the movement between enough/not enough, between present/absent, between near/far. Nature is never absent, but it is never simply present as a clear referent or guide. Whether it is "enough" or not depends upon the political project we are pursuing.

So much for distance. What of intimacy? Nature may be distance, the unreachable referent of our desire or need, but it is never really far at all. What would distance really mean in a world where habit is nature, where nature is cultivated? The distance of nature is the smallest possible distance. Nature is, in fact, present, but not as a thing or a transparent history, not as a simple origin or as a clear telos. This is seen by Nietzsche, who develops the idea of "second nature" as a way of understanding change that is not simply "conventional," that is not a matter of adopting roles but of transforming the self. Nature is distance in its ungraspability, but it is always that in which we live as what we are. We are nature, just as surely as we are unnatural. Neither the distance of nature nor its constant presence is avoidable.

Perhaps intimacy is better understood if we contrast it to immediacy. Immediacy has connotations for political theory of the transparent, that without distance. In contrast, *Webster's* defines "intimate" as "intrinsic," "belonging to or characterizing one's deepest nature," involving "close association, contact, or familiarity." While these definitions illustrate the interconnections between words such as *nature*, *intimacy*, and *close*, intimacy does not involve the elimination of distance as does immediacy. Rousseau is often read as the theorist of immediacy; indeed, Hegel's argument against immediacy has been read for close to two centuries as a critique of Rousseau. However, I would argue that Rousseau in fact is groping for intimacy, not immediacy. Intimacy allows room for ambivalence, for mediation, for complex relations with the not-self (whether another human or the nonhuman world).

What are the political implications of conceiving of nature as intimate distance? First, and most important, such a conception makes explicit the ambiguities and paradoxes in our current usages. It makes clear that nature is always a double standard, never with a univocal meaning by which it can legitimate some political aims and delegitimate others. As a consequence, such an idea fosters a certain humility in our rhetorical and political use of nature. It does not remove nature from the armory of Western political discourse, as some have hoped to do, but it cautions its users that nature is always double-edged, introducing a new humility to its usage. As a result, political contestants may begin to develop other arguments for their aims, arguments that move beyond existing liberal/conservative uses of nature.

Two examples will help to make this point:

1. On the day that I write this, a friend tells me of a gay man he knows who dresses as a woman, refers to himself with a woman's name and pronouns, and insists that he "feels like a woman inside." My friend asks, is

this unnatural? When I ask what he means, he clarifies: (a) Is this person "pathological"? (b) Could there be a physiological basis for his/her sense of him/herself? I answer by shifting the questions. I talk about the ways in which gender and sexuality are associated in our society, so that many gay men experience themselves as "female" by a simple process of elimination (man = desires women, woman = desires men). I mention the relatively greater social acceptance of women who dress "like men" or "act like" men, stemming from the greater social esteem of men and "male" activities/behaviors. I talk about my own uneasiness around male transvestites, stemming from my own socialization into gender roles. Most important, I wonder again about the stakes in calling transvestism or any other social difference "natural" or "unnatural." My friend seems to think that if he can answer such questions he will know how to judge people, and he shares this belief with doctors and policymakers across the United States.

Debates about human nature have also pervaded lesbian and gay theory. While liberals have often pointed to the advantages of the nature argument ("they just can't help it" and therefore should not be persecuted), many contemporary theorists are challenging this, arguing that such arguments only constrain us in a fixed identity with its own "truth." [48] Basing our arguments upon nature is dangerous, unless nature is reformulated.

2. The literature of ecofeminism covers a range from full-blown reification of nature as origin and telos to considerations of the cultural constructions of "nature" and "woman" as well as their rhetorical linkage. The simple celebration of women as natural usually carries with it an indictment of capitalist patriarchy for dominating both women and nature,[49] but no critique of these categories or their theoretical articulation. As a result, women become both the vanguard of the environmental movement and the victims of its antimodernist impulses, reinforcing and submitting to romantic pictures of housewives baking and sewing. Other ecofeminists acknowledge the problems with the simple opposition between nature and culture, but even the more constructionist positions eventually fall back to conceptions of nature (and women) as unproblematically distinguishable—"I know it when I see it." "Nature" usually comes to mean "nonhuman," even when humans are acknowledged to be "members of an ecological community." [50] Karen Warren's description, in which humans are also "different from" that ecological community, does not problematize the ecological community as such, but only points to the peculiar status of humans within it. However, this precarious position is the result not of something about humans and their activities, but of a conception of ecological communities that contains an implicit definition of them as static, self-contained, and defined in opposition to human activity. While this conception seems strategically strong, providing a bulwark against en-

croachment by humans, its strength rests on a rigidity that leads it to break continually.

Carolyn Merchant's groundbreaking work *The Death of Nature* also attempts to steer away from essentialism. She is aware of the problem, and asserts that "there are no unchanging 'essential' characteristics of sex, gender, or nature." [51] She is concerned with interpretations and constructions of nature and women rather than with "nature itself." She describes beautifully the cost in real women's lives of the discursive links between women and nature. When nature is seen as the bountiful mother, real mothers are called upon to be bountiful and giving, not demanding things for themselves. When nature is a disorderly, dangerous woman, real women are suppressed and constrained. [52]

However, she too then proceeds to treat nature unproblematically as that which is not human, not social, not conventional. Never does she question what nature "is": like "beings" for Aristotle, "nature" for Merchant is too obvious a referent to occasion real awe. While she urges us to engage in "a radical critique of the categories *nature* and *culture*," [53] she herself never suggests any basis for that critique. She rejects the mechanistic view of nature, but never inquires into the nature of nature in any way.

Merchant is not alone in this failure to ask the nature of nature. The environmental movements as a whole have not done this. Whether it is the fully essentialized "Nature" of the deep ecologists or simply the "nature" of the National Resources Defense Council, environmentalists talk as though they know what nature is. What has distinguished ecofeminism is the challenge to traditional gendered assumptions about nature and resistance to the gender traditionalism of many other movements such as deep ecology. The romantic movement back to the land and to preindustrial modes of life is also a movement back to prefeminist gender roles, in which women are the nurturing mothers of the earth. This is not a true confrontation with the dislocation of nature, but a flight from it.

While paying lip service to feminism, deep ecologists such as Devall and Sessions never address *male* dominance or linkages between contemporary Western masculinity and science. [54] They call us to the premodern, the "primitive," to nature as origin, with no interrogation of the problems posed by modernity. They do indeed treat humans as natural, trying to avoid the nature/culture distinction, but their purpose is to recall all of human activity within the bounds of an authentic nature.

Bringing intimate distance to the fore would alleviate (not resolve) this problem by foregrounding the construction of the ecological community as a human activity, and by seeing humans not as "members" or as "different from" nature, but as elements of a dynamic and never fully locatable process. The questions to be asked then are not, What should humans do (or not do) to nature? but instead, How do we understand ourselves and our world? How ought we to negotiate our relationships with ourselves? The questions of sexuality and ecology, to name only two fields of nature discourse, can never be resolved by simply opposing human activity/ies to "nature." This formulation maintains the very oppositions that most ecologists hope to overcome. Nor can we deal with them by assimilating ourselves unproblematically into nature. The only nature that we can lay full claim to is the intimate distance of human existence, a nature that belies any full claims.

These examples make clear that seeing nature as intimate distance places judgment in the foreground. Intimate distance can be explored and evaluated only contextually, within a particular time and place; it does not admit of regulations and checklists. These shortcuts and substitutes to personal judgment are precisely Nietzsche's targets and, in de Man's reading, Rousseau's as well.[55]

Nature is a foundational category for the West, but the course of modernity is a course of internal conflict for that category. As we become more aware of the ways in which nature functions, not only to limit discourse, but to reflect our alienation and aspirations to become whole, we see more clearly the price of reliance upon it. The challenge to the category of nature made by feminist and postmodern or poststructuralist writers is bound to recognition of the limiting role nature has played in discourse and politics.[56] The avoidance of the chasm of distance is the source of ideologies that reify and reduce nature, including human nature, in the service of clarity and order. Nature as telos and natural right have continually served to repress and oppress, to justify hierarchies; nature as origin has been the expression of our longing, our "homesickness" for an intact, just world.[57] We see all these uses in Rousseau and Nietzsche, as manifestations of differing impulses and needs. These two thinkers also show that nature is too slippery to be confined to any one definition; they show us that the intimate distance of nature is not something to be collapsed or avoided.

Instead of attempting to eliminate nature in political discourse, I would argue for the mediation of intimate distance, a continual reflection and contest over the category. The elimination of nature can only further the solipsism of modern Western civilization, in which the earth becomes "standing-reserve" for appropriation by humans who have themselves become nothing but resources in a global economy.[58] What is needed is a reconceptualization that heightens respect and care without a return to medieval piety. Recognition of nature as intimate distance reminds us simultaneously that nature is us and our lives, but that those lives are the greatest, most mundane mystery we will ever face.

# Notes

1. Paul de Man, *Allegories of Reading: Figural Language in Rousseau, Nietzsche, Rilke, and Proust* (New Haven, Conn.: Yale University Press, 1979), ix.

2. Ernesto Laclau, *New Reflections on the Revolution of Our Time* (London: Verso, 1990), 39.

3. See Genevieve Lloyd, *The Man of Reason: "Male" and "Female" in Western Philosophy* (Minneapolis: University of Minnesota Press, 1984); Susan Griffin, *Women and Nature: The Roaring Inside Her* (New York: Harper & Row, 1978); and Sandra Harding, *The Science Question in Feminism* (Ithaca, N.Y.: Cornell University Press, 1986).

4. See James Madison, Alexander Hamilton, and John Jay, *The Federalist Papers*, ed. Clinton Rossiter (New York: Mentor, 1961); and Thomas Hobbes, *Leviathan*, ed. Michael Oakeshott (New York: Collier, 1962).

5. Jane Flax, *Thinking Fragments: Psychoanalysis, Feminism, and Postmodernism in the Contemporary West* (Berkeley: University of California Press, 1990), 235.

6. Shane Phelan, *Identity Politics: Lesbian Feminism and the Limits of Community* (Philadelphia: Temple University Press, 1989), chap. 2.

7. Leo Strauss, *Natural Right and History* (Chicago: University of Chicago Press, 1953), 81.

8. Ibid., 82.

9. On the ways in which Allan Bloom uses nature to attack feminism, see Jean Bethke Elshtain, *Power Trips and Other Journeys: Essays in Feminism as Civic Discourse* (Madison: University of Wisconsin Press, 1990), chap. 8.

10. William E. Connolly, *Political Theory and Modernity* (Oxford: Basil Blackwell, 1988), 62.

11. Jean Ehrard, *L'Idee de Nature en France a L'Aube des Lumieres* (Paris: Flammarion, 1970).

12. Jean-Jacques Rousseau, *Emile, or On Education*, trans. Allan Bloom (New York: Basic Books, 1979), 40, and *The Social Contract and Discourses*, trans. G. D. H. Cole (London: J. M. Dent & Sons, 1973), 177–78.

13. Asher Horowitz, *Rousseau, Nature, and History* (Toronto: University of Toronto Press, 1987), 36–37.

14. Rousseau, *The Social Contract and Discourses*, 156–57.

15. Ibid., 44.

16. Ibid., 68.

17. Ibid., 44.

18. Connolly, *Political Theory and Modernity*, 47.

19. Rousseau, *The Social Contract and Discourses*, 248.

20. Rousseau, *Emile*, 37.

21. Ibid., 40, 38.

22. Ehrard, *L'Idee de Nature en France*, 394, 417.

23. de Man, *Allegories of Reading*, 249.

24. Ibid., 248.

25. It is useful to contrast de Man's reading of Rousseau with that of Allan Bloom's "Introduction" to *Emile, or On Education, by Jean-Jacques Rousseau* (New York: Basic Books, 1979), and to reflect on the different political implications of the reading. Whereas de Man stresses the openness and complexity of Rousseau's "nature," Bloom denies the problems lurking in that complexity. For Bloom, nature is a simple standard, both an origin and a telos, though one that can be deformed. This use of nature is linked to his conservative educational politics by Jean Elshtain in *Power Trips*. She finds similar uses of nature in his *Closing of the American Mind*.

26. Ehrard, *L'Idee de Nature en France*, 394.

27. Michel Foucault, *The Order of Things: An Archaeology of the Human Sciences* (New York: Pantheon, 1970), 310.

28. Friedrich Nietzsche, *The Will to Power*, ed. Walter Kaufmann (New York: Viking, 1968), 73.

29. Ibid., 148.

30. Friedrich Nietzsche, *The Use and Abuse of History*, trans. Adrian Collins (New York: Macmillan, 1957), 21.

31. Friedrich Nietzsche, *The Portable Nietzsche*, ed. Walter Kaufmann (New York: Viking, 1968), 552.

32. Ibid., 21.

33. I thank Tracy Strong for clarification of this idea.

34. Friedrich Nietzsche, *The Gay Science*, trans. Walter Kaufmann (New York: Vintage, 1974), 169.

35. Ibid.

36. See Mark Warren, *Nietzsche and Political Thought* (Cambridge: MIT Press, 1988).

37. Nietzsche, *The Will to Power*, 529.

38. Ibid., 428.

39. Ibid., 199.

40. Friedrich Nietzsche, *The Birth of Tragedy and the Genealogy of Morals*, trans. Francis Golffing (Garden City, N.Y.: Doubleday, 1956), 154.

41. Nietzsche, *The Will to Power*, 74.

42. Ernst Cassirer, *The Question of Jean-Jacques Rousseau*, trans. Peter Gay (New Haven, Conn.: Yale University Press, 1989), 54.

43. Paul Bove, "The Ineluctability of Difference: Scientific Pluralism and the Critical Intelligence," in *Postmodernism and Politics*, ed. Jonathan Arac (Minneapolis: University of Minnesota Press, 1986).

44. Jacques Derrida, *Spurs: Nietzsche's Styles*, trans. Barbara Harlow (Chicago: University of Chicago Press, 1979), 49.

45. Jacques Derrida, *Of Grammatology*, trans. Gayatri Spivak (Baltimore: Johns Hopkins University Press, 1976), 186. Neither I nor Derrida seeks to establish the presence of metaphors of distance in Rousseau and Nietzsche. What I hope to achieve here is a means of conceiving their dilemmas as internal to the term itself.

46. Ibid., 163.

47. For example, the first usage occurs in "supplements" to a text, helpful but not necessary; the second is the basis of vitamin supplements, which supply something needed but perhaps missing in regular diets.

48. See Diana Fuss, *Essentially Speaking* (New York: Routledge, 1989); Judith Butler, *Gender Trouble: Feminism and the Subversion of Identity* (New York: Routledge, 1989); and Phelan, *Identity Politics*.

49. Judith Plant, "Ecofeminism," in *The Green Reader*, ed. Andrew Dobson (San Francisco: Mercury House, 1991).

50. Karen J. Warren, "The Power and the Promise of Ecological Feminism," *Environmental Ethics* 12 (1990): 142.

51. Carolyn Merchant, *The Death of Nature: Women, Ecology and the Scientific Revolution* (New York: HarperCollins, 1990), xvi.

52. Merchant (*The Death of Nature*, 138) gives the particularly terrifying example of two villages in the Bishopric of Trier in Germany, which in 1585, after the witch trial fever ran through town, were left with one female inhabitant each. Overall, statistics for Europe indicate that approximately 83 percent of those tried for witchcraft were women.

53. Merchant, *The Death of Nature*, 144.

54. Bill Devall and George Sessions, *Deep Ecology: Living as if Nature Mattered* (Salt Lake City: Gibbs M. Smith, 1985).

55. Kevin Paul Geiman, "Lyotard's 'Kantian Socialism,'" *Philosophy and Social Criticism* 16, no. 1 (1990): 23–37, and Bill Readings, *Introducing Lyotard* (New York: Routledge, 1991), both describe the debt that Lyotard owes to the Kant of the *Critique of Judgment* in terms that are strongly reminiscent of my reading of Rousseau and Nietzsche; Kant provides one of the links in the sequence of "dislocation" that I illustrate here. The function of judgment and its link to a limited, not really knowable nature is an important topic, one deserving of a separate paper.

56. See Jean-François Lyotard, *The Postmodern Condition: A Report on Knowledges*, trans. Geoff Bennington and Brian Massumi (Minneapolis: University of Minnesota Press, 1984); Jean-François Lyotard and Jean-Loup Thebaud, *Just Gaming*, trans. Wlad Godzich (Minneapolis: University of Minnesota Press, 1985); Donna Haraway, "A Manifesto for Cyborgs: Science, Technology, and Socialist Feminism in the 1980's," *Socialist Review* 15, no. 2 (1985): 64–107; and Donna Haraway, *Simians, Cyborgs and Women: The Reinvention of Nature* (New York: Routledge, 1991).

57. Connolly, *Political Theory and Modernity*.

58. Martin Heidegger, *The Question Concerning Technology and Other Essays* (Boston: Beacon, 1977), 3–35.

# Part II

Animal and Artifice

Chapter 4

# "Manning" the Frontiers:
# The Politics of (Human) Nature in *Blade Runner*

Michael J. Shapiro

> The Four Errors—*Man has been educated by his errors. First, he always saw himself only incompletely; second, he endowed himself with fictitious attributes; third, he placed himself in a false order or rank in relation to animals and nature; fourth, he invented ever new tables of goods and always accepted them for a time as eternal and unconditional: as a result of this, now one and now another human impulse and state held first place and was ennobled because it was esteemed so highly. If we remove the effects of these four errors, we should also remove humanity, humaneness, and "human dignity."*
>
> Friedrich Nietzsche, *The Gay Science*

## "Human Sentiments"

Ridley Scott's film *Blade Runner*, like the Philip Dick novel on which it is based, places heavy pressure on the long-held assumptions that moral sentiments are uniquely human and that they provide an unambiguous boundary between humans and other creatures.[1] One of the most thoroughgoing inquiries into the "moral sentiment" was Adam Smith's eighteenth-century treatment of morals—an inquiry that still reflects many contemporary notions of both the psychology and geography of moral concerns. In Smith's *Theory of Moral Sentiments* a markedly secularizing impulse is in operation. He substitutes social space for transcendent, spiritual space as the venue for morals. For him, the moral life is to be firmly located in the common life, and its dynamic is to consist in the exchange of sentiments. While the boundary between the sacred and the secular is the primary one upon which Smith's views have an impact, there is another boundary implicated in his way of treating the moral sentiment. Smith identifies two dimensions of the interpersonal exchanges in social space. First, there are the passions a person evinces as a result of the passions exhibited by others, and second, there are the judgments of others' actions made possible by a person's ability to adopt the perspective of an "impartial observer."

Inasmuch as Smith held primarily a sensationalist view of sentiments (for him the major constituents of moral sentiments are the passions produced by sympathetic bodily sensations), the question of the capacity for moral practices must inevitably be raised for other embodied creatures. Because animals are creatures that both invite sympathetic passions and are themselves capable of them, it is not surprising that Smith was led to a consideration of the place of animals in the exchange of sentiments. In this regard, he notes that in *all* animals, the things that cause pain or pleasure "immediately excite [these] two passions of gratitude and resentment," and goes on to suggest that given their ability to experience those sentiments, animals are "less improper objects of gratitude and resentment than inanimated objects." But despite being "less improper," and although they are capable of feeling those sensations, animals are not "complete and perfect objects either of gratitude or resentment," because they lack one important dimension involved in the human exchange of sentiments.[2] When there is a "concord" perceived between one's sentiments and those of another, there is a reassurance that one is being esteemed:

> What most of all charms us in our benefactor, is the concord
> between his sentiments and our own, with regard to what interests
> us so nearly as the worth of our own character, and the esteem
> that is due us. We are delighted to find a person who values us as
> we value ourselves, and distinguishes us from the rest of mankind,
> with an attention not unlike that with which we distinguish
> ourselves.[3]

Smith denies animals a human place in the exchange of sentiments because they are not able to make critical judgments of worthiness. Their passions do not weigh in as heavily in the human prestige system because those upon whom they bestow their sentiments are not able to feel sufficiently esteemed as a result.

Two important and overlapping interpersonal economies are evoked in Smith's reference to the place of animals in the exchange of sentiments. First, he locates them as both subjects and objects in the system of exchange but devalues their sentiments. Second, in devaluing their sentiments, he locates the primary social economy to which the exchange of sentiments is connected, the exchange of esteem. In this perhaps more fundamental economy, only humans can participate meaningfully and plausibly.

Like Smith, many contemporary thinkers are drawn to a consideration of the human-animal boundary, for they develop their notions of the social bond on the basis of both embodiment and a capacity that transcends it. For example, there is this recent formulation: "Man's uniqueness consists in his capacity to *control* his animality, a capacity which is denied to the rest of the animal world."[4] In general both before and since Smith, theories of morality have been most often predicated on ontologies in which the essentially "human" involves a capacity to transcend embodiment or "animal nature" (e.g., Smith emphasized the stoic virtue of "self-command").

## Humans, Androids, and Electric Sheep

Traditionally, when thinkers have emphasized the transcendence of animality involved in self-command, they have been thinking of an effort of will, judgment, or some wholly autonomous exercise of a human capacity. But the traditional moral thinker would lack the usual props if dropped onto Philip Dick's dystopic earth planet, early in the twenty-first century, for the conditions of possibility for thinking about human identity and moral conduct are altered there. Dick's novel is politicizing in a special sense; by altering the context in which human attributes function, they take on a different significance and therefore change from implacable facts about "human nature" to highly contingent dimensions of human subjectivity. One aspect of the altered context is a result of technology. In the very first scene, Rick Deckard and his wife, Iran, are arguing over the settings on their "Penfields" (mood organs). In Adam Smith's universe people's sentiments tend toward a natural harmony. Indeed, the musical metaphor so dominates Smith's discourse on the social bond that in one of his explications he has the sentiment of one in pain "beat time" with the level of sympathy the individual can reasonably expect from an observer.[5] In stark contrast, in Dick's futuristic universe, sentiments are harmonized not naturally but through manipulation, and the music is the noise of the Penfield as the novel opens:

> A merry little surge of electricity piped by automatic alarm from the mood organ beside his bed awakened Rick Deckard.[6]

Deckard's argument with his wife ensues when she refuses to set her Penfield at a compatible level (his is at a cheerful and energetic "D" setting and hers at a grumpy and lethargic "C").

Another major alteration in the identity structure in Dick's world is the cast of characters. In addition to humans and (live and artificial) animals, there are "rogue androids." Because of a global atomic war, most of the animal/others are extinct, and many humans, including Deckard, have artificial ones. Owning only an electric sheep, Deckard tries unsuccessfully to get his neighbor, who will soon have two "real" horses, to sell him one. Failing that, and unable to find an affordable pet in the national catalog of live animals or on "animal row," a string of retail outlets of live pets, Deckard decides to take a difficult assignment in his role as a "bounty hunter." This brings him into a confrontation with androids.

The androids were produced by a large corporation as part of the strategy to encourage emigration from earth's deteriorating condition. Those who emigrated did so to avoid mental deterioration from the radioactive fallout and to enjoy a better life-style, which would include the ownership of android servants, on another planet. Occasionally, however, androids would resist the docile roles for which they were invented and return to earth as dangerous killers. Bounty hunters were hired to eliminate them. Deckard's assignment is particularly difficult, for the escapees he is pursuing are advanced models that exceed many humans in intelligence and, most significant, cannot be unambiguously detected with the use of an empathy test that had been successful in detecting previous models.

It is the androids' lack of human empathy that sets up the complex pattern of identity relations structuring Dick's story. The people remaining on earth are involved in a fierce struggle to maintain their human identities. The primary identity threat is mental deterioration. A human who degenerates below a particular level of mental competence is regarded as "a special," and, "once pegged as a special, a citizen, even if accepting sterilization, dropped out of history. He ceased, in effect, to be part of mankind." [7] The other significant identity threat stems from the difficulty of distinguishing androids from humans. Because androids lack empathy, they are not sympathetic to or sentimental about animals. Humans use their pet ownership to help maintain their human credentials, and if it is discovered that a pet is artificial (the threat that Deckard is facing), the rationale for the pet is obviated.

Therefore, structuring Dick's narrative is an identity triangle with humans, animals, and androids at the corners, and positive or negative valences along the sides. To disassociate themselves from androids, humans must associate themselves with animals (which are in turn disassociated from androids if they are "real"). Accordingly, Deckard attempts to retire rogue androids in order to be able to afford a live pet, which he wants in order to distinguish himself from androids. Apart from the identity logic in which the three different types are implicated is the fact that Dick's world is Smithian; the social bond is based on moral sentiments. However, in this case there is an additional dimension, an instability in the identities that determine who or what is a worthy object of sympathetic identification. Given that humanlike and animal-like creatures have been made as well as or better than what "nature" can produce, nature can no longer be counted on to inscribe its work clearly.

The animal remains an important identity sign within the human social bond, but the activity involved in appropriating the sign is more feverish and disturbed than it was in the predystopic earthly condition. And, given the presence of the pseudohuman android, the animal-as-sign must play an additional role. Throughout human history (and "prehistory"), humans protected the privilege of their identity by distinguishing themselves from (mere) animals while, at the same time, distinguishing among themselves on the basis of relations with animals. In Dick's cruel new world, there is an additional frontier to police, and the animal/other must play a role in helping humans to maintain the android as other.

In Ridley Scott's film, the animal more or less disappears, and the identity problematic is centered on the man-android (or "replicant") distinction. However, before turning to the film, which retains the sentiment or empathy problematic, the man-animal relation bears further scrutiny.

## The First Frontier

Humanity's concern with its ontological condition may have always involved speculation about the human-animal relationship. According to Georges Bataille, evidence of this exists in the prehistoric wall paintings in the Lascaux caves. Resisting the view that the preponderance of the hunting thematic suggests the food fantasies of hungry hunters, Bataille sees the paintings as evidence of humanity's attempt to achieve separation as beings from animals:

> Resolutely, decisively, man wrenched himself out of the animal condition and into "manhood": that abrupt, most important of transitions left an image of itself blazed upon the rock of this cave.[8]

What is the evidence for this interpretation? Among what Bataille sees in the paintings are prohibitions relating to death rituals and sexuality, and it is through this domain of normativity, he argues, that humans are distinguished from other sentient beings. Here, as in other later texts, humans recognize their animality, but something is added in the form of a troubling normativity: "The enduring animality in us forever introduces raw life and nature into the community: prohibitions exist to quell these uprisings and spread oil on the sea of insurgent animal passion and unruliness." The step from animal to "man" "is conditioned upon recognizing prohibitions and upon violating them."[9]

According to Bataille, therefore, the Lascaux cave paintings are to be read symbolically rather than materialistically. They are imaginative enactments in which humans are extracting their identities from animality rather than meditations on the importance of the hunt in producing the food necessary for human survival. One detail Bataille uses in making this case for his interpretation bears special attention here because it arises in Ridley Scott's filmic text. It is the presence of an imaginary animal in the paintings, a unicorn whose presence suggests that animals are being treated in terms of the relationship to an ontological concern, the relationship of a creature to truth.

If we accept Bataille's view that the human use of animal/others has had primarily an identity-constituting function, that humans have always located animals within the discursive economies with which they distinguish themselves, it should be evident that the meanings assigned to animal-human relationships are associated with heavy symbolic investments. The borders constructed as prehistoric humans distinguished themselves from animals have therefore since been assiduously patrolled.

This has been nowhere more apparent than in the continuing fascination with monkeys and apes, who, by dint of their upright postures, humanoid appearance, and social capabilities, have presented the most serious challenge to the policing of the human-animal frontier. Aware of this fascination, Franz Kafka mocks humanity's striving to distinguish itself from apes in a story in which an ape, desperate to escape its confinement, carefully studied the human behavior in proximity to its cage and, in time, "managed," as the ape puts it, "to reach the cultural level of an average European." [10]

Putting it less ironically but nevertheless aptly, Donna Haraway has also noted the human preoccupation with simians:

> Monkeys and apes have a privileged relation to nature and culture
> for western people: simians occupy the border zones between
> those potent mythic poles. . . . The commercial and scientific traffic
> in monkeys and apes is a traffic in meanings. [11]

This trafficking has been apparent in a variety of writing genres. For example, Edgar Rice Burroughs's commercial success with his Tarzan stories is not unrelated to the boundary flirtation that Tarzan, the "ape-man's," ambiguous background and behavior represent. In the very first Tarzan story, Burroughs plays with the boundary in an episode in which Tarzan, behaving as an animal/predator, kills a local black tribesman and is on the verge of treating his victim as fresh meat. At the moment he is about to dine, Tarzan is apparently without the "moral sentiments" that Adam Smith and others have seen as distinctive to humans, even though Burroughs has given him the raw materials for such sentiments—various aspects of human embodiment and their associated capacities, and even added class distinctions:

> How may we judge him, by what standards, this ape-man with the heart and head and body of an English gentleman, and the training of a wild beast?[12]

The question of judgment quickly becomes moot, however, as Burroughs has immanence substitute for training. "A qualm of nausea" inhibits Tarzan, as human norms (which Burroughs seems to treat as universal) manifest themselves in the form of a counterinstinct:

> All he knew was that he could not eat the flesh of this black man, and this hereditary instinct, ages old, usurped the functions of his untaught mind and saved him from transgressing a worldwide law of whose very existence he was ignorant.[13]

Burroughs's Tarzan stories play with the human-animal boundary but maintain it nevertheless. For Burroughs, as for Bataille, the human is extracted from the domain of the animal by virtue of the prohibition.

Social science discourses, like those in the literary/commercial domain, also provide evidence for Haraway's suggestion that scrutiny of apes and monkeys is a "traffic in meanings." When it is discovered that simians appear to transgress a boundary used to maintain human distinctiveness, a new frontier is created to protect it. For example, in a recent discussion of the nature of the social link for baboons and humans, the authors grant not only that baboons have a relatively well articulated social order but also that, as among humans, their social order is "performative"—they actively negotiate its structures. Once this is admitted, however, the frontier must be "manned." Accordingly, they pose the question, "When we transform baboons into active performers of their society, does this put them on a par with humans?" [14] Their answer is no. Unable to use either sociality or linguisticality to maintain human distinctiveness, they turn to the "practical means" through which humans versus baboons perform the social and argue that while humans have material resources and symbols, baboons have "only themselves, only their bodies as resources." [15]

This argument is more dogged than convincing. Haraway undoubtedly has it right when she says:

> By the late twentieth century in United States scientific culture, the boundary between human and animal is thoroughly breached. The last beachheads of uniqueness have been polluted if not turned into amusement parks—language, toll use, social behavior, mental

events, nothing really convincingly settles the separation of human and animal.[16]

The border war continues as strategies for maintaining the frontier are altered each time new evidence impeaches earlier modes for distinguishing humans from animals. The frontier shifts, but a distinction remains. Paradoxically, however, the human desire to be distinguished from animals has often required greater intimacy with them. For example, the mentality involved in maintaining the historical gulf between urban bourgeois classes and the peasantry has been based in part on the mode of intimacy with animals.

As bourgeois classes developed, especially in the nineteenth century, part of their notion of their distinctiveness was based on the greater degree of segregation between their living quarters and those of animals, and they expressed contempt at the animal-like existence of the peasantry who allowed farm animals into their living quarters. "The whole upbringing of the nineteenth-century bourgeois was based upon a notion of moral superiority to the more bestial lower classes. He had mastered the animal within." [17] However, as one historical analysis has shown,

> at the same time that the urban bourgeoisie was complaining
> about the cohabitation of men and animals in the peasant villages,
> distinctions were being created between animals. Pets became
> very important in nineteenth-century society. ... While it was
> considered highly improper to have piglets or hens running
> around in the living room, a lapdog in bed or a kitten on one's
> knee was something quite different.[18]

Part of the reason for this is the above-noted connection, made by writers from Adam Smith to Philip Dick, between keeping pets and having good moral sentiments. "Caring for animals was thought to make people into better human beings." [19] Thus, the special value placed upon owning pets, their importance in the boundary maintenance behavior of the humans who remain on earth in Dick's *Do Androids Dream of Electric Sheep?* has a continuity with the mentality of bourgeois city dwellers in earlier periods.

## The Second Frontier

In Dick's novel and Scott's film the altered cast of characters, notably the presence of cyborgs, "creatures simultaneously animal and machine, who populate worlds ambiguously natural and crafted," [20] produces an immense complication for the construction of a stable and distinct human identity. And this is not the kind of problem one should consign to "science fiction," for it resonates with more contemporary identity problematics. The human-cyborg frontier that Dick and Scott explore has already been opened up. It has existed in prototypic form in the social and political discourses that have attempted to distinguish an authentic humanity from that which is manifested in modernity's increasingly instrumental modes of rationality, within which calculable and subservient forms of subjectivity are in evidence. In both Dick's novel and Scott's film, the theme is very contemporary. However, rather than simply lamenting the losses humanity experiences as a result of modern technology, which is a traditional, conservative critique of modernity, Dick's novel and Scott's film deconstruct the primary opposition, that between nature and culture or artifice, with which the traditional criticism works.[21] The "manning" of the second frontier takes place in a world in which technology has all but effaced this opposition.

Where can one turn to examine the impetus for the making of this second frontier, which is foregrounded in Scott's film? Just as an anthropological imagination was helpful in disclosing the identity concerns directing the constitution of the human-animal frontier, it can profitably be applied to the human-cyborg frontier. When humans have tried to distinguish themselves from animals, the primary strategy has been to locate humanity in a meaning frame in which they have a capacity that transcends the merely physical—hence the special emphasis on "moral sentiments," the capacity for which involves more than mere physicality.

However, in the confrontation with the cyborg, the strategy has been partly reversed; cyborgs, it would seem, are machines, made in contrast to humans, who are "physical." But "the boundary between physical and nonphysical is very imprecise for us,"[22] and, indeed, the replicant Roy Baty (in *Blade Runner*) says, "We're not machines . . . we're physical." This claim is reflective of the many ambiguities that develop as Deckard tries to do his job of "retiring" replicants, a job he can manage only as long as he is able to maintain an unambiguous distinction between humans and replicants.

Deckard's practice is merely more focused than the ordinary human-cyborg policy. In a variety of domains of practice, this second frontier is being "manned." *Blade Runner's* problematic functions primarily within this second frontier. Because of his extraordinary role in the policing process (certainly not because of his cognitive complexity), Deckard is forced into reflecting on what humans are and what sense their institutions make, given the special boundary problems with which they must cope.

Therefore this film (and all science fiction involving the fictive production of the alien) provides an opportunity to intensify reflection on border issues. As one commentary on the genre has noted, "The story of the alien is always a story of borders and the institutional forces that try to neutralize and control those borders in the name of a certain political economy." [23] That "certain political economy" involves identity currency. In *Blade Runner*, official policy is organized around a citizenship/sovereignty impulse, which is manifested in a securing of the identity boundaries of the state. Keeping the alien/others outside human territory requires that the alien be both normatively and spatially contained. Hence, in *Blade Runner*, the replicants, who are dangerously close to humans in appearance and function, must be kept outside the territory spatially (they are an "offworld" work force) and normatively—they cannot be allowed to replicate humans, so they are programmed for a shortened (four-year) life span lest they learn to take on human sentiments and efface the last significant distinguishing characteristic.

Therefore, when some of them escape from their spatial alienation (they return to earth from their offworld work venue) and seek to escape their normative alienation, to renegotiate their longevity limits, the humans try to destroy them in order to save themselves—that is, to preserve their uniqueness. Deckard is the blade runner, the one who is given the assignment to protect humanity, and his inability to maintain the motivation and perspective necessary to function in his job—to police the frontier effectively—is the primary narrative in Scott's film version of the story. The human-animal frontier is largely neglected in the film (except for some hints left by the character Gaff in the form of origami figures he creates).

### *Blade Runner:* **The Story**

The dramatic visual aspects of *Blade Runner* cannot be neglected. The dystopic city of Los Angeles in 2019 is represented as a poisoned, crowded, polyglot cacophony of dialects and noises from people and from flying advertising vehicles broadcasting offers of rewards for emigration to the "offworld." Complementing the sounds is a confusing blend of sights—neon signs with mobile displays, flames and sparks shooting off everywhere, and a bazaar-type street scene punctuated with piles of rubble and dirt.

From a political point of view, the most significant aspect of the cityscape is represented as a sharp contrast between the reality of the bustling, confused street life and the tall, templelike structure of the Tyrell Corporation towering well above the street, appearing as a kind of transcendence looming over the ethnically and linguistically heterogeneous mob of people who are barely intelligible to each other. This corporation seems to rule what is left of the world not only in a bureaucratic sense but also in a theological sense. The heteroglot speech practices are a reminder of the

Tower of Babel episode in Genesis. It seems as if some human attempt at boundary crossing is being punished by a god who has "baffled their tongues" (Yahweh's punishment in Genesis).

As the cityscape is presented in the opening scene, the camera zooms into the Tyrell Corporation's interrogation room. Within the first few moments one of the film's dominant tropes is presented — an eyeball. We see the Los Angeles skyline, smoke, fog, and shooting flames reflected in the eyeball of Holden, a police functionary about to administer the Voigt-Kampff empathy test to Leon, a suspected replicant. The test measures emotions by monitoring various physiological reactions to questions that, in a human context, are expected to evoke powerful emotional responses. Foregrounded during this scene is one of Leon's eyes, for part of the test measures involuntary movement of the pupils. There is a strange, nonreflective quality to Leon's eye.

What place does the eye, which is a pervasive visual imagery as well as a focus for various parts of the script, have? If we attend to the sound rather than the grapheme, an ambiguity presents itself. Can the eye be doing double duty, representing both vision as the "eye" and identity as the "I"? A number of details move toward coherence if we answer this in the affirmative. Certainly, as a whole, the story involves both human (if Deckard is a human) and replicant attempts to achieve a coherent subjectivity — an I. Leon, who like all replicants has no extended past, has collected pictures of others in an attempt to simulate an identity with a temporality that reaches back to a childhood. And Rachael, a Tyrell replicant/employee, who thinks she is human until Deckard's visit to the corporation during which he gives her the Voigt-Kampff test, has been given memories and, unlike other replicants, has no known termination date. Her extended temporality plays an important part in her passing as human.

Another important detail is the extreme thickness of the glasses worn by Tyrell, the head of the corporation and "maker" of the replicants. Indeed, it is an ironic reversal that the cold, distant (his eyes/I are behind a shield), and rationalistic Tyrell, who displays no human sentiments, presides over a world in which his kind are supposed to be distinguishable from his creations on the basis of a capacity for sentiment. Moreover, the thick glasses emphasize Tyrell's eyes (he is the head, human I) but at the same time, that I is virtually inaccessible.

The eyes become significant again as representations of the self in two instances in which the replicants are attempting to kill humans. Leon is shot by Rachael before he manages to kill Deckard by pressing his thumbs in Deckard's eyes (almost ending him as an I), and the leader of the escaped replicants, Roy Baty, slays Tyrell (the head I) that way.

Finally, and perhaps most telling, is the scene in which the replicants, Roy and Leon, enter the small factory of Mr. Chew, who does subcontracting for the Tyrell Corporation. Baty and Leon, in their quest for longevity, hope to get some clues about their pseudogenetic coding. Chew manufactures eyes for the latest, Nexus 6 replicants, of which Leon and Baty are "models." Chew is seen lifting eyes out of tanks with chop sticks and peering at them through a microscope. For him, the eyes are the achievements of his craft, and, taking pride in his work, he says, "Ha ha, so beautiful."

When Leon tugs off the life-support hose attached to Chew's protected suit (he's working in subzero temperature—to protect the eyes), Chew turns sharply and utters the double entendre, "Where did you come from? What the hell do you think you are doing?" Baty picks up on the hell imagery, and in an ironic reversal of a Blake poem, responds, "Fiery the angels fell, deep thunder rolled around their shores, burning with the fires of orc." Blake's line from his "America, a Prophecy," reads, "Fiery the angels rose." Because the poem is about freedom and independence, the reference to it helps to thematize Baty's quest to be free of Tyrell's programming.

The eyes play into this thematic; after Chew says, "I made your eyes," Baty responds with, "If you could only see what I have seen with your eyes." Here Baty is taking some control by noting that whoever the creator may have been of his (eyes/I), it has been his use that has made them significant. This politicizing of vision effects a coherence between the eye of vision and the I of identity. Throughout the film, the control of the gaze is at issue. For example, the long scene in which Deckard subjects a photograph of a room with a woman to close scrutiny with a highly calibrated, voice-operated viewing machine dramatizes the extent to which the human gaze has been subordinated to a policing-oriented technology. The subjugation and narrowing of the gaze's function and orientation is underscored by the still photograph ("hard copy") that Deckard obtains from the machine. The picture of the woman and room is reminiscent of paintings from an earlier century in which the gaze applied to interiors and their inhabitants operated in behalf of a more sympathetic, aesthetic practice. It seems clear that who or what controls the gaze is at issue, but it is unclear whether humans have more control over their ways of seeing than do replicants.

More generally, while the primary level of signification treats the control over vision, the thematic as a whole involves control over the authorship of one's experience, the ownership of the I or self. The eye/I theme therefore moves the problematic in the same direction as the memory theme. Part of one's sense of self, one's ability to maintain a coherent identity, is based on the ability to endure (hence Baty's quest), but part is also based, as has been suggested, on what one has already endured. One's self-understanding as a human is based on the idea that one is now the same person who developed from childhood, adolescence, and so on. That the replicants are seeking a human-type subjectivity, to endure in both a past and future sense—that is, to be able to remember and to anticipate—blurs the boundaries between them and humans.

Leon, who collects pictures of someone else's past in order to manufacture a past he has not lived, tries to return to his apartment (after shooting Holden) to get them. But Deckard and Gaff, a police detective, are already there looking through his photos. Deckard, who also has photos around his apartment, expresses surprise at Leon's interest in this ersatz past. And later, Rachael displays a lot of interest in Deckard's photos, which seem to reach back over several generations. At a minimum, the issue of the photographs encourages reflection on the human-cyborg boundary by evoking a strong similarity between Deckard and Leon as collectors of photos.

Rachael is the one replicant with a manufactured memory and, because she has been kept ignorant of being a replicant, has played the dual role of a Tyrell employee as well as product. During a conversation with Deckard in his apartment, after she suspects she is a replicant, Deckard tells her that her memory is an "implant" and proves it by reciting details he could only have seen in a Tyrell Corporation file. The purpose of the implant was to make her think she is human. This is not surprising, for human self-understandings are organized in the form of narratives. If one compares the meaning structure of visual arts with that of human identity, as one analyst has, it becomes clear that self-knowledge and coherence require more than simply "wide-angle introspection" to "afford a coherent idea of one's personhood." What must be included is a story, a "life story," for narrative plays an essential role in the development of a unified individual identity.[24]

However, as has been argued, there is that which forms identity by being integral to it—and narrative plays a part here—and there is that which forms identity by containing it and setting it apart from otherness. In the context of the social network on earth in *Blade Runner*, a narrative going back to childhood makes a self coherent by giving it temporal extension, but it has an additional significance. The fact of having had a childhood is a form of distinction with special value because of the nearness of replicant/others who have not had one.

Before the film is over, however, both dimensions of the coherence structure of the human are called into question. What does it mean to have real memories or a real past? Although this question is never explicitly raised in the film, the postmodern, dystopic world within which the action takes place—a world that is overcoded, that contains an unmanageable jumble of advertising appeals from disembodied voices along with a heteroglot of language and speech styles that threaten both self-understanding and mutual intelligiblity—makes an implicit point. It is that the stuff from which memory can be made, expressed, rehearsed, and so on is not owned by anyone. The issue of the ownership of signification has always been complex and problematic, and in the world of *Blade Runner* it is even more difficult to claim that a person can control meaning structures. Once reflected upon, it becomes evident that memory is never "natural," for codes are human inventions. Inasmuch as one cannot have a past without codes—without ways of inscribing and giving significance to it—it is problematic to say that one "has memories." The Los Angeles of 2019, in which the very humanity of the inventors of the codes is being called into question, places an additional tax on the ownership of memory.

Where memory fails as a distinguishing characteristic of humans, so does the motivation to which it is connected, the desire to endure in the sense of having a long future. Even what seems to be the primary drive of humans to continue living is shared with replicants, who develop that motivation by themselves. This shared and pervasive desire is emphasized when, at one point, one of the flying advertising vehicles promoting emigration to the offworld with the slogan "Live on the offworld" has its sound system malfunction. The message comes out with the endlessly repeated, "Live on, live on, live on, live on . . . "

The failure of past and future orientations to distinguish adequately between humans and cyborgs moves in the direction of the primary deconstructive effect of the filmic story as a whole, which focuses on the identity boundaries humans use to maintain their coherence and exclusivity. The fact that Deckard is so obtuse to what is happening (as his expectations about the differences between humans and replicants are violated) helps to produce a plot that takes the shape of a *roman d'education*, Deckard's sentimental education. He has sentiments that have a potential for spilling over the human-replicant boundary, but his job requires a strict control over those sentiments, for they are always in danger of being inappropriate lest they be deployed on nonhumans. Reflection sets in slowly as he observes the way that replicants cling to life and the props that humans use to give life meaning and coherence. As he begins to discover the various dimensions of his own sentiments, he also learns how similar they are to those of replicants, saying at one point, "Replicants weren't supposed to have feelings, but neither are blade runners. What was happening to me?"

There is a parallel narrative that also helps to efface the human-replicant boundary. Tyrell, the designer and manufacturer of replicants (the "creator"), is shown as unredeemably unfeeling, and so is Bryant, the police chief who refers to replicants as "skin jobs" and is no more sympathetic to Deckard, whom he enlists against his will in the job of retiring replicants.

Deckard, by contrast, is not only a redeemable human being (there are moral sentiments there waiting to come out), he is in fact redeemed, and the role of the replicant, Roy Baty, is very much one of a redeemer. Baty is, indeed, a Christ figure, and it is Deckard who is ultimately saved.

However, before he confronts his redeemer, we witness his capacity for empathy or moral sentiment deepen while, at the same time, his identity distance from replicants lessens. Two intimate scenes with Deckard and Rachael are relevant here. In one, Rachael plays the piano, and Deckard says, "*You* play beautifully," with the "you" very subtly emphasized. In effect, Deckard is employing a grammar that gives Rachael agency; the implication is that it is she, and not her implanted routines, who is producing the music. Her humanity is further suggested in an identity pose as she and Deckard are both shown in profile as they sit together at the piano.

Deckard's linguistic strategy for humanizing Rachael also takes a more aggressive form than a mere grammar of agency. In a violent love scene in which Deckard forces himself on Rachael, he also forces her discourse: "Say kiss me," he prompts, and she says, "Kiss me." "I want you," he prompts further, and she says, "I want you." She then adds, unprompted, "I want you . . . put your hands on me." Although within some interpretive frames what we are witnessing is a rape, in the context of the primary narrative of the film, Rachael is here crossing the replicant-human frontier, moving toward the human identity she ends up sharing with Deckard.

Another boundary tension between replicants and humans is represented in the interaction between Sebastian, a Tyrell employee, and Pris, Baty's girlfriend who has been described to Deckard as "your basic pleasure model" when he is shown images of the replicants he is to retire. Pris, who is befriended and taken in by Sebastian, and subsequently Baty when he shows up later, pretends to be taking refuge in Sebastian's apartment in order to use him to get to Tyrell. Several ambiguities are foregrounded in the scenes in Sebastian's apartment. Sebastian is a replicant maker, but his locution "There is some of me in you" suggests identity rather than the kind of distance affected by the head maker, Tyrell. Sebastian shares something else with the replicants. He has the human version of being a short-timer, suffering from the "disease" of accelerated decrepitude. He looks a lot older than his years would warrant.

Added to these ambiguities is the fact that Sebastian is also a maker in his spare time. His apartment is full of small, humanlike cyborgs who march around speaking to each other and greeting new arrivals to the apartment. When Sebastian first ushers Pris into his apartment and they are greeted by his creations, he says, "These are my friends, I made them." His giving new meaning to the phrase "making friends" exemplifies the irony surrounding speech practices when contexts are ambiguated.

There are many such discursive moments, including the remark by the replicant/nightclub performer Zhora—Deckard's first retiree—who responds to Deckard's moralizing remarks about the sexploitation that may be involved in her work, asking, "Are you for real?" In any case, ersatz friends are fine for Sebastian, for he seems to respect all beings, from the austere and distant Tyrell to his own creations, his "friends," and the replicants he has helped to construct. He is strangely mystified about how to characterize the replicants when he questions Pris and Baty about their abilities, and Pris deepens the ambiguities when she remarks, "We're not computers, Sebastian, we're physical." Sebastian is not motivated to police boundaries. He seems to be in awe of all creatures, even those he himself has made.

Even one of the police officers is not disposed to do boundary policing. Gaff, who works for the police and is Chief Bryant's arresting officer who brings Deckard in early in the film, ends up subverting the identity policy involved in retiring replicants. He, like Sebastian, has an imagination not controlled by the official stock categories of creatures. An identity between Sebastian and Gaff is effected also by their shared interest in unicorns. Recall that for Bataille, the inclusion of a unicorn in the Lascaux cave paintings constituted evidence of the exercise of imagination about creature identity. Among the "machines" in Sebastian's apartment is a small mechanical unicorn. Gaff, like Sebastian, makes creatures, but he does it with origami. *His* speculations on identity boundaries are represented by the origami figures he makes throughout the film—animals, a person with a tail, and, finally, a unicorn.

Deckard discovers the unicorn outside of his apartment, just before he and Rachael leave together in the last scene. The unicorn is, at once, evidence that Gaff has been to the apartment and of his view of the various boundary distinctions. Despite knowing that Rachael is now a rogue replicant, he had decided not to apprehend her, an attitude he signaled to Deckard earlier when, after Baty's death, he said to Deckard that he had now gotten them all. When the unicorn is discovered outside Deckard's apartment, there is a voice-over with Gaff's voice repeating his earlier remark, "Too bad she won't live, but then, who does?" The unicorn simply underscores the other gestures with which he refuses to commit himself to a rigid distinction between the "natural" and artificial.

Ultimately, however, it is Roy Baty who is the film's strongest, most exemplary character. As a physical presence, Baty (actor Rutger Hauer) is at times glowering and menacing—a Nordic, angular, cold, chiseled face and a powerful-looking body. But in his philosophical and emotional moments (e.g., bending over the dead Pris) he becomes sympathetic. His speech style involves a variety of modes, shifting from poetic to theological to scientific and philosophical discourse. And he is pervasively ironic because of all the characters, he is the most mindful of the boundary issues involved in a world shared between humans and replicants.

One dimension of his irony is the reversal of imagery as in the above noted reversal of the Blake poem—"Fiery the angels fell" instead of "rose," a line that contained another irony because of its positioning; he had just been asked what the hell he was doing. This is exemplary of the major aspect of Baty's ironic remarks, which are based on his play with context, his subtle manipulations of the discursive spaces that control meanings. Perhaps most exemplary in this respect is his remark to Sebastian when he first enters his apartment: "I like a man who stays put." At a simple level, it can be interpreted as a reference to the fact that Sebastian has not emigrated to the offworld, but at another level it evokes the boundary-crossing thematic. As a human, Sebastian is more or less stable within the symbolic order.

However, the major manipulations Baty engages in are connected with his attempt to get to Tyrell, who is positioned to know the vital code he is seeking. He ultimately gains admission to Tyrell's penthouse apartment in the Tyrell Corporation building through Sebastian, by encouraging him to continue his ongoing chess match with Tyrell. As they are seeking permission to come up to the apartment from a lower floor, Baty instructs Sebastian in the chess moves he is making over the phone to Tyrell.

At the level of the game, Baty reverses the positions of the master and pawn by finding a mate in two moves with the use of a pawn, and at the level of life, he is both, himself, changing positions with the master and, not incidentally, elevating Tyrell's pawn, Sebastian, into a winning position.

Once he gains admission, however, the imagery shifts from gaming to theology, as Baty says to Tyrell, "It's not easy to meet your maker," and after being asked about what is troubling him, "I want more life, fucker" (it could have been "Father"), and, as a prodigal son (a designation Tyrell uses), adds the admission, "I've done questionable things." Tyrell defeats Baty's hopes with an ambiguous line. Referring to the "facts of life," he tells Baty that there is no way to reverse his extinction date. The reference to "facts" is discordant. It hovers ambiguously between what is natural or given and what has been invented. Facts ordinarily refer to what is given in a natural sense, yet here they refer to artifice, to what has been made to be unalterable. Here, as throughout *Blade Runner*, the venerable distinction between *physis* and *techne* is under pressure.

It would appear that Baty never quite overcomes his ambivalence toward Tyrell. At the end of their encounter he kisses him first, acknowledging him as a father. Then he kills him. The ambivalence manifested by the two actions appears to operate more within a psychoanalytic than a theological frame. At a simple level, it seems that Baty kills Tyrell out of frustration and for vengeance because his father will not give him what he wants. At another, however, the killing is an act of purification (with ritual significance within a theological frame or rivalrous significance within a psychoanalytic one). Whatever narrative one allows to govern the significance here, Baty seems changed. He is more at peace with himself and is resigned to his imminent death.

He has, as it turns out, one more task, the redemption of Deckard, although at this moment he is not prepared for this particular outcome. However, much of the imagery works in the direction of making of him a Christ-like figure in the last encounter with a human rival. The fight scene with Deckard begins with contention and difference and moves in the direction of identity as Deckard and Baty together efface the human-replicant boundary.

Back in Sebastian's apartment after killing Tyrell (and apparently Sebastian), Baty, with a kiss, bids farewell to the dead Pris, whom Deckard has killed there. This leaves blood on his face that looks like Indian war paint. Thus decorated for the final battle, he runs past Deckard's line of sight, and, as Deckard's shot misses, he shouts, "Aren't you the good *man*." He manages to grab Deckard's arm, remove the gun from his hand, and then break two of Deckard's fingers, indicating that it is vengeance for the deaths of Leon and Pris. He replaces the gun in Deckard's crippled hand and then drives a nail into his own hand, right through the palm. This gesture operates at two levels. First, it seems to be a calculated effort to stimulate his energy, to produce a pseudoadrenalin rush so that he can finish his last task before expiring; second, it is a mortification of the flesh, which further identifies him as a Christ-like redeemer.

The fight continues with both of them having crippled hands. As Baty watches Deckard fight on against overwhelming odds—much of the imagery here evokes a chess game context, with Baty's head breaking through a checker-board-painted wall and ending up on what appears to be a square of a checkered board—it becomes clear to Baty that they both want the same thing, to endure. They have been in the same game with the same stakes.

Finally, chased and harassed onto roof tops, Deckard is about to lose his grip and plunge to his death. But Baty relaxes his rivalrous posture and grabs Deckard's wrist, just as he loses his grip on the edge of a roof top. Then, seemingly composed, Baty sits opposite Deckard and speaks to him of what his brief life has been like, saying, among other things, that he has seen things "you people wouldn't believe." He expires just after saying, "And now, it's time to die."

Deckard's voice-over after Baty's death retains the cadence of a some-what slow thinker, but his words nevertheless evidence some edification, recognition that he and Baty are not different after all, that one cannot un-ambiguously distinguish the "natural" from the made. Perhaps this is an ambiguity that has its most exemplary resonances in the word "creature," which comes from an anachronistic, theological discourse that is predi-cated on the idea that all living things have a transcendent maker. But Baty is also a creature whose maker was a godlike father. In the last analysis, all human attempts to police the new frontier between this kind of creature and themselves have failed.

What remains is a scene within a very different visual setting, as Rachael and Deckard leave together, after Gaff's reprieve. They leave the city, with its sharp verticality, represented in the difference between the tall, temple-like Tyrell Corporation building and the polyglot street scene on the dying planet—between a controller maker and diverse creatures living under a death sentence. What they leave, therefore, is an old theology, and what they glide into is a "natural" setting of trees, mountains, and lakes that flit by the windows of their flying vehicle. But there has been no basis left to speak of the "natural."

What, then, can it mean for them to be suddenly out in nature? It is not at all clear what it means, but we can turn to Nietzsche again, who is full of cautions about expecting nature to yield answers as if it exists as a set of intrinsic norms, a holder of meanings and answers, ready to respond to human queries. Modern "man," Nietzsche says, has sought to "understand the lawfulness of nature in order to submit to it," but this is hopeless be-cause "man is the *rule*, nature is *without rule*." [25] Like Roy Baty, who mocks Deckard's struggles to survive with such ironic remarks as "That's the spirit" and "Show me what you're made of," Nietzsche disparages the idea that there is a special spirit behind the physical. So Deckard and Rachael end up "out in nature," which humans like, says Nietzsche, "because it has no opinion of us." [26]

## Notes

1. Philip Dick, *Do Androids Dream of Electric Sheep?* (New York: Ballantine, 1968).

2. Adam Smith, *The Theory of Moral Sentiments*, ed. D. D. Raphael and A. L. Macfie (In-dianapolis: Liberty Classics, 1982), 94, 95.

3. Ibid.

4. Werner Stark, *The Social Bond*, vol. 1 (New York: Fordham University Press, 1976), 7.

5. Smith, *The Theory of Moral Sentiments*, 22.

6. Dick, *Do Androids Dream of Electric Sheep?*, 1.

7. Ibid., 3.

8. Georges Bataille, *Lascaux; or the Birth of Art*, trans. Austryn Wainhouse (Lausanne, Switzerland: Skira, 1955), preface.

9. Ibid., 37.

10. Franz Kafka, "A Report to an Academy," in *The Complete Stories*, ed. Nahum N. Glatzer (New York: Schocken, 1946), 258.

11. Donna Haraway, *Primate Visions: Gender, Race and Nature in the World of Modern Science* (New York, Routledge, 1990), 1.

12. Edgar Rice Burroughs, *Tarzan of the Apes* (New York: Ballantine, 1963), 71.

13. Ibid., 72.

14. Shirley S. Strum and Bruno Latour, "Redefining the Social Link: From Baboons to Humans," in *Primate Politics*, ed. Glendon Schubert and Roger Masters (Carbondale: Southern Illinois University Press, 1991), 78.

15. Ibid., 79.

16. Donna Haraway, "A Manifesto for Cyborgs," *Socialist Review* 15 (March/April 1985): 68.

17. Jonas Fykman and Orvar Lofgren, *Culture Builders* (New Brunswick, N.J.: Rutgers University Press, 1987), 85.

18. Ibid., 78–79.

19. Ibid., 79.

20. This characterization belongs to Haraway, "A Manifesto for Cyborgs," 66.

21. This argument is made in Michael Ryan and Douglas Kellner, "Technophobia," in *Alien Zone*, ed. Annette Kuhn (New York: Verso, 1990), 63.

22. Haraway, "A Manifesto for Cyborgs," 70.

23. Michael Beechler, "Border Patrols," in *Aliens: The Anthropology of Science Fiction*, ed. George E. Slusser and Eric S. Rabkin (Carbondale: Southern Illinois University Press, 1987), 26.

24. David Novitz, "Art, Narrative, and Human Nature," *Philosophy and Literature* 13 (1989): 59, 62.

25. Friedrich Nietzsche, *Human All Too Human*, trans. Marion Farber (Lincoln: University of Nebraska Press, 1984), no. 11, 84, 81.

26. Ibid., no. 508, 237.

Chapter 5

## *Brave New World* in the Discourses of Reproductive and Genetic Technologies

Valerie Hartouni

"The final and most searching revolution ... the really revolutionary revolution, is to be achieved not in the external world, but in the souls and flesh of human beings"—so wrote Aldous Huxley in a foreword to his novel *Brave New World*.[1] This foreword Huxley attached to his work some fifteen years after its initial publication in 1931. While it contains passing gestures in the direction of acknowledging some of the novel's artistic and prophetic shortcomings, its primary purpose appears to have been to reintroduce the tale to a world whose immediate past and present circumstance lent it a reality and plausibility well beyond what Huxley himself could originally have anticipated. Of more pressing concern to the author than the novel's many failures of form or foresight was the vulnerability of an only recently liberated postwar world and the treacherous new beginnings to which this world seemed irreversibly committed with the rise of the totalitarian state, the unchallenged construction of death centers for the "unfit," the completion of the Manhattan Project, and the entrenchment of Cold War relations.

When situated against this background and the many staggering questions that had begun to emerge with the war's end about what had happened and how and why, the story *Brave New World* told was fundamentally transformed. Regarded initially by some as a "mildly pornographic fantasy," [2] and by others as a somewhat reactionary diatribe concerned more with the democratizing potential of technology than with its potential for dehumanization,[3] the work became somber political commentary on dangers postponed but not canceled. "Out of the realm of mere slavish imitation of nature, into the . . . world of human mastery and control," [4] the penultimate revolution or that revolution about which men had only dreamed at least since Bacon had, in Huxley's estimation, begun. Through the development and application of ever more sophisticated therapies and technologies, the body and the body politic together would be normalized, stabilized, modified, and "cured" of their many disorders; human suffering in all its various forms would be alleviated finally and forever. "All things considered," wrote Huxley, "it looks as though Utopia were far closer to us today than anyone, only fifteen years ago, could have imagined. . . . If we refrain from blowing ourselves to smithereens in the interval . . . , it is quite possible that the full horror will be upon us within a single century." [5]

If *Brave New World* seemed at one time to shed critical light upon a world poised at some kind of crossroads, a world that was not only recovering from but beginning as well to revel in the realization that "all things were possible," that light has since dimmed considerably. Indeed, today, one could say that it has been all but extinguished, so "old world" does Huxley's "new world" now appear. Its inhabitants, its technology, its organization of knowledge, social relations, and desire direct our attention not toward the future but to an age now long past—to the world of our parents and their parents as well. Its nightmares are not those of one living in the late twentieth century, nor precisely are the fears, terrors, and various fantasies the work conjures and parodies. We are not free of political nightmares, and much about the present configuration of life in the late twentieth century is quite terrifying, but the tale itself hardly sounds the depths of either.

It is rather curious, then, that *Brave New World* should be positioned so prominently in an emerging, ever-expanding discourse on the new technologies of human genetics and reproduction. In an otherwise diverse and contesting set of literatures spanning medicine, law, ethics, feminism, and public policy, as well as in popular discourse and debate over the proper use and potential abuse of these new technologies, *Brave New World* is a persistent and authoritative presence. Routinely rehearsed to frame multiple, competing sets of claims regarding the implications of genetic and reproductive manipulations, the work is as frequently invoked only in passing or by title. In either case, the authority and centrality of the text are simply assumed, as is its relevance. Within the context of these literatures and popular culture more generally, it is as if Huxley had become a master cartographer and his novel, a base map from which contemporary thought and imagination confidently took its bearings. Out of the technoculture of one age he is said to have drawn, in astonishingly accurate detail, the contours of another, not yet our own perhaps, but similar enough in the wake of radically new and expanding biotechnical possibilities as to be both its map and measure.

What I intend to do in this essay is offer a reading of the place that *Brave New World* holds both in popular debate and across a range of contending literatures concerned with the development and deployment of new reproductive and genetic technique. Whether proffered as illustration, prophecy, or specter, invocations of Huxley's tale clearly function as a kind of shorthand for a host of issues having to do generally with the organization, application, and regulation of these new technologies. They also mark in abbreviated fashion an equally broad range of issues generated by the use or anticipated use of these technologies having to do with formulations and configurations of freedom and power as well as human nature and identity. Still more interesting, however, and in many ways more significant, than the place the novel holds is the world it holds in place— discursively, semiotically, politically. Within the context of debates over new reproductive and genetic techniques, the novel provides a universe of fixed meaning that stabilizes and rehabilitates the many disturbed and unsettled cultural narratives that frame these debates and form their substance. In this respect, it is a reactionary discourse, recirculating notions of nature, power, choice, identity, and freedom that contemporary reproductive and genetic practices disrupt.

Consider, by way of example, the original ruling handed down by the New Jersey Superior Court in the case of "Baby M." In the opening pages of his opinion, Judge Sorkow links the emergence and appeal of alternative methods of reproduction to what he describes as a growing epidemic of infertility and "dearth of adoptable children." [6] Noting the "social and psychological importance people attach to the ideal of having children who are genetically theirs," or "bear[ing] a child naturally," the judge proceeds to detail medical science's response—"the development of new techniques and alternatives for non-coital reproduction"—and to observe that while these new techniques present "awesome opportunities," they also have far-reaching social consequences for, among other things, the organization and meaning of "family." [7] Following his description of several new procedures, Judge Sorkow concludes his account by juxtaposing it with another. "We are not dealing with Huxley's *Brave New World*," he declares. [8] Whatever "brave new world" is, present modes of intervention, however socially and culturally disruptive, are nevertheless *not* this. While certainly unique and, as the judge has read and presented them, technically exceptional, these methods restore and foster "natural" relations—they enable people to "bear a child naturally" and thus to constitute a "natural" family—even as they may also transform or modify them; according to the judge, new reproductive techniques are not about genetic manipulation but rather about genetic fulfillment.

Although Judge Sorkow invokes Huxley only in passing, the invocation establishes a contrast that works to (re)naturalize and thus stabilize precisely the conventional relations, orders, and identities that reproductive interventions, in this case commercial surrogacy arrangements, disrupt and expose. On the one side Sorkow situates genetic fulfillment, the "natural" family, primal desire, the innate drive to reproduce blood lines and through procreation achieve a certain immortality. In opposition to this, the judge situates as a matter of legal truth or finding of fact, a fiction, what "we are not dealing with": "brave new world," genetic manipulation, things conventional, "artificial," and political, or questions having to do with how reproduction in the United States is organized, valued, and positioned in this last quarter of the twentieth century. On the one side are "natural" processes—conception, gestation, and birth—and their "handmaid," medical science.[9] On the other side are social practices, relations of power, the specter of state regulation and control. The latter are not only part of a conversation we are not having; designated the stuff of "brave new world," they are part of a conversation we must safeguard against. Within the context of Sorkow's ruling, the novel holds an important place and a world in place—why else would it matter whether we were dealing with "brave new world" and in what sense really might the answer count as a "finding of fact"?

I will explore other citings of the novel in subsequent pages of this essay. However, before moving on to a fuller reading of the significance of these citings, I want to draw attention to the curious way in which the novel itself, while proffered as a means of expanding our field of vision, actually narrows or circumscribes it. The power of the text and clearly much of its authority and perceived contemporary relevance have something to do with, as one commentator put it, echoing others, "the [apparent] accuracy of so many of [its] projections."[10] Constituted and incorporated within much contemporary discourse as a kind of "blueprint for the future,"[11] as "prophecy" rather than "mere fantasy,"[12] Huxley's vision seems to have become a means of extending our own, of seeing or imagining ourselves beyond the present (historical) frame, concretely situated in a future that certainly looks "real," even if it is not yet realized, that is also known, and that, being both "real" and "known," is within our power to control. From the vantage point the text provides, indeed, with the text as its map, "the future" presents itself as an already inscribed geography, as marked terrain that can be read but also reconfigured. We need, however, to ask what it means to think of the future as something predicted rather than invented. In what sense is "history" geographical or, to put the matter differently, in what sense is the technoscape of "brave new world" something fixed and forever given, as indeed it must be regarded if the invented future is exchanged for the predicted one? In what terms are we led to organize and render the contemporary world when we read that world against and through Huxley's? What happens when Huxley's vision — or the social and political relations and identities, meanings, categories, assumptions, and understandings that the novel maps — comes to set the parameters of our own? What is foreclosed, displaced, or decentered when that vision dominates contemporary imaginings and becomes the discursive frame through which issues raised by currently evolving genetic and reproductive technique are figured, "policy" with respect to these new technologies is formulated, and new "principles" governing their use are fashioned?

Sorkow's passing invocation of the tale in the "Baby M" ruling works to legitimate one set of conversations and questions while rendering another set quite irrelevant. "We are not dealing with *Brave New World*," he asserts, thereby reconstituting with this assertion a politically contested boundary between things natural and artificial or between things given and contrived — precisely the boundary that surrogacy arrangements in particular and reproductive technologies more generally expose and explode. But there is more at stake here than breached boundaries — issues that cannot be formulated within a Huxleyan framework and formulations that are, politically speaking, precisely at issue. *Brave New World* is not merely a tale around which commentators have gathered, but a master text or discourse — a way of enunciating and adjudicating questions and answers with respect to the development and deployment of new reproductive and genetic techniques that constructs and configures people and practices. Following a brief account of the novel, and an equally brief presentation of instances from law review and science journals, the popular press, the bioethics literature, and feminist writings in which the tale is invoked, what I propose to do is to look at how this text operates as discourse to produce a world it also simultaneously reconsolidates. Specifically, I want to look at what happens to three elements of political conversation and practice when each is read against and through Huxley's novel. Considered critical in the debates surrounding reproductive and genetic intervention, these three practices are freedom, power, and "human nature."

## Brave New World Visited

The primary feature of life in the twenty-first century, as Huxley imagines it, is its one-dimensionality: totalitarian rule by a "world-state" that maintains itself not through brute force, but through the therapeutic control of the minds, bodies, desires, and judgments of its members. Indeed, in this new order, the state has seized control of the means of reproduction and, according to Huxley, finally joined to it the principle of mass production. All the essential choices have been made: humans are objects of design, ectogenetically produced as needed and to precise requirements, in standardized, uniform batches. Each member is a sterile, stabilized part of a sterile, stable whole, predestined biologically as well as socially, engineered according to a particular set of technical specifications for a particular set of social purposes, and conditioned physiologically as well as psychologically "to like their inescapable social destiny." [13] "Life is literally a gift from the state [and] not only life, but happiness." [14]

Now, of the many aspects of this new world that incite contemporary commentators, two aspects in particular are frequently singled out as especially depraved. Both are linked to the fundamental reorganization of reproductive and genetic processes that distinguish this future and include the abolition of the nuclear family and the installation of a rigid, biologically rooted and reinforced caste system. In Huxley's new order, the family has been rendered obsolete with the disintegration and reallocation of its material base and content; the state has absorbed its economic and procreative functions, and the community, its affectional ones. Its dissolution, however, Huxley presents as having been foremost a matter of practical rather than material necessity. "Do you know what a 'home' was?" Resident Controller Mustapha Mond asks a group of students touring the Central London Hatchery and Conditioning Centre:

> a few small rooms. . . . No air, no space; an understerilized prison; darkness, disease, and smells . . . as squalid psychically as physically . . . hot with the frictions of tightly packed life, reeking with emotion. What suffocating intimacies, what dangerous, insane, obscene relationships between members of the family group! . . . Our Freud had been the first to reveal the appalling dangers of family life. The world was full of fathers—was therefore full of misery; full of mothers—therefore of every kind of perversion from sadism to chastity; full of brothers, sisters, uncles, aunts—full of madness and suicide. . . . Family, monogamy, romance. Everywhere exclusiveness, a narrow channelling of impulse and energy.[15]

In Huxley's new world, by contrast, "every one belongs to every one else." All alike are decanted and raised in state conditioning centers where the identity and place of each prenatally socialized infant is fixed through a process of intense psychological and social conditioning. No feature of development escapes regulation; early "pavlovian" reflex conditioning is augmented with sleepteaching or suggestions from the state, until "at last the child's mind *is* these suggestions and the sum of these suggestions *is* the child's mind. And not the child's mind only. The adult's mind too—all his life long." [16] In the end, each member becomes, socially, what they have been bred or predestined, biologically, to be—a functioning part of the collective whole, "future sewage workers or . . . future World controllers," future Alphas and Betas, Gammas, Deltas, and Epsilons. [17]

These are the five, biologically distinct, classes or castes that make up brave new world and of these five only those of Alpha and to a lesser degree Beta "heredity" retain some semblance of their old world counterparts. While stunted physiologically and psychologically, members of the select Alpha class are nevertheless capable of making choices and assuming responsibilities; they possess the last vestiges of humanity, of distinctly "human" yearning and, for Huxley clearly, distinctly "human" possibility. Gammas, Deltas, and Epsilons, by contrast, are made up of genetically reduced beings, "deliberately bred downward or backward on the evolutionary scale." [18] As Resident Controller Mustapha Mond explains, these genetically reduced beings "are the foundation upon which everything else is built." They perform all socially necessary but mundane tasks. Having been bred to perform these tasks and, thus, being most "naturally" suited to perform them, they do so as no one with greater emotional or intellectual capabilities could—and that, of course, is precisely the point. "We believe in happiness and stability," Mond reflects:

> Imagine a factory staffed by Alphas—that is to say by separate and unrelated individuals of good heredity and conditioned so as to be capable (within limits) of making a free choice and assuming responsibilities. . . . It's an absurdity. An Alpha-decanted, Alpha-conditioned man would go mad if he had to do Epsilon Semi-Moron work—go mad or start smashing things up. Alphas can be completely socialized, but only on condition that you make them do Alpha work. Only an Epsilon can be expected to make Epsilon sacrifices, for the good reason that, for him, they aren't sacrifices. [19]

Although the genetically reduced, "subhuman" Gammas, Deltas, and Epsilons bear the weight of degradation, regression, and mutilation in Huxley's imagined future and thus constitute the tale's most potent political symbol, the moral crime this brave new world perpetrates is not necessarily against them, the working masses. The novel does not challenge their fate or champion their lost humanity. The moral crime this world perpetrates, as Huxley presents it, is rather against the exceptional few, those with "good heredity" who have somehow become, in the spirit of John Stuart Mill, "too self-consciously individual to fit into community life." [20] Huxley's convictions and thus those of the novel unfold through the sufferings and struggles, indeed, the rebellion, of an elite few: Bernard Marx, a specialist in "sleepteaching"; Helmholtz Watson, a distinguished "emotional engineer"; and John Savage, an alien of Alpha/Beta descent and, significantly, a man of woman born. Their story is the significant story; their protests, the last possible and, for Huxley, least diluted expression of "pure" human nature and need.

John Savage has been raised outside the control of the World State on a reservation somewhere in the North American Southwest. A "vacation spot" for citizens of the first world eager to observe the "primitive past" or the spectacle of the "natural" in all its squalid, savage splendor, the "pueblo of Malpais" is the mirror image of Huxley's futuristic society — it is a world "run riot with all the impulses and forces that the World State, in order to exist, must repress and banish": time, death and God, puritanism and asceticism, personal identity, human development, instability.[21] John is the viviparous offspring of a World State citizen who was separated from her companion while on holiday at the reservation and left for dead. He grows up an emotionally, psychologically, and physically tortured and isolated child, suffering what Mond describes as the foul intimacies of family life: "every kind of perversion from sadism to chastity." Thoroughly identified with pueblo life and ostracized from it because of his fair skin and literacy as well as the promiscuous sexual practices, at least by pueblo standards, of his mother, John is caught between two worlds, "a most unhappy gentleman," as he describes himself to Bernard Marx upon their first encounter at the reservation, a "primitive who speaks the language of Shakespeare." [22]

Unlike John, who does not merely experience the world or himself, but suffers both with passionate abandon, Bernard Marx and Helmholtz Watson are men struggling "to feel something strongly." Helmholtz yearns to feel "intellectual sensations," a sense of discovery, invention, creativity, and tragedy; Bernard longs to experience "passion" and freedom, freedom having something to do, as he understands it, with being "singular" or "more me," "not enslaved by my conditioning, not so completely a part of something else, not just a cell in a social body." [23] Although neither Bernard nor Helmholtz has fully escaped his conditioning, each has developed well beyond the infantile fixations that circumscribe even the lives of the elite Alpha class; each is the product of a "decanting" error or chemical imbalance in his blood surrogate. As a result of their atypical genetic makeup and their Alpha Plus programming, neither develops "normally." Both have desire—for things noble, fine, and heroic, for things "grander" than happiness. Both seek "virtue" and a kind of manliness each believes is ultimately meaningless without some kind of affliction—temptation, misery, misfortune, doubt:

> "Do you like being slaves?" the Savage was saying as [Bernard and Helmholtz] entered the Hospital. . . . "Do you like being babies? . . . Don't you want to be free and men? Don't you understand what manhood and freedom are? . . . I'll teach you; I'll *make* you be free whether you want to or not." And pushing open a window that looked on to the inner court of the hospital, he began to throw little pill-boxes of *soma* tablets [a euphoria-producing, cure-all substance] in handfuls out into the area. . . . "He's mad," whispered Bernard. . . . "They'll kill him. . . . Ford help him." "Ford helps those who help themselves." And with a laugh, actually a laugh of exultation, Helmholtz Watson pushed his way through the crowd.
>
> "Free, free!" the Savage shouted, and with one hand continued to throw the *soma* in the area while, with the other, he punched the indistinguishable faces of his assailants. "Free!" And suddenly there was Helmholtz at his side—"Good old Helmholtz!"—also punching—"Men at last"—and in the interval also throwing the poison out by handfuls through the open window. "Yes, men! men! . . . You're free!" [24]

Bernard, Helmholtz, and John Savage yearn for precisely the things Huxley presents as having been purged from this world: the unpredictable and potentially destabilizing, the mortal and unsure, the right to be unhappy, "the slings and arrows of outrageous fortune." [25] As Huxley puts it elsewhere, "[Man's] dignity . . . consists in his ability to restrain himself . . . , and . . . raise obstacles in his own path," and this, of course, is what Bernard and Helmholtz attempt to do—exercise restraint, frustrate want in order to enhance and extend it. [26] "Isn't there something in living dangerously?" John queries, "Nothing costs enough here." In their desires and the antisocial actions that they foster—solitude, celibacy, and the writing of poetry in Helmholtz's case; monogamous, romantic, and ascetic impulses in Bernard's—both men come to be regarded as deviants and, in the end, are deported to an island where, in the words of Resident Controller Mond, "the most interesting set of men and women to be found in the world" reside: "All the people who aren't satisfied with orthodoxy, who've got independent ideas of their own. Every one, in a word, who's any one." [27] John Savage is not permitted to join Bernard and Helmholtz in exile. He

nevertheless retreats from the hedonism and commercialized pleasures of
the World State to a deserted lighthouse. There he engages in a series of
purification rites that culminates in suicide.

Huxley's is a cautionary tale, openly and primarily didactic, and from it
a set of teachings having to do generally with human dignity and nature,
progress, power, freedom, individualism, and manhood is fairly easily de-
duced. The protests of the protagonists Huxley clearly presents as the protests of a "stripped-down" human nature, reduced but "pure." Likewise,
the truth these men utter is the truth of "pure" human need. Human nature and need Huxley treats as transhistorical, and individualism as a fixed,
given, indeed genetically rooted aspiration toward which the "human
spirit," however amputated or flattened, naturally and necessarily inclines.
Wherever there is an opening, a possibility, he implies, this spirit—the
yearning for freedom or individual self-expression, as Huxley defines
freedom—will bloom spontaneously and triumph. It is a familiar conviction, rooted in the same founding political and ontological mythology that
inspired mainstream American journalistic representations of the "democratic" uprisings in Tiananmen Square in 1989 as well as the more recent
uprisings that swept eastern Europe and Moscow and led to the "collapse
of communism." As in these representations, Huxley casts freedom and individualism, tolerance, charity, and democracy not as historically mediated
practices, but as abstract political principles or the telos of human life, part
of the essential nature of human beings that, for this reason, cannot help
but prevail under the most abject circumstance—in the face of tanks, bul-
lets, and totalitarian repression whatever its form—if given even the most
remote opportunity.[28] To kill the spirit, you must either kill the man or radically modify him, genetically; but even death, Huxley seems to suggest,
cannot extinguish the yearnings and aspirations of man qua man—the liberal-democratic, indeed "Millian," man that is "authentic" man.

What Huxley thus offers in this tale is an unequivocal denunciation of
those forces principally responsible for what he takes to be the moral and
social deterioration of "authentic man": consumer capitalism and the mutilated psyche it produces, a psyche occupied with material gratification
and consumption; scientific rationalism or "science's tendency . . . to make
the world manageable by reducing it to its own logic";[29] and, finally, a developing technological reality that requires the mechanization, regimenta-
tion, standardization, and administration of human life and labor. Ironically, however, and in contrast to those who would in subsequent decades
use this as a starting point for a critique of the domination of liberalism
entwined with a capitalist market economy, Huxley reinvents the very
world the tale simultaneously denounces and problematizes, the liberal
world of values and meaning. And this he does "as though the horror

which transfixes the novel were not itself the monstrous offspring of individualist society." [30] Moreover, in organizing the world into a series of simple oppositions — individualism, choice, and freedom on the one side, totalitarianism, conformity (or domination), and collectivism on the other — Huxley involves his readers in a similar act of invention, soliciting from them an allegiance to one side of the antinomy through the gruesome specter of its opposite. As we shall see, contemporary invocations of the tale function in an analogous fashion: when refracted through the novel, social relations, meanings, and practices and the conflicting claims and contests that structure each are condensed and ahistorically configured as questions of principle rather than practice. In this way, they escape critical scrutiny; they become the assumed terms of a discourse while posing as its object.

## Brave New World in Contemporary Discourse

"The road to Brave New World is paved with sentimentality — yes, even love and charity. Have we enough sense to turn back?" With this question, biologist and bioethicist Leon Kass concludes one of his three oft-cited essays condemning what he refers to as the "technological conquest of nature, conducted under the banner of modern science . . . for the betterment of mankind." [31] In the absence of sustained public deliberation over "ends" and "ultimate ends," and of "humility in the face of our awesome powers," Kass opposes the further development and application of new reproductive and genetic techniques as well as "technologies springing from the neurological and psychological sciences"; indeed, even with such deliberation he counsels caution and restraint. The stakes as he regards them are high: while these technologies are "the fruits of a large, humane project" dedicated to alleviating human suffering and to enhancing human life, they distinguish themselves from earlier practices in that "the object upon which they operate is man himself." [32] Without a sense of boundaries or a coherent set of values and standards that might "guide and restrain the use of [their] awesome power," [33] without the wisdom or the means to limit and control the many new forms of human engineering now or soon to be made possible by the rapidly expanding arsenal of biomedical technologies, we could, in Kass's view, "unwittingly render [ourselves] irreversibly less human." [34] "It will be difficult to forestall dangerous present and future applications of this research and its logical extensions. . . . Defensible step by defensible step we could willingly walk to our own degradation." [35] Thus he asks:

What ends will these [new] techniques [of reproduction,

neurobiology and psychobiology] serve? . . . What kinds of
creatures will we become . . . ? What kind of society will we have?
    We need only consult Aldous Huxley's prophetic novel *Brave
New World* for a likely answer to these questions. There we
encounter a society . . . peopled by creatures of human shape but
of stunted humanity. . . . our techniques, like theirs, may enable us
to treat schizophrenia, to alleviate anxiety, to curb aggressiveness.
We, like they may indeed be able to save mankind from itself, but
probably only at the cost of its humanness. In the end, the price
of relieving man's estate might well be the abolition of man.[36]

If allusions to *Brave New World* figure prominently in Kass's writings, so
also do allusions to another world equally as mythical. This is the ancient
Greek world, with, as Kass reads it, its sense of place and proportion, its
preoccupation with preserving the "distinctly human," and its regard for
things good, just, and beautiful. The teachings of the ancients Kass positions as antidote to what he describes as a multiply constituted failure of
nerve: to challenge the prevalent assumption that biomedical techniques
and technologies are a source of largely unqualified benefits, "the final solution to the miseries of the human condition," to question "the reason-
ableness of the desire to become masters and possessors of nature, human
nature included,"[37] and to accept "the idea that [these techniques and
technologies] make possible many things we should never do."[38] He laments, nevertheless, that the moment for "doing" and "asking" may already have passed. According to Kass, the likely outcome of this contemporary failure of nerve is not wisdom à la the ancients, but dehumanization
à la *Brave New World*, the creation of "happy slaves with a slavish happiness."[39]

If "brave new world" is invoked as specter by individuals like Leon Kass
who see an increasingly striking resemblance between Huxley's world and
our own, it is invoked as well by other commentators, for example, Peter
Singer and Deane Wells, who pursue the comparison but see no compelling resemblance at all. The story that Singer, an ethicist, and Wells, a member of the Australian Parliament, tell about the new technologies of reproduction and genetics is one of continual progress and increased
proficiency. As Singer and Wells read them, these new technological innovations express or fulfill rather than diminish what is most distinctively human about human nature. Indeed, their story, unlike Kass's, locates social
responsibility in the continued development and application of new techniques and offers a guardedly optimistic prognosis, informed by the belief
that in the West's democratic legacy and institutions lie precisely the constitutional and political restraints necessary "to ensure that we can easily
have the new biotechnology without having Brave New World."[40] Careful

to distinguish between what they refer to as "political and moral ideals" and technological capabilities, Singer and Wells dismiss the specter of Huxley's Central London Hatcheries, confident that our political constitution will preserve the distinctly human essence suffusing our biological one:

> Since major advances in biotechnology are taking place all around us, it is more illuminating to consider the nature of the social system in which these advances are occurring. The major IVF [in vitro fertilization] centers are in Australia, the United States and Western Europe. . . . [Each nation] subscribe[s] to equality before the law. All hold democratic elections. Every adult has an equal vote. All allow free speech and freedom of assembly. All agree that the state exists to serve the citizen, rather than the other way around.[41]

> The Brave New World's caste system could hardly appear without the sweeping away of all sorts of constitutional and political restraints that guarantee citizens' equality in certain respects. Any Huxleyan program to do away with the family would hardly get off the ground. . . . Advances in biotechnology alone will not plunge us irrevocably into the depths of Huxley's nightmare. A technology is only a tool. How a society chooses to use a tool will be influenced by the characteristics of the society in question. In the societies with which we are here concerned, there are deeply embedded obstacles to the pursuit of Huxleyan programs.[42]

Echoing Singer and Wells, the editor and director of the Hastings Center's genetic research group, Tabitha Powledge, similarly contends that the aspirations of the state to regulate the type and number of its citizens is virtually nonexistent. Powledge is nevertheless troubled by the commercial pressures currently shaping reproductive technologies and the burgeoning field of genetic engineering and questions the desirability of leaving the various new means of reproduction once they become more precise and controllable in the less socially responsible, less publicly accountable hands of "private developers." What would happen were the laboratory and the market to merge fully, she asks? What will happen when activities, entities, or processes currently sequestered from the market become subject to the vicissitudes and vulgarities of its profit-driven relations?

> Unless our form of government changes radically, we can dismiss from our minds the idea that our government will impose even the smallest version of a reproductive Brave New World upon us. . . . But this doesn't mean that we are not moving toward a form of the Brave New World. . . . we have been led to expect that test-

tube babies and human genetic engineering would be imposed on societies through their governments. The great irony is that the very opposite has occurred. We now look to government to protect us against the Brave New World.[43]

Similarly concerned with exploring some of the potential conse-quences of recent research pertaining to the genetic engineering of embryos—specifically, the extent to which this research conducted on be-half of women might ultimately contribute to women's further oppression—feminist Shelly Minden begins an essay with a long passage from *Brave New World*. The passage Minden singles out is a detailed de-scription of the controlled and ordered space of the laboratory and the conveyor-belt production of human beings, *Brave New World*'s replication of gestation and the birth process. Minden reflects:

> Today, science fiction merges into reality with the development of techniques for the laboratory fertilization and culturing of human ova, and the successful transfer of genes into the embryos of other animals. The barriers to genetic engineering of the human embryo are rapidly becoming social and political rather than technical. How will our society be affected by this technology?[44]

Having deployed Huxley to initiate, indeed frame, her analysis, Minden has, in some important sense, already begun to answer the question she poses about the possible future effects of the new reproductive technolo-gies. What looms as specter throughout her essay are Huxley's hatcheries and the world they both contain and create.

In much the same way as Minden, a recent issue of *Time* magazine sim-ilarly framed an examination of "the opportunities and dilemmas created by the new genetic knowledge" with an invocation of Huxley. "Lurking be-hind every genetic dream come true," *Time* observed, "is a possible Brave New World." [45] And, in response to a 1980 Supreme Court ruling permit-ting the patenting of laboratory created life forms, an alarmed public in-terest group is reported by the *New York Times* to have declared, "The Brave New World that Aldous Huxley warned of is here now." [46] Judge Sorkow invoked the fiction to find fact in the opening pages of the Baby M ruling; legal scholar John Robertson invoked it in the context of efforts to determine what a constitutionally coherent concept of procreative liberty might encompass. Indeed, in the process of mapping "the legal structure of the new reproduction," Robertson takes his bearings from the map of another:

> Beyond fear of harm to embryo, offspring, family or collaborators is a more generalized concern that technologizing conception

demeans human dignity and exploits women, and may lead down a slippery slope to complete genetic and technical control of humans.

A powerful image of these fears is Huxley's description in *Brave New World* of state hatcheries where babies with predetermined characteristics are decanted from bottles with pre-assigned social roles. Such images influence perceptions of IVF and the public policy that should control its use.

IVF may be the first step toward such a world, but a host of factors independent of noncoital reproduction would have to coalesce to bring about that dystopia. Such a hypothetical possibility does not justify denying married couples safe and effective infertility treatments now. . . . But [it] do[es] caution us to use noncoital technology safely and reasonably, taking steps to avert the most likely kinds of harm.[47]

These few examples drawn from diverse and contesting literatures suggest that it is largely against or in terms of Huxley's dystopic vision that issues raised by the new technologies are framed, that policy with respect to these technologies is formulated, and that new principles governing their use is fashioned. We hear legal scholar Robertson candidly assert that the specter cast by the novel informs the making of public policy—from it, Robertson reflects, steps can be taken to avert the most likely kinds of harm. But, to return to a question posed earlier, is the "harm" that Huxley envisioned necessarily the most likely harm confronting us today, and what might the stakes be in regarding it as such? If it is against Huxley's world that we currently measure our own, we need to look closely and critically at what is being measured, and how, and by what scale. Huxley's mapping is, as we have seen, a political mapping, and the geography charted, indeed inscribed, is that of social relations and meanings. We need then to ask what the discursive dominance of the text—the way in which the text constitutes and reflects a dominant political discourse—potentially forecloses. What exactly is displaced, decentered, and distorted by reading the contemporary world against and through Huxley's? What questions, formulations, conversations, and configurations does Huxleyan discourse legitimate and stabilize? What questions, formulations, and conversations does this discourse render irrelevant, invisible, illegitimate, even impossible?

## Reinventing Modernity

We have already developed something of a purchase on these questions, having seen, in previous sections, the way in which the social world, refracted through the prism of the novel, is organized into a series of simple oppositions—individualism, choice, freedom, and nature on the one hand, and totalitarianism, conformity, collectivism, and technology on the other. Reviewing contemporary invocations of the novel, we have also begun to see the way in which questions about the development and application of new reproductive and genetic techniques and their potential future abuses, when mediated by the tale, are likewise simplified and formulated in ways that place beyond interrogation precisely those aspects of the world, the very categories, meanings, relations, and practices these new techniques disrupt and demystify. In this vein we have heard asked whether the new reproductive and genetic technologies diminish humanity or fulfill it; whether they enhance life or enslave it; whether they promote women's liberation or impede it; whether they extend and express human nature or degrade and dehumanize it. We have also heard asked whether brave new world is here now or yet to come; indeed, some now wonder whether "artificially" produced humans, or "brave new babies" as they are sometimes called, born of human ingenuity, are more essentially human than their naturally conceived counterparts.[48] What each of these questions presupposes is a world of fixed and given meanings—a world in which what counts as human, constructs freedom, constitutes power, or separates "the artificial" from "the natural" is given, stable, and intact. Such a world is precisely what new reproductive and genetic practices profoundly disturb. It is also, and significantly, what invocations of Huxley's novel both construct and (re)consolidate. In the context of contemporary debate, *Brave New World* works, simultaneously, to produce and hold constant a universe of fixed meanings, a specifically liberal ensemble of values and assumptions, that in turn frame and inform what gets problematized and how. To get a clearer, somewhat more concrete sense of the questions and conversations Huxley's mapping frames and forecloses, and of the implications of this mapping for contemporary discourse and debate, we can look at what happens to three practices—freedom, power, and human nature—when these practices are read against and through his text.

In the discourse of the novel, as we have seen, freedom is about constituting and "realizing" oneself as a fully human individual through the choices one makes. It is, in Bernard's words, about "being more me." Individual choice is championed as both an expression and measure of freedom so that the more choices one has or the more discretion one exercises, the greater will be one's freedom. Huxley's is a fairly standard liberal rendering of freedom, not so very different from contemporary formulations that equate freedom and choice and constitute both as the condition for individual autonomy, self-expression, and self-realization. With Huxley's rendering in mind, listen to philosopher Michael Bayles on the subject of freedom in the opening pages of his textbook on "reproductive ethics." "One substantive moral assumption," Bayles writes, "is implicit in our method: Freedom is a basic value of rational persons. . . . The presumption is always in favor of freedom. Those who want to limit it by ethical and policy norms must carry the burden of persuasion." [49] Bayles, like Huxley, construes freedom in a narrow but familiar way as individual "freedom of choice," the freedom to use to one's own advantage, in an informed, autonomous, and implicitly "rational" fashion, available reproductive and genetic techniques. To circumscribe "freedom of choice" or thwart the fulfillment of personal desire that these new techniques make possible—the interests, for example, of infertile women or "people desiring to have only a few healthy, genetically normal offspring"—by regulating, limiting, or simply banning their use requires, in Bayles's words, "sound arguments . . . to show that the value of freedom is outweighed." [50]

Where does this formulation leave us in terms of thinking about the construction and production of freedom with specific regard to developments in reproductive and genetic technologies? If freedom is understood only or largely in terms of expanding and protecting individual choice, what escapes interrogation are the conditions that enable and restrict choice, the social arrangements and relations that limit and define the parameters within which individuals make choices, indeed within and through which "individuals" are made. In the liberal-Huxleyan formulation of freedom, the social, material world is not a constituent of freedom but a backdrop to it or field of operation. Not only is the historically, socially, economically, and politically situated and mediated character of individual choice rendered irrelevant, but so too are questions regarding what these choices construct as the needs and wants of individuals, or what kinds of subjects are constructed by the choices offered them. Also rendered irrelevant and invisible are the ways in which choices about the new reproductive and genetic technologies—which technologies to develop and which to use—do not merely implement a given set of values or facilitate a particular way of (individual and collective) life, but also quite conspicuously alter both.[51] It is useful to recall here a central, critical insight about the construction and production of freedom in modernity proffered by Rousseau, Marcuse, and Foucault that the expansion of "choice" does not in itself necessarily guarantee "freedom" but may in fact signal its erosion or absence.[52] Indeed, these critics discerned not only that what we call freedom can be expanded at the same time that domination is intensified, but that the proliferation of choice can itself be a vehicle of domination.[53] Within the semiotic framework of Huxley's novel, questions and formulations such as these remain unintelligible; within that framework, domination is not concealed by choice but situated in simple opposition to it.

To develop this point further, we can look at how "power" is configured when the practice itself is read against Huxley's text. Let us take as a starting point one of Foucault's insights about the nature and operation of modern forms of power in bureaucratic, disciplinary, liberal social orders. According to Foucault, power does not emanate from one center or source, nor is it to be found in or flowing vertically from any one set of hands; rather, it circulates everywhere and through everyone. As Foucault conceives it, power moves diffusely, locally, and continuously through social practices and lived systems of value and meaning. Irrigating the entire social body, "present in the most apparently trivial details and relations of everyday life," [54] and exercised from innumerable points, its operation, he maintains, "is ensured not by rights, but by technique, not by law, but by normalization, not by punishment, but by control." [55] While the state clearly remains one of its visible embodiments, power operates "on all levels and in forms that go beyond the state and its apparatus." Says Foucault, "We must eschew the model of the Leviathan — in political thought and analysis, we still have not cut off the head of the king." [56]

With Huxley framing our focus with respect to power, our eyes are trained solely on the state and its apparatus. Indeed, the state is, for Huxley and for those reading the contemporary world through his, the seat of sovereignty; it is the instantiation of power while power is itself treated as a phenomenon whose operation can be inspected, critically scrutinized, censored, and contained. From one standpoint, therefore, the standpoint, for example, of Peter Singer and Deane Wells, who are concerned to show why "we can easily have the new biotechnology without having a Brave New World," the liberal state is a source of reassurance. In those countries in which the major advances in biotechnology are taking place, the state exists only by virtue of free elections and to serve the citizen. By their account, its presence and liberal democratic practices forestall a "brave new world." From another standpoint, watching or monitoring the state allows us to anticipate and avert what legal scholar John Robertson refers to as the most likely kinds of harms that might follow from the application of new reproductive and genetic techniques — the state seizing or assuming eugenic authority, science serving "ideology" rather than "humanity." [57]

From the vantage point of both accounts, the state is positioned as the sole source and site of power and its potential abuse. It stands in contrast to the clinic or that arena of research and application regarded by these thinkers as outside power's field of operation and therefore both safe and reasonable. The state is the place where power is brokered; the clinic, the place where humanity is served. However, the problem with this account of power and its exclusive orientation toward the state is that "power" will rarely be revealed even while its operation and abuse are precisely what commentators claim we are looking at and for, talking about and preparing to guard against. This lack of articulation, in turn, not only permits certain vectors of power, like gender power, to persist and even intensify, it renders their production and application for the most part invisible.

Consider the clinic, that place where "technology is simply being used in the service of humanity."[58] In the clinic, according to fertility expert Carl Wood, physicians are "repairing nature" or "overcoming its defects"—treating women who consider their infertility a kind of "deformity" and themselves less feminine because of it, and who, by Wood's account, are driven by their "innate wish" to procreate.[59] Indeed, it is this "innate wish," "biological drive," or "natural desire" that not only creates the demand for the new technologies but legitimates them. Listen to the way the late Patrick Steptoe, "father" of the first in vitro conceived or "test-tube" baby, put the matter: "It is a fact that there is a biological drive to reproduce. Women who deny this drive or in whom it is frustrated show disturbances in other ways."[60] In the development and application of some of the new reproductive technologies, specifically those designed to "remedy" infertility and restore the "maternal nature" of "denatured women," we see encoded in the project itself women's "failure" as women along with "the belief that motherhood is the natural, desired and ultimate goal of all 'normal' women and that women who deny their 'maternal instincts' are selfish, peculiar or disturbed."[61] However, in addition to the inscription of age-old assumptions regarding what women are and are for, we see as well a perfect instance of Foucault's insight that while subjects are constituted by power, they are at the same time its vehicle.[62] Beyond this, we see in the clinic increased surveillance—facilitated by the increasingly common use of "peering" technologies (ultrasound)—and, more generally, an increase in the medical management of women's reproductive capacities. Accompanying this increased management, we see finally an extension of legal regulation over women's bodies and lives or the close monitoring and criminal prosecution of pregnant women who engage in an ever-expanding range of activities deemed "reckless" and detrimental to fetal life. What is taking place in the state and in the clinic are not coincidently related, but two interconstitutive moments in a particular, cultural construction of women. In Foucauldian terms, disciplinary power and juridical power operate conjointly as a distinctly modern technique of power.[63] However, from within a Huxleyan framework such power and its effects cannot be accounted for or seen. Indeed, from within a Huxleyan framework the clinic simply "repairs" women while the (liberal-democratic) state "protects" them.

To conclude this analysis of some of the implications of Huxley's mapping for contemporary discourse and debate over the new technologies of genetics and reproduction, we have finally to consider Huxley's rendering of "human nature," a notion whose basis and boundaries most commentators agree is gradually disintegrating in the wake of reproductive and genetic interventions. As one commentator put the issue, "The advances made in human genetics [as well as reproduction] are moving us rapidly to a world in which human features and faculties might be altered almost at will. ... we can ill afford to ignore the implications of these developments for traditional definitions of human nature. At the least, a clarification of the term ... , is critical at this juncture." [64] Were Huxley to be the vehicle of such clarification, we would be led, as we have seen, not only to (re)invent, as does he, the liberal subject—the autonomous, self-determining, rational being, self-made and male, possessed of free will and a moral sense—but to reconstitute the world that subject requires to flourish, the liberal world of value and meaning. For Huxley, human nature and need are situated as an essential core within, fixed and given properties that drive the human spirit, however mutilated, while technology and power are external forces that operate from without through domination and repression. This, at least, is part of the tale Huxley rehearses, and some of the assumptions that tale stabilizes. However, it is also a teaching the novel subverts, for when read against the technoculture of late twentieth-century North American life, what Huxley identifies as "natural" and transhistorical properties are clearly revealed as the markings of historically and culturally specific social and political relations.

Consider the people we encounter in the novel. As we might expect, given Huxley's assumptions, these people are entirely out of sync with the sophisticated technology that surrounds and is practiced upon and by them: within the Huxleyan ontology, there exists no deep or direct relationship between who we are and the world we make. However, what we would not expect, given these assumptions, is that the "who" and "what" of their "essential" identity and need as humans would differ in any dramatic way from those of their late twentieth-century counterparts, and yet of course both do. Both clearly bear the markings of an age that precedes even our own. While they are manufactured entities, little distinguishes these beings from their viviparously produced forebears of the late nineteenth and early twentieth centuries; indeed, what Huxley inscribes as universal with respect to gender, sex, and the distinctly "human" mirrors the social mores and milieu of an era we recognize only as quite foreign to our own. What even Huxley's text suggests, therefore, in contradiction with its ostensible didactic message, is that the "who" and "what" of identity and need are not dictates of nature or transhistorical essence. Along with the discourse that produces them, they are the effects and artifacts of specific configurations of power. To put this in postmodern terms, who and what "we" are is socially constructed by the world we construct, or, following Marx's insight, in changing the shape of material life, we always also change ourselves.

In contrast to the ontology that Huxley's novel constructs and that contemporary invocations of the novel reinscribe, we are not simply creatures of nature or creatures with a nature who have suddenly acquired technologies that only now permit us to rewrite and thus remake ourselves fundamentally at the cellular level. Neither are we creatures upon whom technology has simply been applied or imposed. Rather, we are creatures who have and who continue to constitute ourselves and our world through our social and technological practices even as we are also constituted by these practices. Such a recognition is vital for apprehending both the problems and the possibilities posed by the development and application of new technologies of human genetics and reproduction within the specific configurations of power constructing late twentieth-century North American life. As the foregoing suggests, viewing ourselves through and against the narrow prism of Huxley's world inclines us not only to misidentify what these problems and possibilities are or might be, but to reinvent the discursive world that obscures them.

## Conclusion

In 1988, the Office of Technology Assessment of the U.S. Congress issued a special report, *Biology, Medicine, and the Bill of Rights*. This report sought to map some of the many challenges that new reproductive and genetic practices as well as other, novel, biology-based technologies currently and potentially pose to the Constitution and its anchoring assumptions regarding human nature, individual agency and responsibility, freedom, and equality.[65] While traversing for the most part an already well-trodden terrain of hesitation and hope, the report nevertheless launches its cartographic efforts from an unexpected site: while extraordinary advances in biomedical science and technique permit us now to intervene in human life processes that "only a few decades ago were mysteries to science," these advances have also rendered that life unrecognizable, both politically and ontologically.[66] Indeed, the "person" hypostatized by the Constitution according to this government study—the rational, consenting, divinely ordained, self-determining, and free-willed being, endowed with inalienable rights and inescapable responsibilities—can no longer be said to exist today.[67] While there are clearly "persons" in the world and while the Constitution exists to secure the rights of "persons," the sign and the signified no longer stand in easy or obvious relation: beyond the chemical and anatomical, it seems we do not know what exactly a person now is. Noting that this fissure may ultimately precipitate a reexamination of "key constitutional concepts," the Office of Technology Assessment nevertheless concludes the prefatory remarks of its report with a set of reflections clearly intended to reassure. Even as we appear now to be less than what "we" once thought ourselves to be as "persons," "we" are, in some respects, also more: since the eighteenth century, what is called "person" has undergone a subtle but significant transmogrification with the inclusion of "women, and men and women of all races and classes." [68] With the advance of scientific knowledge and technique, this transmogrification continues. While we can no longer say with certainty who or what "we" are in some irreducible, essential sense, whoever we are in the end, whatever entity we turn out to be, that entity will still be protected by the Bill of Rights. [69]

One need not read a document on biology and the Constitution to sense the depth of the confusion of government with respect to what makes or sustains persons; the domestic policies of the last two administrations and their, until recently, popular appeal speak a confusion more deadly than profound. What is striking about this document, nevertheless, is its clear if tentative suggestion that a privileged political narrative has ruptured, that the stories "we" have told ourselves about who and what "we" are can neither frame nor contain the material practices and processes that constitute "persons" in this closing decade of the twentieth century. Indeed, what this document suggests is that the kinds of "choices" we often think of as yet to be made, "choices" that will profoundly alter our identity as human beings and the identities of the communities we occupy, we have always, already, been making.

The development and deployment of the new technologies of human genetics and reproduction and other biology-based technologies may boldly stage and dramatize such "choices." However, the revolution of the flesh they are said to be inaugurating, Huxley's "really revolutionary revolution," is enacted daily and less dramatically in legislative and legal domains, the formation of public policy, the setting of health care priorities, and the funding of particular research agendas. Following Foucault, it is enacted as well in the disciplinary practices and processes that constitute what is otherwise called "modernity." The humanist project of the eighteenth and nineteenth centuries was a practice of power operating in and through the souls and flesh of human beings to produce what it would liberate, the "naturally free and rational subject." [70] Although we are no longer certain that this is what we are, the revolution that this "naturally free subject" made and was made by is precisely the revolution Huxley feared most and championed: his final and most searching revolution or revolution of the flesh was modernity, and we are its effects. The question confronting us now is not whether we should alter our identities and the identities of the many communities we occupy. The question about these incessantly fluid configurations is rather "how," "in what ways and combinations," and "subject to what conditions"? What sort of people(s) and society are we and are "we" likely to become, should we become that sort of people(s) and society, and how do "we," whoever and however "we" are and are configured, individually and collectively, decide?

## Notes

I would like to thank Jean Bethke Elshtain and Peter Euben for reading and commenting on early drafts of this essay. Thanks also to Wendy Brown, who repeatedly discussed the arguments of the essay with me at length and whose critical responses to its many versions were invaluable.

1. Aldous Huxley, *Brave New World* (New York: Harper & Row, 1946), x.

2. Raymond Clayton, "The Biomedical Revolution and Totalitarian Control," in *On Nineteen Eighty-Four*, ed. Peter Stansky (Stanford, Calif.: W. H. Freeman, 1983), 79.

3. Mark R. Hillegas, *The Future as Nightmare: H. G. Wells and the Anti-Utopians* (New York: Oxford University Press, 1967), 120. See also Robert S. Baker, "Critical Reception," in *Brave New World: History, Science, and Dystopia* (Boston: Twayne, 1990).

4. Huxley, *Brave New World*, 10.

5. Ibid., xiii–xiv.

6. Superior Court of New Jersey, "In the Matter of Baby M," *Opinion* (March 31, 1987): 14.

7. Superior Court of New Jersey, "In the Matter of Baby M," 16. One has to wonder just what exactly Sorkow had in mind when he spoke of surrogacy as a new medical technique. The procedure itself requires no medical expertise and nothing as yet more remarkable, sophisticated, or high tech than masturbation and the use of a syringe.

8. Ibid., 15.

9. Ibid.

10. Krishan Kumar, *Utopia and Anti-Utopia in Modern Times* (New York: Basil Blackwell, 1987), 272–73.

11. Peter Firchow, *The End of Utopia: A Study of Aldous Huxley's Brave New World* (London: Bucknell University Press, 1984), 39.

12. As Kumar puts it, "The new developments in biotechnology are indeed the most compelling evidence to date that Huxley's vision of 1932 was no mere fantasy." Kumar, *Utopia and Anti-Utopia*, 276.

13. Huxley, *Brave New World*, 10.

14. Martin Kessler, "Power and the Perfect State," *Political Science Quarterly* 72 (1957): 571.

15. Huxley, *Brave New World*, 24, 25, 26.

16. Ibid., 19.

17. Ibid., 8.

18. Alexandra Aldridge, *The Scientific World View in Dystopia* (Ann Arbor: UMI Research Press, 1984), 54.

19. Huxley, *Brave New World*, 151.

20. Ibid., 154.

21. Baker, *Brave New World: History, Science, and Dystopia*, 119.

22. Ibid., 115.

23. Huxley, *Brave New World*, 20.

24. Ibid., 145.

25. Ibid., 162.

26. Huxley, cited in Firchow, *The End of Utopia*, 50.

27. Ibid., 154.

28. Huxley offers a more elaborate formulation of this position in *Brave New World Revisited* (New York: Harper, 1958), especially chap. XI, "Education for Freedom."

29. Aldridge, *The Scientific World View*, 52.

30. Theodor Adorno, "Aldous Huxley and Utopia," *Prisms*, trans. Samuel Weber and Shierry Weber (London: Spearman, 1967), 115.

31. Leon Kass, "Making Babies: The New Biology and the 'Old' Morality," *Public Interest* 26 (1972): 56, 18.

32. Leon Kass, "The New Biology: What Price Relieving Man's Estate?" *Science* 174 (November 1971): 779.

33. Kass, "The New Biology," 785; "Making Babies," 55.

34. Kass, "The New Biology," 785.

35. Ibid., 56.

36. Ibid., 785.

37. Kass, "Making Babies Revisited," *Public Interest* 54 (1979): 59.

38. Kass, "The New Biology," 787.

39. Ibid., 785.

40. Peter Singer and Deane Wells, *Making Babies: The New Science and Ethics of Conception* (New York: Charles Scribner's Sons, 1985), 31–32.

41. Ibid., 30.

42. Ibid., 31.

43. Tabitha Powledge, "Reproductive Technologies and the Bottom Line," in *Embryos, Ethics and Women's Rights: Exploring the New Reproductive Technologies*, ed. Elaine Hoffman Baruch et al. (New York: Harrington Park, 1988), 209.

44. Shelly Minden, "Patriarchal Designs: The Genetic Engineering of Human Embryos," in *Made to Order: The Myth of Reproductive and Genetic Progress*, ed. Patricia Spallone and Deborah Lynn Steinberg (New York: Pergamon, 1987), 102.

45. *Time*, March 1989, 70.

46. *New York Times*, June 17, 1980.

47. John A. Robertson, "Embryos, Families, and Procreative Liberty: The Legal Structure of the New Reproduction," *Southern California Law Review* 59 (July 1986): 1023.

48. Whereas Leon Kass ("The New Biology," 49) would argue that laboratory procreation of human beings is no longer *human* procreation, Joseph Fletcher of "situational ethics" fame would insist on quite the opposite. In Fletcher's own words, "The real choice is between accidental or random reproduction and rationally willed or chosen reproduction. . . . Laboratory reproduction is radically human compared to conception by ordinary heterosexual intercourse. It is willed, chosen, purposed, controlled and surely those are among the traits that distinguish *Homo Sapiens* from others in the animal genus, from the primate down." Fletcher cited in Singer and Wells, *Making Babies*, 29.

49. Michael D. Bayles, *Reproductive Ethics* (Englewood Cliffs, N.J.: Prentice-Hall, 1984), 6.

50. Ibid., 5, 6.

51. For a more detailed discussion of this last point, see Lawrence Tribe, "Technology Assessment and the Fourth Discontinuity: The Limits of Instrumental Rationality," *Southern California Law Review* 46 (June 1973): especially pp. 642–660; Robert Blank, "Ethics and Policy: Issues in Biomedical Technology," in *Technology and Politics*, ed. Michael E. Kraft and Norman J. Vig (Durham, N.C.: Duke University Press, 1988); and Langdon Winner, *The Whale and the Reactor* (Chicago: University of Chicago Press, 1986), chaps. 1–3.

52. Jean-Jacques Rousseau's account is to be found in the *Discourse on the Origins and*

*Foundations of Inequality*, trans. Roger D. and Judith R. Masters (New York: St. Martin's, 1964), and *Emile, or On Education*, trans. Allan Bloom (New York: Basic Books, 1979); Herbert Marcuse's in *One-Dimensional Man* (Boston: Beacon, 1964); and Michel Foucault's in "Two Lectures," in *Power/Knowledge: Selected Interviews and Other Writings 1972–1977*, ed. Colin Gordon, trans. Colin Gordon et al. (New York: Pantheon, 1980).

53. Consider what *Newsweek* has referred to as the "new gender option"— (postconception fetal) sex selection or the use of prenatal testing to screen for gender. While designed to reduce the incidence of sex-linked diseases, prenatal testing has also been used increasingly in the United States to identify and abort fetuses on the basis of sex. While "gender is the only nonmedical condition for which prenatal tests are widely available," *Newsweek* speculates that testing will soon be developed to enable prospective parents to screen for other traits and features as well as "conditions," for example, stuttering, obesity, and reading disorders, all of which have traceable genetic markers. *Newsweek*, "Special Edition: The 21st Century Family," Winter/Spring 1990: 94, 98, 100.

There are clearly ways in which the language of reproductive choice and preference not only masks and reinforces, in the case of sex selection, deeply embedded values and assumptions about gender—study after study reveals a pronounced preference for male children on the part of both men and women—but allows us to fetishize it further. Put another way, the language of "choice" and "preference" obscures "background" structures of domination and hierarchy, the basis of gender as a vector of power.

54. Nancy Fraser, "Foucault on Modern Power: Empirical Insights and Normative Confusions," in *Unruly Practices: Power, Discourse and Gender in Contemporary Social Theory* (Minneapolis: University of Minnesota Press, 1989), 26. See also Shane Phelan, "Foucault and Feminism," *American Journal of Political Science* 34 (May 1990): 421–40.

55. Michel Foucault, *The History of Sexuality*, vol. 1 (New York: Vintage, 1980), 89.

56. Michel Foucault, *Power/Knowledge*, 102; also *History of Sexuality*, 89.

57. On the quite considerable scope of the modern liberal state's eugenic interests and agenda(s), see Rosalind Petchesky, *Abortion and Woman's Choice: The State, Sexuality, and Reproductive Freedom* (New York: Longman, 1984); and Michel Foucault, *History of Sexuality*. The distinction drawn here between "science in the service of humanity," or "positive eugenics," as it is sometimes referred to, and "science in the service of ideology," or "negative eugenics," is one that runs throughout the literature and certainly gives one pause. Among Anglo-American eugenicists of the late nineteenth and early twentieth centuries, positive eugenics marked the approach that "aimed to foster more prolific breeding among the social meritorious," while negative eugenics targeted the socially disadvantaged and sought to reduce or stop breeding among individuals so identified. Although contemporary use of the distinction is clearly intended to set off or distance contemporary research and practices from those of the late nineteenth and early twentieth centuries, the resonance is unmistakable. For a more detailed discussion, see Daniel J. Kevles, *In the Name of Eugenics* (Berkeley: University of California Press, 1985); and R. C. Lewontin, Steven Rose, and Leon J. Kamin, *Not in Our Genes: Biology, Ideology, and Human Nature* (New York: Pantheon, 1984).

58. William Walters and Peter Singer, eds., *Test-Tube Babies* (Melbourne: Oxford University Press, 1982), 137.

59. Carl Wood and Ann Westmore, *Test-Tube Conception* (Englewood Cliffs, N.J.: Prentice-Hall, 1984), 96.

60. Cited in Michelle Stanworth, "The Deconstruction of Motherhood," in *Reproductive Technologies: Gender, Motherhood, and Medicine*, ed. Michelle Stanworth (Minnesota: University of Minnesota Press, 1987), 15.

61. Ibid. For a fuller discussion, see also V. Hartouni, "Containing Women: Reproductive Discourse in the 1980's," in *Technoculture*, ed. Constance Penley and Andrew Ross (Minne-

apolis: University of Minnesota Press, 1991), 27–56.

62. Foucault, *Power/Knowledge*, 98. My point here is not that women are simply passive victims in the repro-tech drama, but that women become vehicles for the powers we are constructed by. Listen to "Jan," who is infertile and for this reason considers herself at 27 to be someone with a "disability." Jan "feels that somehow you [aren't] a real woman unless you are fertile," and fears that her husband, "Len," "might not love me as much if I can't have a baby" ("he wouldn't consider me as feminine"). And then there is "Isabel": "I have been attempting to conceive for the past 17 years. . . . The only way I can give quality to my child's life now is by giving him a body through which he can live. The only alternative is to destroy him. Who can help this mother practice euthanasia on her deformed child? How can you bury a child who hasn't known life, who is held back from any attempt at realizing his life because of his mother's deformity?" Both of these accounts appear in a collection aimed at demystifying the technical aspects of laboratory-assisted reproduction, clarifying the range of moral questions raised by its practice, and establishing the demand that legitimates their further development and use. Walters and Singer, *Test-Tube Babies*, 15, 127.

63. "It is precisely in the extension of medicine that we see, in some sense, not so much the linking as the perpetual exchange or encounter of mechanisms of discipline with the principle of right. . . . sovereignty and disciplinary mechanisms are two absolutely integral constituents of the general mechanism of power in our society." Foucault, *Power/Knowledge*, 107–8.

64. Robert Blank, "The Changing Nature of Human Nature: DNA Probes and the Human Genome," unpublished manuscript, 1988, 19.

65. Office of Technology Assessment, *Biology, Medicine, and the Bill of Rights* (Washington, D.C.: U.S. Government Printing Office, September 1988), 35.

66. Ibid., 3.

67. Ibid.

68. Ibid., 4.

69. Ibid.

70. Michel Foucault, *Discipline and Punish*, trans. Alan Sheridan (New York: Vintage, 1979), 135–69.

# Contributors

**Jane Bennett** is associate professor of politics at Goucher College. Her works include *Unthinking Faith and Enlightenment* (New York University Press, 1987) and articles that explore the relationship between literary and theoretical portrayals of contemporary political issues. She is currently working on a book on Kafka.

**R. McGreggor Cawley** teaches environmental politics and public administration at the University of Wyoming. His research and publications focus on federal land policy. He is currently finishing a book on the Sagebrush Rebellion.

**William Chaloupka** teaches American politics and political theory at the University of Montana. He has written *Knowing Nukes: The Politics and Culture of the Atom* (University of Minnesota Press, 1992) and, with William Stearns, coedited *Jean Baudrillard: The Disappearance of Art and Politics*. He is currently working on a study of cynicism in American political culture.

**Romand Coles** is the author of *Self/Power/Other: Political Theory and Dialogical Ethics* (Cornell University Press, 1992), as well as numerous articles. He is currently writing a book on ethics of differential generosity that engages Kant, Hegel, Marx, Nietzsche, Habermas, and Adorno. On a less philosophical plane, he is working on issues of political economy and democratic theory as they relate to ecological problems.

**William E. Connolly** is professor of political science at The Johns Hopkins University, where he teaches political theory. He is the editor of *Contestations: Cornell Studies in Political Theory*. His two most recent works are *Political Theory and Modernity* (Basil Blackwell, 1988) and *Identity/Difference: Democratic Negotiations of Political Paradox* (Cornell University Press, 1991).

**Jan E. Dizard** teaches sociology and American studies at Amherst College, where he is Charles Hamilton Houston Professor of American Culture. His most recent book (written with Howard Gadlin) is *The Minimal Family* (University of Massachusetts Press, 1990). The issues he explores in "Going Wild" will be amplified and extended in a book by the same title to be published by the University of Massachusetts Press in 1993.

Chapter 6

# Going Wild: The Contested Terrain of Nature

Jan E. Dizard

When Thoreau left Concord to seek meaning on the shores of Walden Pond, he wanted respite from the contrivances of civilization. He sought nature, which he assumed was separate from Concord and its artifice. But it is clear that Thoreau discovered something other than "pure nature." Though he permitted himself, at least for expository purposes, the conceit that what he encountered was the natural order itself, it is abundantly clear that human beings had been altering nature long before he began building his simple cabin and recording his minute observations of nature's ways. In fact, human modifications of the environment had been going on for thousands of years before the first European set foot on what was to become Massachusetts soil.[1] Moreover, Thoreau brought with him a whole repertoire of assumptions and taxonomies with which to apprehend nature. The "wildness" that Thoreau engaged was, in other words, highly mediated, both by human presence and by the systematic knowledge that Thoreau's culture had amassed about the natural world.

Thoreau's knowledge was not the only way of knowing nature, as he himself was quick to admit. Thoreau observed other humans on the shores of Walden, rustic folk engaged in subsistence fishing:

Early in the morning, while all things are crisp with frost, men

come with fishing-reels and slender lunch, and let down their fine
lines through the snowy field to take pickerel and perch; wild
men, who instinctively follow other fashions and trust other
authorities than their townsmen, and by their goings and comings
stitch towns together in parts where else they would be ripped.
They sit and eat their luncheon in stout fear-naughts on the dry
oak leaves on the shore, as wise in natural lore as the citizen is in
artificial. They never consulted with books, and know and can tell
much less than they have done. The things which they practice are
said not yet to be known.[2]

Thoreau clearly envied the knowledge of these folk. He could invoke
complex taxonomies and thereby put things "in their place"; the fishermen knew a different order of things and accordingly felt and saw things
that Thoreau, for all his observational skill, did not. Though Thoreau and
those who would come to be called "swamp Yankees" both took nourish-
ment from Walden Pond, literally and figuratively, clearly the pond represented very different things to them.

Nature—that which appears in some substantial way separate from and
a priori to human existence—just might be the original Rorschach. Nature
is, after all, an evocative mix of amorphous stimuli onto which we are invited to project our innermost longings and anxieties. For Thoreau, nature
was exquisitely pure: truth prevailed and stood in stark contrast to the de-
ceits and conceits of Concord. Nature was also, again in contrast to civilization, exquisitely balanced. Each organism, however minute or grand,
was accorded its place, its function in the scheme of things. To be fitted in,
certain in knowing and feeling one's purpose—this is the prospect close
appreciation of nature offered. For transcendentalists such as Thoreau, the
discovery of nature was also self-discovery.[3]

Thoreau's immersion in nature released him from convention—at least
some conventions—and permitted him, in his wide travels in Concord, to
savor "the West" and, if you will, even Africa.[4] For him, the "wild" was of a
piece, whether encountered on a faraway continent or within earshot of
the railroad connecting Boston to Concord and points west. Wilderness
was as much a state of mind as it was a physical setting. His thoughts could
travel the steel rails west but not be constrained by the rails' fixed path.

Less than seventy miles west of Concord, and little more than one life-
time after Thoreau's, in the Swift River Valley of central Massachusetts, a
large earthen dam was erected in the late 1930s to form a vast impoundment for the purpose of supplying water to Boston and environs, including
Concord. Modern-day Thoreauvians repair to the Quabbin, as the reserve
surrounding the reservoir is called, much as Thoreau depended upon Walden, to contemplate the wonders of nature, savor the mysteries of wilder-

ness, and restore and even reinvent themselves. And, like Walden Pond, the Quabbin means different things to different people.

In this essay, I will explore the different meanings people who have become deeply involved in the fate of the Quabbin attach to "wilderness." I will also show how these projections onto nature are embedded in fundamentally divergent assumptions. This divergence sets in motion a cultural and political dynamic that defines the parameters of environmental policy. In order that the reader might appreciate the drama that is unfolding at the Quabbin, I will first provide a brief overview of the reservoir and how it came to be the center of intense controversy.

## Managing a "Wilderness" for Water

By the turn of the century, planners knew that population growth and commercial development of the Boston area would have to stop unless a very large and dependable source of water could be secured. Water had been diverted and reservoirs and aqueducts built in several stages over the course of the nineteenth century, but growth was outstripping these supplies. Capping growth, of course, was unthinkable, as was the prospect of moving people and industry to water. It was easier to contemplate moving water. Given topography and state boundaries, the search for water moved west. As luck would have it, there was a lovely but not particularly thriving river valley, the Swift, that met all the geological and engineering requirements for a large impoundment and that had the added virtue of being sparsely settled—no large politically or economically powerful interests would have to be confronted, and properties could be taken at acceptable cost.

Rumor spread through the communities of the Swift River Valley and before long the deal was done. The state began acquiring the land and engineers began surveying and planning construction for what would become, when it finally filled up in the late 1940s, the largest body of fresh water in New England. As construction of the dam commenced, crews of depression-idled men began to demolish the houses and barns that could not be moved and to clear the basin of trees.

In order to protect the reservoir from sundry contamination, 55,000 acres of land surrounding the water were purchased as well, forming the largest tract of publicly owned undeveloped land in southern New England. Initially, this property was closed to the public. The Metropolitan District Commission (MDC), the agency established to oversee the reservoir and watershed, maintained a large police force to patrol the Reservation in order to discourage unauthorized visitors. In some areas pine plantations were established to stabilize the soil. In other areas, native species of oak, birch, ash, and maple were thinned in order to stimulate new growth. In substantial measure, however, the place was left alone. In a surprisingly short time, it was reclaimed by woods.[5]

Trees were not the only living things that thrived in the vacuum created by state fiat. Beaver, virtually extinct in the area since the middle of the nineteenth century, somehow found their way back into the valley. Coyotes, too, resumed a residency that had been rudely interrupted by the agriculturists of the preceding century. Loons, arguably the most reclusive of water fowl, also established a small breeding population in the more secluded reaches of the reservoir. Moose, by the 1980s, were seen in the Reservation, though it is not certain if a breeding population has become established. And reliable sightings of the eastern mountain lion, long believed to be extinct, have grown steadily more frequent along the periphery of the Reservation.

The Reservation also became the site of deliberate attempts to restore wild species. The fishery was augmented by salmon and varieties of feed fish to sustain the population of sport fish. Peregrine falcons once again hunt for fish up and down the valley and, most spectacularly, elaborate efforts to establish breeding sites for bald eagles have paid off: several breeding pairs of bald and golden eagles now make the Quabbin their home and are joined in the winter by as many as forty of the great birds of prey.[6]

Given this incredible transition, the emergence of what one author has called an "accidental wilderness," it was not long before the public began to press for access.[7] Sport fishermen were the best organized, if not the most insistent, of the constituencies eager to have access to the Reservation. By the mid-1950s, legislation was passed that allowed sport fishing on the reservoir. The MDC nonetheless maintained strict supervision of fishing, regulating the hours, the points of access to the shore, and the nature of the boats and motors to be used. Picnicking remained forbidden, as did swimming, canoeing, and sailing. Over time, the MDC relaxed its prohibition on pedestrian access, though this was an informal, not legislative, arrangement. As a result, nature lovers of all sorts, ranging from the occasional walker to the most dedicated professional wildlife photographers, began to visit the Reservation. Wildlife could be observed in abundance and, for many, the Quabbin became a monument to a world we had lost and, perhaps more important, an example of the world we might recapture on a larger scale if only we had the will.

The MDC also took great pains to accommodate the feelings of the people whom the waters had displaced. Former residents of the five towns that were flooded were permitted to visit the reservation with fewer restrictions than applied to the general public; cemeteries were moved, and the MDC continues to help maintain the relocated memorials (and former residents continue to be buried in the new cemetery); and the MDC supports groups such as the Swift River Historical Society who are devoted to keeping the memory of the valley alive.

In all these efforts, the MDC built a diverse constituency interested in preserving the Quabbin as a more or less pristine area. The fishing fraternity was, in this regard, most problematic, since they pressed for more access and relaxation of restrictions on eating, horsepower of motors, and the like. But through such groups as the Friends of Quabbin, a loosely knit group of individuals committed to the preservation of the Quabbin as the largest area of undeveloped land in the state, as well as more broad-based environment groups such as the Audubon Society, the MDC cultivated a strong lobby for its efforts to manage the Quabbin as a preserve.

Management, of course, meant more than restricting human access and use of the Reservation. From the beginning, the MDC planted and cut, built roads or maintained existing roads for use in fire control as well as forestry, wildlife study, and patrolling for the inevitable poachers, illegal campers, marijuana growers, and the like. The goal of this management has remained constant: to sustain a high-yield watershed capable of reliably supplying now roughly two and a half million people with safe, high-quality drinking water. Though the goal has been constant, strategies for reaching this goal have varied over time, reflecting changes in knowledge, adjustments to changing climatic and larger environmental forces (such as acid rain), and shifts in projections of population growth and demand for water.

At one point, in the late 1960s to the early 1970s, demand soared. As luck would have it, this rise in demand coincided with several years of below-average rainfall. In response, the MDC did some clear-cutting in hopes of increasing water yield. They have since turned away from this practice, but the clear-cuts still rankle and are frequently pointed to as an example of how MDC intervention is misguided and bumbling and not to be trusted. Small-scale logging, aside from the very modest foray into scattered clear-cutting, has also been a key component of the MDC management strategy. Some of this cutting is strictly governed by fire suppression concerns. Other cutting is driven by the desire to reduce the risk of disease and to enhance the age and species mix of the forest.

The prevailing ideal of the MDC is to see that the forest becomes as diverse as it can be. The assumption is that diversity is like an insurance policy—the risk is spread out and thus the impact of any particular disruption, whether from blight, drought, fire, or storm, will be dispersed and buffered. A forest that is homogeneous, with respect either to species or to age, so the reasoning goes, is highly vulnerable to catastrophe. A catastrophic episode would almost certainly place the reservoir at risk.

None of these interventions would likely have caused more than a very occasional grumble here and there were it not for one inhabitant of the Reservation: the white-tailed deer. The forestry practices of the MDC over the years had created and then sustained almost ideal habitat for deer. Deer thrive on the edge that marks succession, that is, the advance of woods into cleared areas. Native Americans understood this and used fire to clear sections of woodland in order to create this kind of successional edge to attract deer and small game. As the former fields and pastures of the valley returned to woodland, the deer multiplied. Exposed to few predators and protected from hunters, the herd quickly expanded. It is estimated that the herd peaked in the late 1940s or early 1950s at somewhere around seventy to eighty per square mile, at least six times more dense than the population outside the Reservation.

The clear-cutting that went on for a time augmented the food supply for the deer. At the same time, winters were becoming less severe, reducing stress on the deer and making it easier for them to scratch for mast and shoots during the winter. Taken together, all this has meant that the herd has stabilized at a very high population density. By the mid-1960s, it became clear to the foresters that the deer were seriously affecting tree regeneration. Young shoots were being eaten as quickly as they grew through the earth's surface. Shoots that survived to sapling stage were being nibbled and pruned such that twenty-year-old oaks were gnarled and stunted, barely shoulder high. Where there should have been a profusion of "sticks," all one could see was a sea of ferns beneath the canopy of mature trees. Deer don't like ferns.

To the untutored eye, the forest looks primeval, and the ferns, with their soft leafy greenness, convey an air of tranquility and restfulness. To a forester, particularly one charged with maintaining a watershed, the scene is anything but restful—it more closely resembles a nightmare. The MDC kept hoping for a return to normal winters, which would increase deer mortality. And when coyotes appeared as permanent residents of the Reservation, it was hoped that they would bring the herd down to a point where trees could regenerate. But the succession of hard winters have not come and the coyote appetite is clearly no match for the fecundity of the deer. The forest continues to be managed, but more and more of the management is being driven by the nutritional needs and dietary preferences of the deer, not by the need for water.

The MDC began to study alternative means of controlling the deer. Some small test areas were fenced. In a short time, the contrast between the area inside and outside the fencing was dramatic. Inside, there was a profusion of growth; outside, ferns. But fencing 55,000 acres is no small matter, and without some way to drive large numbers of deer off the Reservation, fencing by itself would do little. Birth control, too, was explored but rejected as impractical for so large an area. Increasingly, the options narrowed to the use of some form of lethal intervention, either sharpshooters or hunters.

The MDC, left to its own devices, no doubt would have preferred sharpshooters. Mercenaries, as it were, could be tightly monitored, reducing the human impact on the watershed, and their work could be carried out with a minimum of fuss and publicity, like the forestry practices themselves. But two problems arose. First, the experience with sharpshooters is not encouraging, except in very confined settings. And even if sharpshooters could be effective in so large an expanse as the Quabbin, there was the problem of what to do with the carcasses. Predators, including eagles, would devour some, but the number of deer that would have to be killed in order to give the forest respite was so large that there would almost certainly be a large number of rotting carcasses around, posing some serious hazard to water quality. Moreover, there is no small uncertainty about the very term *sharpshooter*. Who qualifies? How are they to be tested and screened? How much do they charge for their services?

Were this not trouble enough, the Division of Fisheries and Wildlife, whose jurisdiction includes the deer, had clear research and experience backing up the claim that ordinary sport hunters are the most effective and least costly regulators of deer populations. The division lobbied hard for opening the Reservation to the state's licensed hunters. In the end, the MDC and the division began to collaborate on arranging what both agencies came to call a "controlled hunt." Hunters were to be drawn by lot from a pool of applicants. All game laws would be in force but, in addition, a set of MDC rules governing the areas to be hunted, the hours of the hunt, use of sanitary facilities, and the like would be in effect. In all, slightly more than 900 hunters were selected for the first hunt, which took place in early December 1991. The MDC had estimated that 150 to 200 deer would be taken from the Quabbin in the nine days of the Massachusetts deer season. As it turned out, nearly 600 deer were taken over the nine day season.[8]

Well before the hunt actually commenced, however, years before in fact, controversy and criticism leveled at the MDC began to swell, reaching its apex in 1990-91, the period during which the MDC narrowed its options to reliance on sport hunters. As the MDC grew increasingly alarmed about the impact of the deer on the forest, they began more intensive study and self-scrutiny. In the course of several major reviews of watershed management practices, the groups and individuals who, over the years, had been drawn into active involvement with the MDC began to question some aspects of the management program.

At first the critics targeted logging, particularly the logging that seemed to go beyond that needed for fire suppression. As the MDC edged its way toward labeling the situation a "deer problem," criticism grew, and when solution to the problem narrowed to hunting, opposition reached a flashpoint. Animal rights and antihunting forces added their voices to the opponents of logging. Major organizations, most notably the Massachusetts Society for the Prevention of Cruelty to Animals and Massachusetts Audubon, offered comprehensive critiques of prevailing MDC practices. And a new grass-roots organization, the Quabbin Protective Alliance, was formed by a diverse group of "Quabbin lovers" who shared the common desire to see a drastic reduction in human intervention in the Reservation.

In effect, the defenders of the Quabbin were splitting into two camps, some moving toward a "no management" stance and others who accepted the need for consistent, hopefully modest, interventions in order to keep the Reservation stable. In an effort to build support for its policies, the MDC scheduled a series of public informational meetings across the state. At each meeting, a panel of people representing the spectrum of positions, pro and con the proposed deer hunt, presented their views and then fielded questions from a highly partisan and quite divided audience. Letters to the editor columns in newspapers across the state regularly included attacks on and defenses of the MDC plan to stage controlled hunts to reduce the deer numbers on the Reservation. These public forums made it abundantly clear that people assign multiple and conflicting meanings to the terms *nature* and *wilderness*.[9] Using these public utterances as well as information gathered from more than sixty hours of interviewing interested parties, we can examine the ways people came to understand the interactions among humans, deer, and the forest of the Quabbin. Then we can explore the range of meanings attached to *nature* and *wilderness*.

## Responses to "the Problem"

While most people caught up in the debate about the proposed hunt agreed that there was a problem with forest regeneration on the Reservation, some of the most adamant critics of the MDC insisted that there was no problem at all. Rejecting the most basic premise of resource management, that intelligent human intervention can improve upon nature, these partisans argued that the deer and the forest would, if simply left alone, achieve a sustainable, mutually beneficial balance. Here's how one of the leading grass-roots activists put it:

> Sure, I agree that with the present deer population they may want to reduce [the deer] initially to get some regeneration started.

[But] I'm not convinced that that's really necessary. I think left to nature that in time that would . . . correct itself. . . . I can't believe that their managed and manipulated forest is going to do a better job than a natural forest.

These sentiments were echoed by an animals rights advocate:

I think that the Quabbin Reservoir, if left alone, would just naturally return itself to some sort of equilibrium and natural order that would not have a negative effect on water supply or the animals, the creatures that are there or anything.

Phrases such as "nature takes care of itself" and "nature knows best" occurred frequently in the interviews with opponents of the hunt. For some, this faith in nature bordered on a religious sanctification of nature's "plan." Left to itself, nature not only heals, it expunges evil. One animal rights advocate was explicit on this:

The need to control [nature] stems from fear. We both [the respondent's companion and herself] admire Albert Schweitzer and share his idea of reverence for life. . . . let's try the hands-off approach. I bet we'll be surprised at how much would change for the better. We'd be much better off . . . more happy, more peaceful.

Indeed, I was singularly struck by the reverential tone in which virtually all the persons I interviewed spoke of the Quabbin. The fact that it had been made off-limits for so long meant that it had become, de facto, a "sanctuary." A former resident of Enfield, one of the flooded towns, and an active member of the historical society that keeps those towns a part of living memory, observed that the peacefulness of the Quabbin, which stood, in his view, in stark contrast to everything around it, was the most fitting way of memorializing the lives and livelihoods of those who had had to suffer dislocation and wrenching disruption so that the reservoir could be built:

People walk there [the Quabbin] for the peace and quiet. . . . It's a sanctuary. . . . this is one place that should be left alone, at least not allow guns. . . . What could be more of a tribute to the people who lived there?

Obviously, the prospect of gunfire in so hallowed a place would be nothing short of sacrilege, even to a person who had himself hunted, fought in war, and had no philosophical objection to hunting.

For others, the violence of hunting *was* an issue. The most consistent rejection of the claim that the deer are a problem came from animal rights advocates. From their vantage point, each animal life is precious. No individual creature should have pain or suffering imposed upon it for the transitory and thoughtless convenience or pleasure of humans. If the deer did, ultimately, have an adverse effect on water quality or quantity, then humans should adjust themselves to the new reality. The animal rights advocates insisted that we should learn to adapt our lives, our values, our needs and behavior to the requirements of what, to them, is an ethically sound relationship to the animal kingdom.

Many opponents of the hunt stopped short of endorsing the animal rights position, even though they agreed that we should stop compelling nature to adapt to us and instead begin to adapt ourselves to nature. This view was often couched in terms of commonsense notions of fair play. As an avid amateur wildlife photographer who was deeply involved with taking his two young boys on regular field trips to the Quabbin put it:

> We've been taking from nature for so long that it's not funny. It's high time we begin to appreciate nature. Leave it alone. . . . learn to live more simply.

From vantage points such as these, it becomes clear that the opponents of the hunt were not so much denying the existence of a problem; they were insisting that the problem at the Quabbin is, as one of the opponents of the hunt put it, "a people problem, not a deer problem." The most publicly outspoken critic of the MDC, himself a former hunter and now someone far more devoted to the preservation of deep woods and old-growth forests than he is worried about deer, was again and again blunt on this: the MDC, he argued, has set in motion what amounts to addictive management. They first created ideal habitat for deer. Then their logging helped maintain ideal conditions. And now, in order to keep the policy of logging viable, the MDC has to intensify their intervention by extending it to the deer. In our interview he spelled it out in these terms:

> If the MDC were to say, "Okay, we're going to stop managing the forest," then [I] would have no problem with them electing a short-term hunt . . . to get the deer herd down initially. But only if they leave that forest alone.

Inept management, in other words, created the large herd. If the forests continue to be logged, the deer will remain abundant and the need for hunting to regulate the herd will become permanent.

Whether the focus of concern was animal suffering or the desire to see the trees left alone, opponents converged on a condemnation of MDC management practices. For some, the problem was the particular management policies of the MDC. For a large number of the opponents, however, management *sui generis* was the problem. One young woman expressed a trepidation that was widely held among opponents of MDC management. Rooted in a skepticism of science, at least insofar as it applied to intervention in nature, she feared that our manipulations of the environment would lead to disaster:

> I think that . . . the further scientists go with trying to control these natural cycles, the worse catastrophe there is going to be in the end. . . . Eventually something is going to blow up. I mean *in a major way*.

At bottom, opponents are, for the most part, deeply pessimistic about the future, not only the future of the Quabbin, but the future of the planet as a whole. For many, part of the "people problem" lies in acquisitive values and selfishness, which they see deeply ingrained in humans. It is also a problem of sheer numbers—there are many too many people, and we are growing far too rapidly, for the planet to absorb. Our need for water, oil, building lots, and the like is screwing things up—changing the climate, polluting the sea, atmosphere, and land. Just a few comments convey the flavor of this attitude:

> I know some people who estimate that there are now ten times as many people as the earth can comfortably sustain. That's why I don't have any children, incidentally.

> I don't have much hope . . . for the world. I feel really scared . . . and when my children say, "I don't think I want to have any children," I say, "I understand." I think our life will live out the next thirty years or so and we'll probably be okay. I think our grandchildren are not going to be okay, it's going to be really awful—environmental stuff, overpopulation being one of the worst.

With everything pretty much going to hell, it is easy to see why passions might be aroused by the prospect of a hunt at the Quabbin. Opponents, whatever their philosophical stance toward hunting, spoke of their efforts to save the Quabbin as a last-ditch effort, as if losing the deer hunt fight would sound the death knell for the Reservation. For some, the desecration was no more complex than gunfire breaking the still air and the scene of imagined tranquility. For others, the irretrievable loss was wrapped up in the conviction that the hunt would give the management forces a virtual lock on the Reservation, transforming it by degrees from the "accidental wilderness" they saw it becoming into a highly artificial playground—a playground for putative experts to try their fanciful ideas about managing

natural forces and for self-styled sportsmen who will fish and hunt to their
heart's content:[10]

> If they allow hunting and continue to log, the deer will keep
> reproducing and will have to be hunted regularly. We don't want
> to see that happen. It'll [the Quabbin] get trashed up, pure and
> simple, and it's the only place of any size in that state that you can
> go for escape. The serenity of the place and the special feelings
> that people have about the place will be seriously altered. I don't
> have a particular problem with killing deer but I don't want that
> activity going on at Quabbin. The whole thing is sad.

Opponents of the hunt by no means monopolized pessimism. The
hunt's proponents also labored with their share of foreboding and gloom.
Some of this pessimism was rooted in the same sorts of concerns the opponents voiced—worries about human profligacy, overpopulation, greed:
the usual suspects. But the proponents also saw other perils, nature herself
for one. However awe inspiring and magnificent natural forces may be,
they are also destructive and threatening. For the proponents, human interaction with nature is more contest, more closely zero sum, than it is for
the opponents. And as in any contest, the "other side" plays tricks and
breaks the rules. To keep society viable, from this point of view, we have to
plan for the tricks of nature, such as droughts, hurricanes, and blights.

Adapting to nature had a certain appeal to the proponents of the hunt,
but they were far less idealistic than their counterparts on the other side of
the issue. There is some irony in this—most of the proponents of the hunt
were "outdoors people." The wildlife biologists, foresters, and other professionals working for the MDC, as well as the researchers who have
helped the MDC study the flora and fauna of the Quabbin, all indicated that
they were attracted to their work because of their love of the outdoors.[11] In
many respects, the proponents were nearer to being able to live in harmony with nature than many of the more urban opponents of the hunt. Be
that as it may, the proponents nevertheless insisted that if present populations are to be fed, clothed, and sheltered, nature and natural resources
have to be managed. Period.

> We're so far into manipulating already, we've done so much to
> manipulate it, that we'd better recognize that only by/through
> science and constant research can we learn what will take us in a
> bad direction and what will take us in a good direction. We have
> to bring nature into the directions that we need it to go. . . . you
> know there's the extreme point of view that says, "Let nature take
> care of the problem," but one of the things that goes along with
> that, and I'm not necessarily opposed to this, is that there would

need to be some drastic reductions in our own population to correspond with that. Unmanaged nature can't sustain us.

To be sure, none of the people I spoke with who actually did the managing made large claims for their prescience. As often as not, they spoke of all that they did not yet understand about how environments function and they freely admitted having erred and miscalculated about the effects of this or that intervention. The only unreserved endorsement of management came from a spokesperson for sportsmen. He found nature in its pristine state "ugly." Speaking of a woodlot that has been left alone for "quite a while," he observed:

It's the most pitiful-looking thing there is. Branches out to here [extending his arms wide]. . . . Branches all over the place . . . all broken, the trees all scarred to hell where the branches fell down and broke. Oh God . . . if you saw a guy with his arm broken off, hanging down, and yet he can't go to the hospital to be maintained? That's beautiful? Well, that's just like that poor tree, all ripped and blood coming down, the sap is running out of him. That ain't right.

Such unabashed enthusiasm for improving on nature was rare. More typical was the heartfelt comment of one of the foresters I interviewed. He confessed:

I mean I have a terrible time when I go out to check on a logging job. I still have a hard time hearing the trees crashing down to the ground. I'm not crazy about seeing a beautiful big tree go from this [expanding his arms upward] to something inert on the ground.

In fact, as I proceeded through interview after interview, I came to the sense that proponents felt condemned to manage, almost as if it were punishment for original sin. Having been exiled from the Garden, we are left no alternative but to muck about, always half in the dark, trying to recapture at least a semblance of equipoise between humanity and nature.

But the metaphor is a bit too tempting. In fact, the professionals and lay people among the proponents were quite confident that sound management practices could produce a very acceptable ecological wonderland in the Quabbin. If not "wilderness" in any true sense, the Reservation could nevertheless be maintained as an enduring oasis of "wildness," where people could repair to get some intimation of what things were like back when. . . . There was more than once a tone of exasperation in the voices of the experts when I posed the opponents' arguments to them. Most, for example, flatly rejected the notion that there was any *scientifically* (i.e., objectively measurable) demonstrable difference in biological diversity as between an unmanaged forest and what they could achieve at the Quabbin once the deer were brought under control and the forest could resume more nearly normal regeneration. In the words of one wildlife researcher:

> Here on the Quabbin some of those forests are getting about as old as they ever got, at least in the last four or five hundred years. . . . I think somehow people view that the current management would prevent us from getting old growth and I don't view that as happening. . . . [Present management practice] going on out there is . . . actually accelerating that advance toward old growth. At least the structure of old growth.

To be sure, were it not for the mandate to keep the water of the reservoir as clean and ample as possible, many of those favoring the hunt might well have switched to the other side. But this is by no means certain. By the time the deer had become publicly controversial, a number of the MDC personnel and the environmentalists who knew the Reservation well had come to regard the deer as pests. Preferring thick forest to fern glades, they resented conceding to the deer the management of the forest. While the opponents of the hunt cast the choice as between management versus no management, proponents saw two sets of managers: deer and humans. Though ignorance and the rest of human frailties leave human management open to critique and radical shifts, letting the deer manage things is folly, they argued:

> From twenty-five years in the woods, I can tell you that red maple and white pine is not biologically nearly as interesting as a forest that has ash and oak and other things. And now the deer are simplifying that forest . . . to their own detriment and the detriment of most of the species that we really like.

Another person, a prominent local environmentalist, put it more dramatically:

> The only thing regenerating there [Quabbin] is cherry and black birch and that is not a satisfactory forest. And when push comes to shove I want to see a healthy forest. I don't want it to look like England. They have so-called woods in England. Totally bare. There's nothing growing in those woods. And that's 'cause the sheep are all over hell and gone. . . . If I saw this lack of regeneration on a piece of western land that was being grazed by sheep or cows or goats I would say get those creatures out of there. . . . Why should I feel differently because it's deer? And as

for management, once you've started there really doesn't turn out to be much of an alternative but to keep doing it.

In sharp contrast to the idealizations of deer that the animal rights activists were promoting, the proponents of the hunt disparaged deer. They saw deer as utterly greedy and selfish. One hunter, attempting to ridicule the "bambi lovers," noted how merciless adult deer can be when pressed for food:

> Why, you know, the mother will chase her fawns away from food, just make 'em starve so she can get something to eat. How's that for kindness?

Of course this fierce survival instinct also makes the white-tailed deer a most challenging animal to hunt. As a destroyer of habitat, the deer is condemned; as prey, the deer has virtues to be extolled. Beauty is, after all, in the eye of the beholder.

It would be wrong, however, to characterize the proponents of the hunt as enthusiasts of hunting. Far from it. Most of the proponents of the hunt whom I interviewed were, if pressed, decidedly cool to hunting. More than a few were philosophically opposed to hunting.[12] But this personal philosophy rubbed up against the reality of what the deer were doing to the forest. For the proponents, the desire to stabilize the forest and thereby to ensure the integrity of the reservoir took precedence over personal values. And so, grudgingly, they conceded hunting its place, along with the other morally vexing decisions managers of our natural environment must make.

Opponents of the hunt were caught up in the discourse of rights—the right of animals to be left alone, the right of forests to grow unimpeded by our sense of aesthetics or desire for wood products, the rights of people to have places that are off limits to all but the most passive, least intrusive forms of human contact. By contrast, proponents were enveloped in a discourse of responsibility—the MDC is responsible for ensuring a water supply for millions of people, humans must take responsibility for regulating their use of resources, we must assume responsibility for maintaining the viability of as diverse a biotic community as our knowledge and resources permit. Embedded in these two discourses on nature are very different conceptions of nature itself and of our relationship to nature. It is to these matters that we need to turn before we can explore the implications of these divergent discourses.

## What Is Wild?

*Wild* has a ring to it. It calls forth images of chaos and destruction. At the same time, we readily associate beauty and exhilaration with the wild. When the opponents of the hunt at the Quabbin invoke wildness or wilderness as something they value, they almost invariably associate the wild with a condition of balance, harmony, and order. In the wild, everything is functionally related—there is no wasted motion, no scrap of meat or vegetation goes unused in the endless cycle of degeneration and regeneration. Some take this to the extreme of believing that, were it not for humans upsetting things, lions would lie down with proverbial lambs.

Though most opponents of the hunt would not be prepared to endorse so Edenic a view of nature, they do maintain, all in all, a view of nature as essentially benign. In phrases such as "nature takes care," "nature provides," and "the balance of nature," respondents conveyed a clear sense that if left alone, if we stopped managing and polluting, nature would cleanse itself and, in terms of the Quabbin controversy, deer and forests would achieve a mutually sustaining equilibrium.

Left to themselves, forests can achieve long-lasting stability, according to this view. Moreover, old-growth forests are host to a rich and interactive biotic community. Each organism has its niche and acts, however subtly, as a check on the other organisms in the system. There is hierarchy—oaks dominate birch and coyotes eat rabbits, not the other way around—but it is not an invidious hierarchy. No one thing is more important or blessed than another. Everything is fitted together. One of the opponents drew from this the implication that the opponents all shared:

> I've reached the point where philosophically I feel the animals
> have a lot more rights than what we've given them. The things I've
> learned over the years, over the past few years from doing these
> studies having to do with deer and deer hunts and old-growth
> forest, has really made me so much more conscious of the entire
> ecosystem and the animals and what they all stand for. And you
> know, I look at it now and tell myself *leave nature alone* because
> it is beautiful as it is. Let's leave it alone and enjoy it the way it
> was meant to be.

Under such circumstances as these, it is easy to see how someone could emphasize the importance of individuals—individual animals, particular trees—or of specific tracts of land and attribute to them rights, especially the right to be left alone. Virtually any tampering, whether deliberate or inadvertent, is likely to throw things out of kilter. Since system and individual are in balance, there is no tension between what is good for the individual and what is good for the system. There is, in this view, no equivalent in nature to the dilemma Garret Hardin denotes "the tragedy of the commons." [13]

Thus, when I posed the problem to animal rights activists, they refused to accept the possibility that deer were at least as incapable as humans of self-regulation for the common good:

> I have a pretty spiritual attitude about that. I think we should always be evolving towards a more peaceful state with our nature, with animals, with ourselves.

Those among the opponents of the hunt who were more open to the possibility that individual species could overrun and ruin a habitat were willing to concede that some reduction in the herd might have to be accomplished to undo an imbalance *created by misguided human attempts to manage nature*. For this group of MDC critics, the system as a whole is central. Individual members of a species are less salient, certainly less so than with the animal rights advocates, and could be expendable if the larger system's health required. But it is natural systems, not the contrived and distorted systems that managers produce, that should be preserved.

To be sure, when pressed even slightly, opponents of the hunt acknowledged that the Quabbin really is not wild or natural and, given its mandate to keep the water flowing to Boston, the MDC could never politically sustain a complete hands-off policy. Nevertheless, critics saw the Quabbin as a place to "hold the line," a point from which to begin to change priorities and redirect environmental policy. Most critics also acknowledged that the Quabbin, though large, is far from large enough to be immune to the consequences of human activity outside the Reservation. Pollution from autos, acid rain, heavy metal contamination of fish—all this and more means that the Quabbin can never be truly pristine, even if the MDC were to adopt a "benign neglect" stance.[14] But, from the critics' point of view, management only *compounds* these external insults. We must stop blundering around and begin to accord nature the right to heal herself. In the process, we just might be redeemed as well.

By contrast, the proponents of the hunt viewed nature as anything but benign and tranquil—and they regarded the idea of harmonious balance with suspicion bordering on ridicule. Stability is illusory, proponents argued, at best a fleeting moment between disruptions and abrupt changes. Storms, volcanos, secular shifts in weather patterns, fires, all these and more are continually modifying the ecological dynamic of any particular area. Species come and go; dominants rise and fall; vegetation advances or contracts its range: all of this is in response to subtle long-term as well as sudden dramatic shifts in the complex blend of microbes, climate, soils, and the biomass that constitute any given ecological system.

There is no doubt that, with the arrival of humans on the scene, another source of dynamic appeared in the shape of increasingly deliberate and often sweeping manipulations of the environment. From primitive slash-and-burn techniques to sophisticated terracing and irrigation projects, humans have been altering the face of the world. This has been going on for so long that there is no place on the globe that can now be considered pristine—unaffected by human activity. To take a hands-off policy now, the proponents claim, would be irresponsible—too much has been altered. In some instances, management ought to be devoted to undoing the effects of previous interventions—cleanups, restorations, and the like. In other instances, management is needed to even out what would otherwise be unacceptably large swings in resource availability—food, water, and wood products, for example. If human populations are to survive in their present numbers, we will need all our ingenuity and resourcefulness to extract from nature all that we need, especially if we are to avoid depletion and mass die-offs of all sorts of species, ours included.

From this point of view, nature is more chaotic than orderly.[15] As one forester noted:

My feeling is that if you look at the history of forests, especially in the Northeast, you will find disturbance is absolutely the norm. And disturbance of a pretty significant nature, including hurricanes.

These views were echoed by others, professionals and laypersons alike. Some saw nature as Tennyson described it: "red in tooth and claw." Others simply insisted that nature ought not be seen as benign or tranquil. Similarly, they were exceedingly suspicious of attempts to characterize nature as "balanced." To be sure, changes in one factor trigger changes in others. But this "chain reaction" does not necessarily restore the status quo ante any more than it necessarily leads to a new equilibrium. Nowhere is it scripted that this complex system of interactions will produce results that humans appreciate or from which we can take comfort.

Finally, proponents embraced what might be called a pragmatic realism. However much they regretted the rapid growth of human populations in general and the profligacy of Americans in particular, they felt obliged to respond to the world as it is—a world where the demand for natural resources is rising, a world in which the desire to have a "wilderness experience" also increases, a world, in other words, in which human pressures on the land produce a lopsided competition with all sorts of biota. Few denied that things would be better if everyone could accept a simpler lifestyle. In the meantime, however, we have to manage resources and the ways humans use resources. Indeed, it would be *irresponsible* not to do so, even though we will inevitably make mistakes. Despite the complexities of stewardship, too much alteration of nature has occurred, and the unintended consequences of human activity are too great, to permit indulging in the fantasy that if we would only stop managing, nature would cleanse and restore itself. As the forester quoted above remarked, reflecting on a campaign to block a hydroelectric dam:

> We can't make environmental decisions justified by an appreciation of nature instead of an honest attempt to study and understand and know what's the correct way to move nature in a particular direction. For example, environmental groups are jumping on the opportunity to challenge relicensing of hydro-dams to let the rivers run wild again. I hate the dams too but right now we have "x" demand for power and that's not going to suddenly change. Hydro is "free" power once you've made the capital expenditure for the dam, and it's nonpolluting. So if you drop hydro, we'll rely more on coal and oil, which are nonrenewable, expensive, and cause acid rain. And there's always nuclear in the background. So that's where some of the well-intentioned environmental efforts are taking us — to nukes. It drives me crazy.

## The Discursive Construction of Rights and Responsibilities

As it turns out, the dispute over the proposal to reduce the deer herd at the Quabbin was about much more than deer. Even those who were motivated to act by the prospect of killing deer had a much larger agenda. What separated on the matter of deer was not bambi loving but something far more profound and far less easily resolved: there are two quite diametrically opposed discourses regarding nature and our place in the scheme of things. One is a discourse of rights. The other is a discourse of responsibilities. Each is constituted in a view of nature that is antagonistic to the other.

To assign rights to animals and to nature itself makes sense only to the degree to which one thinks that, left to itself, nature produces a world where, in the words of folksinger Bill Staines, "all God's children have a place in the choir." By according all of creation the right to be left alone, the right to live out existence with as little intrusion from humankind as possible, one also implies that the outcome will be one in which all of creation is ensured permanence in a balanced and stable system. Otherwise, claims to rights will inevitably collide and winners will take all.

The discourse of rights of nature, then, is constituted in images of balance and harmony, in the belief that the greatest good for the greatest number can be achieved in nature by what amounts to a posture of laissez-faire — management is to the advocates of the rights of nature what regulation is to the advocates of free markets. Each must believe in a "hidden hand" that transforms the selfishness, shortsightedness, and obliviousness to unintended consequences that surely characterize plants and animals as much as they characterize human action. For some, of course, the hidden hand is God's.

But this is hardly a straightforward proposition among the holders of the rights position. In the Judeo-Christian tradition God enjoins humans to dominate and exploit creation—if you will, to manage it for human purpose. He places us, as it were, at the top of the food chain. The result of the unpleasantness produces tension within the ranks of the rights advocates. Some freely borrow from Native American and Eastern traditions. Others are drawn to faith in nature herself, using the vast store of natural history to point to systems in stable balance over long periods of time as well as systems that have corrected themselves after a period of disruption. But whether deist or not, the discourse of rights of nature requires serious skepticism with respect to the claims of what, following Kuhn, we might think of as contemporary "normal science." [16]

In particular, the prevailing sciences of forestry and wildlife biology are regarded with deep suspicion. The reason for this is straightforward: these fields have long been closely associated with resource users. Schools of forestry have long worked closely with the commercial users of wood products. For their part, wildlife biologists have a long association with state fish and game departments and with the ethos of game management for food and sport uses. These "patron-client" relationships weaken claims to objective or value-free science and expose experts in these fields to the increasing wrath of environmentalists.

Several of the critics of the hunt, in fact, had been trained in forestry and wildlife biology and by no means rejected scientific claims out of hand. But, at least as regards the Quabbin controversy, the preponderance of opposition was rooted in a sweeping suspicion of scientific claims coupled with an openness to claims rooted in nonorthodox science (Gaia, holistic amateur naturalism) or in forms of religious or at least supernatural cosmology.

The point, here, is not to examine these beliefs so much as to indicate that the assertion of rights has to be accompanied, implicitly or explicitly, by the conviction that the constituent elements will behave in ways that justify the claim to rights. Thus, in the most elaborated versions of the rights-based approach, the animal rights position, the assertion is that bad humans have upset good nature and made some animals unnaturally aggressive and mean. If only we humans would relent, nature would return to harmony.[17]

The proponents of the hunt, as we have seen, rejected this view of nature. Because they saw the natural order as subject to abrupt disruptions (by no means all of which caused by humans) and in no way described as tending toward stable harmony, Edenic or otherwise, they had to construct a discourse of responsibility, a discourse that obliges humans to take an active role in shaping the natural environment. We do this consciously or unconsciously, by our mere presence as an inevitably dominant species. Indeed, our dominance, accorded us by our brain, is itself a product of natural forces. As one respondent observed, it would be unnatural for us not to manage and manipulate our environment.

Management, whether "natural" or not, is, in the eyes of proponents, our responsibility—and ours alone. Though we have not done a particularly good job of management, we have to do the best we can to reduce the adverse effects of past and present practices and to ensure that renewable resources remain ample. There is, from this vantage point, absolutely no basis for assuming that nature, left alone, will consistently and predictably provide. Moreover, there is no basis for believing that deer, or anything else for that matter, will behave "responsibly," that is, will reliably moderate their activity for the larger good of others. Deer will browse until there is nothing left to eat: for themselves, for beaver, or for nuthatches. It is our responsibility to ensure that this does not happen, not only for our own self-interest, but in the interests of the other creatures that share habitat with the deer and presumably cannot, in any reasonable sense, protect themselves. From the point of view of the hunt's advocates, the discourse of rights is a discourse of irresponsibility, of surrender to the blind forces of nature.

## Can We Ever Be One with Nature?

The opponents of the hunt saw themselves as defenders of nature against yet another misguided attempt to second guess and guide natural forces. Again and again, in interviews and public statements, they pleaded nature's case and wished that humans could be made to understand the urgency of their cause. If we could appreciate more fully nature's wonder and her perfection, perhaps we would learn to live with nature instead of constantly doing battle with her. The results, they felt, would be salutary: not only would nature have respite and begin to heal the manifold wounds we have inflicted, but people themselves would likely be more understanding and tolerant of one another. The struggle over the management of the Quabbin had, for the critics of the MDC, implications that went well beyond deer and the water supply.

It is hard not to sympathize with such lofty ideals, especially when the record of human efforts to improve upon nature has been so shabby. Indeed, it might well be argued that it is our sorry environmental record that makes the desire to live in harmony with nature so recurrent a theme in human affairs. The clash over the deer hunt at the Quabbin is simply a recent example of a debate that has been going on for decades. Indeed, as historian Roderick Nash has observed, Thoreau anticipated the debate over the Quabbin when he took the side of the shad whose migratory run up the Concord River had been blocked by a dam. The shad, he argued, had a right to the river at least as weighty as any right asserted by humans.[18] Thoreau was among the first in the United States to urge that we should respect nature by ending our efforts to tame and exploit her.

This ideal, to be one with the natural order, is as powerful as it appears to be elusive. It is, it would seem, impossible for humans to abstain from attempting to assert control over nature. Even Thoreau's observations of nature represent a form of control—to catalog and place things in a scheme is to assert power over the things named. Thoreau, for all his disdain for the conceits of civilization, was nevertheless unwilling to forgo many of the fruits of human intervention in nature. John Muir may have come closest to a sustained harmony with elemental nature, setting off, as he did, for months at a time with scarcely more than the clothes on his back. But even Muir, arguably our most forceful advocate for preserving wilderness, knew that the most to be hoped for was the preservation of select areas that were striking in one or more respects.

It seems that we are trapped. Indeed, the terms of the debate have changed little over nearly two centuries. Even the compromise of designating some areas parks or reserves has failed to protect them from human interference and degradation. This has led some to argue that all human activity should be banned in some areas in order that they remain "natural." But if humans must be banned, does that mean that we are declaring ourselves "unnatural"? To project purity and balance onto nature, and the opposite onto humanity, has appeal. But however appealing, there is no serious basis for thinking that undisturbed nature can either be recaptured in any genuine sense or that, if recaptured, it would produce anything like the harmony and balance that the protectionists dream of. To keep an area "natural," it seems, we would have to manage like mad.

In this context, the attraction of the rights position is clear. If we agree that nature has a right to be left alone, we are spared such troubling choices as that between deer and tree regeneration. By letting nature decide, we are absolved of responsibility for the outcome. Ours would then be a morally simplified world, just like the world of the laissez-faire economist who is content to let the impersonal market decide the social good. But this is not the world we inhabit.

The world we inhabit is one that requires our active intervention. Some of this intervention clearly needs to be restorative, aimed at rectifying past mistakes and ending current abuses. Other interventions will inevitably be directed at ensuring stable and continuous supplies of essential resources, such as water. All of this will entail agonizing moral choices. Not all damage can be repaired. Deer may have to be controlled to protect forests. Cruel trade-offs seem inescapable.

Nature, in the sense of that which is a priori, is finished. We will never get it back. But does this mean that we cannot somehow learn to live more harmoniously with nature? I do not see why. The critics of resource management are correct, if not in their characterization of the MDC as thoughtless and interested only in justifying a forestry operation, then in their more general sense that resource management has really been little more than an ideological mask for resource exploitation and the quick dollar. But if we are to be less invasive, less exploitative, it will not come from the extension of rights to the natural world, with the implicit reliance on a faith in nature's benign equilibrium that the rights position entails. It will, instead, have to come from an enlarged sense of responsibility, of stewardship. This will mean devoting more energy and resources to managing ourselves, that we might moderate our efforts to manage nature. It remains to be seen whether we can curb our appetites and control our numbers as effectively as we can control deer. Much more than the fate of deer hangs on the question.

## Notes

This essay would not have been possible without the cooperation of dozens of people who, despite their often deep disagreements, care deeply about the environment in general and the Quabbin in particular. Officials of the Metropolitan District Commission and the Division of Fisheries and Wildlife were also cooperative beyond measure. It is rare to find public agencies so willing to make staff accessible to the prying questions of researchers. I am most grateful. I would also like to record my gratitude to the Trustees of Amherst College, who have given me both a grant and time off from my teaching duties to conduct the research on which this essay is based. Brenda Hanning worked patiently through the endless hours of transcription. Without her painstaking work, all would have been for naught. The ideas in this essay first began to take shape in a course, "The Imagined Landscape," that Tom Looker and I taught together at Amherst College in 1990. Conversations with Tom and with our students helped me frame the project upon which this essay draws. This chapter is based on a longer manuscript that will be published by the University of Massachusetts Press in 1993.

1. See William Cronon, *Changes in the Land* (New York: Hill & Wang, 1983), for an account of the manifold ways in which native Americans in southern New England manipulated the environment for their own ends.

2. Henry David Thoreau, *Walden and Other Writings of Henry David Thoreau*, ed.

Brooks Atkinson (New York: Modern Library, 1965), 254.

3. The flavor of this is especially clear when Emerson's essay "Nature" is read alongside Thoreau's "Walking." This is made easy by a lovely new edition of these two essays introduced by John Elder (Boston: Beacon, 1991).

4. See Thoreau's essay, "Walking," 71–122.

5. One of the wildlife biologists I interviewed observed that New England "wants to be forest." Rainfall, soils, and climate conspire, despite the continued interventions of humans, to create an area of irrepressible herbaceous growth—at least so far. The advent of acid rain may alter this significantly.

6. Ambiguity mixes with inspiration in this tale. As it turns out, eagles were in all likelihood no more than passersby in the Swift River Valley. The river and its tributaries were far too small to be of much interest to the fish-hunting birds. As with many of our attempts to "restore" and "re-create," we operate in terms of what we like to believe things were like "back then." I say this not to chide smugly or to raise the flag for some purist standard. As we shall see repeatedly, any choice we make with respect to environmental intervention (or nonintervention) is laden with ambiguity. In this sense, to speak of "restoration" is probably little more than soothing mystification. Alston Chase explores these matters as well as anyone I have read. See his analysis of the management of Yellowstone National Park, *Playing God in Yellowstone: The Destruction of America's First National Park* (New York: Harcourt Brace Jovanovich, 1987).

7. Thomas Conuel, *Quabbin: The Accidental Wilderness*, rev. ed. (Amherst: University of Massachusetts Press, 1990).

8. The high kill, exceeding predictions by a factor of three, is being read, not surprisingly, in diverse ways. With good reason, some have argued that the MDC staff had significantly underestimated the size of the herd. Others, with equally sound assumptions, insist that the deer were so tame and unsuspecting that they were virtually lambs at the slaughter. The only way to get a sense of this is to ask the hunters about deer sightings and the behavior of the deer once the hunting commenced. This research is under way, in collaboration with Robert Muth and David Loomis, colleagues at the University of Massachusetts.

9. The public character of this controversy also made it possible for me to identify the most active and outspoken partisans and thus to approach them for interviews. Without going into elaborate detail, I attended and taped the proceedings of all the public meetings held in 1990 and 1991. In addition, I conducted interviews with each of the panelists the MDC had invited to its informational meetings, as well as with the principle MDC and Division of Fisheries and Wildlife officials responsible for framing the deer management policy, and with a range of people selected from among those who spoke out at one or another of the public meetings or wrote letters to the newspaper about the proposed deer hunt at the Quabbin. In all, I carried out thirty-five interviews, most lasting well over an hour, with men and women who, while not themselves in any way representative, nonetheless represented the full spectrum of opinion so far as I can tell. The only refusals to be interviewed came from people strongly identified with animal rights (two refusals) and with antihunting (one refusal).

10. As I noted early on, many of the opponents had long been supporters of the MDC restrictions on use of the Reservation, restrictions that were largely responsible for the Quabbin resembling a "wild" tract. As a result, the controversy ruptured some long-term friendships. It also led some opponents to characterize various MDC personnel as having betrayed their original mission. Opponents freely speculated about the personal motives and agendas of MDC officials in often quite unflattering terms. Environmentalist ranks were also split over the deer hunt and old alliances and personal friendships were strained, in several instances past the breaking point.

11. I did the bulk of the interviewing for this project during the summer of 1991, so I had

to stitch interviews around peoples' vacations. Most of the proponents vacationed in remote spots—wilderness backpacking in the Rockies or Alaska, canoeing wild rivers, and the like. For men who spend their working lives outdoors, in and around what others think of as a primeval forest, the fact that they choose to vacation in the woods is testimony to their embrace of nature.

12. It is important to note here, to be picked up again in the conclusion, that what separates animal rights advocates from those who are privately against hunting is the desire to see one's personal philosophy codified into law. The animal rights activists want their ethical system enacted into law. Those among the hunt's proponents who disapprove of hunting recognize that those who do not share their ethical view have a right to think and behave differently.

13. Hardin's oft-cited essay, "The Tragedy of the Commons," is reprinted, along with commentaries and elaborations, in Garrett Hardin and John Baden, eds., *Managing the Commons* (San Francisco: W. H. Freeman, 1977).

14. A few of the more "romantic" of the critics, particularly those who were uninvolved in the process of policy formulation, remained hopeful that wolves and mountain lions could be introduced into the Reservation and would quickly bring the deer population down. They could not accept the argument that the Reservation is not large enough to sustain resident (as opposed to transient) populations of these large predators.

15. For a rendering of this, see Eliot Porter's stunning photographic accompaniment to James Gleick's essay in Porter and Gleick, *Nature's Chaos* (New York: Viking, 1990).

16. Thomas Kuhn, *The Structure of Scientific Revolutions* (Chicago: University of Chicago Press, 1962).

17. Desmond Morris, for example, disputes the notion that wild animals are ferocious. He writes, speaking here about what we can learn from those who have kept "exotics" such as leopards as pets: "All too often in the past the savagery of such animals has been caused by the brutal way they have been treated by humans rather than by some inherent viciousness in their characters. The 'savage beast' is largely the invention of the cowardly big-game hunter." *The Animal Contract* (New York: Warner, 1990), 65.

18. Roderick F. Nash, *The Rights of Nature* (Madison: University of Wisconsin Press, 1989), 166–67.

# Part III

## Environmentalist Talk

Chapter 7

# Restoring Nature:
# Natives and Exotics

John Rodman

## Three Cases

The October 1988 issue of *Fremontia*, journal of the California Native Plant Society, carried three succinct articles on coastal dune restoration projects occurring in the 1980s, in addition to several notes and one letter on the control of various exotic (alien, nonnative) species of plants. The link, of course, is that the control, removal, and sometimes eradication of exotic species of plants and animals is the negative moment in the dialectic of ecological restoration, in complement to the positive moment of planting, reintroduction, and so on. But what does it mean to be an exotic, as distinct from a native, and why is this important?

In this first section the three texts are examined, not to evaluate the actual projects, but to raise questions about how we think and what we presuppose when we use the categories "native" and "exotic." The next section shifts the scene from the revegetation of coastal dunes to the defense of desert riparian areas against invasion by tamarisk. Throughout this chapter, the focus is primarily on plants, but the argument leads to a concern with larger ecological systems. It is not my intention to reduce the complex process of ecological restoration to the replacement of exotic by native species, but rather to focus on this particular aspect of ecological restoration, leaving the discussion of other problematic aspects to other times and places.

## Case 1

Andrea Pickart's article, "Dune Revegetation at Buhne Point," describes the re-creation of a 20-acre sand spit in Humboldt Bay in northern California.[1] The Buhne Point spit had eroded over the course of a century and finally washed out to sea in 1982, leaving a fishing village exposed to storm waves and flooding. Re-creation of the spit was undertaken as a state-of-the-art "shoreline erosion demonstration project" funded by Congress and carried out by the Army Corps of Engineers *(sic)* in collaboration with state and county governments.

Until very recently, the state of the art for dealing with shoreline erosion consisted of building protective jetties and stabilizing the dunes by planting *Ammophila arenaria,* an introduced European beach grass. (One cause of the long-term erosion of Buhne Point, of course, was the construction of the Humboldt Bay jetties in 1899; like flood control dikes, jetties protect the immediate area and pass the problem along.) The new Buhne Point project continued the reliance on jetties, but, instead of seeding the newly imported sand with European beach grass, used instead a seed mix of plant species typical of the "dune mat" vegetation of the northern fore-dune community as it was found in its "most pristine" form on the Lanphere-Christensen Dunes Preserve, a 450-acre area located on the North Spit of Humboldt Bay, owned and managed by the Nature Conservancy. The Buhne Point project aimed not simply at creating a sand spit with stable dunes by revegetating with whatever would work, or even at restoring the sand spit as it had existed before the 1982 washout, but at creating a sand spit on the model of the best available paradigm of what a native fore-dune community was like. (The project director at Buhne Point was the manager of the Lanphere-Christensen Preserve, but I cannot fault her choice of models.) Subsequently, the Buhne Point project became a model used by the California Coastal Commission and by Oregon State Parks in cases where coastal development was permitted on the condition that disturbed dune areas be restored as a mitigation.

The project manager's account does not suggest that revegetation with European beach grass would have been an ineffective way of stabilizing dunes. The defect of that approach was rather that "the spread of this introduced plant away from the stabilization sites was resulting in the dramatic loss of diverse natural communities." In short, the exotic plant was a threat to native plant communities—first, presumably, by replacing (or at least taking up space that could be occupied by) natives, and, second (and apparently more important), by escaping the stabilization sites and invading various natural communities present in the region. Evidently, exotics are bad when they behave invasively; but, since what they do when they invade is to replace natives, we may suppose that the presence of an exotic is bad per se, and that invasive behavior compounds the original sin. Alternatively, we may speculate that the key is to be found in the adjective *diverse* (assuming that the phrase *diverse natural communities* means not only various kinds of natural communities, but also communities that are characterized by a significant degree of internal diversity), and that what is bad is the diminishing of biological diversity (at both species and community levels) by the introduction of something approximating a monoculture, which occurs first at the stabilization site and later more widely when it spreads.

Which of these interpretations is correct? What is the primary value at stake — nativity or diversity? To what extent do they come to the same thing, and to what extent can they differ? Since we can all think of examples of exotic plants that are difficult to grow on some site or other, or that survive only in garden or greenhouse conditions (e.g., tropical orchids in the Mojave desert), "exotic" cannot be equated with "invasive" any more than "native" can be equated with "drought tolerant." But can natives be invasive?

## Case 2

Linda Miller's analysis, "How Yellow Bush Lupine Came to Humboldt Bay," begins with an anomaly in Paradigmland. "For ten years a war has been waged against yellow bush lupine (*Lupinus arboreus*) in The Nature Conservancy's Lanphere-Christensen Preserve."[2] The low-growing, herbaceous "dune-mat" community, containing some forty species, including Menzies's wallflower (state listed as endangered), was in the process of being taken over by this "aggressive" and "invasive" perennial, woody shrub, which, unlike European beach grass, was a California native species.

*Native* and *exotic* are, of course, very relative terms. Presumably, every plant is native somewhere and exotic somewhere else. (For example, Hooker's evening primrose, whose portrait graces the cover of this issue of *Fremontia* as an example of the native dune community in northern California, is a somewhat invasive exotic in my part of inland southern California.) Anyone who has picked up at a botanic garden's sale of "California native plants" some beauty whose ancestors were at home in the fog of the Channel Islands and has managed to fry it in San Bernardino or Riverside knows that true statements that are vague ("This is a native plant") or cast at an inappropriate level of generality ("This is a California native plant") can be as disastrous as ignorance or falsehood. So, on reflection, we arrive at a range of concentric contexts: a species may be native to the Western Hemisphere, to North America, to California, to northern California, but is it native to the foredune community on the North Spit of Humboldt Bay? Logically, there is no limit to this process: a species could be native to the south side of the North Spit but exotic to the north side of the North Spit. The ability to say whether this would be a meaningful statement or not would depend on one's knowledge of the geography and ecology of the North Spit and on the purpose of the statement. In practical terms, the two most common questions that people in general have are, Will it grow here if I plant it? and Will it grow here too well (become invasive)?

After almost a decade of waging "war" against yellow bush lupine, the Nature Conservancy decided to fund research by Linda Miller "to determine the history of the introduction" of the shrub. The wording suggests that the research presupposed the likelihood that bush lupine (observed to be invasive) was exotic and therefore introduced; the question was how and when. According to Miller, "most local botanists" believed the plant to be locally nonnative "because of [undocumented] reports of its introduction around the turn of the century and because of its aggressive behavior." Now, "aggressive" or "invasive" behavior is often a sign or consequence of exoticality, but it cannot be a defining characteristic for two reasons—one empirical (not all exotics behave aggressively) and one logical (if aggressive behavior automatically made bush lupine an exotic, there would have been no issue, yet "some botanists [who presumably did not deny that bush lupine behaved aggressively] still considered the bush lupine to be a native of Northern California"). Perhaps, also, the bush lupine seemed to Miller and others suspiciously, and paradoxically, too well adapted, too successful, on the foredunes of the North Spit, with its roots penetrating deep into the soil and clothed with nitrogen-fixing bacteria to compensate for the sandy soil's lack of nutrients. One wonders also if there was less than universal agreement on the preserve management's policy of trying to eradicate "this showy and fragrant shrub," so that research was commissioned to somehow legitimate the policy of lupine eradication to which the management was already committed.

The evidence unearthed by Miller (reports of botanists, recollections of early residents, aerial photographs, and so on) supported the introduction hypothesis. It seems that Theodora Cobb, wife of the operator of the fog signal station on the south end of the North Spit, collected bush lupine seeds on a trip to the San Francisco Presidio in 1908 and planted them around the station and in her yard. (If there had been bush lupine close at hand, presumably Ms. Cobb would not have bothered to bring in seeds from San Francisco.) Later, in 1917, the Corps of Engineers took bush lupine seeds from the fog signal station and planted them along the railroad on the lower spit to prevent sand from blowing onto the tracks. Subsequent aerial photographs show "a clear northern migration and overall increase in the area of bush lupine between 1939 and 1984," with the increase averaging 6.4 acres a year. The evidence, concludes Miller, "strongly supports the theory that the plant is not native to the North Spit and helps to justify a decade of eradication efforts at the Lanphere-Christensen Dunes Preserve."

But what if the California Geological Survey of 1860–67 had listed bush lupine as being already present in Humboldt County? Better yet, what if Archibald Menzies's journal had recorded the plant at nearby Trinidad Bay in 1793? How long would bush lupine have to have been known to be in the area (and how precisely must we specify "the area"?) to be considered native? In her concluding paragraph, Miller appears to suggest that something like one hundred years is the critical time frame: "It is difficult to prove that bush lupine did not grow here a century ago, but the evidence strongly supports the theory that the plant is not native to the North Spit." Why a hundred years? It is a round number, but seems scarcely time enough for a plant species to adapt and become a member of a community.

How much weight is borne by the case for deliberate introduction by Ms. Cobb and the Corps of Engineers? Evidence of this degree of specificity is unusual in the history of plant introduction; in the absence of such evidence, what should we assume? Is human agency (intentional or not) the critical factor? If so, would accidental introduction via seeds carried in the wool of exotic sheep brought into an area by humans render a species exotic, whereas seeds carried in the fur or intestines of wild animals moving under their own power would be considered a case of plant "migration," and a plant species that extended its range in this way would be considered native throughout its range? It may matter whether an area not adapted to heavy grazing is overgrazed by sheep, and whether an area so disturbed is colonized by one or more invasive plant species, but what does it matter (other things being equal) on which animal, wild or tame, native or exotic, human or sheep, the plant hitched a ride?

Suppose, contrary to Miller's findings, there was evidence (comparable to that of the aerial photographs) that bush lupine had "migrated," not simply from the south side of the spit to the north side of the spit in fifty years, but from the San Francisco-Sacramento area to Humboldt Bay (a distance of about 180 miles) in the course of the two centuries that separate us from Menzies's journal. Is it unreasonable to think that a plant that could "migrate" northward at a rate of 6.4 acres per year could have "migrated" in the same direction at a rate of slightly less than one linear mile per year without human assistance? How much space can a plant cover in how little time before we characterize it as an invasive exotic? (A full consideration would have to include climate change during the time period, as well as the different kinds of habitat occupying the space covered.) Perhaps this is more important than whether Theodora Cobb or the Corps of Engineers, rather than sheep or coyotes or birds or whatever, introduced bush lupine to the North Spit.

Above all, how is it, exactly, that support for the theory that "bush lupine did not grow here a century ago [and] is not native to the North Spit . . . helps to justify a decade of eradication efforts"? If Miller had discovered evidence that bush lupine had existed on or near the North Spit a century or two ago, would the Nature Conservancy then have abandoned its policy of bush lupine eradication? If not, what is the real purpose of the "war" against bush lupine? Is it not enough that bush lupine, however long it has been on the North Spit, and however it got there, is aggressively invasive and poses a threat to the northern foredune community? If, then, nativity is not the real issue, what is? How easy it is to fall back on Menzies's wall-flower (a state-listed endangered species), as if the ultimate issue were a private conflict between one species (the robust invader expanding its progeny and domain) and another (the wimpy victim diminishing in numbers and shrinking in range). The Endangered Species Act is not only an act of Congress but an act of habitual conceptualization that reflects in a twisted way (individual species, species as individuals) the atomistic metaphysics and social theory of modern Western culture, even when the evident issue before us is whether to allow an aggressive species to disrupt and convert a diverse, differentiated community into a homogeneous mass society.

Different ways of formulating the issue can have implications for practical policy. If being nonnative makes bush lupine bad per se, perhaps it should be eradicated in *all* those areas where it is nonnative. If it is bad only where it threatens an endangered species (such as Menzies's wall-flower), then we may have no business waging "war" on it in other situations. If it is bad where it threatens to disrupt and impoverish one or more native communities (like the northern foredune community) or ecosystems, then it can legitimately be fought on a broader front, but the objective may be best formulated in terms of control, which may or may not involve eradication, depending on the situation. An analogy of sorts may be made with the shift in "pest control" philosophy from total chemical war waged to eradicate bad insects to the more limited ambitions of integrated pest management, which uses a variety of approaches to control or "contain" pest populations within tolerable limits.

## Case 3

Marylee Guinon's account, "Dune Restoration at Spanish Bay," describes the restoration of 65 acres on Spanish Bay in Monterey County, where coastal dunes had been mined as a sand quarry for some forty years.[3] The dune restoration (including foredune, mid-dune, and hind-dune areas) was a mitigation required by the California Coastal Commission as a condition of permitting a golf course/hotel/condominium development in the regulated coastal zone.

Before "dune construction," a program of eradicating exotic plants was undertaken, targeting at least eight species ranging from ice plant to pampas grass, Kikuyu grass, French broom, and two species of *Acacia*. Primary attention was given to ice plant and pampas grass, "since these were the most abundant and aggressive exotics found on the site and would pose significant maintenance problems." After dune construction, a mix of some fourteen plant species was hydromulched, using seed collected on or near Monterey Peninsula. With one exception, all the species used were "members of the native coastal strand community and . . . believed to have once inhabited the Spanish Bay site."

The exception was sea rocket (*Cakile maritima*), an exotic annual chosen for use "because it is an early successional species capable of rapidly establishing on dunes and stabilizing sand." Native plant species, in comparison, were seen as too "slow to germinate and produce extensive root systems." Why such a hurry to stabilize (at least some of) the dunes? Because the golf resort was being constructed simultaneously, and because "some restored dunes would be adjacent to golf greens, tees, and fairways, and, in many cases, also would serve as the golf course's 'rough.'" Hence, stabilization was of pressing importance. The role of sea rocket was envisaged as temporary: it would stabilize the dunes while the natives became established, but was not expected to persist more than a season or two, because "nurse crop annuals do not normally occur in sand dunes," and because the project design called for capping the decomposed granite fill with three feet of pure sand.

Alas, the golf course architect redesigned some of the dunes after they had been constructed, and "their sand caps were disturbed and mixed with soil." A similar disturbance occurred when an irrigation system was belatedly installed. Also, the initial hydromulch mix turned out to contain too high a proportion of sea rocket seeds. The result was that, especially in areas where the sand cap had been disturbed, "an almost uniform, thick, and verdant stand of the [exotic] nurse crop had grown up and many native plants had perished or were weakened." This led the project manager to

reduce the ratio of sea rocket in subsequent hydromulchings and to eliminate it in the seeding of low-erosion sites, out of fear that "the nurse crop
would thrive and possibly persist for a number of years." It also led to a
greater emphasis on "an ongoing exotics eradication program" to be included in the maintenance manual for this (it was hoped) "self-sustaining
dune complex."

What are the elements of interest for us in this story—aside from obvious lessons, such as that haste makes waste, that the means can affect the
end, that, failing coordination, the left hand can undo the work of the right,
and that introductions of species are often attended by unpredicted and
undesired consequences? In the account of this project, we cannot fail to
be struck by the juxtaposition of an ambitious program of removing exotic
plants with a program of deliberately introducing another exotic plant.
What makes this intelligible is the classification and ranking of exotics going on. Recall that, among the exotics to be purged from the site, ice plant
and pampas grass were given priority as "the most abundant and aggressive exotics," which is to say the most dangerous to the native community
being re-created. Other exotics on the priority hit list were woody shrubs
(e.g., French broom and two species of *Acacia*), and all were perennial
species. Sand dunes, like grasslands, are susceptible to invasion and take-
over by perennial woody shrubs, which convert the area to a dominantly
different type of vegetation and, in the case of dunes, can stabilize them to
the point of immobility. By contrast, an herbaceous annual such as sea
rocket, even though exotic, was thought not to pose a long-term problem.
In the context of the task at hand, its aggressive, invasive, "weedy" tendency became a virtue, so that one referred to it not only optimistically in
terms of one of its hoped-for community functions ("nurse plant") but also
respectfully as "an early successional species capable of rapidly establishing on dunes and stabilizing sand," [4] and even as "a non-native, non-inva-
sive pioneer species . . . used because of its colonizing ability." [5] Sea rocket's aggressiveness could be seen as a virtue as long as one believed that, as
an annual not adapted to growing in sand, it would not survive many seasons in competition with native plants atop sandy dunes and therefore
would not be invasive in any long-term sense. Like "the dictatorship of the
proletariat," the reign of sea rocket was envisaged as a necessary transi-
tional stage that would serve its function and "wither away," leaving utopia
to flourish. Those with the vision did not control events, however, and sea
rocket got out of control to the extent that the Spanish Bay project was being criticized in 1989 as "revegetation in the guise of restoration." [6]

Implicit in this discussion are two complementary ways of looking at
plants—substantively and functionally. In terms of the substantive composition of a plant community, nobody doing strict ecological restoration

work (as distinct from mere revegetation, reforestation, or land reclamation) wants to include an exotic species. In terms of function, some exotics are more subversive to native communities than others, and the use of some may arguably be worth risking in certain circumstances when a function needs to be served (e.g., dune stabilization, ground cover, or shade for seedlings) and no natives are suitable or available for the job. In some situations, the species that historically played one of those roles may have become extinct, and anyone trying to restore the system to the extent possible may search for a functional substitute, which may be nonnative. We are not confronted with that type of situation here, however, and one lesson of the Buhne Point project, even making allowance for differences between the coasts of Monterey County and Humboldt County, is that one need not have recourse to an invasive, exotic species (such as European beach grass or sea rocket) in order to stabilize dunes.

As the Spanish Bay project suggests, the decision to risk using an exotic species as a means, when the goal involves reestablishing a native community, sometimes arises from time constraints. While nearly all restoration projects are characterized by constraints of time, as well as of money and labor, especially severe time constraints tend to be involved in "multiple-purpose" projects that involve development as well as restoration, golf resorts as well as coastal dunes. In a development-oriented society, "time is money," and it seems too expensive to do the dune restoration first and patiently, using only native species and giving the restoration project manager co-control over the "architecture" of the dunes. In this type of situation, the notion of the useful exotic appears as a "shortcut," a way of getting the revegetation work done rapidly so that development can proceed. This reflects, on the mundane project level, the larger, world-historical sense in which introductions of exotic species are shortcuts in evolutionary time. To this theme we now turn, by way of a brief excursion into the arena of the tamarisk invasion and its control.

## The Tamarisk Invasion

We remove "saltcedar," the deciduous tamarisk shrub, from desert riparian areas of the southwestern United States because it is an invasive exotic. On public lands managed by the Bureau of Land Management the key term is *invasive*, taken together with the particular consequences that follow in this case—namely, depletion of water supply through lavish evapotranspiration, obstruction of channels with consequent flooding, and impoverishment of wildlife habitat.[7] In Nature Conservancy preserves and in national parks there is an additional motivation: since the restoration and preservation of native ecosystems is a primary management objective, saltcedar should be removed simply because it is exotic, regardless of how invasive it is, and regardless of the kind of impact it has on wildlife habitat, water supply, or flood protection.

In practice, of course, whether resources are allocated to the control of exotics at all, and, if so, which ones, is apt to depend on how invasive they are perceived to be, on the consequences of that invasion, and on the estimated degree of probability that control efforts could make a significant difference. In desert riparian areas, saltcedar scores high on the first two counts; the only question is whether the invasion is too far advanced to reverse. Hence, on many preserves, efforts are devoted to saltcedar removal while other exotics that exhibit less invasive behavior or have a less devastating impact are tolerated or ignored. On preserves where "athel" (*Tamarix aphylla*), the evergreen, tree-size tamarisk, exists along with the deciduous, shrubby "saltcedar" (*Tamarix chinensis, T. ramossisima*), the priority of eradication work is normally given to saltcedar for the simple reason that, although both species "waste" water and provide poor wildlife support, athel does not reproduce sexually in this climate and is, therefore, although exotic, not significantly invasive. An occasional athel that happens to be unfortunately located (e.g., next to a visitor center or along an entrance road, where it is an embarrassing symbol of the preserve's distance from reaching its goal of restoring native ecosystems, or next to a spring that supplies water for endangered desert pupfish) may be targeted for removal. But, generally, athel removal is a luxury, whereas saltcedar removal is urgent. The two species of tamarisk occupy very different priority niches in the ecology of preserve management, even though they appear to be equally exotic to the American Southwest.

The family *Tamaricaceae* and the genus *Tamarix* are generally regarded as native to a zone stretching from northern Africa and southern Europe through the Middle East and South Asia to China and Japan, with a few species in disjunct parts of western and southern Africa. There is also general acceptance of Baum's view that it is "most probable that the earliest *Tamarix* species ... developed in the southeastern part of the Indo-Turanian Centre [India, Pakistan, Afghanistan, Soviet Central Asia, Iran]," given that half the total number of species are still found there, including a disproportionately high number of the "primitive" forms.[8] Baum also postulates a secondary site of speciation in the eastern Mediterranean area (Turkey, Lebanon, Israel, Egypt). If Baum is correct, the pattern of migration was roughly thus: from South Asia eastward to East Asia, and from South Asia westward to Europe and Africa, both directly and via the eastern Mediterranean. What Baum's "diagrammatic representation of the principal migration routes of *Tamarix*" does not show is the later movement from western Europe to the United States, Canada, and Latin America, and across the

United States from New York to California. Why? In what sense is a genus that starts out in India "native" to China or Spain but "exotic" to the United States? Does movement across land constitute "migration" and allow the plant to be everywhere native, whereas movement across a sea makes it an introduced exotic? If so, why does the Atlantic Ocean count but not the Red Sea? How wide must a sea be to turn a migration into an introduction, a native into an exotic?

Perhaps more pertinent than the difference of degree in space is the difference of degree in time. Imagine that it took millions of years for *Tamarix* to migrate from the Indian subcontinent across Persia into Iraq, and on to Spain. Imagine also that *Tamarix* underwent repeated speciation as it adapted to different environments along its path, and that in each environment it gradually became part of a system of checks and balances that included insects and pathogens and perhaps grazing animals that eventually limited it. Then imagine that some individuals of at least two tamarisk species living in Europe were suddenly taken out of context and transported to the United States, where they were propagated and planted, and where there were no natural (preexisting) controls for them. In areas where conditions were unfavorable or marginal they failed to survive, survived only in cultivation, or hung on as noninvasive, even nonreproducing, anomalies. Where they found climate and habitat for which they were preadapted, they flourished and spread like an Old World virus discovering New World bodies. In this process, saltcedar genes proved far more adaptive than those of athel. In fact, there is no consensus on whether saltcedar (the deciduous, shrubby, incredibly prolific form of tamarisk) should be thought of as one species, several distinguishable species, or a group of highly adaptive, rapidly speciating forms.[9]

Research by Robinson suggests the suddenness of saltcedar's introduction and spread in the United States.[10] It was not brought from East Asia by "Native Americans" crossing the Bering Strait, or even from Europe by the early Spanish explorers coming via Latin America, but was first introduced in the 1820s and 1830s via the nursery trade in eastern seaport cities such as New York and Philadelphia. Nurseries in the San Francisco area were offering it by the 1850s, and by 1880 it had escaped from cultivation and turned up in Texas and Utah. In subsequent decades it was planted here and there, sometimes as an ornamental, sometimes for erosion control. In the 1920s Aldo Leopold had tamarisk in his front yard when he worked for the U.S. Forest Service and lived in Albuquerque, but that was probably an athel planted for shade. Since the 1920s, and especially the 1940s, saltcedar has colonized riparian areas in the West, particularly the Southwest, forming dense, monocultural thickets in the drainages of river systems such as the Colorado, the Gila, the Arkansas, the Rio Grande, and the Pecos, as well as in numerous desert oases, gaining notoriety on occasions such as when it dried up spring-fed ponds in Death Valley.

Saltcedar control is difficult for many reasons: saltcedar's long season of prolific production of tiny wind- and water-dispersed seed; the versatility of its root system, which can either use surface water or put roots down to the water table; its ability to cope with high levels of salinity; its preadaptation to fire, which enables the root crown to resprout after burning or cutting; and, of course, the absence of any biological control. Attempts to control saltcedar have involved burning, bulldozing, flooding, cutting, and poisoning. In some areas, saltcedar has been controlled through laborious hand cutting and careful poisoning of the stumps; on the Coachella Valley Preserve, where I shared in the volunteer work, this process took five years. There are other, vaster, more densely infested areas where this approach would be so labor-intensive and take so long as to be unthinkable, and the main alternatives involve some form of biological control. Either one tries to adopt the perspective of evolutionary time, imagining some future in which the wave of the tamarisk invasion, like some great world religion, has crested and begun to subside and be absorbed into the larger regional ecology, or one becomes a participant in the process of research and lobbying that aims at deliberately introducing a biological control. The process of identifying possible control agents is well under way, and the prospects for species- or at least genus-specific control agents are good because no members of the tamarisk family are native to this hemisphere.[11] Experimental testing of possible tamarisk control agents for effectiveness and safety is an expensive process, however, and funding tends to go to controlling insects that threaten human food crops, rather than to controlling plants that impoverish wetlands and wildlife. Meanwhile, we work and wait and explore some of the interesting questions that the possibility of biological control raises.

Suppose that the essence of exoticality is existence outside a community, lack of membership in a community of mutual dependence and mutual controls. The potential for aggressive, invasive behavior is inherent in the status of being an exotic (which is why the use of exotics, such as sea rocket, is always fraught with danger), but the right match with climate and environment is needed for this potential to be actualized. Several intriguing possibilities now arise. If/when a system of biological control emerges in a new setting, should the exotic be reclassified as a native? If some already-existing New World control were to prove immediately applicable to an introduced exotic, would the new arrival be an instant native? And what if an exotic control agent should arrive upon the scene, either accidentally (like the Eucalyptus beetle in 1985) or as part of a deliberate biological control program (like the wasp that has been introduced by scientists at the University of California, Riverside, to control the Eucalyptus beetle, or the other wasp introduced to control the ash whitefly)? Can three exotics—the Eucalyptus, the beetle, and the wasp, all from Australia—make each other natives of California if they balance out, without causing disastrous side effects? Would saltcedar become native to the United States if we were able to control it by introducing, say, the foliage feeder *Agdistis arabica* from Pakistan?[12] Perhaps the ultimate issue is not whether or when a species is (labeled) native or exotic, but whether and when and to what extent species behave as members of communities, how we can help reconstruct communities using new parts, and what membership in a multispecies community involves.

Plants resemble people in that many "natives" are immigrants that have been in a country long enough to become members and citizens of a community. It is important not to absolutize the native/exotic dichotomy by writing as if there were some "original" time (before agriculture, say) when "the flora of the earth was ... made up only of native plants."[13] On reflection, the contrast of native and exotic presupposes the separation long ago of a continuous land mass into distinct continents that functioned for millions of years as islands where distinct patterns of adaptation and speciation developed. It also presupposes the modern age of exploration and "discovery" from the Renaissance on, when Europeans colonized the world with their surplus people, their plants and animals, and their germs, while sending back samples of New World flora and fauna for their own gardens and zoos. In Charles Elton's classic formulation, "We are living in a period of the world's history when the mingling of thousands of kinds of organisms from different parts of the world is setting up terrific dislocations in nature. We are seeing huge changes in the natural [age-old?] population balance of the world."[14] But we live at a stage of this period when we have become more conscious of the colonization process, the legitimacy and utility of native floras (whether of California or of Amazonia), and the importance of self-regulating communities whose balance is threatened not only by the continuing introduction of exotics from other continents but also by our species' multiplication, mobility, greed, and impatience. The greatest of the ecological "explosions" involves ourselves.

Whereas the native/exotic dichotomy arises out of our retrospective understanding of the whole modern period of world history, in contrast to the continental isolation that preceded it, our preoccupation with aggressive and invasive behavior leading to impoverished and unstable monocultures seems to reflect a more recent, twentieth-century way of regarding the world—a world characterized by "world wars" and by "totalitarian" movements that periodically arise and spread, eliminating or repressing (for a time at least) some basic form of human diversity (e.g., ethnic, socioeconomic, or religious) in order to create the precarious utopia of a racially pure *Reich*, a classless society, or a purely Islamic state. The deeper political meaning of the native plant movement is not, I think, a nativistic fear and dislike of immigrants, but a commitment to the defense, preservation, and restoration of indigenous, balanced communities. The priority of form over content appears when, all else failing, we are willing to introduce another exotic in an attempt to reestablish a balance that we perceive to be lost or threatened. What is most difficult is to recognize our own responsibility for the loss of balance—for example, how by damming Glen Canyon and managing water releases primarily for hydroelectric power production for a continually multiplying, economically expanding, energy-intensive society, we have changed the hydrologic regime in a way that set up the Grand Canyon for tamarisk invasion.[15] The tamarisk explosion in the American Southwest is, then, at least in part, both a result of and a metaphor for the human explosion. When we look at the tamarisk invasion, we look as if in a mirror and realize that restoring the balance must, in large part, come from within.

## Conclusion

This essay provides more questions and suggestions than it does answers. The intent is not so much to redefine or debunk the notions of "native" and "exotic" as to tease out some of the issues that underlie our use of these notions. The reader may feel that, in the process, I have merely substituted one set of problematic categories for another. Instead of "natives" and "exotics," we get notions such as "community" and "balance." Neither social theorists nor ecologists agree on what a community is, or whether there is any analogy, parallel structure, or common pattern between biological systems and human societies. (See Worster for the individualist/collectivist split within ecology.)[16] Yet the pervasive patterns of metaphor that see vegetative politics in terms of aggression, invasion, colonization, war, defense, containment, and migration, as well as community, suggest an intuition of some kind of common or parallel structure that needs more exploration. When the direction of metaphor runs also the other way I will be more sanguine about the joint future of plants and people. Meanwhile, it may be useful to consider what might be involved in our becoming more aware of ourselves as members of a multispecies community, or network of communities, in which we not only play restoration politics like Metternich, balancing other "powers" against one another (e.g., the lacewings against the aphids), but also strive for a greater measure of balance within ourselves. As for ecological restoration, it is at bottom not so much about natives and exotics as about restoring balance in a disturbed world, and restoring our place in the balance of the world.

## Notes

1. Andrea Pickart, "Dune Revegetation at Buhne Point," *Fremontia* 16 (October 1988): 3–5.

2. Linda Miller, "How Yellow Bush Lupine Came to Humboldt Bay," *Fremontia* 16 (October 1988): 6–7.

3. Marylee Guinon, "Dune Restoration at Spanish Bay," *Fremontia* 16 (October 1988): 8–11.

4. Ibid.

5. David Allen and Marylee Guinon, "The Restoration of Dune Habitat at Spanish Bay: Preliminary Results," in *Proceedings of the Second Native Plant Revegetation Symposium, San Diego, CA* (Madison, Wis.: Society for Ecological Restoration, 1987).

6. Suzanne Schettler and Mary Ann Matthews, "Revegetation, Not Restoration," *Fremontia* 16 (January 1989): 29.

7. For a fuller analysis of the tamarisk invasion and its consequences, see John Rodman, "Reflections on Tamarisk Bashing," in *Restoration '89: The New Management Challenge: Proceedings of the First Annual Meeting of the Society for Ecological Restoration, Oakland, California* (Madison, Wis.: Society for Ecological Restoration, 1990). See also Michael R. Kunzmann et al., eds., *Tamarisk Control in the Southwestern United States: Proceedings of Tamarisk Conference, 1987* (Tucson: NPS Cooperative Unit, University of Arizona, rev. 1990).

8. Bernard R. Baum, *The Genus "Tamarix"* (Jerusalem: Israel Academy of Sciences and Humanities, 1978).

9. Bernard R. Baum, "Introduced and Naturalized Tamarisks in the United States and Canada," *Baileya* 15, no. 1 (1967): 19–25; Jerome S. Horton and C. J. Campbell, *Management of Phreatophyte and Riparian Vegetation for Maximum Multiple Use Values* (USDA Forest Service Research Paper RM-117) (Washington, D.C.: U.S. Government Printing Office, 1974).

10. T. W. Robinson, *Introduction, Spread, and Aereal Extent of Saltcedar* (Tamarix) *in the Western States* (U.S. Geological Survey Professional Paper 491-A) (Washington, D.C.: U.S. Government Printing Office, 1965).

11. C. J. DeLoach, *Technical Proposal to Conduct an Analysis of the Harmful, Beneficial, and Ecological Values of Saltcedar and Assess Its Potential for Biological Control* (Temple, Tex.: USDA Grassland, Soil, and Water Research Laboratory, 1986).

12. Ibid., 27.

13. Elizabeth McClintock, "The Displacement of Native Plants by Exotics," in *Conservation and Management of Endangered Plants*, ed. Thomas S. Elias (Sacramento: California Native Plant Society, 1987).

14. Charles S. Elton, *The Ecology of Invasions by Animals and Plants* (London: Methuen, 1958), 18.

15. Donald Worster, *Nature's Economy: The Roots of Ecology* (San Francisco: Sierra Club Books, 1977).

16. R. Roy Johnson and Steven W. Carrothers, "External Threats: The Dilemma of Resource Management on the Colorado River in Grand Canyon National Park, USA," *Environmental Management* 11 (January 1987): 99–107.

Chapter 8

# Green Consumerism:
# Ecology and the Ruse of Recycling

Timothy W. Luke

The production, distribution, and consumption of material wealth are the effects of innumerable technical decisions made by product designers, industrial engineers, corporate managers, public administrators, and marketing executives. And, in exchange for a constantly increasing level of material comfort and economic security, virtually every client and customer of this global capitalist economy accepts the outcome or impact of these decisions with little or no protest. Larger cultural trends, then, in global economic and social rationalization tend to proceed apace without any popular representation that they are so determined.[1]

The scope of these powers in everyday life is quite extensive. Such forces determine who gets what, when, and how in the most immediate material sense. Yet, the political dimension continues to be mystified in discourses of technical expertise, economic imperatives, or social necessity that all allegedly exert their effects beyond the realm of ordinary politics. Most mainstream analyses of politics ignore such subtle contradictions, but, since the 1960s, small social movements based upon an ecological politics or environment radicalism have contested these cultural dynamics and challenged their highly institutionalized authority. By exposing the many mystifications of environmental balance with issues of technology and industry, ecological radicals have struggled to win popular representation within, or even popular control over, these processes of rationalization.[2] But the political terrain in this battle is always shifting.

In today's ultrahyped scientific debates and political discourses, the spin placed by the mass media upon concern for the environment shifted profoundly from Earth Day 1970 to Earth Day 1990. Twenty years ago, any serious personal interest in the environment often was seen as the definitive mark of radical extremism.[3] To deter the attacks of environmentalists, big business frequently argued that growth was good, any legislation aimed at limiting pollution meant cutting jobs, and ecologists were crackpot limousine liberals willing to put the existence of snail darters before modern humanity's material progress.[4]

However, by 1990, assumptions in the popular discourse about nature, ecology, and environmentalism had changed significantly. Of course, there are holdouts from the old school who still, for example, rhetorically pit the material welfare of loggers against the survival of the spotted owl or dramatically tout the necessity of real estate development over protecting of coastal wetlands in this or that corner of the nation. But, on the whole, Earth Day 1990 saw "environmentalism" become a much more legitimate or even mainstream public good. Many major corporations now feel moved to proclaim how much "every day is Earth Day" in their shop, what a meaningful ecological relationship they have with nature, or how their products are manufactured with constant care for the biosphere.

In most respects, these claims are still largely false. Thus, this elaborate change in ideological emphasis by corporate political discourse is very significant. What has changed in the social imagination of ecology and environmentalism that makes these astounding rhetorical ploys not only possible, but also apparently somewhat convincing? As this study will indicate, one vitally important change was the domestication of some types of ecological radicalism as "green consumerism."

Ecological handbooks and self-help guides that urge consumers to "go green" have provided the most accessible and widely distributed discussions of the environmental crisis in recent years. This study examines the rhetorical commitments and political practices of green consumerism, and then asks if the popular understanding of the ecological crisis has been altered or reconstructed by them. Have these ideological maneuvers acquired rhetorical legitimacy and popular acceptance? Answers to such puzzling questions can be found by critically reconsidering green consumerism's interpretations of what are some of the late twentieth century's most trusted articles of faith, namely, ecology, environmentalism, and recycling.

## Shifting Rhetorics: From Production to Consumption

In the 1950s, 1960s, and 1970s, corporate managers and government bu-
reaucrats often tried to crush ecological protests, figuring that such direct
political strategies might roll back the symbolic assaults of troublesome
"tree-hugging" nature lovers. A rhetorical counterassault sought to convince the general public that belching smokestacks still were signs of material progress and not the stigmata of industrial pollution.[5] During the
early 1970s, however, President Nixon and the U.S. Congress rapidly re-
acted to mounting popular pressure for environmental reforms with a series of major legislative initiatives, passing the Clean Air Act, the Clean Water Act, the Endangered Species Act, and the Resource Conservation and
Recovery Act. In addition, they also authorized the establishment of the Environmental Protection Agency.[6]

By many objective measures, these laws did begin to have a discernible
impact on pollution levels in many areas. Similarly, the elaborate oversight
mechanisms of the EPA began to create at least the appearance of corporate
compliance with government environmental codes. And, finally, of course,
the flight of factories from the United States to the Third World in search of
cheaper labor and more lax pollution laws often made production less of
a worry. Therefore, environmentalist organizations frequently found that
the image of the ecological enemy had to be rhetorically expanded and
intensified. In an ideological turnaround—ironically aided and abetted by
some ecological activists—the discourse of blame began to include individual consumers, in addition to the more obviously dirty polluting factories and hungry lumber mills. Indeed, with the regulatory fig leaf provided
by EPA regulations and federal environmental law, the rhetoric of ecological responsibility slowly shifted from a vernacular of "Big business is dirty
business" to dialects of "Factories don't pollute. People do."

To contain the emergence of new, and perhaps more radical, measures
of ecological transformation, the corporate-run circuits of mass consumption refunctioned the rhetoric of ecologists who favored green consumerism as a means of reducing material consumption. In a remarkable switch,
factions in the ecology movement were transformed into a new special
subsystem of mass consumption. In these rhetorics of reform, as they are
used by both environmentalists and corporate public relations, major
corporations—such as Exxon, General Foods, and Phelps Dodge—are not
responsible for pollution. Rather, each individual consumer or family
household is now the key decisive ecological subject, whose everyday economic activities are a blow either for environmental destruction or for a
greener Earth. The environmental movement, once united in opposition to
producing more material goods, now has a wing that accepts guided mass

consumption and embraces subtly engineered preferences. Environmentalism has gained greater acceptance and visibility in the 1990s by presenting itself, in part, as a new set of material choices, a fresh guide for mass consumption, and a revolutionary reengineered set of "green" consumer preferences.

Throughout the go-go 1980s, this vision for solving the ecological crisis largely was ignored; but, in the aftermath of the 1989 Exxon *Valdez* tanker accident, the mass media and oil industry spin doctors seized upon these alternative life-style agendas to construct a narrative of collective guilt that could explain why that tragic shipwreck and oil spill "had to happen." Once launched, these counterrevolutionary ecological rhetorics also gained tremendous momentum from 1989 to 1991 with a rush of new mass-marketed handbooks for ecological living, whose authors and publishing companies sought to capture the growing green market arising from the increasing levels of hoopla for Earth Day 1990.

Clearly, guidebooks have been produced for decades to help consumers make buying decisions in accord with logics of thrift, style, and safety. As part of the 1990 Earth Day mobilization, however, even the infamous Heloise of syndicated newspaper feature fame issued her ecologically oriented *Hints for a Healthy Planet* (1990) to help her millions of now green-leaning readers cope with the demands of environmental housekeeping.[7] In turn, a whole new crowd of even more elaborate consumer guidebooks joined Heloise in 1989, 1990, and 1991 to lead consumers to a green future as their authors urged readers to forsake a long march toward the institutions for a short shopping trip through the malls to revolutionize modern society. Hence, in hundreds of Waldenbooks or B. Dalton's bookstores across America, thousands of concerned consumers could ring up another purchase to learn how to save the planet.

## Looking at Guidebooks for Green Consumption

Saving the earth or preserving the environment are extremely complex challenges, and there are no easy or simple solutions. Yet, in complete fulfillment of the fallacy of generalization—namely, if every X did Y, then Z would certainly follow—the Berkeley, California-based Earth Works Group confidently markets a whole series of self-help manuals based upon "50 simple things" that everyone can do to "save the Earth." The first book, *50 Simple Things You Can Do to Save the Earth*, alleges that it "empowers the individual to get up and *do something* about global environmental problems."[8] "Most of the 50 Things," the reader is told, "are unbelievably easy. They are the kind of things you would do anyway to save money—if you knew how much you could save" (p. 6). Hence, the book claims that rather

than allowing negative media coverage of the environmental crisis to drive
one to despair, each consumer can do some "unbelievably easy" things to
conserve their cash as well as to solve "intractable environmental problems" (p. 6). Thus, if every consumer bought this one book and followed
its directions, then ecological salvation would surely follow.

How does the Earth Works Group's solution hope to work? First, by
openly acknowledging the real powerlessness of consumers, and, second,
by whittling vainly away at major supply-side irrationalities through urging
consumers to make slightly more frugal and marginally more rational
choices about obtaining the material wherewithal needed for their day-to-
day survival. Instead of thinking about how to reconstitute politically the
mode of modern production to meet ecological constraints, the book, like
most tracts of green consumerist agitation, bases its call for action upon
nonpolitical, nonsocial, noninstitutional solutions to environmental problems "that cumulate from the seemingly inconsequential actions of millions of individuals. My trash, your use of inefficient cars, someone else's
water use—all make the planet less livable for the children of today and
tomorrow" (p. 7). Consequently, the corporate institutions that produce
goods wrapped in this trash, that restructured cities to require travel in
their inefficient cars, and that build appliances, homes, and cityscapes
based upon wasting water are excused from the outset, except insofar as
individuals choose to use fewer of their products or decide to purchase
alternative merchandise.

The logic of the group's resistance, then, just like the logic of the average consumer's initial compliance, is centered upon the still largely passive sphere of *consumption* rather than upon the vital sites of *production*.
The ecological battle lines are drawn at the gas pump or in the supermarket aisles, not at the factory gates or in the corporate boardrooms. The
Earth Works strategy asserts, both wrongly and rightly:

> Few of us can do anything to keep million-barrel oil tankers on
> course through pristine waters. All of us can do something,
> everyday, to insure that fewer such tankers are needed. None of us
> can close the hole in the ozone layer above Antarctica. All of us
> can help prevent its spread to populated areas by reducing our
> use of chlorofluoro carbons (CFCs). (p. 6)

This characterization of environmental conflicts rightly notes, on one level,
that using less gasoline and fewer underarm sprays in the United States
might well lessen oil tanker traffic and reduce the hole in the ozone layer.
But, on another level, it wrongly suggests that people cannot really expect
to use collective political means to keep tanker accidents from happening
or to eliminate CFCs totally. The whole ecological crisis is reinterpreted as

a series of bad household and/or personal buying decisions. That is, "as much as we are the root of the problem, we are also genesis of its solution" (p. 7).

The aggregate effects of the ecological crisis, therefore, can be framed only in terms of the accumulated impact of consumers' choices. The key dimensions of the crisis, according to Earth Works, are the greenhouse effect, air pollution, ozone depletion, hazardous waste, acid rain, vanishing wildlife, groundwater pollution, garbage, and excessive energy use. Individual consumption patterns now seen as the cause of all these problems, can, at the same time, solve them if individuals simply shift to reasonable levels of individual conservation. Conservation, ecological sustainability, frugality "can be accomplished by simple, cost-effective measures that require little change in lifestyle" (p. 18). Here is the other major flaw in the Earth Works logic. A strong case can be made that the reckless individual consumer—along with ecological disaster—is a symptom, not a primary agent, in the process. In fact, more reasonable patterns of individual consumption were once quite common, but corporate imperatives to stimulate more consumption of mass-produced goods have overridden these traditional restraints with many of today's throwaway life-styles. Corporations have spent decades on developing complex, cost-effective (but environmentally disastrous) techniques that have required massive changes in each consumer's life-style. The reconstruction of everyday life around the automobile is an excellent example of how a capital-intensive, resource-wasting consumer good has transformed most people's individual ecological impact and consumer behavior.

After defining the ecological crisis as essentially a struggle over how elites go about shaping tastes in the everyday lifeworld of material consumption, the Earth Works Group outlines a three-stage strategy for reshaping these patterns of taste, which are organized around three different levels of relative effort required from consumers. First, there are really only twenty-eight "Simple Things" to begin doing, like stopping junk mail, keeping automobile tires fully inflated, giving up styrofoam cups, refusing to buy ivory products, or using energy-saving light bulbs. Second, there are twelve things that "Take Some Effort," like recycling glass, using cloth diapers, planting trees, and carpooling. And, third, there are eight things "For the Committed" that require bigger, and actually more necessary, changes, like driving less, eating less meat, replanting one's house lot in xeriscaping, and getting involved in community associations working for ecological change. Most of these recommended changes, while requiring personal sacrifices, do nothing to change the infrastructure of consumption. Instead, they involve resurrecting an ethic of frugality, thrift, or common sense. This ideological line perhaps is most obvious in the Earth Works Group's *The*

*Recycler's Handbook: Simple Things You Can Do.*[9] Yet, those far-reaching changes that push beyond the limited agenda of recycling would appeal to very few people because they would require more than a "little change" in life-style.

Indeed, the Earth Works Group implicitly recognizes these limitations given that it also has produced a follow-up book, *The Next Step: 50 More Things You Can Do to Save the Earth*, that suggests "snipping six-pack rings may be a start, but it's not the solution. . . . It's time to reach out to the community." [10] This handbook does begin to ask some political questions, but its style of politics is posed almost entirely in the basically tame dialects of Naderite public interest insurgency.[11] The "next step" of "50 more things to save the Earth" simply takes green consumerism down already familiar tracks, like using affinity group charge cards, pushing for local curbside recycling programs, starting a ridesharing system, buying only recycled goods, urging retailers not to sell ozone-damaging goods, or starting a municipal yard composting program. It hints at promising political action, but the political activities being advanced mainly are directed at motivating more people to start doing the first fifty simple things to save the Earth. This weak reformist strategy even is affirmed in the Earth Works Group's appeal to more radical youth audiences, *The Student Environmental Guide: 25 Simple Things We Can Do.*[12] To paraphrase Marx, Earth Works environmentalism fails because it recycles one interpretation of the world, when the real point is discovering how to change it.

Indeed, the real intellectual limits of the Earth Works Group's environmental transformation is most obvious in its latest work, *50 Simple Things Your Business Can Do to Save the Earth.*[13] Rather than directly attacking the obvious ecological irrationalities in most businesses' production processes, this manual "recognizes the realities of business" by claiming the Earth Works approach "can yield dividends in this fiscal year — in cost savings, lower taxes, improved company image, and in increased employee satisfaction and productivity. This is a textbook case of 'doing well by doing good' " (p. 9). Thus, each business is treated mainly as "a super consumer" that can, like other individual consumers or private households, contribute to ecological change by doing the same "simple things," such as reorganizing the office coffee pool to use ceramic mugs, recycling office paper, buying green cleaning supplies, changing to low-energy light fixtures, fixing company toilets to use less water, composting landscape by-products, or remodeling the office with plants, nonrainforest wood products, and solar climate control.

Unfortunately, the logic of resistance behind these changes is wholly defensive. The Earth Works Group accepts the modes of industrial production as they operate now, but urges that employees engage in their own environmental policing to avoid running afoul of the prevailing legal, bureaucratic, and public relations problems that regularly befall many companies. Green is good because it saves money, it is good public relations, and, of course, it is good for the environment. Rather than pushing waste elimination, the Earth Works Group stands for waste reduction. Instead of advocating economic transformation, it accepts weak bureaucratic regulation of present-day polluting processes. Unable to support the reconstitution of today's productive forces, it advocates piecemeal reforms to lessen, but never end, their most environmentally destructive activities.

The Earth Works Group also fails to identify the key potentialities of workers and management in modern businesses for realizing ecological changes. On the one hand, Earth Works notes, "If you work in an office, a workshop, a factory, you are the backbone of your company. You and co-workers can use your collective influence to mold policy decisions" (p. 8). These claims sound, at first, quite impressive, but with this allegedly immense collective influence, they direct workers to make decisions about essentially insignificant choices: "Should you throw out that piece of paper ... or recycle it? Is it too much trouble to wash out a mug so you don't have to use a disposable cup? Should you leave a light or copier running ... or turn it off?" (p. 8). Plainly, if the nerve centers of corporate America are misdirected into agonizing over policy decisions such as these, then the truly critical ecological choices about what to produce, how to produce it, when to market it, and where to distribute it all will be left to those managers in high positions who know "it's not possible to turn well-honed products and processes topsy-turvy to protect the environment and still function as a business" (p. 9).

The Earth Works Group, then, winks at prevailing practices of antiecological management, privileging the passive acceptance of corporate managers' expertise and the legitimacy of not troubling executives as they discharge their tough decision-making tasks. Instead, it pushes ineffectual window-dressing practices on ordinary employees to green a few marginal aspects of their firms' office ecologies or their companies' public images. The fact that everyone in some company uses ecologically correct ceramic mugs and recycles office memos does not lessen the environmental destruction that this same firm might be spreading by building gas guzzlers, selling CFCs, mowing down rainforests, or manufacturing plastic playthings.

Along with the Earth Works Group and its widely distributed books, Jeremy Rifkin's edited volume *The Green Lifestyle Handbook: 1001 Ways You Can Heal the Earth* has been a major hit in the nation's book stores.[14] In spite of its frothy political pitch, it, too, largely pushes household strategies to propagate the virtues of an "ecological lifestyle." Combining the sepa-

rate household, student, and business product lines of three books from
the Earth Works Group, Rifkin's one anthology invites readers to join the
green revolution by embracing an ethic of voluntary simplicity or purpose-
ful frugality. In the opening section of the handbook ("back to basics"),
various contributors sketch out the virtues of curbing home energy use,
using green household cleaning products, shopping with an ecological attitude at the supermarket, and reorganizing office waste streams for recycling. The second section, on "lifestyles," bids the reader to acknowledge
the importance of eating down low on the food chain, returning to simple
idleness for leisure, and investing in a socially responsible fashion, while
the third section, "cultivating solutions," affirms the ecological wisdom of
personal gardening, tree planting, low-impact agriculture, and preserving
genetic diversity.

This consumeristic treatment of ecology, of course, tends to cover the
same individual-centered ground as the Earth Works Group's "50 simple
things" "at home" and "in business." Picking up on the public interest citizen lobbying initiatives of the Earth Works Group's *The Next Step*, Rifkin's
handbook in the last section underscores the critical importance of "getting organized" to realize a local, grass-roots "environmental democracy."
By targeting corporate polluters, utilizing boycotts of antiecological products, lobbying elected representatives, and becoming informed about environmental litigation, Rifkin's handbook suggests, an "organized citi-
zenry" following these obvious techniques of ordinary citizenship can win
"a place at the bargaining table to ensure that local corporations stop local
poisoning and preserve the planet's limited natural resources" (p. 130).
The fact that such places are rarely won, that their occupants also typically
have little voice, or that local poisoning, if stopped, is only moved elsewhere is not discussed. Still, Rifkin invites all of his readers to push
through these sorts of negotiations, because public interest environmental
advocacy should gain "more influence over the activities of companies that
threaten the environment. Also, we must organize to insure that local, state,
and federal legislators pass the necessary laws to help save the planet" (p.
130). Of course, this call to activism is not really all that new; this set of
tactics has structured the agenda of mainstream environmentalism since
the mid-1960s.[15] Sometimes it works successfully for a bit on the margins,
but mostly it falls short by a very wide mark.

Another best-seller, Jeffrey Hollander's *How to Make the World a Better
Place: A Guide to Doing Good* also promises "over 100 quick-and-easy actions," as if ecological revolution were an instant cake mix, to show "how
you can effect positive social change."[16] This book can be read, as the author's foreword suggests, "in any order you choose," so that one will not
"get bogged down by all the introductory facts" and anyone can "always

skip ahead to the action" (p. 9). Arguing that it is not yet another journalistic description or just one more academic analysis of the world's ecological crisis, this handbook offers ways to link everyone's "sincere and noble desire to help and the concrete, effective actions necessary to effect change" (p. 19). Like Rifkin and the Earth Works Group, Hollander asserts, "The shape of the future is in our hands. It is our responsibility, for it can be no one else's. The world won't be destroyed tomorrow, but it can be made better today" (p. 21).

How these hitherto unattained radical advances toward global ecological harmony will be wrought "is designed to generate the greatest impact in the least amount of time" and, miraculously, "results are guaranteed without marching on Washington, quitting your job, or giving away your life savings" (p. 21). On one level, Hollander's endorsement of Naderite public interest lobbying tactics allegedly ensures that his readers will learn "how to help build low-income housing, use recycled products, contribute to a food bank, invest money in a socially responsible manner, free prisoners of conscience, pass legislation through the U.S. Congress, and encourage world peace" (p. 21). And, even more fortunately for today's harried average consumer, Hollander claims, like an ad for taped foreign language lessons or some new tummy reducer, that "only a few minutes are needed for many of the actions that will result in positive social change" (p. 21). Therefore, on another level, Hollander makes the ultimate radical claim for today's socially concerned, but fundamentally passive, consumer. That is, the ecological revolution really can be made essentially by doing nothing more than ordinary everyday things. In other words, you can learn how "to make the world a better place as you wheel your cart down the aisle of a supermarket, travel on business or pleasure, select an insurance policy, open a bank account, prepare dinner, relax around the house, and even as you soap up in the shower" (p. 21).

While it may be true, as Hollander holds, that "the actions of those now living will determine the future, and possibly the very survival of the species" (p. 31), it is, in fact, mainly a mystification. Only the actions of a very small handful of the humans who are now living—namely, those in significant positions of decisive managerial power in business or central executive authority in government—can truly do something to determine the future. Hollander's belief that those many thousands of his readers who actually will replace their light bulbs, water heaters, automobiles, or toilets with ecologically improved alternatives can decisively affect the survival of the species is pure ideology. It may sell new kinds of toilets, cars, appliances, and light bulbs, but it does not guarantee planetary survival. And the absurd claims that average consumers need only shop, bicycle, or garden their way to an ecological future merely moves most of the responsibility and much of the blame away from the institutional centers of power whose decisions actually maintain the wasteful, careless ways of material exchange that Hollander would end by having everyone recycle all of their soda cans.

Yet, Hollander does not stop there. He even asserts that everyone on the planet, not merely the average consumers in affluent societies, are to blame for the ecological crisis. Therefore, he maintains, rightly and wrongly, that "no attempt to protect the environment will be successful in the long run unless ordinary people—the California executive, the Mexican peasant, the Soviet factory worker, the Chinese farmer—are willing to adjust their life-styles and values. Our wasteful, careless ways must become a thing of the past" (p. 31). The wasteful, careless ways of the California executive plainly must be ecologically reconstituted, but the impoverished practices of Mexican peasants and Chinese farmers, short of what many others would see as their presumed contributions to "overpopulation," are probably already at levels of consumption that Hollander happily would ratify as ecologically sustainable if the California executive could only attain and abide by them.

Finally, Marjorie Lamb takes the demands of mounting a green revolution from within the sphere of everyday life down to the bare minimum in her *Two Minutes a Day for a Greener Planet: Quick and Simple Things You Can Do to Save Our Earth*. Her manifesto speaks directly to the harried but still very guilty modern suburbanite:

> We are all busy people. Let's face it, we don't have the time or desire to climb smoke stacks or confront whaling vessels. But there are lots of things we can do differently every day. Without effort and with very little thought, we can make a difference to our planet Earth.[17]

This astounding revelation is, of course, precisely what every consumer wants to hear. Like ecological destruction itself, ecological salvation is possible "without effort" and "with very little thought."

Only "two minutes a day" are needed by today's one-minute managers to execute the "quick and simple things" needed to save "our Earth." To fill the bookstores at the mall with yet another cookbook for ecological transformation, Lamb has expanded her original "Two Minute Ecologist" radio spots, first developed for the CBC's *Metro Morning* radio broadcast, into a pocketbook guide to green liberation. And, once again, she stresses the vital importance of recycling aluminum, refusing to buy overpackaged goods, and composting kitchen/household waste. But, interestingly enough, Lamb also honestly remarks that much of her advice is essentially remedial consumer education. Indeed, as Lamb notes, many, if not most, of the simple hints that she, Hollander, Rifkin, and the Earth Works Group are spelling out were once held within a widely practiced tradition of popular common sense. Lamb credits "the Depression generation," or those who grew up prior to 1945, with an ethic of thriftiness that actually approximates many of the virtues she assigns to the coming "Age of the Environment." On the other hand, "the Baby Boom generation," and now their offspring, have embraced all of the unsustainable habits of mass consumption that corporate capital once encouraged, but now allegedly finds are at the root of today's ecological crisis.

In part, Lamb's analysis is true, but it ignores how corporate capital, big government, and professional experts pushed the practices of the throwaway affluent society on consumers after 1945 as a purposely political strategy to sustain economic growth, forestall mass discontent, and empower scientific authority. People did choose to live this way, but their choices largely were made from a very narrow array of alternatives presented to them in the consumer marketplace as rigidly structured, prepackaged menus of very limited options. And now, ironically, all of these green guides to ecological consumption are moral primers pitched at resurrecting—through their own green but still nicely designed plans of commodified ecological revitalization—the responsible habits of more frugal consumers or autonomous citizens, which corporate capital and the mass media have been struggling to destroy for nearly a century.

## Green Consumerism as Marketing Demography

Campaigns for individual change, like these mobilizations for green consumerism, rarely change society in any fundamental sense. However, they often do diversify today's already complex consumer markets in new and exciting ways by generating new psychodemographic niches of need. The Roper Organization, for example, recently conducted a series of public opinion surveys that profiled the entire American public as members in one of five different behavioral bands when it comes to questions of ecology and recycling. In 1990, 78 percent of all Americans supported "improving the environment." [18] However, only 11 percent were "True-Blue Greens," or those who were regular recyclers, members of environmental groups, and serious supporters of stringent environmental regulations. Another 11 percent were "Greenback Greens," or persons who failed to practice recycling regularly and remained diffident environmental supporters, although they would willingly buy "green" products. A healthy 26 percent were "Sprouts," who recycle regularly but doubt that it really does much good as a purely individual effort. And the large antienvironmental majority of 52 percent were divided between "Basic Browns," 28 percent, and

"Grousers," 24 percent, who either do nothing for the environment or who simply make excuses for not recycling and buying green products.[19]

Green consumerism, as these sociologically constructed market segments reveal, is not an insignificant force. Indeed, the allied bloc of True-Blue Greens and Sprouts adds up to 36 percent of the nation's mass markets. This indicator closely parallels other market studies that reveal about three out of every ten consumers buy products because of green advertising, ecological labeling, or environmentalist endorsements. Therefore, green consumerism, which allegedly began as a campaign to subvert and reduce mass marketing, now ironically assists the definition and expansion of mass marketing by producing new kinds of consumer desire.

To reach nearly a third of all contemporary consumers, no savvy advertiser or manufacturer can ignore the need for retooling existing systems of promotional hooks and lures. For example, green advertising can buy time on a national news program that displays file footage of bird and seal corpses, soaked in Exxon crude and floating in Prince William Sound, to run ads for Conoco's double-hulled tankers that apparently move sea mammals, seals, and birds to jump, leap, and flap in exaltation to the beat of Beethoven's Ninth Symphony and Schiller's chorale "Ode to Joy" as a celebration of the DuPont Corporation's "ecological concern." But oil continues to be lifted, shipped, and sold to burn in thousands of personal automobiles that all are still pumping more carbon dioxide into the atmosphere. Likewise, green interpretations of ordinary manufacturing can rhetorically transform "a woman's selection of a nightgown made of 100 percent cotton into an 'environmentally responsible' purchase of a product made from a 'renewable resource.'"[20] But the cotton is still likely to be grown, harvested, and produced using inefficient and dangerous inputs of oil-based pesticides, fertilizers, and fuels that ravage local soils, watercourses, and biotic communities. The seamless domination of modern mass consumption proves itself capable even of turning an antithetical assault on all of its material premises into yet another psychodemographic space of highly segmented, but nonetheless still consumeristic, behavior.

Yet, even big business now is sensitive enough to recognize that a crisis of ecological credibility already exists in the green market. Any company can put "ozone friendly," "ecologically approved," "environmentally sound," or "dolphin safe" logos, usually printed in green ink, on any product. The proportion of new products that claimed green pedigrees increased from 4.5 percent to 11.4 percent of all new packaged goods from 1989 to 1990. By the same token, the number of advertisements with green tie-ins more than quadrupled.[21] Yet there is no common legal and scientific definition of *recycled*, *biodegradable*, or *ecological* available for standard use in labeling or advertising. Hence, many products claim to be all of these good things while being none of them. Fortunately, however, different advocates of green consumerism are coming to the rescue. Dennis Hayes, the chair of both the 1970 and 1990 Earth Day celebrations, has organized Green Seal in Palo Alto, California, to issue a "Green Seal" mark of environmental soundness. By allying with Underwriters Laboratories for product testing, and by building coalitions with a few major producers, Green Seal hoped to begin certifying new products in 1992. A second group, Green Cross of Oakland, California, already has agreements with several large retail outlets, and has already certified nearly 400 products with its "Green Cross." [22] While there are considerable differences between the two groups over how to certify a product (immediate ecological impact in consumption versus impact over the entire production life cycle), this sort of eco-labeling is winning support.

Green consumerism will most likely culminate in some mix of "safe seals" or "wholesome hallmarks" certifying ecological purity. Indeed, the Blue Angel seal of environmental soundness has been used on thousands of products in Germany for more than a decade, and comparable government-backed programs are beginning in Japan and Canada.[23] Because being an effective environmentally conscious consumer demands much more than two minutes a day, these different underwriting laboratories of credibility creation already are battling over the right to certify authoritatively whether this or that product is "ecologically correct." This development, of course, is simply the final stage in the pacification of ecological protest—"two minutes a day" becomes "two seconds per purchase." A consumer scans a product, finds the socially accepted seal of approval, and tosses it into the shopping cart with no muss, no fuss, no never mind. The seal suspends the need for environmental consciousness or ecological reasoning; it too already has been expertly engineered by the manufacturer. Yet, beyond adding the seal, very little, if anything, may have actually changed anywhere in the cycle of producing, distributing, consuming, and disposing of the product. The consumer society still draws resources from all over the world to the detriment of biomes, animals, plants, and other humans all around the globe, all in order to produce new profits through green indulgences for those who can afford to buy them. A range of ecologically diverse societies of immediate producers, environmentally well matched to the peculiarities of their various bioregions, does not develop; indeed, its basic plausibility only becomes even more fantastic as "green" goods marked by the appropriate seals of good planet-keeping pile up, first as merchandise and then as trash in the consumer society's supermarkets, recycling bins, and landfills.

The amazing popularity of recycling, thanks to Lamb, Hollander, Rifkin, and Earth Works, also actually might be, at the same time, undercutting its legitimacy. The symbolic importance of every household "doing some-thing," especially if it is quick and easy, makes recycling a pervasive prac-tice. Yet, in certain instances, recycling actually may be less efficient or cost-effective than some other resource conservation strategy. Certain papers, for example, can be recycled only so many times. Rather than emphasizing paper recycling, there should be more emphasis on reducing or eliminat-ing paper in packaging, record keeping, and transmission of information. Similarly, recycling can fix into place many prevailing packaging or re-source use technologies, which may be irrational or inefficient in compar-ison to alternative techniques, by providing a new, cheap, voluntary infra-structure for their retention. Recycling also can create recycled resource gluts of newsprint, glass, plastic, or paper waste that certain communities must pay to collect and store. However, they may be unable to complete the critical cycles of actual reuse due to saturated markets, a lack of recy-cling plants, or excessive transportation costs for moving recyclable com-modities. Hence, these semirecycled resource stocks actually might have to be landfilled anyway.

Incinerating recycled resources can provide a short-term solution for some combustible products, but this practice also creates air pollution, ash by-products, and new transaction costs. Raising landfill costs can reduce waste by forcing communities and households to conserve their creation of trash, but this option also will only generate more incineration or recy-cling. Thus, only in recycling does the real source of the problem now per-haps emerge, namely, the manufacturers that continue to package their products excessively, irresponsibly use nonrecyclable materials, irratio-nally waste energy resources, and unfairly externalize production costs. By shifting the costs of coping with their inefficiency and irrationality to newly motivated recycling households and municipal waste management agen-cies, producers can continue the exploitative practices of old wave tradi-tional industrialism as their negative effects are mitigated by new wave green consumerism. Once again, a core supply-side changelessness is pre-served by enveloping it in a demand-side mobilization for marginal change.

## Earth Day as the Holiday of Green Consumerism

Green marketing and ecological consuming, in turn, feed directly into the organization and administration of spectacles, such as Earth Day, to affirm occasionally or even to ritualize permanently the practices of green con-sumerism. Just as mainstream consumer society finds its most complete af-firmation in the highly commercialized festival day of Christmas, green consumerism has been woven into the mythologies and rituals of its own commercial festival, Earth Day. Arguably, the Earth Day celebration does serve to promote worthwhile environmental changes and to popularize meaningful ecological lessons among mass audiences who might otherwise ignore them. Yet it also feeds directly into the same destructive logic of such consumer days as Presidents' Day, Memorial Day, Labor Day, or Columbus Day as well as Mother's Day, Father's Day, Grandparent's Day, or Secretary's Day. Corporate marketing departments create or reengineer these celebrations to encourage consumers to make another trip to the mall. As a specially valorized day to boost consumption by "showing you care" or "telling someone how much you love them," Earth Day becomes a day to mark how we can save the planet by producing and consuming spectacles about planetary salvation. In turn, major retailers rack up huge sales of can crushers, composters, newspaper bundlers, bicycles, and green guidebooks to fulfill consumer desires to possess the correct icons for observing the day's rituals. Otherwise, like the 1980 celebration, it is either totally ignored or marked only by a few nature lovers in total obscurity out in the woods.

So, ironically, what began as a special festival to call planned mass consumption into question now can survive only if its designers allow it to be packaged as yet another organized event based upon specially planned mass consumption. Wendell Berry's fear that environmentalists are too cautious in their protests as they approach the earth as "nature under glass" is not a problem here. Instead, Earth Day commodifies nature and concern for nature as still another set of carefully coded products to circulate in the contemporary marketplace as "nature under plastic." Most important, Earth Day, which began as a popular resistance to unfettered capitalist markets, today promotes green capitalism as if it were an effective mode of meaningful political resistance.

James Speth, the president of World Resources Institute, observed in 1989 that since the first Earth Day there has been a "steady and sometimes spectacular growth of worldwide public concern about environmental degradation, and of citizen action and participation to meet these challenges." [24] Perhaps, but such mass-mediated measurements of spectacularly growing concern do not translate into ecological revolution. Earth Days might mark new levels of "intense public interest," as marked by thousands of marchers in Earth Day parades or by proenvironmental sound bites on the nightly news, but, in practice, most consumers' behavior, beyond recycling soda cans or refusing to buy African elephant ivory products, is not really changing. In part, there can be only minor changes because change can happen only if the products offered in the marketplace are manufactured in a more environmentally correct manner; and, in part, there will be no radical change because the broadly mobilized version of green consumerism still is a form of corporate capitalist consumerism.

After twenty years of ecological consciousness, for example, the average per capita daily discard rate of garbage has risen from 2.5 pounds in 1960 to 3.2 pounds in 1970 to 3.6 pounds in 1986.[25] By 2000, despite the impact of two decades of recycling, this figure is expected to rise to 6 pounds a day.[26] Similarly, even though ecological concern is rising, the average gas mileage of new cars declined 4 percent from 1988 to 1990, and the number of miles driven annually continues to rise by 2 percent year by year.[27] In 1979, 47,000 square miles of tropical rainforest were cut down; 88,000 square miles were cut down in 1989.[28] Japan more than doubled its per capita output of carbon from fossil fuel emissions from 1960 to 1987, Saudi Arabia almost quadrupled its levels, and the United States increased its output by almost 25 percent.[29] Consequently, it becomes apparent that "worldwide public concern" may be nothing but Green Cross packaging wrapped around the same old antienvironmental goods and services.

## Conclusion: The Ruse of Recycling

As dogmas for attaining not only personal but planetary salvation, some of today's most common discourses about ecological activism (or even environmental consciousness) ironically reaffirm tenets of consumption rather than conservation. In the ruse of recycling, green consumerism, rather than leading to the elimination of massive consumption and material waste, instead revalorizes the basic premises of material consumption and massive waste. By providing the symbolic and substantive means to rationalize resource use and cloak consumerism in the appearance of ecological activism, the cult of recycling as well as the call to save the earth are not liberating nature from technological exploitation. On the contrary, they cushion, but do not end, the destructive blows of an economy and a culture that thrive upon transforming the organic order of nature into the inorganic anarchy of capital.

Green consumerism has been at work daily for many years in many millions of households and thousands of firms at least since the energy crisis of 1973, and, after decades of careful ecological concern, myriad campaigns for recycling, many days of rational shopping, and much thinking about source reduction, the biosphere still suffers from intense ecological exploitation. The earth is not greener or safer, but deader and more endangered. Of course, on one level, one must acknowledge that green consumerism actually may have a slight positive impact on the global environment. After all, and if only for a short time, the planet probably is better off with a few more people using fewer resources at slower rates of consumption. Yet, on another level, these marginal benefits are counterbalanced by the substantial costs of remaining structurally invested in thoroughly consumerist forms of economy and culture.

The green consumerist variety of environmentalism is virtually meaningless as a program for radical social transformation; it has become an agenda of conservative ideological containment. In the final analysis, these campaigns for propagating green consumerism also are almost completely anthropocentric. The well-being and survival of other animal species, plant life forms, or bioregions virtually are ignored. Of course, shoppers for a better world enjoin themselves and others not to buy consumer products made from endangered species or rain forest beef, but this injunction largely is driven by other green consumerist needs that run parallel to these goals. That is, one cannot be a happy ecotourist if there are no longer any rhinos, hippos, or elephants in African game parks, and the rain forests probably contain exotic plants that someday will cure cancers for ailing green consumers. When every group from Worldwatch to the American Forest Council, Greenpeace to Exxon, the Sierra Club to the Chemical Manufacturers Association claims to be on the same ecological path to green salvation, as today's green consumerism handbooks or Earth Day celebrations indicate, then the most threatening specter haunting the world today is no longer ecologism. Instead, this era of reconciliation shows how decades of rhetorical exorcism directed against radical ecologism have successfully worked their spell by caging this surly antagonistic spirit and refracting its radical revolutionary animus out into the ghostly moonbeams of friendly green consumerism.

### Notes

1. Timothy W. Luke, "Community and Ecology," *Telos* 88 (Summer 1991): 62–72.

2. Timothy W. Luke, *Screens of Power: Ideology, Domination, and Resistance in Informational Society* (Urbana: University of Illinois Press, 1989), 207–39.

3. See Barry Commoner, *Science and Survival* (New York: Viking, 1966); and Murray Bookchin, *Postscarcity Anarchism* (Berkeley: Ramparts, 1971).

4. John G. Mitchell and Constance L. Stallings, eds., *Ecotactics: The Sierra Club Handbook for Environmental Activists* (New York: Pocket Books, 1970).

5. Samuel Hays, *Beauty, Health, and Permanence: Environment Politics in the United States, 1955–1985* (Cambridge: Cambridge University Press, 1987); and Frank E. Smith, *The Politics of Conservation* (New York: Pantheon, 1966).

6. Hays, *Beauty, Health, and Permanence*, 137–245.

7. Heloise, *Hints for a Healthy Planet* (New York: Perigee, 1990).

8. Earth Works Group, *50 Simple Things You Can Do to Save the Earth* (Berkeley: Earthworks, 1989), 6. Page numbers for further quotes from this work appear in text.

9. Earth Works Group, *The Recycler's Handbook: Simple Things You Can Do* (Berkeley: Earthworks, 1990).

10. Earth Works Group, *The Next Step: 50 More Things You Can Do to Save the Earth* (Kan-

sas City: Andrews & McMeel, 1991), 7.

11. Robert D. Holsworth, *Public Interest Liberalism and the Crisis of Affluence: Reflections on Nader, Environmentalism, and the Politics of a Sustainable Society* (Boston: G. K. Hall, 1980), 28–72.

12. Earth Works Group, *The Student Environmental Action Guide: 25 Simple Things We Can Do* (Berkeley: Earthworks, 1991).

13. Earth Works Group, *50 Simple Things Your Business Can Do to Save the Earth* (Berkeley: Earthworks, 1991). Page numbers for quotes from this work appear in text.

14. Jeremy Rifkin, ed., *The Green Lifestyle Handbook: 1001 Ways You Can Heal the Earth* (New York: Henry Holt, 1990). Page numbers for quotes from this work appear in text.

15. Holsworth, *Public Interest Liberalism*, 28–72.

16. Jeffrey Hollander, *How to Make the World a Better Place: A Guide to Doing Good* (New York: William Morrow, 1990). Page numbers for quotes from this work appear in text.

17. Marjorie Lamb, *Two Minutes a Day for a Greener Planet: Quick and Simple Things You Can Do to Save Our Earth* (New York: HarperCollins, 1990), i.

18. *St. Louis Post-Dispatch*, July 8, 1991: 1BP.

19. Ibid.

20. Ibid.

21. *Consumer Reports*, October 1991: 687.

22. Ibid., 689.

23. Ibid.

24. *New York Times*, April 22, 1990: 24.

25. Ibid.

26. *Roanoke Times & World News*, April 22, 1990: 5.

27. *New York Times*, April 22, 1990: 24.

28. Ibid., 25.

29. Ibid.

Chapter 9

# Green Fields/Brown Skin:
# Posting as a Sign of Recognition

Cheri Lucas Jennings and Bruce H. Jennings

## Environment in the Context of Race and Class

While the relationship between pesticides and consumer health has been widely discussed, this discourse has neglected some of the most basic issues of agrarian practice. Consumer organizations continue to press for stronger residue testing programs and greater basic toxicology research but ignore an international policy that creates farm zones drenched with pesticides of the more highly toxic, nonpersistent sort whereby produce can be washed relatively "clean" by the time it reaches grocers' shelves. Similarly, one effect of "wilderness" preservationist strategies has been to generate "social pollution zones" [1] where it is permissible to poison tens of thousands of migrant farm workers and their communities. In place of agrarian reforms in which those who work the fields have the right to determine labor conditions or secure protections for their families' health, many land-grant scientists support programs of "sustainability" that systematically strip farm workers of those rights. These new wave, environmentally sensitive experts legitimate a "managed" environment in which regulators negotiate "acceptable" doses of poison. The immediate life expectancy of farm workers is estimated to be twenty years below the national average,[2] yet other social concepts in agriculture—such as housing, nutrition, and working conditions—lie largely if not totally outside the focus of modern agrarian research.

If we set out to study the effect that various chemical inputs have upon plant and animal life and the general environment, would not their claim on human lives—particularly those lives most heavily affected by immediate and large-scale exposure—be an intrinsic part of such study? Yet contemporary agrarian and environmental sciences actively exclude the impact of techniques on people of color and Third World populations as a research focus, even as their innovations objectively worsen those populations' households. In fact, innovations in nonpersistent pesticide applications supply the kitchens of certain powerful northern constituencies while subjecting minority populations to an even larger volume and variety of inherently hazardous chemicals, disease, and displacement.

## "Improving" on Nature

When Newton discovered the law of gravity, he observed an apple falling from a tree. In a sense he acted as interpreter or translator for the fruit, recording for posterity what it did when it engaged in the actions he later imbued with the qualities of "gravity." Newton named this event and called these interactions "laws." What had been a random intercourse among height, weight, volume, and the leap of faith into which a ripe apple might seasonally plunge became a tool—after Newton observed it, called it something, and then attempted to reproduce it elsewhere—by which natural relations might be altered toward particular purposes.

The apple is not the only seasonal worker dependent on the cycles of nature and the "laws" of scientists. Much as Sir Isaac acted as interpreter for the relationship between the fruit and the ground in the enterprise called "physics," modern science interprets and replicates relations between the fruit and its consumer and calls these "nutrition." The distinct relations between the fruit and its smallest predators are examined as "entomology." Relations between the fruit and competing nonedible plants are studied as "botany." The diseases to which this fruit might fall prey are resisted as a "plant pathology" (a fascinating term all by itself), and the relative size and complexion of the fruit become the focus of "marketing." We no longer simply partake of the apple as part of the bounty of nature, but constitute the fruit as an entity defined by its social and scientific purposes. Yet what do we name the relationships between the fruit and those who tend it? What branch of science examines the interplay between soil and ownership, access and nutrition, ecology and human health? The professional discourse of science that now guides this inquiry focuses away from the social dimensions of the enterprise, a science that actively excludes minority participation as an element of agronomic relations, a science that systematically disavows its impact upon Third World cultures. Soon, agronomic scientists may accomplish their defined task by designing a genetically engineered plant. This research proceeds irrespective of whether any of the world's malnourished are able to eat these foods. What profit is there in the study of produce absent the populations who tend it, of health in consumption absent harm in production, of ecology absent sociology?

As Jim Hightower notes in *Hard Tomatoes, Hard Times*, modern fruit "can no longer be perceived as existing in nature." [3] It serves the volatile purposes dictated by an expanding market economy. Yet we pursue the development of increased yields as if they guarantee broader distribution. We know that capital-intensive production techniques are furthering the rural exodus of small-scale farmers. We know that displacement of traditional agroecologies often results in the exposure of local communities to pesticide hazards. Yet scientists continue to fixate on the plant in isolation, as if the conditions of production are separable from its social and ecological consequences.

Marc Reisner illustrates how a "Cadillac desert" was created in the most arid region of Los Angeles, solely because vast expanses of inexpensive land were available. [4] The agroscience community found itself no longer at the river's bank, but involved instead in studying how to grow massive amounts of produce in the desert and in saline-decimated soils. The decision regarding where the crops would be grown—and thereby what conditions the scientists would study—had been made without consideration of what would be ideal for the plant, best for the soil or the aquifer, or fair to the people using the land from which the water was diverted and to whom the crops had been bound.

The needs of traditional communities are undermined by practices that require the produce to act in clearly "unnatural" ways by any definition: to fall up, directly into the harvester, and ripen fully away from the limb; to stave off decay without wisening; and, not unlike other domesticated pets, to sit on command, without rolling over. Eventually, society sought to effect *The Death of Nature*—to simulate the growth process in laboratories, under our control, with a few modifications and "improvements" here and there. [5] The mythology is that advanced agricultural technologies so pursued will provide abundant, nutritious foods accessible to all. Yet the inability of inner-city minority populations to reap this bounty and the effects of intensive chemical applications on migrant labor populations are but a reflection of the hazards in store for populations worldwide.

With the development of gene splicing, new species, and unprecedented "shelf lives" for foods, scientists have come close to creating in agronomy the killer tomato that threatens to consume the vast majority of

the world's resources while leaving disease, infection, and increased malnutrition in its wake. Many of the most strident proponents of environmental reform refer to "conquering" nature as a goal, as if it were something
outside, beneath, or northeast of us that can be rearranged for market convenience without jeopardizing the fundamental source of our collective
livelihood.

## Sustainable Agriculture: Whose Sustainability?

The modernization of U.S. agriculture, particularly its technological face,
has as one of its most important foundations the publicly subsidized research at the fifty state universities created at the turn of the century. By the
late twentieth century, the techniques perfected at these land-grant colleges became the subject of much criticism. Vastly increased food production also contributed to massive ecological destruction—the loss of top-
soils, wetlands, groundwaters, natural predators, and genetic diversity.
Gradually, agricultural scientists acknowledged some "problems" in past
research, and "sustainable" agriculture programs were created in California, Iowa, Texas, Pennsylvania, and other states to examine a complex of
factors related to the fruit and its interplay with "production factors" such
as soil, water, and climate. However, virtually none of these research programs in sustainability addressed the role of workers—not in terms of labor rights, immigration, housing, or welfare, or of their importance in
maintaining low pricing while increasing distribution. Particularly striking
in its absence was any systematic examination of the health status of predominantly brown-skinned fieldworkers routinely exposed to hundreds of
toxic substances.

Various bureaucratic agencies, such as the EPA's Office of Pesticide Programs, were established in the 1970s to monitor and regulate the effects of
chemical applications upon national health. The U.S. Department of Agriculture hailed the benefits of pesticides for the producer, while the FDA
calculated permissible residues for food processors. Both tasks proceeded
despite profound ignorance about complex chemical synergies referred to
as data gaps. Land grants addressed the need to develop integrative systems for the intensive use of capitalized inputs. Environmentalists warned
of the impact of pesticides on "wildlife" and pathologists studied their consequences for plant diseases, but who was to speak to the effect of these
innovations on the field labor and migrant communities so essential to
production?

Since the 1960s the investigation of labor in agriculture has resided with
the United Farm Workers (UFW), other labor unions, and public interest
organizations. Massive uses of a particularly infamous group of soil fumi-

gates (DBCPs) initiated a reconnecting of farm workers and consumers in l978, when

> workers began to suspect they were suffering from sterility as [a] result of exposure to the chemicals they worked with. In casual conversation the men at the plant had found the wives of the ones who worked with [DPBC] frustrated in their attempts to conceive children. A union officer arranged for sterility tests to be done on the men ... and the publicity the union helped to arrange forced the company to admit that it had data, sixteen years old, that indicated the pesticide caused sterility and that it probably caused cancer. [A] test program for rural wells in California's Central Valley showed disturbingly high levels of groundwater contamination. [A] nation wide ban came two years later when [this pesticide] was shown also [to] constitute a threat to consumers.[6]

The United Farm Workers have spearheaded a decade-long boycott of grapes, wine, and lettuce. Dolores Huerta, Cesar Chavez, and other UFW organizers have circulated unprecedented amounts of information on the direct social effects of traditional polycultures that have been so systematically suppressed as to cause researchers, scientists, environmentalists, and the general public to be blinded to the importance of their continuing presence on the landscape. For Huerta, Chavez, and other union members the issue embodied in the flesh of the grape is *the relationship among production practices, farm worker health, and consumer habits.*[7] For migratory labor and the displaced farmers the grapes do speak. They "speak" to the plight of farm workers who must hollow their beds out of tainted soil as they migrate north to pick them. They speak of the communities displaced and resources diverted to grow them. They speak of families torn apart as the stem is harvested from the plant. Indeed, if we judge by their common absence in the debate over certifiably "healthy" and nutritious foods, the conditions that the certifiably "organic" marketer guarantees are conceived as quite separate from the practices under which food is planted, tended, diverted, and delivered.

The circumstances to which Huerta and Chavez object expose a practice of culling environmentally sound "green" products for our children's health from a wholly unsound "brown" environment fostered in their production. Brown is the color of the insecticide wash engineered to be rinsed from the peel without a trace by the time it reaches our table. Brown is the color of the irrigation ditch and contaminated soil left behind. And brown is the color of the "other" skin incidentally present in the field when growers spray the fruit. How did the presence of other skins come to be eliminated systematically as a source of concern in *The Greening of America*[8] and what price have minority populations paid for this breach between social and "scientific" issues in the production of so-called clean food in the last two decades?

## The Movement for Organic Agriculture: Brown or Red Skins?

Beginning in the 1970s, a small group of farmers (probably no more than several thousand across the United States) identified themselves as "organic" growers. While the term had no sanctified meaning, most who adopted it meant to distinguish their operations from the land-grant ideal, particularly with respect to the absence of toxic chemicals. Organic farming practices constituted a small (and diminishing) percentage of food production until the late 1980s, when a report was released by the Natural Resources Defense Council that immediately became a story on *60 Minutes*. This report detailed the potential cancers that America's children might suffer from applications of Alar, also known as the pesticide daminozide, used for ripening apples. The televised interviews with EPA's administrator confirmed for millions of viewers the impression that thousands of Americans could be expected to develop childhood cancers in order that apples might have shiny red skins. Despite the flurry of interest surrounding pesticide residues for consumers, reporters generally ignored the news that tens of thousands of fieldworkers faced even greater hazards when cultivating and harvesting these same foods.

Within one year the label "organically grown" suddenly became the sign of idealized food for millions of consumers. The sleepy headquarters of the California Certified Organic Farmers was transformed into an internationally sought source. CCOF, within the course of six months, received as many applications for new membership as had been submitted over the previous decade. Celebrities took the cause of organic production methods to the morning news, and national marketing chains ran newspaper ads as well as radio and television commercials touting sources of wholesome foods that would neither harm consumers' children nor restrict their life-styles. In early 1990 at their annual gathering, organic farmers celebrated their newly discovered popularity by forging a document titled the *Asilomar Declaration*, which proclaimed all manner of good things to follow from a new agriculture that was "socially responsible, environmentally safe, and nutritious."

The organic label was thus positioned to extend agrarian justice and promote positive effects for fieldworkers and surrounding communities as issues intrinsic to the maintenance of a generally healthy environment. Questions that deeply disturbed the gathering of New Age cultivators about the role of field laborers and minority communities in these costly new marketing strategies remained prominently unresolved. Whose justice would such practices vanguard? Whose health would the sale of "organically grown" products ultimately protect? Would certification be limited to Yuppie Chow lettuce for a small number of elite households and health food restaurants at regional farmers' markets, further isolating these practices from the larger nutritionally deprived underclasses? Would pesticide-intensive production simply be exiled to new locations abroad, further removing health hazards from consumers while actually increasing health risks to those who work the fields?

As if foreshadowing this debate, the organic farmers' keynote speaker, Wes Jackson, called for the adoption of a further resolution that CCOF oppose large agribusiness by circumscribing "a scale of farming operations that even if environmentally-sound, should be rejected as socially destructive." [9] Jackson's advocacy underscored the harm that one group of consumers in promoting an "organic" food might cause for others, such as farm workers, who lack control over the toxics applied in their workplaces.

Vandana Shiva points to the accomplishment of so-called traditional cultures in terms of their sheer longevity. [10] By just *Staying Alive* she asserts that Third World nations have experience to offer to a rapidly encroaching Western appetite bent on exhausting what was once thought to be an inexhaustible fount of global natural resources. Pointing to a community of women in India who consider their own livelihood and "rights" inseparable from the forest they cull, Shiva notes that native cultures and the vast majority of those who have occupied the planet regard nature not as "resource" to be redefined or mastered but as "home" to which care must be given and within which life is regenerated and sustained by interdependence. Shiva describes a growing international apartheid in which northern nations regard so-called undeveloped southern landscapes as "fallow" and therefore generally available for entrepreneurial purposes, thus exposing their dwellers to massive health risks that informed workers of the northern provinces are no longer willing to take.

Indeed, the World Bank has recently suggested that the relatively pristine landscapes and lungs of the Third World could better bear the teeming excesses of First World waste. In the tradition of colonial military conscription, where the upper classes could pay peasant counterparts to assume military duties and risks in their stead, the international economic director of the World Bank suggested in a spring forum that Third World countries might be provided similar economic incentive for burying our toxic waste in their soils, putrefying their ground water with our runoff. When objection was raised that peoples of underdeveloped countries would thus be exposed to the risks of Western technology with none of its adherent benefits, and that such exchange would precipitate manifestly greater health risks and more limited life expectancies in southern populations, this official reasoned that the trade-off was still an advantage in areas where "life expectancies are presently at greater risk from poverty or imminent starvation."[11]

Entrepreneurial regard of landscapes as undeveloped resources to which native inhabitants bear illusory and often illegitimate claim is not, of course, confined to hemispheric apartheid. It defines relationships between North Americans and "native" Americans as well. Where sovereignty is claimed internationally, it is much harder to deny responsibility for health and environmental devastation occurring within our own shores, among our own population. To do so requires one of two tactics. The first is a familiar form of racism that involves constituting Mexican-American migratory laborers as the "other" and then denying that "they" in fact are American. Despite the fact that citizenship claims between Mexico and California are becoming more and more unclear, this tactic has endured.

The second approach is more insidious, and denies that "they" are even involved in the transaction, that they are even "using" any resources or implementing any "practice." The latter approach is used when entire valleys in India are designated as undeveloped lands, as if entire settlements were not even there. So, too, with migrant farm labor in the United States. We literally look around them and beyond them to "discover" our resources. Shiva describes scientists' expeditions to the field to observe plant behavior in this way:

> In the course of their observations of the way crops grow
> alongside one another, they ask those who have been growing
> plants in just that way for generations "How did this one come to
> be so hearty?," or "How did that strain come to grow with so little
> water?" discovering our ideas in much the same way you speak of
> Columbus "discovering America" [already a very real continent to
> its inhabitants]. These individuals hurry north to claim these
> practices as "theirs" by placing a patent on their use, and do not
> even recognize them as "ideas" until they have had them.[12]

In a very real sense, northern-trained agriculturalists consider themselves to be engaged solely in the activity of observing the plant at their field sites. They seek to discover something about growing conditions from plant behavior or soil behavior or their intercourse with the elements. They are engaged in commissioned scientific inquiry that (by its very license) the untrained cannot perform. The idle peasant beside them in the field serves as a sort of translator for the plant. It is the observer who then "reflects" on this activity, creates the idea of it by instituting a systematic practice to replicate it, reconstitutes that practice as a science through patenting, and redistributes that agricultural science in the form of hybrid strains and loans. What the World Bank often "lends" back to indigenous people are the very resources recently expropriated and the very knowledge claims that were eroded and unrecognized when embodied in the person of the native.

## Organic Agriculture: A Sign for Whom? A Sign of What?

Agricultural research in the United States reflects an entirely myopic concept of scientific inquiry. Land grant colleges staffed by agronomists, plant pathologists, and geneticists pursue a narrowly focused mission to increase production while largely ignoring ecological and social consequences. Other researchers maintaining a critical perspective, such as Jack Kloppenberg and Miguel Altieri, beckon the land-grant scientists to step back from the soil they so busily exploit and recognize in whose hands it is held and to whose families its bounty is bound. With his nose in the southern soil, Norman Borlaug, the Noble Prize-winning "father" of the green revolution, defines agricultural research as an essentially apolitical enterprise:

> Often these individuals . . . seem to be the same utopians that criticize plant breeders for having been unable to produce grain varieties that will grow well and produce 8 tons/hectare yields on small farms, but yield only 2 tons/hectare when it is grown with the same technology on a large farm. Unfortunately, this has been unachievable up to now because plant varieties are both apolitical and impersonal.[13]

Even the most altruistic of soil scientists thus restrict their "mission" to the economic abundance of the crop, losing sight of the overall social goal of their operations: to provide more food for an increasingly displaced and hungry population. By virtue of their focus, they are blinded to the kinds of social relations that finance-dependent inputs create—where only those with the largest hectares and access to the most nutrient-rich soils can take advantage of large-scale, single-crop technologies. From behind their microscopes, plant breeders literally cannot see the fields for the crop. They are unable to see that increasing levels of production of certain foods by capital-intensive methods means further displacing small shareholders who cannot compete and ultimately displacing entire harvests (in favor of export crops that could pay the bill for production loans).

Immersed in inquiry as to the plant's nature, these scientists do not see the "pathology" in the study of a plant as if its production techniques existed apart from and indeed above needs defined by hunger or some other complex of social forces. Here, "more than just the production of crops, agricultural scientists succeeded in defining (and altering) relations between laborers and the land worked, the hungry masses, their right to secure food, and the knowledge necessary for making decisions in the public interest." [14] That odd term, *pathology*, accurately describes the way the researcher comes to regard the plant's fixation on traditional (and largely outmoded) ways of forming its fruit, growing to size, yielding to "deforming" disease and the ravages of age. These effects they promptly modify, encouraging it to return to the more "natural" state only as it falls into the hands of the consumer.

The clever marketing strategies of several large upscale supermarket chains (e.g., Vons and Raley's, in the Pacific Northwest) sometimes even celebrate the disconnection of their "clean" produce from "simple" farming processes. In their television campaigns, scientists in white lab coats study cellulose mash under microscopic scrutiny, assiduously searching for traces of chemical residue remaining on the fruit the chains sell. One commercial featured greens tossed about in a small agitator to effect the image of "clean" produce. These marketing strategies have fostered the widespread use of nonpersistent pesticides that can sit full strength on the plants in the field but are rinsed off to a bare "trace" by the time market testing kicks in. A robust, well-tanned newscaster is then confident in assuring that produce is "free of harmful residues," at least by the time it graces consumer tables.

This perhaps more than any other guarantee belies the nagging flaw of modern agriculture. Once toxins are created for productive use, where can they be disposed of with minimal harm? Even if they were to vanish into thin air, we breathe that air and drink its moisture. But they do not vanish. These secondary toxins wash into the unprotected soil in which we grow our food and emerge as part of unprotected water supply from which we draw further irrigation and in which fieldworkers bathe and from which they drink and sustain life. These toxins hover in the air they breathe and, as is their purpose, remain on the leaves of the plants they tend, often causing all manner of illness but little alarm — until some other sector of the population is affected. This infusion of whole rural communities is sometimes dramatic:

An entire valley in the state of Hidalgo [was] heavily contaminated with Parathion due to the wreck of a Bayer Chemical Company truck [that] left many of the packages ruptured with the contents spilled along the road. The insecticide had been carried by wind and water through the valley. Intact packages had been stolen by peasants anxious to acquire free . . . a miraculous product. . . . after a guard was posted, the guard himself became an illicit sales agent for the chemical . . . until the public health team discovered it. . . . by that time numerous mysterious deaths with all the symptoms of organophosphate poisoning had occurred . . . because the valley produces an especially large corn husk prized by housewives as a wrapping for fine, large tamales served on special occasions. The sickness of groups of friends and family at parties and the death of one person led to an autopsy investigation that would not have occurred had the victims been poor.[15]

We put those poisons that Angus Wright documents as having caused *The Death of Ramon Gonzalez* (among thousands of other migrant laborers) directly into their bare hands and bare faces without even providing gloves or masks or boots as shields. But what if manufacturers were to provide barefoot, bare-faced brown workers with plastic boots and goggles? What if owners were to provide sufficient warning of the presence of deadly toxins by posting signs written in English and Spanish for all occupants of the field to read? Would "posting" that intention — thereby allowing farm worker families opportunity to exhale upon saturation spraying[16] — really allow those who must necessarily live and sleep in the fields they work opportunity to escape the powerful toxins upon which production relies? And when we provide sufficiently heavy boots, goggles, gloves, and masks for the workers who hold the canister sprayers, do we also provide enough heavy clothing for their families who live nearby? If we pay the workers a "living" wage (which necessarily implies living away from the toxin-drenched fields) does the cost of produce delivered out of season now rise to a point where U.S. consumption diminishes and our "tostadas" approximate their Mexican counterparts?

## Posting as a Sign of Recognition

For the past decade a series of proposed laws — posting bills — have been considered by both the California Legislature and the U.S. Congress. These have been defeated in their many incarnations. When certain designated "toxic" chemicals are to be sprayed in an area, this legislation proposes that a sign be posted to inform those at work in the fields, detailing the potential hazards of the chemicals applied. The protections afforded operate on the same principle as the warning label on a package of cigarettes, and are thus in no way intended to restrict the sale or distribution of the product. They simply pose a warning of potential (and likely) hazard: Let the user beware.

At first glance, it may seem odd that these bills have been vigorously opposed and defeated. For consumers, a form of posting already exists in prominent signs lurking beneath sprayer nozzles in supermarket produce sections that assure us "no detectable residues" of the pesticides used in production remain on the fruit. But these disclaimers also announce (by exclusion) that the toxic pesticide applications that may have been made to the typically brown skin of harvesters are of neither short- nor long-term concern to the grocer.

Proposed agricultural posting is threatening because it reconnects the grocers' practice with production sites and methods. Liability requires intention, and intention requires recognition. Pesticide manufacturers could not be held responsible for health effects that government exempts as "acceptable risks," but posting laws reallocate that government exemption. Warnings posted comprehensively (and in Spanish as well as English) would provide recognition on the part of producers, scientists, and the institutions employing them that there are other heads among the lettuce, other skins beside the apple's that toxic inputs affect. If we begin to understand that our enterprise is circumscribed by larger ecological relations—including the skin of the farm worker as well as the skin of the fruit—then agricultural posting would constitute a first step toward an expanded, politicized recognition of the ways we are altering "our environment."

Since the 1960s, following the upsurge in chemical applications, farm worker advocates have insisted that fieldworkers should receive written warnings of potential dangers, posted in fields where they work. The struggle for the farm workers' right to know about the hazards of their workplace continued with little success during the 1970s, and most of the 1980s. But even "successes" in posting such information in some U.S. fields raised other doubts. The act of giving workers sufficient information to judge the very character of their occupations does not grant them control to choose some other job. And U.S. warnings could not extend to labor camps such as the ones found in Mexico, where laborers must work and live under direct exposure to chemical inputs, while still growing produce for U.S. markets. Here not just workers but entire communities are affected by nonpersistent chemicals:

> The father of the family had severe laryngitis and . . . a skin rash covering much of his face and running down his neck, to where it disappeared under his jacket. His wife and children were lying on the floor in the cubicle, each suffering from some . . . cold and

flulike symptoms. The only furniture were metal pesticide containers used as stools and another for drinking water storage. . . . A spray gun containing a DDVP compound lay next to the stove. I asked what it was for. "Flies. The flies are unbearable in here." He picked up the gun and gave it a few pumps . . . to demonstrate. I asked him if he was aware that the chemical in the gun and containers could be dangerous to himself and his family. "So they say," he croaked through his raspy throat. "So they say. But sir we are a very poor people. Very poor people. We must do as we can. And we have nothing to buy pots and pans with so. . . . We pick up the containers left in the fields because they are free. This is it. This is our life as you see it here." [17]

Indeed, various of the farm workers' activists suggested that in place of a skull and crossbones, with the words "Danger! Peligro," more explicit signs might be erected in the fields. These signs might explain that health effects for thousands of pesticide products are not known with any certainty. And the signs might note that whether field hands might suffer cancer, reproductive damage, or other long-term disabilities is also one of the "effects unknown." Further, these signs might detail that regulatory scientists (as distinct from other kinds), even where they can provide information about single chemicals, are almost never able to explain the synergistic effects of two or more chemicals in combination or consequences of routine, continuous exposures for the nervous or immune system.

And where would be the appropriate places to post such information? Farm workers' advocates began to visualize a trail of signs that would extend from petrochemical facilities to outlying fields, to adjacent communities, to grocers' shelves in the United States and abroad. And what would be the appropriate message for these warnings? Advocates first suggested that, rather than featuring a universal skull and crossbones, much larger signs might be erected that could be seen from nearby highways, or perhaps from the air, that would read: "THIS FOOD GROWN WITH CANCER-CAUSING SUBSTANCES." This produce was grown by predominantly brown-skinned people, thus reflecting the composition of California's harvesting populations. The posted warnings could describe "hazardous labor camps" where those in this work force are forced to spend much of their money each season on high rents for structures that barely keep out the heat and cold, have only the barest types of bathrooms or kitchens, and are crammed with many individuals at once.

Still other signs could indicate the "community exposure" to many of the same chemicals applied in the fields. These could denote the communities where "clusters" of children have developed cancers or describe studies conducted by California's Department of Health that would ascribe "seasonal flu" to the fact that air basins are widely contaminated. And more signs showing "RURAL EXODUS TRAIL" might indicate the path millions of fieldworkers have taken for several decades from such places as Michoa-cán, Oaxaca, Morelos, and Chiapas. Or historic signposts of terrain for thousands of villages throughout Mexico and the American Southwest could indicate "CULTURES DECIMATED BY MODERN PRACTICES."

But how would common people—particularly illiterate peasants—be expected to appreciate the significance of these deleterious warnings? With so many, soon signs for California's agrarian work force might approximate the absurd landscape suggested by Gabriel García Marquez in the Colom-bian countryside, demanding "so much vigilance and moral strength that many succumbed to the spell of an imaginary reality, one invented by themselves: Less practical but more comforting," as

> with an ink brush he marked everything with its name: *table, chair, clock, door, wall, bed, pan.* . . . He went to the corral and marked the animals and plants: *cow, goat, hen, cassava, banana.* . . . Little by little, studying the infinite possibility of memory loss, he realized the day might come things would be recognized by their inscriptions but no one would remember their use. . . . The sign that he hung on the neck of the cow was exemplary proof of the way in which the inhabitants of Macondo were prepared to fight against the loss of memory: *This is the cow. She must be milked every morning so she will produce and the milk must be boiled in order to be mixed with coffee to make coffee and milk.*[18]

The day has come when foods are recognized by their potential uses over their effects, their size and color before their taste, their number above their nutritional value. In our new posting system, instead of the function we would employ signs that would explain the consequences of productive relations. Perhaps there would be different signs for needs of marketers, such as "THIS TOMATO MUST SIT WELL WITHOUT ROLLING OVER," reflecting the need for genetic engineering, and different signs yet marking the relations among growing conditions, insecticides, and labor-ers that would warn, "THIS SOIL PERMEATED WITH CHEMICAL POISON-OUS TO MOTHER'S MILK," and finally grocery and restaurant signs like the ones that have recently appeared heralding the use of tomato bits and meat substitutes at fast-food restaurants advertising the relationship of the end product to the customer palate, such as "THIS IS A GENETICALLY AL-TERED FACSIMILE VEGETABLE" (that does not necessarily perform as a real fruit might), so that the potential consumer could be informed of all of the practices he or she is supporting in choosing that particular food.

Environmentalist groups have begun to map ecological consequences of agricultural activities for raptors, sea otters, and mountain lions. Animal rights advocates decry the dangers of testing unknown substances on laboratory research animals. Isn't it time that a new mapping be required to make more explicit the social ecology of modern agriculture, where instead of labeling warnings geared solely toward consumer habits we warn against the health and moral consequences of larger production practices as well?

## Nonpersistent Chemicals: "Clean" Food and Dirty People

Posting legislation was first introduced in California in the early 1960s, yet none of numerous bills made its way to the governor's desk until 1986, and then the successful measure was vetoed. In 1988 the CDFA (California Department of Food and Agriculture) "agreed" to post approximately one dozen labor-intensive crops—leaving unregulated at least three dozen others. An anterior and more significant way in which land-grant ecology purposely overlooks the participation of minority laborers has to do with the classification systems for chemical pesticides. There are chemicals such as DDT, BHC, aldrin, chlordane, and lindane (with half-lives measured in years) that "persistently" refuse to break down. It is the chemicals classified as "persistent" in the environment and on the produce that have become the focus of many environmental campaigns. The "Circle of Poison" legislation introduced in Congress, for example, seeks to limit chemicals banned or not registered for use in the United States, but produced here and detected on produce imported from abroad. The catalysts for alarm, of course, are the multiple long-term threats to species ranging from brown pelicans to consumers. Yet legal "nonpersistent" pesticides, such as organophosphates, are even more insidious than the largely illegal persistents such as DDT. For the past three decades, worldwide applications of "legal" pesticides amounted to billions upon billions of pounds of chemicals possessing largely unknown ecological and health characteristics. Despite considerable efforts by multinational corporations and their university researchers to instill confusion and ignorance, evidence of negative ecological consequences have been steadily and rapidly mounting concerning the legal uses of nonpersistents. These include the following:

the contamination of tens of thousands of drinking water sources throughout the world with aldicarb, alachlor, atrazine, and related pesticides;
the extinction and endangerment of thousands of plant, animal, and insect species caused by the application of pesticides with unknown ecological effects on a global scale;

the routine exposure of millions—with one well-respected study
citing twenty-five million pesticide poisonings each year;
and, if critical U.S. studies provide any guide, thousands to
hundreds of thousands of victims of pesticide exposure every year,
suffering cancer, reproductive failure, and organ damage.[19]

It is the prudent use of these chemicals that private testing agencies
such as Nutri-Clean certify when they assure their clients, advertising that
they are "working with science to bring you wholesome and nutritious
fresh fruits and vegetables [where] we encourage our growers to use pesticides prudently, leaving no residues in our food." This specter raises concern as to whether less wholesome, chemically tainted produce actually
addresses the nutritional needs of those populations they do reach. Even
*were* FDA testing adequate to ensure safety against a wider range of pesticides, even were there more extensive testing for hundreds of substances
currently uncategorized, and even were such results provided in time to
institute appropriate standards, these programs would serve only to protect predominantly white, urban consumers.

Thus, it is entirely possible that we may severely abuse farm workers
and the environment with toxic pesticides while producing crops with relatively small quantities of residue but that are still terribly dangerous to
people (nonconsumers), animals (nontarget species), plants (nonweeds),
and (beneficial) insects. Nonpersistent chemicals linger in the dust from
applications in and around the home.[20] They remain in the soil and flow
with the water that travels through it.[21] They are contracted through the
skin into the mother's womb and may lead to neurological impairment,
congenital limb defects, or childhood leukemia.[22] They are infused into
our diets at accelerated rates, with the anterior effects of such exposures,
especially to formative childhood development, unknown. They permeate
rural *campamentos*, the drainage ditches in which families bathe, and the
canisters in which they store their water.[23] How great then are health risks
of certifiably "clean" foods and production techniques? For some they are
unequivocal. Yet we do not regard inert or even acute toxic poisonings as
direct results of a fundamentally flawed set of agricultural practices. We attribute these effects to numerous other factors (including poor prenatal
care in general and the effects of poverty in particular) partly because of
latent manifestation and largely because they tend to occur outside of our
circumscribed realm of personal responsibility.

## The Child Poisoning Prevention Act: Who Is Affected?

It is the growers who are responsible for the crop, the breeders who are responsible for nutrition, the manufacturers who we hold responsible for the use of toxics, and the parents to whom we look to safeguard the health of their children. Even were we to post an infinite number of warnings about potential dangers of organophosphate applications occurring in the fields, these would not compel manufacturers and growers to alter their agricultural practices for the benefit of fieldworkers and their surrounding communities—quite the opposite. Scientists, growers, and agribusinesses consistently use floracentric techniques, thus eliminating powerless field-workers as referents in a professional discourse of productivity.

Far more effective in deterring use of certain common chemicals than the efforts of the United Farm Workers has been the campaign launched by public health advocates. Children and infants are also at greater risk of developing disease caused by toxic residues on food as a result of consuming substantially more produce (as much as twenty-two times the apple products as adults) in proportion to their body weight.[24] Campaigns such as those represented by the Child Poisoning Prevention Act make higher levels of private risk for affluent American children the focus of public alarm. That migrant labor finds itself at similar or greater levels of risk from measurable increases in chemical exposure is not "news." As one *Wall Street Journal* reporter observed, "Unfortunately nobody in the U.S. is going to get excited about the health of migrant farmworkers or a bunch of migratory birds killed by pesticides in Mexico. You have to hit people where it hurts them directly." [25] Those people and "their" problems do not receive the sort of alarmed public attention that celebrities can bring to focus on those latent dangers among "our" children.

The most positive effect of another piece of California legislation with the goal of minimizing infant exposures, the Birth Defect Prevention Act, is that it is preventive. It proposes we limit chemical use not on the basis of known risks but on the basis of the unknown risks with which our children may have to live for generations to come. Daminozide apples and the toxic chemical residue on more than 19 percent of all dairy products and 48 percent of fish, seafood, and meats[26] may not only be putting our children at twenty-two times the risk of adults similarly exposed, but unrestricted foreign export and application of more persistent, acute toxics are certainly putting "their" children at similar risk. The conversion of small plots of land and open forests beyond the southern meridian to agribusinesses that advantage northern consumers has certainly put "their" children at even greater risk of malnutrition or death. Yet these are not part of the detectable, measurable health risks factored into assessments of land-grant production practices. They fail to examine the synergistic, cumulative, or low-level impacts, because this history is not considered to be a part of a particular produce under study or to have direct bearing on American health.

## Mirror, Mirror: The Role of Expert

For many observers who have worried about the state of agriculture, the promise of a new technology, a biotechnology, offers the latest, greatest hope. Like the unfulfilled promises of the green revolution, biotechnology is intended to better feed the hungry. Even beyond hunger, it is hoped that biotechnology will provide an answer to the ravages of the chemical age. Corporate and university spokespersons outline projects whereby biotechnology will utilize "natural" substances in place of human-designed toxic ones, and the genetically engineered plants will be integrated with "natural" ecologies.

Even if we were able to accept these pronouncements, the promised lands suggest little change for people of color throughout the world. The advance of modern agriculture through land-grant techniques has been predicated on the destruction of older, more traditional forms. The irony, however, is that modern agriculture finds within them its rescue. Thus, to answer the loss of genetic diversity, scientists send teams to the Third World to "discover" sources of variability that traditional cultivators have built up for thousands of years. The same is true of finding stock for "inventing" new breeds of rice, corn, and other food grains. The actual inventing belongs to peasant farmers who have selected and reselected food crops according to local tastes, climate, and habit. Multinational representatives then claim the rights of "ownership" for traits that have been generations in the making.

Students of traditional Mexican agriculture note that twentieth-century monocrop agricultural practices devised at U.S. land-grant universities threaten to destroy knowledge that for more than 5,000 years provided a basis for ecologically and culturally sensitive production systems. The paradox of Mexico's agriculture at the end of the twentieth century is that traditional polycultures, or the complex mixture of plants on a single plot of land—which have provided foods, fibers, medicines, wood products, fish, and animals—are being coercively discarded in favor of a modern technology that results in the decimation of soils, the contamination of vast bodies of drinking water and aquatic habitat, the annual poisoning of hundreds of thousands of workers, the massive indebtedness of an entire nation, the continuation of low-intensity warfare against landless peasants, and systematic destruction of the peasantry and their thousands of years of accumulated knowledge rich with alternatives for modern agriculture. Scientifically tested, ecologically certified "clean" programs in fact sweep peasant minority cultures aside in the pursuit of the perfect plum.

The intensive land-grant study of the produce as existing apart from the larger ecology of the communities in which it was developed has in fact become an elaborate ruse to divert public attention ("Just keep your eye on the tomato") from the anterior effects we know have been occurring for some time. We know that so-called innovations in sustainability and the development of nonpersistent pesticides have had a most devastating effect on minority communities both in the United States and throughout the world. We know, for example, that the same minority workers who once effectively sustained production in their own *chinampas* with few or no external inputs have been separated from their land, on a massive scale, by agribusinesses that largely mimic the local ecology.[27] It is well documented that

> minority workers are disproportionately represented in industries with high levels of occupational health risks and in the most hazardous jobs within those and in other industries. Workplace exposures to solvents, airborne particles, fibers, lead and other metals, pesticides, and farm chemicals are linked to chronic dermatitis, cancers, respiratory diseases, brown lung, asbestosis, metal and chemical poisonings for persons of color.[28]

We know that inner-city children, particularly those below the poverty level (a condition minority children suffer at triple the rate of their Caucasian counterparts), are at risk of lead paint poisoning in dilapidated tenement dwellings,[29] and yet we divert attention from these risks by publishing pamphlets encouraging minority mothers to "keep a better watch on your children's activities." We build communities of color disproportionately on top of landfills, toxic waste disposal sites, and solid waste incinerators. We know that a variety of food crops have been displaced throughout the world for more economically productive "cash crops," thus fostering starvation by furthering a "strawberry imperialism" in agrarian practices.[30] We know that chemicals banned in the United States are rarely restricted for export, and the annual poisoning of millions of fieldworkers throughout the world is a requirement of modernized agricultural practices.[31]

We know that officials of the World Bank have explicitly advocated hemispheric apartheid through which ever-increasing levels of chemical and solid waste produced in the North will be dumped, for a price, in the South. And we have long been certain that capital-intensive technologies are not simply genetically altering produce size, shape, and composition, but actually contributing to enhanced levels of malnutrition and starvation beyond the meridian. Yet the single greatest rallying cry for organic practices, sustainability and minimization of (certain) toxins, came when it could be shown that middle-class American children were at risk from consuming the legal residues of the pesticide Alar. Consider the apple, the tomato, the sugar beet, the plum. Thus far, these are the only red skins to which we devote massive shares of the world's resources, scientific expertise, and medical concern.

Following the findings by minority organizations that risks of toxins are especially borne by the darker-complexioned people of the United States, the U.S. Environmental Protection Agency has initiated a discussion termed Environmental Equity. The EPA describes its concern as follows:

> In the context of a risk-based approach to environmental management, the relative risk burden borne by low-income and racial minority communities is a special concern. Environmental equity is important to those who may bear disproportionate risks. But everyone has a stake because it is also an argument for better environmental protection generally. Included in environmental equity are the distribution of risks and the environmental policy-making process. The manner in which environmental policies are set must allow the concerns of all communities to be heard, understood and considered.[32]

If what we mean by the "equitable distribution of risks" is that the benefit of greater agricultural productivity must be shared by all persons — majority and minority, small shareholders and large agribusinesses alike — then we are more distant from environmental equity as each new land-grant technique finds its implement. If we mean that minority peoples and Third World populations need increasingly shoulder the consequences wrought by mounting toxic waste and synergistic applications of pesticides, the certifiably "organic" products of which they do not enjoy, then we must devise new methods of creating "clean" foods. Given the routinized poisoning of 2,000 farm workers per year during the 1970s, 1980s, and 1990s, with estimates of more than 100,000 poisonings annually and massive destruction of drinking water sources — more than 2,000 wells destroyed in California from pesticides alone increasing childhood cancers for minority children in such towns as Earlimart and McFarland[33] — it is imperative that we return to a public discourse linking the consequences of green fields to brown skins.

## Notes

1. Bob Higgins, *Race and Environmental Politics: Drawing New Connections* (Dudley, Mass.: Nicholas College, 1992), 23: "Ritual uncleanliness operates in many cultures. Its central characteristic is the identification of situations which constitute threatening irregularities . . .

when environmental pollution is relegated to such appropriately socially-polluted spaces [it] is really 'in its place' and . . . relatively invisible in its physical and cultural separation from predominantly white centers of power."

2. Amicus Brief for NAACP Legal Defense Fund, quoted in Higgins, *Race and Environmental Politics*, 30–31.

3. Jim Hightower, *Hard Tomatoes, Hard Times: A Report of the Agribusiness Accountability Project on Failure of America's Land Grant College Complex* (Cambridge, Mass.: Schenkman, 1973), 12–13.

4. See Marc Reisner, "The Go Go Years," in *Cadillac Desert: The American West and Its Disappearing Water* (New York: Viking, 1986).

5. Carolyn Merchant, *The Death of Nature: Women, Ecology and the Scientific Revolution* (New York: Harper & Row, 1980).

6. Angus Wright, *The Death of Ramon Gonzalez: The Modern Agricultural Dilemma* (Austin: University of Texas Press, 1990), 192.

7. Cesar Chavez, *The Wrath of Grapes: The United Farm Workers of America* (Keene, Calif.: UFW, 1986): "In the 1970's the UFW was in its ascendancy in California. By 1973, the UFW had signed contracts for 40,000 workers on 180 farms. These contracts were mostly for workers in lettuce and grapes, where acutely toxic pesticides are used heavily under conditions that tend to lead to direct worker exposure" (p. 24).

8. Charles Reich, *The Greening of America* (New York: Continuum, 1970).

9. Wes Jackson, *Meeting the Expectations of the Land: Essays in Sustainable Agriculture and Stewardship* (Berkeley: Northpoint, 1984), 25.

10. Vandana Shiva, *Staying Alive: Women, Ecology and Survival in India* (London: Zed, 1989), 74.

11. Lori Ann Thrupp, "Pesticides and Policies: Approaches to Pest Control Dilemmas in Nicaragua and Costa Rica," *Latin American Perspectives* 15 (1978): 7.

12. Vandana Shiva, "Nature as Resource, Nature as Home," recorded lecture, University of Montana Mansfield Lecture Series, Missoula, April 1992.

13. Norman Borlaug, "Green Revolution: Can We Make It Meet Expectations?" *Proceedings of the American Phytopathological Society* (St. Paul, Minn.: APS, 1976), 14.

14. Bruce H. Jennings, *Foundations of International Agricultural Research: Science and Politics in Mexican Agriculture* (Boulder, Colo.: Westview, 1988), 189.

15. Luis Jorge Domante Biello, *Investigacion de un Brote de Intoxicación por Plaguicides* (Guanajuato, Mexico: Guanajuato, 1983), 83: "The Argentine epidemiologist commented this investigation had led him to the realization that pesticides may be a serious health threat in Mexico [and] that there was a systematic cover-up of the pesticide problem by high government officials."

16. Wright, *The Death of Ramon Gonzalez*, 20. The grower's social worker said, "We try to tell them how to protect themselves, to wear the right clothes, to wash the tomatoes before they eat them, and to exhale when the airplane sprays over them while in the field" (p. 55).

17. Ibid., 14. "The best of the camps are built of corrugated sheet metal, sold to growers by firms as poultry sheds. The cubicles . . . are open on the fourth side. Farmworkers often build a makeshift fourth wall from packing crates or blankets" (p. 13).

18. Gabriel García Marquez, *One Hundred Years of Solitude*, trans. Gregory Rabassa (New York: Avon, 1970), 53.

19. Bruce H. Jennings, *Pesticides and Regulations: The Myth of Safety* (Sacramento: California Senate Office of Research, 1991), 13–21.

20. John W. Roberts and David E. Camann, "Test for Assessing Exposure to Pesticides in Household Dust," *Bulletin of Environmental Contamination and Toxicology* 43 (1989): 717–24.

21. J. K. Hawley, "Assessment of Health Risks from Contaminated Soil," *Risk Analysis* 5 (1989): 289–301.

22. Robin Whyatt, "Intolerable Risk: Physiological Susceptibility of Children to Pesticides," *Journal of Pesticide Reform* 9, no. 3 (1989): 5–9: "Although not required by federal regulation, some behavioral tests on . . . low level exposure to organophosphates and carbamates . . . before and immediately after birth can cause delays in reflex and sexual development, eye opening . . . alter nerve transmission function and neuroreceptor development, impair neuromuscular function, alter . . . and affect brain structure" (p. 7).

23. Anne Kricker, "Women and the Environment: A Study of Congenital Limb Abnormalities," *Community Health Studies* 10 (1986): 1–11.

24. Ruth A. Lowengart, John M. Peters, Carla Cicioni, et al., "Childhood Leukemia and Parent's Occupational and Home Exposures," *Journal of the National Cancer Institute* 79 (July 1987): 37–42.

25. Wright, *The Death of Ramon Gonzalez*, 188–89, quoting the reporter.

26. Lawrie Mott, "Residues on Food," in *Federal Food and Drug Administration Pesticide Program* (Washington, D.C.: U.S. Government Printing Office, 1989).

27. *Chinampas* are raised beds surrounded by canals that dredge silt from nearby lakes and marshes and spread it as fertilizer. Willow-pole mat grids sprinkled with precise amounts of water, semiliquid silt, and plant seeds can produce four or more crops per year with minimum-intensity inputs.

28. Higgins, *Race and Environmental Politics*, 7.

29. Jeanne M. Stellman and Susan M. Daum, *Work Is Dangerous to Your Health: A Handbook of Health Hazards in the Workplace and What You Can Do about Them* (New York: Vintage, 1971), 32–35.

30. Ernst Feder, *Strawberry Imperialism: A Study in the Mechanisms of Dependence in Mexican Agriculture* (Mexico City: Ediciones Campesinos, 1976).

31. Wright quotes Dr. Luis Velasquez (of the Social Clinic in Campo Gobierno El Sol de Sinaloa): "It is irresponsible on the part of the bosses to contract children as young as ten years old for agrochemical application tasks which require knowledge, great caution and special equipment, but older people, who have already suffered the consequences, don't want to do it." *The Death of Ramon Gonzalez*, 55; see also 46.

32. "Environmental Equity," *United States Environmental Protection Agency Report* 23 (October 1991): 12.

33. James N. Seiber, *Airborne Concentrations of Selected Pesticides in Three Communities in Kern County, California from Samplings Done in June-July 1987* (Davis: University of California, Davis, Department of Environmental Toxicology, 1988), 42. Seiber's report spurred the UFW's "Wrath of Grapes" campaign. Readers seeking more current information on issues concerning environmental racism are advised to consult the following individuals: Carl Anthony, coeditor of *Race, Poverty & the Environment* (a newsletter for social and environmental justice published by Earth Island Institute, San Francisco, California); Dana Alston, Panos Institute, Washington, D.C.; Baldemar Velasquez, Farm Labor Organizing Committee of Ohio; Luke Cole, California Rural Legal Assistance Foundation of San Francisco; Professor Robert D. Bullard, Department of Sociology, University of California, Riverside; Professor Bunyon Bryant, Environmental Studies Department, University of Michigan; Marion Moses, M.D., United Farm Workers, La Paz, California; Professor Robert Higgins, Department of Human Ecology, Rutgers University; and Jerry Poge, National Institute of Environmental Health Sciences, Research Triangle, North Carolina.

# Part IV

The Order(ing) of Nature

Chapter 10

# Voices from the Whirlwind

William E. Connolly

## Nature and Culture

What is the character of things "below" or "prior to" culture? We will never
answer this question as posed, for every attempt to do so draws upon the
resources of culture. And yet, the attempt to pose such a question is unlikely to disappear either, for every interpretation projects presumptions
about the primordial character of things into its presentation of actuality
and possibility, identity and difference, good and evil. It does so even if it
strives to go "beyond good and evil" and, though more ambiguously and
problematically, even if it strives to call every "metaphysical" or "ontological" assumption into question.

In modern cultures the question of what precedes culture is often
posed through the vocabulary of nature. Some political theorists invoke
nature as a set of regularities potentially knowable and masterable by humans. Others treat it as a meaningful order in which humans participate
through their own embodiment and to which embodied selves can become more closely attuned. These two options together set the table upon
which contemporary debates over identity, ecology, moral sources, sexuality, tolerance, and community are placed.

But the familiar differences between these two alternatives do not exhaust the range of discernible possibilities, even within the history of the "West." The Latin, *natura*, meaning "birth, constitution, character, course of things," suggests other options for exploration, as does the root term *nasci*, "to be born." The closest Greek term, *physis*, folds genesis or "coming into being" into the idea; and it is not perfectly clear that this energy that propels a thing into being was always and everywhere bound close to the theme of an intrinsic purpose governing it.

I will explore a subterranean legacy in this region by considering the stories of Job and Alexina, respectively, the first being a biblical story of a probable pagan living seven or eight centuries before the common era, the second being the memoir of a teenager living in France in the nineteenth century. The stories of Job and Alexina disturb interwoven concepts of divinity, identity, nature, moral order, and suffering governing their respective communities. They do so particularly when each strives to locate h/er suffering within terms established by h/er community, for the suffering of each exceeds and challenges fundamental conceptions through which the community strives to redeem it.

## Job

The Book of Job is the site of a struggle over the interpretation of human suffering. The book is organized into three parts: a prologue in which the Accuser tempts the Lord to test Job's fidelity and receives instructions from the Lord, a middle section in which Job's experience with unrelieved suffering is presented through a dialogue with friends culminating in the engagement with the Voice out of the whirlwind, and an epilogue in which Job is restored to well-being by the Lord while his erstwhile friends are punished. Some scholars believe the epilogue was added after the poem that makes up the core of the book. And most agree that the book was the object of numerous "interpolations" before it acquired the form in which we receive it. The long speech by Elihu inserted at the end of the middle section, for instance, is widely thought (on grounds of style and content) to be a later intervention by a pious priest. It seems designed to subdue scandalous possibilities of interpretation in the theophany immediately following it.

The Book of Job, probably composed around the seventh century before the common era, remains a site of textual struggle, as scholars in later centuries have contested its meaning through the politics of translation and interpretation. Job's struggle is not only with himself, his friends, and his god, but with later friends, scholars, and editors who wish to interpret that struggle in particular ways. The persistence of these struggles signifies the continuing power of the book to inform and disturb. Job compels both because its themes continue to flow through the cultural unconscious of the West and because its energies disturb that unconscious.

Because the text, as we receive it, is splintered by multifarious contestations and clouded by numerous additions, revisions, and interpretations over the centuries, it is an excellent mirror to hold up to ourselves. It reflects demands and ambivalences often concealed in other texts through stabilized traditions of interpretation. Its ambiguities render it a relatively open book through which each individual can try to come to terms with the sources and effects of suffering. The book speaks to us through the incredible power of its rhythms, metaphors, and images; it presses us to respond to its surprises, reversals, and intensifications; it remains open to a diversity of readings; and it resists easy or full assimilation by any single response. Is this power to confound the unanimity of a single reading one of its strengths? I think so, but that judgment already implicates me in a particular reading, with its own agenda, lessons, anxieties, and hopes.

Let us concentrate first on the poem that makes up the center of the book. Job, apparently a man of integrity who has enjoyed uncommon well-being, now suffers immensely. He has lost his sons and daughters, his property, and his reputation, through violent, uncanny events. His body is covered with boils. His wife ridicules him for refusing to "curse God and die." [1] But he perdures in his faith, eventually receiving three friends who come to counsel and console him.

He soon learns—as many have after—that these two functions of friendship do not coincide. Were these visitors, in the earliest version of the poem, defined as friends or as functionaries assigned to squeeze a confession out of one who might otherwise disturb the faith of the community? We will never know. At any rate, the friends, at first diplomatically and then belligerently, interpret Job's suffering through the optics of an intrinsic moral order governed by a god who bestows justice upon human life. A beneficent, providential god rules the world; he rewards the virtuous and punishes the wicked. This being so, Job *must* either admit wrongdoings he has not yet acknowledged or search within himself to uncover wrongs heretofore overlooked. His suffering signifies his vice.

Job resists these instructions, protesting his innocence and virtue. The "friends" insist more actively, even though they must realize they intensify the misery of this miserable man in doing so. Why must they be so insistent? Job thinks he knows:

> You too have turned against me;
>> my wretchedness fills you with fear.
> Have I ever asked you to help me
>> or begged you to pay ransom. . . .
> Look me straight in the eye;
>> is this how a liar would face you?
> Can't I tell right from wrong?
>> If I sinned, wouldn't I know it? (p. 22)

The friends cannot console Job because their investment in the vision of a moral world order drives them to accuse him for suffering. If Job suffers without desert, the same bad luck might befall any of them. And if their current well-being is not the result of their own merit, it cannot be to their credit now and it might vanish later for no reason at all. If these things were possible their moral world would spin out of control. Contingency, luck, and blind fate would replace providence, justice, and order in the cosmos; these blind forces would inhabit every human project from the inside and challenge it from the outside, opening up frightening possibilities. The fate of Job makes them fear the world may be more precarious, fragile, and unpredictable than they had thought, and their reactions to him seek to restore this reassurance in themselves regardless of the toll its restoration might impose on him.

Moreover, the impiety in Job's protestations of innocence is dangerous to those clinging to the comforts of an intrinsic moral order: it is a blasphemy against the divine spider thought to spin the moral web of the world. Even considering this thought—let alone endorsing it—might bring down upon them the wrath that has fallen upon Job. Job, with his festering boils, thus exists as an exemplar of the riskiness in these thoughts. This communal web of faith in an intrinsic moral order presided over by a jealous god possesses an impressive capacity to still doubts among the faithful once its strands have been woven through and around the members. Its impressive capacity for self-restoration is one of its attractions and one of its traps.

Job has become dangerous to the friends through his existential response to suffering. So they become increasingly more insistent in their counsel, progressively shedding the pretense to console him in his suffering. The form Job's suffering assumes drives them to take a punitive orientation to him. They turn the victim of bad luck—or, perhaps worse, the target of earlier communal vengeance—into an adversary of the community.

Job exposes boils festering in *their* souls when he says, "My wretchedness fills you with fear."

The misery of Job is now compounded: he suffers the pain and grief of his condition, the anxiety of doubts about cosmic justice aroused by the experience of these injuries, the blame imposed upon him by friends for (allegedly) bringing suffering upon himself, and the hostility they aim at him for refusing to reaffirm the justice of this god by acknowledging his own faults. "You are undermining religion and crippling faith in God," asserts Eliphaz, one of the friends (p. 41). Job, in turn, now begins to discern how this very conception of a moral divinity provides the impetus through which the sufferer is converted into a stranger and an adversary.

But Job himself is implicated in the web of moral order he protests against, even as he exposes the cruelties it fosters. As the "dialogue" proceeds (the exchanges become too bitter to fit this term well) Job's estrangement from his friends becomes joined to a profound bitterness against his god:

> I loathe each day of my life;
>> I will take my complaint to God.
> I will say, Do you condemn me;
>> why are you so enraged?
> Is it right for you to be vicious,
>> To spoil what your own hands made . . . ?
> Why did you let me be born?
>> Why couldn't I have stayed
> in the deep waters of the womb,
>> rocked to sleep in the dark? (pp. 29–30)

Here, and elsewhere too, Job accuses his god because it does not live up to the ideal of justice he projects into it. "Do you condemn me?" "Is it *right* for you to be *vicious*?" This extraordinary passage recognizes a god who presides over a moral order even while it poses the possibility that this same god is vicious, that is, immoral—not a reliable source of moral order. What the hell is going on here? Does Job's suffering demand a transcendent moral agent capable of being blamed while the character of Job's fate also makes him doubt the truth of this attribution?

Job now doubts that this god is a moral god. His experience belies it. But, still, there ought to be a moral god so that it can serve as the object of blame for failure to live up to the demands of moral order in the world. In appealing to this plaintive "ought to be," Job reinstates at one level the principle he actively doubts at another. He ambiguates his god. This ambiguous god now becomes the source of Job's deepest bitterness. Indeed, without a semblance of faith in this god Job would have no transcendental source to appeal to, but with such a being he suffers the additional burden of rancor against a god who does not consistently enforce its own principles. Even while the dangerous thoughts of Job threaten the self-certainty of his friends, his own thoughts have moved only a short distance from those of the friends. Job's existential rage is subjected to the torture of an ambivalence that renders it possible.

The friends/enemies, then, are disparate voices inside Job as well as members of the community he challenges. And the moral god he denies is also the one he condemns. That is why the debate within the Book of Job is so intense and repetitious. Its torturous ambiguities cannot easily be stabilized. As long as Job retains this existential "ought" ("My god ought to be what I thought he was but now doubt him to be"), he can cling to a slender hope that his suffering reflects a divine mistake or momentary lapse into injustice. But, also, as long as he clings to that slim hope amidst this wretchedness, his relationship to divinity will be one of bitterness. He will rage against a god for injustice he doubts it could commit. He will protect a doubtful moral divinity to provide a dubious target against which to project rage. How many people—suffering, say, as invalids on the way to long, painful deaths—have twisted and turned in this same chamber of torture?

Job's "friends" grasp something of his ambivalence; hence, they keep trying to draw him back to their faith. This is the one response that might convert his bitterness into remorse while reassuring them. So they cling to their project tenaciously, while (a voice in) Job continues to outrage the will to belief they embody. Listen as Job speaks to them again:

> I made a pact with my eyes;
> > that I would not gaze at evil.
> But what good has virtue done me?
> > How has God rewarded me?
> Isn't disgrace for sinners
> > and misery for the wicked?
> Can't he tell right from wrong
> > or keep his accounts in order? (p. 73)

The thought in the last two lines has surely occurred at some time to every believer and doubter, but the friends find it too much to take. Job has become a "rebel" against their god by accusing it belligerently of deficiency; this reprehensible conduct during his suffering reveals to them retroactively how richly Job deserves the fate that has befallen him. His rebellion renders him intolerable. No new deeds have been added to his existential offenses (he has, for instance, neither stolen property nor murdered a member of the community). But these words are deeds enough. His metaphysical rebellion renders him an outcast from the community.

The debate with the friends merely provides a prelude to the main event. The vitriolic debate finally stirs up the voice in the whirlwind. This unexpected effect of Job's existential rebellion is also ambiguous. True, the Unnameable does respond through a powerful whirlwind that sweeps over and above the ground upon which the puny Job stands. But, still, Job's well-aimed arrows do generate a divine response, and this divinity has not heretofore been moved to speak so directly to any number of believers and tormented doubters calling upon it to do so. The poetry reaches its highest level of imagery, energy, and irony as the voice speaks to this courageous rebel, this bitter accuser, this ambivalent devotee. If the friends inhabit Job as well as speaking to him on behalf of the community, is the "whirlwind" yet another voice within Job?

The voice speaks but does not answer. It refuses the questions Job posed to it. Its words recall previous formulations by Job and his friends about the wonder of the world, but it lifts those themes to a level higher than they were able to reach. The voice says familiar things, but delivers a new message through its mode of saying. The poet who crafted these lines must have had an ambiguous relation to divinity,[2] celebrating its power through the lines invested in it but rebelling against the injunction to piety through the very willingness to invest these human words in divinity. Is this ambiguity reversed in the hesitations of later priests and scholars who have worked on this text? Is the theophany too compelling to repress but too dangerous to present to the faithful without cautious editing and interpretation?

Speaking out of a whirlwind, the voice recalls forces and energies in the world that exceed human capacities for understanding and control. A whirlwind—a tornado—is an immense, uncontrollable force, erupting as if out of nowhere, wreaking devastation upon anything in its path, emitting a roar that terrifies, following an irregular path that reveals no rhyme or reason from the perspective of human notions of regularity, merit, and virtue:

> Where were you when I planned the earth?
>
> Tell me, if you are so wise.
>
> Do you know who took its dimensions?
>
> measuring its length with a cord?
>
> What were its pillars built on?
>
> who laid its cornerstone? (p. 79)

The voice bellows questions Job cannot answer. Hence, it crunches the standpoint from which Job's questions, pleas, and accusations have proceeded. Do its ironic questions suggest that it presides over a moral order beyond the full grasp of mere mortals? Or do these dismissive questions crush the self-serving, anthropomorphic demand for an intrinsic moral order itself?

As the interrogative voice proceeds, it calls up images of energy, diversity, strangeness, and uncanniness in nature. On one register it invokes whirlwinds, thunderclouds, lightning, deserts, ocean depths, darkness, ice, wilderness, and the unfathomable stretch of time. On another it calls forth lions, antelopes, wild asses, oxen, the ostrich, the wild steed, the hawk, the hippopotamus, and the crocodile. These energies, forces, and beasts reflect the wonder of an earth more diverse, strange, vital, and vast than anything Job or his friends have been able to digest into their morally ordered cosmos. Consider the Beast, transcribed as Behemoth in most presentations and commonly thought to be the hippopotamus:

> Look now; the Beast that I made:
>
> he eats grass like a bull.
>
> Look: the power in his thighs,
>
> the pulsing sinews of his belly.
>
> His penis stiffens like a pine;
>
> his testicles bulge with vigor.
>
> His ribs are bars of bronze,
>
> his bones iron beams.
>
> He is the first of the works of God,
>
> created to be my plaything.
>
> He lies under the lotus,
>
> hidden by reeds and shadows.
>
> He is calm though the river rages,
>
> though the torrent beats against his mouth.

Who will take him by the eyes
or pierce his nose with a peg? (p. 85)

There is wildness in the world that exceeds the wish of humanity either to moralize or to master it. This Beast was not created for us. It is god's "plaything," certainly not Job's or yours. Its penis does not stiffen according to rules you prescribe. Indeed, the stiffening of a man's penis or hardening of a woman's nipples does not follow a code of propriety either. There is more wildness inside and outside than Job and his friends have heretofore imagined. More important, their responses to the strangeness they do discern is centered upon themselves and their moral projections. They assume that things are ordered according to an ultimate code of justice or, at the very least, that they ought to be. The only god they respect is one who is accountable to their needs and wishes for justice in the last instance. Hence, they are unable to experience the wonder of a world of diverse energies and strange vitalities that whirls around and through them—a world that is more than a moral order.

What about the crocodile (or "serpent")? "Will you pass a string through his nose or crack his jaw with a pin? Will he plead with you for mercy and timidly beg your pardon?" (p. 86). Try to look a crocodile in that eye hovering just above the water line of the swamp. Do you detect recognition of your humanity there? You are a matter of indifference to it when it is full, a prey to be devoured when it is hungry. The eye of the crocodile is a Jobian metaphor for the world—not the only one, but one, perhaps, that deserves more attention from those who demand that "god" or "nature" be designed for them and them alone.

This god is not the designer of a cosmic womb that envelopes the little circle of human categories, wishes, fears, and hopes in its care. It is the instigator of a strange, vast world of internal energies and external forces; they clash, collide, converge, and career through, over, and against one another in multifarious ways. Their multiple lines of intersection often produce unexpected effects. The world invoked by this voice speaks to a protean vitality of being, not to the provincial demand that it embody the particular conceptions of merit and reward of the animal who speaks and ponders its mortality.

It is not only that the world invoked by the theophany is not designed for humans. Humans are not the only *actors* in it. The world flows over with diverse "energies" and "forces" that impinge upon human life in multiple ways and that sometimes react to human impingements upon them in unpredictable and uncanny ways. If a human actor is one who makes a difference in the world without quite knowing what it is doing, then germs, volcanoes, crocodiles, and whirlwinds have some of the characteristics of actors too; the term *actor* now gathers within it a plurality of variable dimensions blurring or ambiguating familiar divisions between nature/culture, humans/machines, will/cause, and creator/creature. Moreover, even within human life, "the will," "the soul," and "the subject" can now be seen to be insufficient or uncertain sources of behavior: the self contains pools of "energy" and "impulse" that flow through and over these officially defined centers of agency. When one emphasizes the metaphorical status of terms such as *energy* and *impulse* in characterizing "drives" within and without the human animal, the corollary metaphorical standing of will and subject begins to shine through more brightly. The Greek idea of "demon" is no more problematic than the Christian idea of "will," it is just that the latter stands at the center of modern conceptions of intrinsic moral order and, therefore, needs to be problematized more actively today for ethical reasons.

The characterization of the world in the theophany is also anthropomorphic, of course. Given that a poet placed these words in the mouth of a god, this is unavoidable. But, still, this poetry gestures beyond the provincial boundaries of moral discourse: it allows the categories through which it grasps the world to fade off into an indefinite set of differences that calls the sufficiency of the categories into question. Such a perspective has disturbing effects on doctrines that demand a close fit between human conceptions of regularity/morality and world formations. Conceptions of nature construing it to be filled with a harmonious moral purpose to which we can become attuned are contested by this theophany. So are those that construe nature to be a plastic substratum susceptible to human mastery and control once its forces and energies have been translated into a matrix of regular laws.

Nature as intrinsic purpose or nature as plastic matter to be used—these two conceptions have competed for hegemony in the history of the West, with the second eventually becoming the majority voice of the modern age and the first receding into the reactive voice of nostalgia for a time when the teleological imagination carried more credibility. The Jobian theophany upsets both of these voices and the respective conceptions of moral order associated with each. Each sounds too much like the other from its vantage point, because each embodies transcendental narcissism. Each demands that the world be *for us* in the last instance, either as a dispenser of rewards for virtue or as a pliable medium susceptible to human mastery. The first invokes a god as mysterious master subject; the second, humanity as technological master subject. The second conception prides itself on its ability to transcend the anthropomorphic moralism of the first, but it remains remarkably close to its favorite opponent. Both demand compensation, either from a god who installs providence into nature or from a plastic world that has lost this god. They demand either equivalence between virtue and reward in the last instance or that the earth be placed at the disposal of humanity. The first vision appears holy to itself; the second, realistic to itself in its refusal of teleological comfort. But both appear provincial, self-enclosed, and narcissistic from the perspective of the Jobian theophany. Its portrayal of whirlwinds within and without repeals the world as intrinsic purpose or plastic matter. The whirlwind is a better metaphor for the difference flowing below, through, and over the structures of cultural organization than either the plowed field or the glow of the sun setting. Or, at least, both of the latter must be experienced in relation to the first before the uncanniness and contingency of nature begins to sink into the presumptions of established practices. Taming and moralizing are necessary ingredients in human life, of course, but everything depends on what projections into being accompany and qualify these formations. The earth is a fireball at its center.

One element in Job's suffering is relieved by the theophany. Job need no longer be bitter about a god who does not dispense the justice expected. That expectation turns out to be a form of cosmic self-indulgence, and its erasure takes away the divine agent one could be bitter against. To subdue the voices within and around us that project such a moral world order is, first, to overcome the existential bitterness that arises when one's virtue is not matched by divine reward and, second, to relieve the demand to convert victims of chance, fate, or human malevolence into scapegoats responsible for the fate they endure or strangers who have lost their right to the comforts and care of the community. Both responses are now exposed as violent tactics of self-protection against victims of bad luck (or human injustice) whose fate would otherwise call transcendental narcissism into doubt. The pious violence of the friends stands out in sharper relief when the vision of intrinsic moral order they endorse is interrogated by the voice in the whirlwind.

My reading of the Book of Job, then, finds the moral picture of the world to be unethical, striving to pry a gap between "morality" and "ethics" that remains to be clarified.[3] It is not, on this reading, that people are best construed as utterly devoid of responsibility for what they do to others or what happens to themselves, but the regulation of others is likely to be intensified and the attributions of responsibility to them to be inflated by those whose response to unorthodox acts, deviant beings, and surprising events is governed by the imperative to defend the vision of an intrinsic moral order.

The theophany, of course, does not dictate the interpretation given to it here. It simply enables it as one possibility to consider in competition with others. While the simple picture of a moral world order, entertained by the friends, seems confounded by the theophany, there is another version that might still be entertained. One might claim that Job and his friends had too simple, transparent a picture of moral order. They expected virtue as (they already understand it) to be matched by punishment and reward (as they already understand them). The theophany, however, might be construed to represent a more complex moral vision, one that appreciates how the god's design transcends the human will to comprehend it, even though human beings can profit immensely from dark signs of transcendent order inscribed in experience and scripture. While the reading endorsed here readily becomes a vision in which faith in divinity, understood in its usual valences, merges into respect for the prodigiousness, strangeness, and grandeur of nature, the "complex" reading of moral order preserves a persistent place for a mysterious divinity whose order one communes with while confessing severe limitations in one's prospects for comprehending it. Augustinianism is one form such an alternative perspective might assume.

Robert Gordis, treating the Book of Job as a critique of the "simple" concept of a moral order, preserves it as a defense of a complex one: "Just as there is order and harmony in the natural world, though imperfectly grasped by man, so there is order and meaning in the moral sphere, though often incomprehensible to man." [4] This retreat to an incomprehensible order protects the idea from devaluation under the hammer of experience, but it also confounds its ability to do very much work except through the authoritative interpretations of an organized priesthood. I support the first reading, then, the one that refuses to treat the god as a moral god, partly because this alternative resists powerful pressures structured into Western culture (and others too) to solidify the moral view by defining as heretics, enemies, sick beings, and evil agents those whose conduct or experience might otherwise destabilize it, partly because my wariness of the authority of priests is ecumenical. Others endorse a complex picture of moral order, partly because they doubt that any viable conception of collective identity and moral life can sustain itself unless it is attached to an external source of authority.

Job himself may leave both possibilities open for debate as he responds to the Voice from the whirlwind:

> I have spoken of the unspeakable
>     and tried to grasp the infinite. . . .
> I had heard of you with my ears;
>     but now my eyes have seen you.
> Therefore I will be quiet,
>     comforted that I am dust. (p. 88)

Is Job comforted amidst his suffering because he sees there is no point in railing against a god for the cosmic injustice of his fate? If you think of the theophany as a voice within him, it is possible to see how it teaches us to bear up under the pressures of contingency and bad luck by cultivating reverence for the beauty and energy of life flowing through and around us. It commends a struggle against the drive to existential resentment that so often haunts life. Does that mean that one must become resigned as well to those actions by the community that contribute to one's suffering? The poem does not respond to this issue, either by specifying closely which portion of Job's suffering flows from communal vindictiveness and which from bad luck or by suggesting very strongly how to sort out responses to his friends from those to his god.[5]

Nonetheless, a good case might be made in favor of a divided response. I might strive to overcome those resentments against my fate and my community that reflect existential resentment, while opposing undeserved burdens and sacrifices the community imposes upon others or me, including those imposed for the conscious or unconscious purpose of protecting the experience of correspondence between its particular organization of life and an intrinsic order of things. But which is which? The Book of Job does not settle that issue, while the multiple voices within it does suggest the value of keeping *this* debate alive.

Still, is not the contemporary insight to be drawn from Job's experience limited because of the radically different context in which it is set? Have "we" not outgrown (or "lost") the very concept of an intrinsic moral order forming the object of debate in Job? I have my doubts. An example closer to home may be pertinent.

## Alex/ina

*Herculine Barbin: Being the Recently Discovered Memoirs of a Nineteenth Century French Hermaphrodite* appeared about twenty-six centuries after the Book of Job.[6] It raises similar issues in a different setting. The autobiography, written around 1863, begins, "I am twenty-five years old, and, although I am still young, I am beyond any doubt approaching the hour of my death" (p. 3). Alex/ina was born to a poor mother in France in 1838. She was soon sent to a convent. She spent most of her youthful years under the tutelage of nuns and in association with other young girls receiving a religious education.

This text, too, has a prologue in which Michel Foucault, who unearthed it from dusty archives, poses the issue of the relation between sexuality and truth. It, too, contains an epilogue, consisting of journalistic reports, the opinions of judges, and the analyses of pathologists, designed to control the range of viable interpretations to be placed on the memoir. These three parts together (the prologue, the memoir, the epilogue) pose the issue of suffering by a modern who does not seem to fit either of the gender/sexual categories available to her.

Her? The first issue posed by this text is the appropriate terms of identification through which to characterize the struggle of Alex/ina. If that issue is not posed, the terms selected will resolve the interpretation before it is launched, for the text speaks to nameless sufferings of one who could not find a place of sexual residence in a culture that maps sexuality onto gender duality and gender duality onto nature. As the reader, responding to the pathos of the memoir, stumbles in deciding among the pronouns *he*, *she*, and *it*, which exhaust the legitimate range of cultural alternatives, this stumbling itself encourages one to ponder the role that the genderization of language plays—particularly in the instances of names and "personal" pronouns, but not there alone—in constituting the genders and sexualities to which it refers. I am not referring simply to the (now familiar) concern over the universal "he" that gives implicit superiority to men over women while claiming to be generic. But the very cultural imperative to say "he" *or* "she" every time a particular human is designated invokes gender as the first and primary mark of identification through which a self is to be characterized. This grammar, first, treats gender as the primary mode of individualization and, second, determines that gender must be divided into two and two only. The position of Alex/ina as Other in the community to which "she" belongs is thus more radical than that of Job in his. Alex/ina's ambiguous position is inscribed in the grammar of the community that constitutes "the hermaphrodite."

Do these terms map a preexisting terrain or do they provide the cultural key through which the terrain is mapped? Is the genderization of grammar part of the process by which gender is first divided and then invested with an intensity that helps to shape everything else in life? And is the naturalization of gender duality part of the process by which bodies and nature are discursively constituted when they are said to be represented? The encounter with Alex/ina suggests the latter possibility in each of these questions. I know of no way to respond to this possibility satisfactorily while remaining "true" to the grammar of genderization. So, I will use the name Alex/ina and the pronouns s/he, he/r in this section to characterize the author of this memoir and others as well, hoping by doing so to flag for a time at least how often these little words recur in discourse and how this repetitive grammaratization of names and pronouns constitutes a subterranean politics of genderization and sexualization demanding problematization.[7] Only a deployment of language that intervenes in the established grammar can begin to loosen the knots it ties.

Why must the knots be loosened? Because the exclusions and divisions sanctioned by those modalities produce sexual strangers required to sustain them? Because the social stabilization of gender duality sustains its purity, first, by translating unsettled differences and ambiguities within the self into definitive differences between selves and, second, by translating those recalcitrant to assimilation into either category into strange, sick, or monstrous beings to be suppressed, treated as mistakes of nature, or surgically repaired until they "fit" one category or the other?

We return, then, to the connection between Job and Alex/ina across all those centuries. They both suffer. They both become adversaries or strangers to their communities. And the definition of each as an adversary to be blamed seems to be bound up with the quest by each community to protect the sanctity of its identity from disturbance. Job suffers the double misfortune of a fate h/is community blames upon him, and h/is suffering is compounded further when h/is engagement with the putative author of that fate offends the sensibilities of h/is friends. Alex/ina suffers the even more intrusive rigors of adjustment to a grammaticocultural definition of gender/sexuality s/he confounds, and h/er suffering is intensified by efforts of friends to silence h/er or to help h/im find h/is true self.

After several years in a convent for young g/irls, studying diligently and entering into fugitive relations of love and pleasure with another student, Alex/ina's experience of h/er own desires and bodily composition, as they relate to h/er cultural expectations, become increasingly strained and filled with shame. "I suffered enormously from this sort of communal living. . . . I would have preferred to be able to hide myself from the sight of my kind companions, not because I wanted to shun them—I liked them too much for that—but because I was instinctively ashamed of the enormous distance that separated me from them, physically speaking" (p. 26). S/he does not fit, and s/he tries a variety of strategies to disguise this condition from others and h/erself.

H/er desires become problematic. At the age of nineteen s/he views h/erself as the only spectator at a bathing party in which everyone else, or so she assumes, is simply a participant. "Of course, they were far from suspecting what tumultuous feelings shook me as I watched their carefree behavior" (p. 39). Alex/ina is becoming a stranger to herself. And she senses that this strangeness would become a scandal and a humiliation if it were to become publicized.

H/er intense relationship with Sara, h/er illicit lover, pulls h/er to the abyss:

My God! Was I guilty? And must I accuse myself here of a crime? No, no! . . . That fault was not mine; it was the fault of an

unexampled fatality, which I could not resist!!! . . . What, in the
natural order of things, ought to have separated us in the world
had united us!!! Try to imagine, if that is possible, what our
predicament was for us both. (p. 51)

"The natural order of things"—Alex/ina affirms as natural an order that
would define h/er to be monstrous if s/he allows the thin veil protecting
h/er (non)identity to slide off. And s/he affirms as a fatality of nature her
inability to fit into this order. This natural order—this order of gender and
sex inscribed in nature—seems through the very desires it produces to
drive together two beings it is designed to separate. There is a fault in this
predicament, all right, but the text cannot settle upon its proper locus. That
is part of the predicament. If it were a willful "fault" in the conduct of the
two young g/irls, guilt would reside with them. If it were a "fault" in nature,
the very conception of nature as a gendered moral order would become
disturbed and shaken. Would guilt reside there? There is, then, a "predicament" here, one that exceeds available terms of specification, one that demands a place to locate fault but can locate only a series of faulty candi-
dates for the assignment. Perhaps, then, the fault resides in the slash? That
is, perhaps this new grammatical mark takes a step toward translating the
mark (lack, division) culturally imposed upon Alex/ina into a mark (lack,
insufficiency) within the grammar through which we are constituted?

The predicament of Alex/ina resonates with the quandary of Job. S/he
sometimes feels blameless, a pawn of fate, but the culture s/he (imperfectly) interiorizes demands that blame for this condition be found within
h/er. S/he can only appeal to the cultural legacy of original sin to resolve
this internal incoherence, appealing to "that feeling that is lodged in the
heart of every son of Adam. Was I guilty, criminal, because a gross mistake
had assigned me a place in the world that should not have been mine?" (p.
54).

What or who made this "gross mistake"? The thought of a *mistake* in
nature is the thought of a divine agent who makes it, or, at least, of an intrinsic design that occasionally lacks the capacity to realize this or that detail of its own architecture. But the thought of an agent powerful enough to
make *this* mistake does not seem congruent with it actually being thoughtless or weak or cruel enough to do so. Alex/ina, like Job, is moved to existential bitterness by a predicament that confounds the terms of reference
each had been taught to revere. H/er interrogative voice retains a place for
a providential god while it scrambles its previous understandings of the
divinity who fills this space. Multiple valences of "nature" pour out of the
text, as Alex/ina tries to pose the right question through which to define

this predicament. "Wasn't Nature being asked to make a heroic sacrifice, of which she was incapable?" (p. 72).

As the pressures mount, Alex/ina is driven to relieve them through confession. The mandate to confess defines the predicament to be a fault or rift within Alex/ina h/erself, rather than, say, a *dissonance* between the cultural configuration of gender normality and culturally inscribed bodies/desires that do not mesh uniformly with this contingent configuration. This interiorization of fault, it seems, defines the politics of confession. Anyway, given that no representatives of the culture come forward to confess arbitrary closure in its gender/sexual configuration, Alex/ina has little choice. S/he offers a confession under cultural duress (as most confessions are) in the hopes of relieving unbearable pressures within and without.

The first priest s/he selects to confess to is horrified by the predicament s/he reports. "It was not pity that I inspired in him; it was horror, a vindictive horror. . . . Instead of words of peace, he heaped scorn and insults upon me" (p. 55). This priest recalls Job's friends, readily enough.

Perhaps the suffering of Job and the suffering of Alex/ina are the same even while the occasions, the sites, and the grammars of the two vary. Each suffers initially from an effect experienced as fate. Each is then blamed to protect the community's cosmic vision of moral order. Job is blamed to protect the community's conception of moral divinity. Alex/ina is blamed because h/er indefinite sexuality and undergendered status—as perceived by authoritative bearers of the culture—threaten to destabilize the experience of gender/sexuality of those who stumble across it. Each is made into a stranger within its community to arrest the cultural destabilization it threatens.

Can you imagine a society in which gender practices are pluralized, say, according to undichotomized standards such as depth of voice, muscular proportions, and variations in percentages of selected hormones? In which the pronouns *he* and *she* are similarly pluralized? This alternative "genderization" of life would not function exactly as gender does now. Nor would it be a utopian condition. The point of gathering these criteria together under the rubric of "gender" might be to differentiate among members according to their probable capacity to engage in, say, arduous labor or military combat, and the cultural need for the old point of "gender" might recede through a series of shifts in technologies of erotic pleasure, conception, and reproduction. The new gender distinctions would overlay the old ones; the old ones might become subordinate voices within the new. There might even be a discernible history of development here in which the new mode is recognizable as an evolution of old practices, and in which the old practices persist as a subordinate feature of the new. The result would be a shift in the practice of gender rather than a replacement of gender by something else altogether. The differences and connections between old and new gender practices would be comparable, say, to those between polytheism and monotheism, only in this case the ."poly" would be the later development.

It is unimportant at the moment whether you would prefer the hypothetical practice to the existing one. Not liking arduous labor myself and being resistant to military combat, I am not drawn to the social priorities this alternative order would reflect. But if you can even imagine such a *possibility*, it helps to expose the role of convention in the construction of gender today and to suggest how sexual and gender strangers are now produced to protect the mapping of gender primacy and duality onto nature.[8] Even the thought of a new possibility, as Nietzsche says, can shake and transform thought. Think, he says, of how thought of the very possibility of eternal damnation transformed the terms of thought for centuries, and, I will add, how it was illegitimate for centuries to treat this revealed truth explicitly as a mere possibility open to debate.

With this thought experiment before us, the vindictiveness and horror in the voice of the first priest can now be heard as a sign of anxiety, an anxiety that will authorize any act of repression to ward off the intensification of self-doubt about correspondence between the cultural map of gender and its natural design. Other voices signify this anxiety in their own way in turn. It is pertinent to note, however, that this priestly horror is not simply self-serving in a narrow sense of that term. The first priest understands that if Alex/ina publicizes this condition in any way in the current cultural setting s/he will become an object of scandal and censure. *If* the cultural practices of gender are untouchable, perhaps it is best to press h/er to re-press the predicament and to live silently with this dissonance. The first premise may remain unthought by the priest, but once it is unconsciously assumed a modicum of concern for the fate of Alex/ina is discernible in h/is hardness. H/e is caught in a bind too.

The next priest Alex/ina consults is kindly and solicitous. H/is counsel:

> You are here and now entitled to call yourself a man in society.
> Certainly you are, but how will you obtain the legal right to do so.
> At the price of great scandal, perhaps. . . . And so the advice I am
> giving you is this: withdraw from the world and become a nun;
> but be very careful not to repeat the confession that you have
> made to me, for a convent of women would not admit you. This is
> the only course that I propose to you, and believe me, accept it.
> (p. 62)

The cultural code of gender primacy/duality is so powerful that Alex/ina *must* be defined as a man or a woman. Because s/he has experienced gender uncertainty as a woman, s/he must be treated as a man whose natural gender was misidentified at birth. This is the first "must." But the cultural line of division between genders is so precarious in its definiteness, so fragile in its fixity, that an inevitable scandal will follow if Alex/ina switches from one side to the other. Alex/ina, the kindly priest decides, must hide out in a nunnery, where those most devout in their worship of this author of moral order reside. This is the second "must."

Horror and kindness; the imperative of a gender switch and the counsel to conceal a previous misidentification; the fear of scandal and the necessity of bearing up under it—these contradictory pairs set the shifting combinations through which Alex/ina is treated by h/er best friends for the rest of h/is life. Each combination dissolves as a viable strategy as soon as its inner dissonances become apparent, but no response can be devised that escapes these terms within the existing cultural matrix. Sophocles might have a field day with this predicament. But Alex/ina is a Christian writer, and, besides, s/he is the one who must bear up under the effects s/he records.

This particular predicament continues, but the problematic role of culture in its definition becomes increasingly more audible. The theophany in the Book of Job—with its (possible) refusal to inscribe a moral design into nature or to treat it as a plastic field that human initiative can reorder at will—may prepare one to disturb the cultural code through which Alex/ina is constituted, treated, and reconstituted. Alex/ina is a real person living in the nineteenth century. But s/he is also a metaphor for a more general murmur of artifice in the cultural constitution of gender duality. The eye of the crocodile, the whirlwind, Alex/ina, the ambiguity of "nature," the insufficiency of grammar: these are metaphors through which subterranean, fugitive experiences of strangeness within cultural configurations might disturb those persistent economies of grammar, moral order, and self-identity.

Things move fast for Alexina after s/he confesses. Suspicions mount against h/er as h/e refuses to heed the kindly priest's advice. A doctor is called in when pain in the abdominal area becomes severe. No priestly stuff from this worldly professional—h/e examines the patient's genitals and promptly announces Alex/ina to be male. H/e then encourages Alex/ina's distraught mother by saying, "It's true that you've lost your daughter . . . , but you've found a son whom you were not expecting" (p. 78).

Alex/ina becomes redefined through a medical examination. H/e becomes a man. The predicted scandal sets in. H/e is sent to Paris. And h/e soon prepares for suicide as h/e finds that the human relationships available to h/im on this side of the gender ledger do not mesh with interiorized expectations of emotional tonality, routines of friendship, intimate relations, and personal demeanor either. Alex/ina is thus subjected to a "terrible, nameless punishment" (p. 93) in which the agents are faceless, the crimes unspecified, and the carriers of punishment often unwitting.

Alex/ina is driven to reject the simple concept of a moral world order through the suffering h/e endures. "The world that you invoke," h/e says to himself in the memoir, "was not made for you. You were not made for it. In this vast universe where every grief has its place, you shall search in vain for a corner. . . . It overturns all the laws of nature and humanity" (pp. 98–99). "Where every grief has its place"—in confessing the absence of fit between h/is constitution and the cultural definition of gender normality, h/e retreats to a more complex conception of moral order, one that promises to deliver h/im from a grief that has no place in *this* world:

> Oh, death! Death will truly be the hour of deliverance for me!
> Another wandering Jew, I await it as the most frightful of all
> torments!!! But you remain to me, my God! You have willed that I
> belong to no one here below, through none of those earthly
> bonds that elevate man by perpetuating Your divine work! Though
> I am a sad disinherited creature, I can still lift up my eyes to You,
> for You at least will not reject me. (p. 93)

Alex/ina officially dies by h/is ow/n hand, though many other hands participate in the preparation of this act. Unlike Job, h/e seeks refuge in the Christian theme of an afterlife in which the experience of natural injustice in this world might be rectified by a god whose providence surpasses the comprehension of those whose suffering seems to "overturn the laws of nature and humanity." No theophany for Alex/ina. No reflection on the diversity of nature and the role of cultural artifice in gender identity. No drive to politicize the naturalization of cultural artifacts. Faith in divine justice in the last instance is wheeled out to replace Jobian affirmation of a world in which no divine hand orders earthly life according to a moral recipe of justice, natural identity, reward and desert. Job remains pertinent to the life and death of Alex/ina, but unavailable to h/im. And does Alex/ina not remain pertinent to the experience of J/ob?

In the absence of a politics that might denaturalize the cultural map of gender and sexuality, suicide emerges as the only viable line of escape for Alex/ina.

## Critical Pluralism

A political constellation informed by (contestable) Jobian presumptions might explore multiple possibilities for life, pleasure, affection, and social relations exceeding the cultural script already in place. It might acknowledge the indispensability of culture to life while affirming the imperative for political contestation of closures in particular cultural matrixes. The paradox of culture, it might suggest, demands a culture in which politicization of fixed maps of identity and nature is a recurrent cultural phenomenon. Such a response discerns strains of unethicality running through these moralities of natural order and gender normality. It observes how scandal is deployed to reassure a culture when its naturalized practices become disturbed by surprising beings, unexpected actions, and unpredicted events. It might contest these terms of self-reassurance by exposing the role that sacrifice plays in fixing the dogmatism of identity. But these sentences are utopian gestures.

I mean to say that these sentences are utopian in the context under review without discounting the role of politics in defining the suffering of both Job and Alex/ina. Each encounter is already marked by the politics of the community in which it occurs. We have discerned this already in the political responses of friends, priests, and doctors to the suffering of both. But this politics of communal self-protection continues after Job and Alex/ina die. We continue to read these exemplary texts, seeking to learn from them; and the epilogues appended to them by authoritative priests continue to police the legitimate implications to be drawn from them. Fortunately, this editorial policing of exemplary texts is susceptible to counterpolicing.

Who knows who penned the brief epilogue to the Book of Job, or when it was written? Its relation to the poem preceding it seems clear: it is designed to domesticate the reading of the explosive text to which it is appended.

The epilogue, four paragraphs long, restores a moral conception of the world by means of a simple reversal: it preserves the divine calculus of reward and punishment by converting Job into its beneficiary and the friends into recipients of divine punishment. The Lord instructs the three friends "to take seven bulls and seven rams and go to my servant Job and offer a sacrifice of yourselves. My servant Job will pray for you, and for his sake I will overlook your sin" (p. 91). By submitting to the total power of his god and recognizing the unfathomable morality of its justice, Job passes the test of loyalty and earns his reward—or so the epilogue insists. It stills the politics of interpretation by appending an official ending to a disturbing story. The "Job" it inscribes is divinely rewarded for endorsing a complex view of moral order; alternative lessons are repressed or muted by the rewards it presents to Job in the name of its god.

The epilogue is the political statement of the dominant community of believers. It protects the conception of moral order that reassures them by justifying divine punishment for the very representatives of the community who brought the original message from the community to Job. It creates a new set of scapegoats to preserve its old faith by clarification. The poet, on my reading, would boil over in h/er grave as Job is divinely showered with sheep, camels, oxen, donkeys, new sons, the most beautiful daughters in "all the world," and a healthy life lasting 140 years. The epilogue depoliticizes the problem of evil by placing a moral calculator in the hands of an inscrutable agent of rewards and penalties. The moral god thus returns, this time as a less fathomable rewarder and punisher, one who needs authoritative priests even more than before to draw the community into close proximity to its mysterious moral order.

While the Book of Job ends with an epilogue that mutes (but does not silence) the most powerful voice it introduces onto the theological register, *Herculine Barbin* closes with one in which secular journalists, a mayor, and pathologists join priests in *pronouncing* the gender of Alex/ina. Does this epilogue, consisting mostly of secular documents, contest the theological message enunciated by the priests and seconded by Alex/ina in the memoir? Many of the pronouncements exude sympathy for the victim, and while some commentators continue to foment scandal, others condemn or surpass it. None, however, tries to contest the map that plots sexuality upon gender duality and gender duality upon nature.

A report by E. Goujon included in the epilogue, published in a journal of human anatomy and physiology in France after the case of Alex/ina became a medical issue, typifies the scientific judgment of the case. Goujon begins by describing a "young man" employed in railroad administration who "committed suicide by asphyxiating himself with carbon dioxide in a wretched room located on the sixth floor of a house" (p. 128). The sympathy with which h/is plight is characterized almost buries the definiteness with which h/is gender is eventually delineated. It is not as though the author doubts there is a "mixture" of some sort here. "In fact, it is difficult . . . to discover a more extreme mixture of the two sexes, as concerns everything relating to the external genital organs" (p. 129).

The report delineates the relevant organs in precise language:

> As we shall see later, this organ was a large clitoris rather than a
> penis; in fact, among women we sometimes see the clitoris attain
> the size of the index finger. As he tells us in his memoirs, it was
> possible for the erection to be accompanied by an ejaculation and
> voluptuous sensations. . . . A vagina ending in a cul-de-sac . . .
> allowed him to play the feminine role also in the act of coitus. To
> this vagina, which was located where it ordinarily is in a woman,
> were annexed two vulvovaginal glands that opened at the vulva,
> on either side, and each next to a little duct that served for the
> emission or ejaculation of sperm. (p. 132)

A scientific description followed by an authoritative medical determination of gender and sexuality—the memoir of the human who lived, loved, suffered, and died with the genitals so described is noted, but only insofar as its characterization of those organs corresponded to the culturally received vocabulary governing the analysis. The specific conjunctions in Alex/ina's life (the years in the convent, the relationships s/he established and interiorized, the literary education s/he received, the contingent structure of desire and habit organized through these conjunctions) is not considered relevant. *Gender* is not a term thought to be open to revision through reconstituted cultural practices. Even more pertinent, the way in which the medical description of organs is drawn from the vocabulary of a culture in which gender duality is lodged firmly in the assumptions of vocabulary is not noted as an element in the analysis capable of disturbing or destabilizing the terms of physiological characterization. The imperative governing the scientific report is to characterize Alex/ina so as to retain confidence that (almost) everyone else corresponds nicely to a natural division between two genders. This division must be naturalized, so that culturally en-gendered terms of bodily inscription cannot be disrupted or shaken through the multiplication of possibilities that scramble them, so that people will not be pressed to interrogate the confident correspondence between the cultural organization that inhabits them and an intrinsic purpose in nature taken to precede it, so that no cultural space will be pried open to create opportunity for "others"—including perhaps the other within oneself—to define modes of life and affectional relations that scramble and pluralize established terms of heterosexual normality and gender duality. The epilogue is a series of exercises in metaphysical reassurance to prevailing cultural practices of sexuality and gender. It is an exercise in power all the more effective because it takes itself to be a neutral representation.

Where, in the domain of gender, does cultural determination end and "raw" nature begin? Nobody knows, and probably no one ever will,[9] but everybody often purports to know. Or, better, *everyone* often invokes a vocabulary inscribed with the mark of this confidence; and most people regularly invoke such a vocabulary with utmost confidence in its sufficiency. The authoritative accounts in the epilogue presuppose the possibility of separating culture and biology into component parts and drawing them back together into a definitive report, while the report itself reveals the impossibility of doing so. The typical political effect of this vocabulary/practice is to produce strangers and scapegoats sacrificed to the altar of an unexamined faith in an intrinsic moral order of gender and sex.

Is the horror Alex/ina encountered in the first priest still detectable within the detached description and kindly manner of the doctor's words?

Listen to the faith of Goujon as he smooths over the disturbing fact that there are "numerous cases" of the sort represented by Alex/ina:

> It would be easy to multiply examples of this kind, and it would even be profitable to science if all the documents that it possesses on this question were brought together . . . , which would become a precious guide for doctors who are called upon to give their opinions and pronounce a judgment concerning people who have been stricken with this kind of anomaly. It would be readily apparent from this work . . . , that if it is sometimes difficult and even impossible to identify the true sex of an individual at the time of birth, it is not the same at a more advanced age, and especially at the approach of puberty. In fact, at this time, inclinations and habits of their true sex are revealed in people who have been victims of an error, and observing those traits would help considerably in marking out their place in society, if the state of the genital organs and their different functions were not sufficient for attaining this end. (pp. 138–39)

Goujon is concerned about the (all too?) numerous cases of people "stricken with this anomaly," but not with the cultural definition of gender that treats these numerous "cases" as anomalies, that is, as mistakes in nature deviating from a design intrinsic to it. That is why surgery presents itself so readily to him as the sufficient response, once the "true sex" of each anomaly has been discerned. He does not ask whether surgery *could* be so precise and extensive, first, to bring innumerable culturally defined elements of bodily composition into alignment with this truth and, second, to draw these elements into consistent correspondence with the contingent development of desires, inclinations, social expectations, and affectional possibilities in particular individuals. He never asks, with Michel Foucault, "Must we *truly* have a *true* sex?" When Goujon writes the scientist/doctor has begun to displace the priest as the culture's guardian of metaphysical comfort, and he plays that new role very nicely.

Is it possible to translate Job and Alex/ina from the discourse of wrongdoers/victims/anomalies/mistakes/rebels deviating from an intrinsic god/nature/norm/virtue/piety into a discourse of signs/metaphors/examples/disturbances calling into question simultaneously the ethicality of conceptions of intrinsic moral order and nature as a plastic medium of human action? If the purposes and effects of the "friends" in such cases were interrogated more actively and impiously, might it be possible to nurture a politics in which the dynamic of cultural reassurance through the production and reproduction of strangers is contested? What if strangeness were treated by more people as indispensable to identity in a world without intrinsic moral design, and, hence, something to be prized as a precondition of identity and a source of possibilities for selective alliances and more generous negotiations with others? And what if more adherents of an intrinsic moral order were to acknowledge the deep and persistent contestability of this projection (along with those that oppose it) so as to allow this issue to become a more overt object of political negotiation and contestation?

Could we create a politics of generous negotiation/coalition/contestation with friends and strangers through cultivation of strangeness residing within our own identities? And a politics of generosity toward the strangeness in ourselves through attentiveness to whirlwinds within and without? Not a generosity growing out of the unchallengeable privilege of a superior social position and moral ontology, but one emerging from enhanced appreciation of dissonances within our own identities and of persistent implication in the differences through which we are consolidated. A refigured generosity.

Does this combination suggest a political pluralism? Perhaps, but not that flat pluralism in which diversity expands indefinitely without imprinting profound effects on the cultural experience of identity and difference. In agonistic pluralism, each constituency would acknowledge its own identity to be bound up with a variety of differences sustaining it. Each identity depends on the differences it constitutes, and each attempt to define identity through difference encounters disturbing responses by those who challenge the sufficiency or dignity of its definition of them. Each identity is fated, thereby, to contend—to various degrees and in multifarious ways—with others it depends upon to enunciate itself. That's politics. The issue is not if, but how.

In a politics of critical or agonistic pluralism, each acknowledges the case for self-restriction in the way it contests those disturbing differences it opposes and depends upon. One aggregate effect of such engagements, collisions, and restrictions is the provision of new political spaces through which to engage strangeness in oneself and others. The aggregate effect of these relations of interdependence and strife, when enough of those engaged in them appreciate the case for self-restriction amidst conflict, may open new spaces for politics and freedom, for freedom resides in the spaces produced by such dissonant conjunctures. It is always fugitive and precarious.

Even fundamentalists—who treat the faith that guides them to be a universal truth and who protect their fundaments by defining every constituency that disturbs their self-confidence as deviant—can participate in such relations of complementary dissonance, to the extent, first, they acknowledge how their own faith appears contestable and offensive in some respects from other points of view, and to the degree, second, they affirm restrictions in the ways they press their demands in the light of this first awareness. Yet, it must be admitted, in the (highly utopian) world of critical pluralism fundamentalists would run the greatest risk of becoming radical strangers. And fundamentalist dispositions inhabit all of us: they are inscribed in the condensations of shared vocabularies, in the obduracy of habit, in the institutionalization of established assumptions, in valiant struggles against mortality, in drives to revenge against those who have jeopardized the self-confidence of our identity most recently, and in a variety of other political tactics through which we reassure ourselves in what we are. The voice of the friends and the priests, my friends, always circulates through and around us, though it may be possible to soften, stretch, politicize, and disturb its insistences to a greater degree.

To say even this much is to admit considerable distance between contemporary democracies and the impossible world of critical pluralism. It is to affirm that such a critical perspective functions mostly as a launching pad from which genealogies of contemporary normality are developed, fixed presumptions about "nature" are disturbed, criticisms of established codes of diversity are pursued, and alternatives for political change are pressed. It does not delineate an ideal susceptible to complete actualization,[10] for any particular form pluralism assumes is itself susceptible to critical strategies of disturbance and deconstruction, partly because its crucial components never fit together as a coherent set at any single time. Thus, at any moment there is always something to be done on behalf of critical pluralism.

Critical pluralism is best presented, then, as a valuable cultural impossibility always susceptible to new possibilities of political operationalization. It is not a sufficient political ideal, but an indispensable component in an admirable ethic of politics. It stands or falls as a critical principle through its ability to expose how advocates of the normal individual and the integrated community (among others) complement one another in concealing violence against the many "Jobs" and "Alex/inas" they produce. And it stands or falls as an ethical spirituality through its capacity to make us ashamed of how dominant identities congratulate themselves through the production and naturalization of strangers. The theophany in the Book of Job suggests possibilities in this regard, without pursuing them. Corollary possibilities are suggested, first, by Michel Foucault's prologue to *Herculine Barbin* and, second, by the subtext of Alex/ina's memoir. When these disparate texts are read together in response to contemporary definitions of nature, identity, responsibility, gender, morality, community, sexuality, monotheism, and secularism—that is, in the context within which this reading has been set all along—subterranean voices become more audible on behalf of the politicization of cultural mechanisms through which strangers are produced and subjugated.

## Notes

1. *The Book of Job*, trans. Stephen Mitchell (San Francisco: North Point, 1987), 6. I use this recent translation partly because it is convenient for use in undergraduate classes, partly because it is refreshing in certain places, and partly because its very newness underlines the continuing process of translation and interpretation in this area. Future quotations from this text will be cited by page numbers in the body of the chapter.

2. Do I project an author into the text? Yes, that is part of the interpretive strategy I am adopting. That is not to say that I know, from independent studies written about "the author," things about him, her, or them, but that my reading of the story includes a projection into the presumptions and moods of the storyteller(s) that may as well be stated rather than hidden. Can other interpretations avoid some such set of implicit or explicit projections? I doubt it.

3. I will not develop this part of the thesis further in this essay. The theme is pursued in William E. Connolly, *Identity\Difference: Democratic Negotiations of Political Paradox* (Ithaca, N.Y.: Cornell University Press, 1991), especially the introduction and chaps. 5–6.

4. See Robert Gordis, *The Book of God and Man: A Study of Job* (Chicago: University of Chicago Press, 1965). Gordis first emphasizes the repudiation of the "anthropomorphic" God in the theophany and then tries to recapture as much of it as possible. "Just as there is order and harmony in the natural world, though imperfectly grasped by man, so there is order and meaning in the moral sphere, though often incomprehensible to man" (p. 133). My reading is closer to that offered by John T. Wilcox, *The Bitterness of Job: A Philosophical Reading* (Ann Arbor: University of Michigan Press, 1989).

5. In *Job: the Victim of His People* (Stanford, Calif.: Stanford University Press, 1987), René Girard argues that Job's suffering is caused by human agents in his own community who envy the authority, reputation, and well-being he has acquired. Their punishment of him is a precondition of their own community and of the closure of dangerous rivalry among them. I find some plausibility in Girard's interpretation, but I also find his symptomatic reading of the text to be too closed and dogmatic. He is certain that all other readings are further symptoms of the sacrificial mentality he opposes. To put the point too briefly, Girard places the "sacrificial crisis" in the (Lacanian) realm of the imaginary, making it too universal and inevitable; he ignores symbolic/discursive modes through which it can be challenged, modified, sublimated, and resisted. In this reading, I want to focus on the relation between political theology and the production of scapegoats regardless of whether the initial suffering is caused by the community or by bad luck. For a book that enunciates the general structure of the Girardian reading of myth, see his *Violence and the Sacred*, trans. Patrick Gregory (Baltimore: Johns Hopkins University Press, 1977). For an excellent critique of Girard's treatment of the Gospels as the definitive recognition and resolution of the logic of sacrifice, see Lucien Scubla, "The Christianity of Rene Girard and the Nature of Religion" in *Violence and Truth*, ed. Paul Dumochel (Stanford, Calif.: Stanford University Press, 1988), 160–78.

6. *Herculine Barbin: Being the Recently Discovered Memoirs of a Nineteenth Century French Hermaphrodite*, introduced by Michel Foucault, trans. Richard McDougall (New York: Pantheon, 1980).

7. Judith Butler, *Gender Trouble: Feminism and the Subversion of Identity* (New York: Routledge, l990), presents the most compelling analysis of this text with which I am familiar. Butler introduces the s/he, h/er terms without commenting on their role in the discourse. Her reading of *Herculine Barbin* is exemplary and I am indebted to it. However, I do not think that Butler's critique of Foucault is quite so compelling, for I do not read Foucault to attribute

to Alex/ina a natural sexuality before the officials tried to reconstitute it. Rather, these "nameless" and "furtive" "pleasures" were socially constituted too; it is just that they were more satisfying for the being constituted by them than the later definitions in that they did not, for instance, suggest suicide as the only line of escape from an impossible life. The general problems posed by the question as to whether one presupposes a conception of "nature" one cannot know to be true are endless; the regresses it generates are infinite. Whatever one says, one appears to constitute a new nature/culture divide ("satisfying," "a being") on a terrain where any such discursive division is always problematic, for the new formulation always draws upon the culture and its grammar one seeks to dig below. One might say, then: the division is both indispensable and problematic, and every formulation that invokes a specific version of it can be problematized through a subsequent gesture. I doubt very much, anyway, that this ambiguity can simply be dispensed with. If not, this condition itself opens every text to the charge that it reinstates its version of the division unthinkingly while criticizing its formation by others. (Or that it installs a new version covertly while pretending to dispense with it.) I have earlier considered the role that the introduction of a text such as *Herculine Barbin* might play in genealogy as a mode of social critique in "Where the Word Breaks Off," in *Politics and Ambiguity* (Madison: University of Wisconsin Press, 1987), chap. 10. The theme there might be summarized in this formulation: "We insist that bodies fit into the duality we impose upon them and act as if we report actuality inscribed in nature. We then treat bodies that differ from these impositions as deviations from the telos of nature" (p. 156).

8. Why do I introduce a possibility I do not endorse to make the point about the constructed character of an identity that has become (always imperfectly) naturalized? Well, partly because I am not writing in this instance about a social position I myself inhabit in a paradigmatic way; I am, rather, striving to open up *responsiveness* to it from an experience containing its own murmurs of dissonance within itself. The "critical pluralism" I will (shortly) endorse as a critical principle is one in which new spaces are produced for alternatives to consolidate themselves and to contest established closures, rather than one in which those outside a particular constituency legislate in advance the form *its* empowerment must take. The point is to expand one's (our) possibilities of responsiveness in some cases while pressing one's (our) own agenda in others. Still, it may be whispered in some circles, "What are you, a 'white,' 'straight,' 'male' 'with tenure,' 'over fifty,' 'teaching at a quasi-elite eastern university' doing on this terrain anyway?" The reply: "Well, Jack, your question reduces me to a set of prefixed categories, either to reassure you in your own dogmatism of identity or, alternatively, to elevate your radicalism to such a height that no one else can climb up there. If you are conservative carrier of 'identity politics,' your characterization reduces me to a self-hating male, professor, etc.; if a radical identitarian, to an inauthentic ally. But, you see, these categories do not quite exhaust me, and hence the alternatives you present do not suffice. Either way, you remain too much of a fundamentalist for my taste, and your politics are too self-encased to be very promising. These categories you enunciate, though, do touch me. Since they enter (differentially along with others you 'forget') into my 'subject position,' as it is constituted in this society, they should be taken into account in the way my responsiveness is articulated." My life experience has encouraged me to move from an appreciation of "Job" to an enhanced sense of the social constitution of "Alex/ina," and thus of the social constitution of my own gender experience, while others might find this trajectory reversed. It is where these two paths *cross* that interesting political possibilities reside, that distinctive alliances and coalitions might become constructible. One point of political reflection, as I see it, is to open up possibilities for alliance where primarily identity and strangeness were before, to pluralize new points of intersection so that the old fixtures of politics become more open to modification. May everyone resist the "subject position" impressed upon them by conservative and radical carriers of identity politics.

9. Judith Butler puts this point succinctly: "Is there a 'physical' body prior to the perceptually perceived body? An impossible question to decide. Not only is the gathering of attributes under the category of sex suspect, but so is the very discrimination of the 'features themselves' "; *Gender Trouble*, 114. I merely add that the introduction of any positive political alternative inevitably invokes presumptions at this level. The appropriate response to this ambiguity, I think, is to make the best *comparative* interpretive case available for the Jobian (as in my case) reading of nature and to resist the persisting temptation to elevate that interpretation into an incontestable discovery of the natural condition itself. To keep *this* irony alive, I want to say, is to appreciate the paradoxical element in politics and to enact one precondition of critical pluralism.

10. I have discussed some of the issues posed in this paragraph more extensively in *Identity\Difference*. Others, most significantly the status of an ethic appropriate to these issues in a world where the thematic of intrinsic moral order is contested, will appear in "Beyond Good and Evil: The Ethical Sensibility of Michel Foucault," *Political Theory* (May 1993).

Chapter 11

# Ecotones and Environmental Ethics:
# Adorno and Lopez

Romand Coles

Hegel, in one of his many perceptive moments, described the modern age as the site of a continual struggle between faith and enlightenment.[1] Put simply, the enlightenment attempts to posit the self as the ground of truth and being, while faith seeks truth and being in terms of a larger absolute Being in which it is submerged, by an act of pure faith in the beyond. The struggle between these two positions is seemingly interminable because, to the embarrassment of each, neither can address the penetrating claims of the other. Reason and the self are themselves principles in which the enlightenment has *faith*, and the enlightenment (increasingly) is aware of the emptiness and weakness of its efforts to come to terms with the larger whole in which it finds itself. Faith, on the other hand, is always making *arguments* and continually discovering (and unable to account for) the unsightly aspects of the self and reason in its own voice. The erosive effects of each with regard to the other diminishes their respective persuasive powers but offers little that is truly constructive. While Hegel brilliantly sketches the terrain upon which we are still struggling two hundred years hence, his solution, the movement toward absolute Spirit, has satisfied few.

Often the various philosophical and practical efforts to come to terms with the ecological crisis exemplify how stuck we are in the dynamic Hegel described. On the one hand we find a pervasive discourse that sticks very closely to the contours of enlightenment. Here, in works like Ophuls's *Ecology and the Politics of Scarcity*, we find affirmed a reason that is essentially instrumental and rooted in the primacy of the survival of the self—in this case the entire human species.[2] Though Ophuls and the genre to which he belongs advocate ethical value changes that would embrace a larger whole, their *reasons for doing so* are instrumental: these new values are ultimately grounded in the self (either individual or social), whose singular survival and ethical centrality remain privileged and unquestioned starting points. Richard Watson exemplifies this reasoning when he writes, "There are very good reasons for thinking ecologically, and . . . to preserve a rich and balanced planetary ecology: human survival depends on it."[3] On this reading it is senseless mysticism to speak in ethical terms whose significance transcends the human realm.

In marked contrast to this is a discourse that submerges itself in and privileges a totality beyond a self that had long been viewed as the locus of value and good sense. Though a variety of voices resound from this position, "deep ecologists" such as Sessions, Devall, and Naess have attempted to gather them together around this theme: "The 'real work' can be summarized symbolically as the realization of self-in-Self where 'Self' stands for organic wholeness."[4] The self finally finds its meaning with respect to a mothering totality. Within this Self, all beings are endowed with "equal intrinsic worth." While we can do much to conceptualize the factual interrelations between beings and the whole, finally, the ethical insights are grounded in "meditative intuitions" of "Earth wisdom,"[5] which in my view closely approximate Hegel's "faith."

I do not mean to dismiss flatly either of these positions; valuable insights have emerged from both, and in the margins of these texts one often finds voices that go beyond their central themes. Yet on the whole they tend to be philosophically and practically unsatisfying. On one hand, they lead to a reductive instrumental rationality that perpetuates a logic deeply entwined with our current ecological and social crises. On the other hand, they lead to a vague holism that offers few persuasive arguments—claims that might allow us to develop basic, specific ethical impulses with at least a modicum of intelligibility, coherence, and sufficient space for distinct selves. Both positions (Ophuls's instrumentalism and the deep ecologists' holism) are dangerous in that they perpetuate the hubris—reason's and faith's—that has led to so many human and ecological disasters throughout history.[6] Instrumental reason's hubris is to place the self at the center in a way that ceaselessly threatens to objectify totally the surrounding world—no matter how intricate and interconnected it conceives this world to be. Faith's hubris is to believe that its "meditative intuitions" constitute a pipeline between it and Truth, and this truth is frequently conceived in terms of a totalizing system of Being within which all beings have a place they must occupy in perfect harmony with all others. This frequently leads to a dogmatic intolerance, an insistence upon consensus without regard to what this eclipses and, generally, little space to appreciate as fundamentally valuable contestations about the order of things. In short, both positions tend toward imperialistic orders of things that a priori reduce that which is "other" to nothingness and error—all to be brought into Being through subjugation or conversion.

In this essay I explore an agonistic dialogical alternative to this terrain through the works of Theodore Adorno and Barry Lopez. The latter's writings allow us to exemplify and in some ways deepen the work of the former; the former allows us to ponder in more general terms ideas that emerge very specifically in the latter. In both cases what emerges is not a set of absolute starting points, principles, or categorical imperatives, but rather something like a *theory of ecological judgment*—a set of agonistic concerns that Adorno and Lopez suggest we must keep in mind if we are to think and act on earth in ways that are conducive to intelligence, freedom, and fecundity.

I should note from the beginning that by *agonistic dialogue* and *agonistic concerns* I do not mean to gesture toward relations whose elements are antagonistic or fundamentally opposed to each other. Rather, I refer to the interminglings, conversations, and negotiations that continually must be pursued between diverse beings. These beings, in their radical otherness, are captured neither by the logic of identity nor that of contradiction, but rather require the difficult elaboration of overlappings, tensions, and paradoxes—all of which are too multiplicitous to ever be reduced. "Agonism" calls us to situate our selves thoughtfully in the midst of the wildly multiplicitous. It refers to a site and a way of inhabiting a site—both of which are conditions of possibility for ecological judgment. I will begin by sketching briefly a couple of essays that point toward a dialogical alternative to the terrain depicted by Hegel. I follow with a more thorough discussion of Adorno and Lopez. I am not interested in discovering the "original intent" of the latter two writers' work, but rather in appropriating it in order to explore an ecological theory of judgment, an environmental ethic.

## Toward a Dialogical Ecological Ethos

Some theorists are beginning to probe beyond modernity's exhausted terrain toward a dialogical view of the relations between the self and the world that breaks with the enlightenment/faith split. One such gesture in this direction comes from John Tallmadge's essay on Buber. In contrast to a technological perspective that approaches the world as an "It," Tallmadge seeks to embrace the world and its beings as a "You" with a dimension of personhood and conceives of the self in a thoroughly relational manner. Following Buber, he understands this relation to originate in a bodily presence in which I and You reciprocally confront one another in the sheer specificity and wholeness of their beings. While this is an interesting start, like Buber, Tallmadge equivocates about the I-You relation, sometimes viewing it as conceptually mediated (as when we view a tree in terms of historical geography), sometimes viewing it as an absolute mystical presence "devoid of qualities." [7] The outcome of this ambiguity is that while his depictions of the awakening one experiences while backpacking are not without inspiration, the dialogical moment either remains purely a mystical presence or involves a conceptual dimension that is unclarified. We are left without a very textured account of what a dialogical relation with the earth might look like.[8] This lack of texture hinders the development of an ecological ethics through which we might improve our relations with the complex earth we inhabit. The latter task calls us to develop the conceptual dimensions of our dialogical relations with the biosphere and beings that are not predisposed to fit neatly into our language. What might a dialogue with the extralinguistic look like?

David Abram's essay "Merleau-Ponty and the Voice of the Earth" takes another step toward a dialogical ethos that begins to address this question. Abram elaborates Merleau-Ponty's notion that "the Earth is the soil or stem of our thought as it is of our life" by discussing our bodily and perceptual intertwining with the world that surrounds us.[9] His description of our bodily participation with the world decenters language from its location in the brain of humans and seeks its emergence in our prelinguistic sensual immersion in the biosphere. "If language is born of our carnal *participation* in a world that already *speaks to us* at the most immediate level of sensory experience, then language does not belong to humankind but to the sensible world of which we are a part." [10] Indeed, it is the world that expresses itself in language on Abram's reading, and hence he speaks of an "Eco-logos." [11]

Yet, while illustrating Merleau-Ponty's dissolution of the dichotomy between language and earth, and thereby providing a deep philosophical basis for some sort of communication between them, Abram does not sufficiently explore (though he does not exclude) the dimension of distance and discord that Merleau-Ponty correctly identifies even in the midst of our intertwining with the world. Merleau-Ponty writes that as inexhaustible "depth," things in the world around us are "beings at a distance." [12] I paradoxically find myself entwined in the same world with them and yet I cannot overcome the distance between myself and them, which maintains them in their transcendent otherness — their inexhaustible being. Merleau-

Ponty's world and beings are incredibly protean, harboring an open richness only the smallest parts of which are revealed to us.[13]

That I am simultaneously in the world and always at a distance means
that though in important and paradoxical ways I speak to the world and the
world speaks to and through me, our conversation is never rid of a significant element of discord and difficulty. Our peculiar intertwining with the
world enables profound expressions of things to emerge, but it also implicates us in perceptual and conceptual transgressions. Perception is "a
violent act."[14] The "sensible" forms through the participation between our
body and the world across distant depths. Yet the sensible always partly
transgresses the world it expresses: "What is proper to the sensible (as to
language) is to be representative of the whole . . . because each part is *torn
up* from the whole, comes with its roots, encroaches upon the whole,
transgresses the frontiers of the others."[15] As we reach into the depth of
the world around us (as this depth reaches us), the sensible and the knowable emerge, yet the "part" that is "torn up" and comes to the foreground
always encroaches (to varying degrees) upon aspects of the otherness that
remain eclipsed, unexpressed, out of reach, and background.

Everything that becomes perceptible speaks of the depths from which it
emerges: as "torn up," it is connected to the whole, but the connections
are not without encroachment, and evocations are always by way of a partly
transgressive tongue. Our perceptual and conceptual relationship with the
world is fraught with this ambiguity. While we can overcome past transgressions, past misconceptions, we cannot overcome the fact that we continue to transgress and conceal dimensions of the world anew. This philosophy holds out the possibility of making better sense of the world, but not
the possibility of being completely present to things such that their difference, our distance, or perception's discordant moment might be entirely
superseded. It is when we begin to face and affirm these paradoxes and
ambiguities that our dialogue with the earth can be brought to higher possibilities. Hints of an "Eco-logos" to which we might listen in any simple
way risk obfuscating the paradoxes and hence concealing important questions that arise concerning our dialogical relationships to the earth.

With this task in mind I think it is helpful to turn to critical theory. Not
that of Marcuse, who sought to "free Nature of its own brutality, . . . insufficiency, [and] blindness, by virtue of the transforming power of Reason,"[16]
nor that of Habermas, who thought we should abandon this ideal and admit that the only cognitively fruitful attitude toward nature is one that se-
cures our instrumental mastery,[17] but rather that of Adorno, whose *Negative Dialectics* is a rich field in which to explore the possibilities and ethical
implications of dialogue with a world that both breathes through us and
remains very elusive, other, nonidentical with our conceptualizations.

## Adorno's Agonistic Dialogics

Like Merleau-Ponty, Adorno argues that "the somatic moment as the not purely cognitive part of cognition is irreducible." [18] We are beings thoroughly entwined with an extralinguistic world that to a large extent constitutes even our language. To simply deny this entwinement—to deny nature, that which is qualitatively specific in our own and other bodies, the otherness within and around us—is to bind ourselves to a quest for an abstract and empty sovereignty that destroys the world and is self-defeating. This denial is, in Adorno and Horkheimer's words, "the germ cell of a proliferating mythic irrationality" in which we discover not our freedom but our enslavement to an insistent and obliterating blindness. [19] If we are to return enlightenment to the promise of freedom that its abstract reifications undermine by eclipsing all that does not fit within a narrowly defined instrumental rationality, we must develop a negative dialectical engagement (which I refer to as "dialogical") with a human and nonhuman world teaming with what Adorno calls "nonidentity"—a specificity and wildness within and around us that exceed our perceptions and conceptions.

Adorno calls us to this engagement because he believes that as beings thoroughly steeped in a world of nonidentity, our freedom and fertility (which we are capable of both receiving from and offering to the world) emerge when we fashion our lives in an increasing consciousness of this world's otherness, not in an obliterating fumbling oblivion to otherness. The greater our oblivion, the greater the likelihood we will destroy the world. And as we obliterate the wild nonidentical textures of our world, we simultaneously reduce the potential richness of our own beings—beings that are entwined with this world. Adorno's link between a fertile freedom and conscious thought and action can be situated within the enlightenment tradition, but with the following important qualification: here consciousness is not simply a knowledge gained within and subordinate to an always already assumed imperative to master the earth, but rather an openness to the world such that one's thoughts, ideals, and practices are continually formed and reformed *through* our multiplicitous dialogue with this world. Lacking the sovereignty posited by the enlightenment in which our thoughts could attain complete Truths affording us autonomous guidance that is either unaffected by or master over all that is "different," we must recognize the ineliminable partiality and contingency of our conceptions and practices in order to partake in a formative dialogue with otherness that moves beyond past blindnesses and affords us the best possibility of living as vitally and sensibly as possible.

Adorno would have us seek our freedom in and live according to judgments that emerge in a dialogue between selves and the nonidentical world around them. What begins to emerge in Adorno, far from an abstract freedom, is a freedom inseparable from and dialogically intertwined with the fertility and richness of the world, a freedom that implies and affirms the freedom and flourishing of other beings. Even *if we could survive* in a world ordered to our utility, a world that no longer teemed with nonidentity would not be the site of our freedom, but an object that, answering "yeah massa" to our every assertion, would merely reinforce the deep reified sleep of a barren self-subjugation. For Adorno it is the world's surprising otherness that provokes and enriches a de-reifying freedom. As wolves and loons are exterminated across most of the United States, as smoggy skies eclipse sun and stars, we die with the elimination of our others—their mysterious provocative howls and shimmering. To say we "die," become less free, less rich, is to say that we lose the possibility of giving and receiving from the world, for human life in any sense worth embracing is in this profound exchange.

These might be easy thoughts in a world designed—by a God or Mother Goddess—so that all things might fit together in an easy harmony. In the relatively postmetaphysical world of Adorno, however, they are more difficult, and his rigorous pursuit of these difficulties constitutes the originality of his thinking. I want to sketch his project first with a very brief summary of the general character of the world as it appears to Adorno and then discuss in more detail the nature of the dialogical relationship he suggests we practice with respect to this world.

For Adorno the world is thoroughly relational. Each thing is a "crystallization" of its relations with others.[20] Yet the language of "crystallization" is as important here as that of "relation." The relational world is not one of pure fluidity and harmony, but one where things crystallize into highly dense, infinitely specific, and often very recalcitrant entities that resist the surrounding world in which they are born. One could say that for Adorno, the first movement toward a dialogical understanding and freedom lies in a recognition of both this relational quality and this recalcitrance. One learns of this recalcitrance through the repeated experience of the way in which the world exceeds concepts we have employed to grasp it, through the continual experience of a world richer than and nonidentical to our concepts that seek its identity. Often this experience involves a tragic recognition that one's thoughts and perceptions did not do "justice" to the radical heterogeneity of that which we sought. "Dialectics," Adorno writes, "is the consistent sense of nonidentity. . . . My thought is driven by its own inevitable insufficiency, by my guilt of what I am thinking."[21]

Spurred by both guilt and mimetic desire, Adorno pursues a philosophical approach to the world driven by and situated within an unresolvable set of paradoxes. On the one side, "dialectics says no more, to begin with, than that objects do not go into their concepts without remainder. . . . It indicates the untruth of identity." Yet, in close proximity with this observation Adorno writes that "the appearance of identity is inherent in thought itself, in its pure form. To think is to identify." [22] As beings in the world we continually attempt to grasp our surroundings conceptually. Yet, like Merleau-Ponty, Adorno argues that our grasp never rids the world of its distance. Even as our thoughts discover past and present reductions and coercions, they do not then simply merge with Truth, but continue to engender new constraints and encroachments. Adorno believes we can — up to a point and without absolute certainty — both decrease and render more desirable the encroachment that remains. Yet the only hope we have of doing so (as I shall illustrate in the section on Lopez) is by thinking, judging, and acting within the field of tension created between identity and nonidentity. Negative dialectics, in a sense that is oversimplified — as we shall see shortly — serves the end of reconciliation, which Adorno understands in simplest terms as a nonantagonistic commingling of a "multiplicity of different things." However, reconciliation is not a completely achievable condition, but rather a dialectical process in which thought goes about "dismantling the coercive logical character of its own course" [23] by seeking to recognize both where it has eclipsed the world and dimensions of that which lies beyond the eclipse.

Some critics who tacitly yearn for a more absolute identity and are troubled by Adorno's insistence that nonidentity is ineliminable see in negative dialectics a helplessness. [24] Others who view the world simply as a correlate of human discourses and practices — having no density and being of its own — see in Adorno's yearning to come to terms with nonidentity a useless ultimately metaphysical quest better left behind. [25] Yet I think both types of critics miss the basic gesture of Adorno's thought, which lies most essentially neither in the yearning for nor in the withdrawal of reconciliation or identity, but in a type of judgment and coexistence that the *paradoxes themselves* (those between identity and nonidentity, between our sense of knowing and our sense of how little we know) engender: a kind of agonistic dialogical thinking, an agonistic art and an agonistic freedom through which — as I shall elaborate below — a reciprocal gift giving passes between the self and the surrounding world. Reconciliation and nonidentity are points in a paradoxical "constellation," the whole of which constitutes the sense of his thought by calling us to pay attention to diverse considerations. Let us explore this more carefully.

If one reads negative dialectics to be driven literally by the goal of reconciliation understood as a multiplicity utterly devoid of encroachment, it becomes empty and even undesirable; it corresponds to nothing we can even begin to conjure. Could anything ever happen in such a world?

Wouldn't aspiring to such a state harbor a tacit will to nothingness, since, as Merleau-Ponty and Adorno show so well, even the simplest perception encroaches upon the world as it brings certain things and aspects of things into focus and plunges others into obscurity? Indeed, thought would be nonexistent in such a world. Wouldn't we be better off guiding ourselves by a goal that acknowledges the ineliminable transgressions of life (e.g., we must identify to think, we consume other living things in large quantities, and so on) and seeks sustainable modes of encroaching being that we can embrace even if somewhat tragically? Here we would at least think upon the terrain of human and ecological possibility.

I think these issues were of great concern to Adorno. Indeed, one could conceive of negative dialectics as a kind of dialogue with the world that seeks to develop the positive dimensions of encroachment (that is, a kind of encounter in which—partly through and partly in spite of encroachment—there is a substantial degree of "justice" and a reciprocal exchange of "gifts"). At the same time, however, this dialogue tries never to lose sight of or conceal the tragic dimension of our encounters. Yet Adorno worried too much about the likelihood that any discussion of "positive dimensions of encroachment" would be appropriated to legitimate an already rapacious subjectivity's transgressions ever to put it in these terms. Instead, he sought to situate thinking within an agonistic set of concerns more likely to engender the effects he sought. In this constellation of concerns—aimed in part at deconstructing various notions of subjectivity devoid of otherness—nothing makes sense or has value, not even agonism itself, without its other. Let us sketch further this constellation by examining the relationships among agonism, reconciliation, and dialogical thinking.

As soon as one approaches a text by Adorno one encounters thought as an agonistic activity par excellence. One finds him ceaselessly turning thought against itself and against a coercive world: its own habits of thinking, social structure, culture, all of this is subjected to strenuous criticism. Indeed, Adorno refers to this critical agonistic activity as the "freedom of philosophy," in which, through a "resistance to that which is forced upon it," the workings, effects, and contingencies of constraint are illuminated.[26] It is through this interrogative resistance that we are able to open a space for the degree of freedom that Adorno thinks is possible. That this agonistic capacity is essential is easy to see in a world where state, economy, and culture bombard selves and the natural world in order to create objects that will function smoothly in an apparatus of ever-increasing "productivity." But perhaps this capacity was not always essential; perhaps there was or will be a time of absolute harmony that renders it unnecessary?

Adorno rejects this latter position, arguing that from the beginning of human existence people have not found *even the nonhuman world* to be one where they could just sit back, relax in its positivity, and be happy campers. Granted that the earth often provides a spectacular abundance of what humans desire and need to live, granted that our efforts to alter its conditions frequently bring about situations far worse than those we sought to avoid; yet the world also presents droughts, deadly storms, poisonous plants, plagues, long-term climate changes, creatures that can eat us or our food, and more. Even though Adorno and Horkheimer's account of "primitive societies" suffers from its acceptance of a European ethnocentric exaggeration of the degree of terror and simplicity in which these cultures lived, their most essential point remains sound, namely, that human existence has always required an element of resistance to an encroaching world: an ability to question, avoid, or alter both social and natural conditions that are unconducive to our flourishing, an ability to pry open that which lies beyond the immediately given in the present.

The problem, Adorno and Horkheimer argue, is that so often this agonistic capacity becomes hyperbolic, becomes an end in itself, and thereby begins to make universal the enthrallment it sought to avoid. Magic and myth—which on their reading begin in part as an effort to participate in rather than simply be subjected to the forces of the world—are ambiguous phenomena for them, illustrating both the desirable moment of agonism and its collapse into blind fear of the other. On the one hand, magic and myth represent a rejection of the claims of our present experience of the world to exhaust things. They tend to open up a space beyond the immediately given for the acknowledgment of nonidentity, of more than we currently grasp. The world ceases to be an immutable force pressing upon the self, and the self's grasp of the world ceases to have the character of an immutable and exhaustive cage as myth acknowledges a surplus that transcends our experience, into which both the self and the world might move. "When the tree is no longer approached merely as tree, but as evidence for an Other, as the location of *manna*, language expresses the contradiction that something is itself and at one and the same time something other than itself, identical and not identical. Through the deity, language is transformed from tautology to language." [27] It is when we can begin to sense not only the genre tree and the concrete identifiable textures and specificities of trees—their bark, leaves, relationships to soil and climate—but also the myriad complexities and open possibilities that lie beyond our identifications, that language moves beyond meaningless self-reference and trees become for us *trees*, rather than object correlates devoid of real otherness.

Yet this space in which an agonistic and fertile dialogical freedom begin to be possible is, on Adorno and Horkheimer's reading, too often closed when magic and myth institute taboos that fix certain dimensions of existence as "antagonistic other"—dangerous alterities to be feared and avoided at all costs. "Enlightenment" takes this tendency to the extreme as history develops, and is "mythic fear turned radical. The pure immanence of positivism, its ultimate product, is no more than a . . . universal taboo. Nothing at all may remain outside, because the idea of outsideness is the very source of fear." [28] In this process a self emerges that defines itself as radicalized agonism in the sense of a blanket rejection and mastery of all that is Other. What begins as a capacity to open a space in which the world's possibilities and otherness might be further dialogically engaged ends in an obliteration of this very space: agonism turns into antagonism.

We have reached a point, Adorno argues, where we no longer need be as threatened by the natural world as we were in times past. Nevertheless, our agonistic capacity remains of vital importance, not only because it thwarts totalizing pressures in the social realm, but because it helps us free ourselves and the natural world from reified conceptions and their accompanying dogmatisms. It is an activity that can expand and enrich our thought.

Yet if the space of nonidentity that emerges for us through our agonistic relationship to the identity of the given is to remain open, if agonism is to facilitate a fertile freedom, it must itself be conceived agonistically—that is, as entwined with and partially animated by *its* other, *reconciliation*. It is in this notion of reconciliation as "togetherness of diversity" that a basic respect and esteem for otherness—as intrinsically valuable and nonhostile—is encouraged that checks the transgressive moment of agonistics from becoming lost in itself. Indeed, animated by reconciliation, the agonistic activity of negative dialectics seeks not to obliterate the other, but rather to "truly give itself" to beings in the world.[29] The language of "giving" is important here, for Adorno writes that "every undistorted relationship, perhaps the conciliation that is part of organic life itself, is a gift." [30] With respect to humans' giving he has in mind thinking and acting toward the nonhuman other in light of an imaginative generosity that seeks to enter the other's voice into the dialogue through which one's judgments and actions emerge. This is a complex thought, and I will elaborate it below when considering speech and the nonspeaking world; here it should simply be noted that the very birth of the agonistic quest for nonidentity arises not simply to facilitate my own freedom but that of the world as well.

However, if agonism becomes worthwhile only in light of its other, the same can be said of the moment of utopian reconciliation. Indeed, the value of reconciliation—and the hope it bears—lies in its negative relation to itself: the continual postponement of its presentation. Just as Judaism has a "ban on pronouncing the name of God," the positive force of reconciliation manifests itself "only with the prohibition against calling what is false as God, against invoking the finite as infinite, lies as truth." [31] On Adorno's reading, the idea of reconcilement and utopian "togetherness of diverse beings" contributes to freedom *only* as a *critical notion* that stirs up a yearning to bring to light and careful consideration that which has been eclipsed, that which suffers and is excluded in our present relations with others and the nonhuman world. In other words, reconciliation should animate an agonistic critical dialogue that explores and aims at improving our relations to other beings. "Dissonance is the truth about harmony." [32] To the extent that it ceases to be in relation with its other, reconciliation—like agonism, which left alone engenders hostility to the outside as such and thwarts both possibility and freedom—turns into its opposite, legitimating and disguising the subjugations of a given state of affairs in a manner that dissuades us from dialogue and hence possibility and freedom. As soon as the notion of reconciliation loses its critical agonistic dimension, it begins to shield the present from contestation and to eternalize it as "reconciled." It is precisely because we are *not* beings who could enjoy an utterly transgressionless existence (whatever this might be) that we need the idea of reconciliation to provoke a dialogical approach to the world in which the gift, justice, and elements of creative reciprocity are most likely to emerge. For Adorno, the fertility of existence depends upon pursuing this dialogical activity—to the extent that we become somnambulists, we lapse into a barren fear of the Other.

Hence Adorno's constellation of agonism, reconciliation, identity, nonidentity, and the thought that emerges in their midst constitutes something like a theory of judgment that calls us toward diverse considerations of which we must not lose sight lest freedom become a sham. I call this a theory of *judgment* because what Adorno offers is not a specific code, set of rules, or prescriptions—the world is far too wild to be thus subsumed—but rather a number of concerns of which we must be continually mindful if we are to dwell conceptually and practically in a manner that contributes to the fertile freedom of humans and earth. Most essentially, these concerns call thought to reflect continually upon its own proximity to and distance from the world around it and, furthermore, to locate itself at the interstice between proximity and distance, identity and difference, for it is at those edges that thought is most supple and capable of the care in which its own fertile freedom and that of the world lie. Nothing in the world is more rigid and careless than a thought blind to these edges—these tensions. Yet if we pursue a dialogical practice there emerges what Adorno called a "morality of thinking." [33] And though Adorno died before he wrote the work on ethics that was to follow his aesthetic theory, one could well argue that it was already written in his earlier works: it is no accident that his epistemology and aesthetics swarm with such concepts as "domination," "freedom," "utopia," "suffering," "guilt," "gift," "balance," and "justice."

But what can a dialogical morality and freedom be, really, in the midst of a world that is so often so silent, a world that utters no words? Adorno writes: "If thought really yielded to the object, if its attention were on the object, not on its category, the very objects would start talking under the lingering eye." [34] This is not to say that he thinks there is some secret language written in the world that thought need only decipher or mirror. It is precisely the absence of such a language that makes nonidentity ineliminable. And yet it is not an utterly plastic *nothing* toward which we hurl our questions, our descriptions—our words. As we face the world we discover a paradox we must live and can never dissolve: something "authoritatively valued and incomprehensible." We find that "nature's language is mute," "silent," "indeterminate," "hostile to all definition," "its substance is precisely its non-generalizability, its non-conceptualizability"; and yet, through our bodily entwinement with the world, it seems to be "trying to say something," seems to have the "peculiar capacity to speak." [35] Crickets, coyotes, leaves wilting in the hot sun, silent hillsides in the wake of the chainsaw's roar—all present the paradox of the mute cacophony.

Whatever it is that is going on in this buzzing, blustery, wild, ecstatic earth we inhabit, this earth that inhabits us, "speech" (in Adorno's reading) is a human activity qualitatively different from the multifarious expressive capacities many other creatures seem to possess. As Merleau-Ponty and Adorno show, no matter how much the earth is the somatic context that always already motivates our language, the earth and its beings only really "speak" (in an important though not the only sense of this term) to us through our efforts to articulate them. And we always say more and less than this protean world with its proximate distance and it can never be any different. The fate of our simplest perception is that it is never simply a reconciled "letting beings be." In the midst of the endless upsurge of identifications that partially eclipse nonidentity, the least obliterative and most fertile thing we can do is pursue a negative dialectical dialogue in which we maintain an actively interrogative and critical attitude to the world as it currently appears and is described. In this way we might remedy past ignorance and develop richer, more complex perceptions, thoughts, and practices. We should not wish to disappear, but to fashion our lives in what Nietzsche (echoing Horace) calls this *"rerum concordia discors"*—the discordant concord of things.[36] The earth provides a lot if we let it, but it also requires a lot of human assertion. To live ethically is to fashion levels and qualities of assertion in the midst of as much of wild Being as we can—or can stand to—hear: to fashion our lives in the midst of the agonistic constellation Adorno describes.

As I argued above, humans are most sensible if they act this way, and our freedom is entwined with maximally sensible activity. In our dialogue with the multiplicitous earth, the earth participates with us in bestowing the gift of this sense. Moreover, it also provides the gift of protean soils in which through dialogical engagement our human being develops richness.

We too, from an Adornoin perspective, have gifts to give to the earth and its beings. On one level, his statement that "thought seeks to give itself to the object" means that it endlessly pursues the difficult task of considering the world, as much as is possible, as an alterity irreducible to thought and worthy of great care as we fashion our lives. More generally, we develop a profound respect for nonidentity as such, for wildness—not only because otherness as otherness can contribute to our fertility and our freedom, but because within itself there is an endless fertile discordant concord/concordant discord that is a kind of metaphor for the highest things we can imagine. (I remember walking with a friend along a narrow path at the base of the cliffs of Pilot Mountain in North Carolina. We came upon a small hole in the midst of this rugged rock, and, peering inside, discovered an entire lush world teeming with lichen, moss, plants I did not recognize—the place was crawling with ants and spiders. I can't write about the meaning of such places any better than I can paint sunsets. But if this or anything I write were to be grand far beyond my powers, in some way it would resemble that hole.)

Our gifts to the world are only partly analogous to its gifts to us. At our best moments we can fashion bits of the world in ways that increase the world's fertility. But is this really a gift to the world? Lest we personify the earth, perhaps it would be better to acknowledge and affirm this as an exuberant gift to ourselves (as a *part* of the earth) in which the earth that is other participates. Finally, I think that we must muster the humility to recognize that we are beings that receive more than we can return in this encounter; that perhaps the most that the respect for nonidentity that wells out of this agonistic constellation can really give to the world is a development of human selves and societies such that our creative activity treads relatively softly where it must and hardly at all (a few hiking trails) where it may. This, however, is not a gift of small proportions. We now—like it or not—hold the fate of the earth in our hands. If we let it flourish in its nonidentity, we—through a somewhat bizarre set of circumstances—are perhaps returning a gift not insignificant in comparison to the one Adorno believes we can receive.

Adorno insists that "the crux, of philosophy, is what happens in it, not a thesis or a position — the texture." [37] In order to illustrate and develop further what has been said thus far by way of a "texture" of thinking that I think exemplifies the best we can draw from negative dialectics, I wish to sketch briefly some of the work of Barry Lopez. In so doing, I wish to follow not with a set of prescriptions, but a style of thinking, an exemplification of good ecological judgment, which I believe is a prerequisite — indeed, the quintessence — of a sound environmental ethic.

## Lopez

> Beyond this — that the interior landscape is a metaphorical representation of the exterior landscape, that the truth reveals itself most fully not in dogma but in paradox, irony, and contradictions that distinguish compelling narratives — beyond this there are only failures of imagination: reductionism in science; fundamentalism in religion; fascism in politics.[38]

Adorno's skies were forever stained dark by the greasy smoke from Auschwitz. He wondered aloud if there could ever be poetry after the Holocaust; he certainly had poetic *moments*, uncomfortably extracting fragments of dark beauty and pleasure as he fashioned his intricate though often turgid prose as an alarm calling us to witness the ominous barbarisms still lurking in our contemporary world. But Adorno was ashamed of these moments — he felt "the shame of still having air to breathe, in hell." [39] In terms of much of our history, Barry Lopez (who is famous for writing such good books in what might loosely be described as the "nature genre," but might just as well be known as a philosopher) knows exactly what Adorno is talking about. From Cortez's destruction of the aviaries and slaughter of the people in the Valley of Mexico to the various types of imperialism in the present, he warns us that we have "become a culture that devours the earth." [40] And yet Lopez inhabits other regions of the negative dialectic; he wanders with a different style. From rural Oregon, where he lives when he is not traveling, he can express dimensions of the world that were barely visible to Adorno. He makes the nonidentical seductive. He exemplifies, I think, a kind of intelligence that is suggested in Adorno's texts, one that emerges at the interstice between identity and nonidentity. To dislodge our devouring culture he seeks to bring to us "the advantage of an altered perspective" — different skies, different types of light: the diffuse light of the Arctic, where even the meaning of "a day" presents an immense alterity, "where airplanes track icebergs the size of Cleveland and polar bears fly down out of the stars." [41] In spaces vast as the tundra, Lopez is able to evoke and practice a kind of fertility and freedom—with all their elusiveness—that brings out dimensions of my reading of Adorno's project in ways Adorno never could.[42] Of course, Adorno knew something profound could emerge in negative dialectics, but in a world where "the founding fathers" sell used cars on prime-time television, the thought of "negative dialectical mouthwash" led him to think its only hope for survival lay in what I think is an overly tenacious negativity.

Lopez's texts are as protean as the earth that swarms his pen. His essays unfold a kind of dance with the world, an endless alteration of movements toward and movements away from the beings he encounters in which a great deal of wisdom emerges. Take his book *Of Wolves and Men*, for example. Lopez pursues the wolf through his own eyes, the eyes of biologists, Eskimos, old Europeans, and so on. He learns a lot about the wolf, revealing from each perspective dimensions of wolves (and humans) that other views conceal. This book exhibits an intense passion to understand the wolf. One finishes reading with a strong sense that if humans guided their behavior affecting wolves in light of Lopez's passion, style of thinking, and specific understandings, both wolves and humans would be better for it. However, intrinsically bound up with the rich identity of the wolf that Lopez presents is a continual homage to the wolf's nonidentity—the vast majority of wolves' beings that lies beyond our concepts and that, by the nature of the distance between our being and that of wolves, will of necessity remain for the most part hidden.

His text reads like a fluidly practiced negative dialectics. Every time Lopez points to something fascinating about the wolf he follows with comments such as these: "The truth is we know little about the wolf." "No one . . . knows why the wolves do what they do." "In a word, not enough is known." "Wolves are wolves, not men." "We know painfully little about wolves. We can only ask questions and guess." [43] Even more profound than his explicit gestures toward nonidentity are the constellations of questions he raises about the wolf for which he has no definitive answers. What happens when the eyes of wolves meet the eyes of their potential prey? Lopez depicts this event not primarily as an answer to the question—though he toys with suggestions—but rather as an event that poses a question that probably exceeds any answer we can ever give. He presents the bits of the world that he can grasp in such a way that they not only unfold a rich knowledge of identities, but—in an *interrogative mode of appearance*—gesture infinitely beyond their identities for us to an inexhaustible surplus of nonidentity. As he ends one chapter, "An appreciation of wolves, it seems to me, lies in the wider awareness that comes when answers to some questions are for the moment simply suspended." [44]

This is not to suggest that he recommends an utterly mystical approach to the world; his texts are too full of what we might call science for anyone to read them this way. His point is rather that "to allow mystery, which is to say to yourself, 'There could be more, there could be things we don't understand,' is not to damn knowledge."[45] Indeed, it is precisely by maintaining the agonistic tension between identity and nonidentity that we can situate ourselves in the world in a dialogical manner that is conducive to knowledge, freedom, fertility. Lopez, like Adorno, knows that the world does not literally speak to us, and yet it seems to be trying to say something. One finds him continually challenging assumptions—others', his own—to see what other words might capture that which lies beyond the ones we currently use. New words will not exhaust the world, but if we are lucky we will grasp something, and perhaps even something to celebrate. Lopez finds himself elaborating his life in a dialogue he cannot quit, with a world that is *both inside and outside* of the conversation. He wants to know about the wolf, but there is an ineliminable distance that houses his "guesses": "Let's say there are 8,000 wolves in Alaska. Multiplying by 365, that's about 3 million wolf-days of activity a year. Researchers may see something like 75 different wolves over a period of 25 or 30 hours. . . . Observed behavior amounts to about three one-thousandths of 1 percent of wolf behavior."[46] The fact is that most of what this absence seems to "speak" of is a difference that is mostly indifferent—even opposed—to the dialogue we seek for both sense and fertility of our lives. (Though, as I argued in the section on Adorno, this dialogue, if rightly pursued, gives the wolf its life and its freedom insofar as both unfortunately depend upon us dispelling our worst myths and developing a reverence for the wolf— things only possible through this very dialogue.)

And yet this antispeech speech, our awareness of the wolf's tenacious absence, is itself one of the most important things that we may hear from selves and other wild beings, both for ourselves and for wolves. For ourselves, it is important because it is here in our presence to the wolves' absence and indifference that we find the alterity of the wolf most profoundly inscribed. It may be precisely in *this* general alterity (its brief appearance as a distant howl, a flash of retreating fur, a shadow in the brush; days and weeks spent looking and finding nothing) that we can instill in ourselves an expectant sense of the more specific alterities that is the precondition of our agonistic dialogue, an anticipatory openness to those alterities that crystallize as questions beyond and partially disruptive of each answer we pose. Yet, if awareness of this deepest alterity is perhaps the condition of our dialogue with the world, I would suggest that it is at the same time agonistic toward dialogue itself: It suggests that, for its own existence, agonistic dialogical dwelling on this earth must recognize not only the limits of what it knows, but the *limits of dialogue itself*. Our dialogue has effects; if it does not check even the insistence lodged in its own dynamics, it could well find that it has destroyed its interlocutor and by implication itself and its possibility for existence as well. We would do well to increase our dialogical observation of wolf-days, but there are real limits here, beyond which the very difference, the wildness, the otherness that we seek to know will begin to cease to be other. A dialogical ethic must be cognizant of both its essentiality *and* its essential limits if its respect for the other is not to become a sham. It is this insight that I believe partly motivated Adorno's not infrequent castigations of even negative dialectics itself.

Having said this, the essentiality of our dialogue remains, for it is only here — in its creations/discoveries, in its discoveries of what it has not yet discovered, and in its discoveries of what if can never discover — that both a reverence for the earth and a knowledge through which this reverence can become meaningful emerge. And it is only here that our lives can move beyond a barren dogmatism that "devours the earth." As long as we find ourselves in this strange position of being capable of subjugating the earth, in the absence of this dialogical ethos, with all its agonisms, there is little hope for the wolves.

In *Arctic Dreams*, Lopez writes of borders, "ecotones." Ecotones are the edges where different ecosystems meet: where forest meets field, sea meets land, salt water meets fresh water. Natural ecologists know that ecotones — with their intermingling borders — are especially fertile, "special meeting grounds" charged with "evolutionary potential." [47] When we combine this knowledge with the etymology of *ecotone*, *oikos* (dwelling), and *tonus* (tension), we evoke an image of the fertility and pregnancy of dwelling at the edge of the tension between different people, beings, landscapes. While our civilization has to a large extent viewed ecotones as anathema, Adorno and Lopez, it seems to me, seek to return us to the ecotone — to the richness of tension-dwelling. "What does it mean to grow rich?" Lopez asks in the prologue to *Arctic Dreams*. [48] It seems to me that he poses one answer to this question through a dazzling display of the biological and metaphorical wealth of Arctic ecotones. Yet the most profound ecotone in the book — and he knows this — is the one that occurs at the dialogical edge between the self and the otherness of the world, between Lopez and the light, the beings, the people of the Arctic. "That attraction to borders, to the earth's twilit places, is part of the shape of human curiosity." [49] The shape of this ecotonal human curiosity — what it means to grow rich — takes form at the proximate distance of the border, and the border itself is a part of why that utter alterity on either side calls for our reverence.

No chapter in *Arctic Dreams* illustrates this ecotone sensibility better than the one on the narwhal. As always, Lopez's text offers an abundant scientific understanding, in this instance on this 3,000 pound whale with a single horn. And yet "the facts" are employed to reveal a site of wonder, mystery, questionability—something to be appreciated and respected. "How different must be 'the world' for such a creature," he writes, "who occupies . . . a three-dimensional acoustical space. Perhaps only musicians have some inkling of the formal shape of emotions and motivation that might define such a sensibility." [50] It is a world of sounds, fluids, pressures, currents, opening and closing ice, a geography where depth and height are central. Lopez's text includes limits ("Perhaps only musicians . . . "), but Lopez throws *all* his readers into an imaginative quest to discern the textures of this different world. In the process we engage not only "the other" but ourselves and the possibilities, limits, and specificities of our more two-dimensional visual world. At the borders between Lopez, his readers, and narwhals, dialogues are engendered in which we learn about the world in quite tangible ways, and also in ways less tangible: ways that have to do with dialogue itself and the nonidentical alterities that make it possible and fructiferous. Through exemplification, Lopez suggests a way of inhabiting the world that is radically different from the constellation of knowledge and interests tending toward the development of Arctic oil production that may threaten the narwhal. If we dwell long enough upon this chapter we begin to get an inkling of the possibility of a dramatically transfigured science that might ask questions now unfamiliar to us, different social and ecological practices, a dialogical ethic.

When we inhabit the ecotone between Lopez and narwhal, a kind of reverence for this dark animal of the sea emerges quite powerfully. Is this a recognition of "intrinsic value"? I think the very term abstracts from the multiplicitous ecotonal interrelationships in which all beings are located and construes value atomistically. Yet we should not move from atomism to a totalizing ecological ethical holism in which particular beings fail to emerge as distinctly worthy of reverence. Rather, I would suggest that we understand value (as a specifically human concept) as that which at best is born in dialogue and the possibilities of dialogue, but at the same time transcends dialogue. Value emerges like breath exhaled under water from encounters between self and other. Discrete bubbles of what we revere appear at a distance and take on lives of their own separate from us; but, for us at any rate, they are born through our opening to the world in the differences of the ecotone. As we finish reading Lopez's account of the narwhal we begin to acquire a strong sense that in addition to its value to us as a site of wonder and edification, it "exists for its own sake." However, I think this "for its own sake" gains its power from the richness of our relations with the narwhal, a text on the narwhal, or at least other beings in the world from which we transfer a sense of reverence to the narwhal. Without dialogical practices our reverence becomes reified, dogmatic, sometimes empty, often dangerous. Through them the "for its own sake" emerges in full strength to animate texts like *Arctic Dreams*. Lest this sound like a re-baked version of an old anthropocentricism, let me add that whatever reverence we ourselves deserve emerges from our capacity to dwell dialogically at the ecotone between self and world; it emerges in how we can and how we do inhabit these borders. The power of our own respectability is entwined with our recognition of the ecotone and the "for its own sake" of the other.

Of course, ecotones are not simply "things in themselves," the pure "Truth" of nature. They are, like all human knowledge, "a metaphorical representation of the exterior landscape," situated with other metaphors in narratives we unfold in effort to make sense of, revere, and enjoy these selves we are and this world we inhabit. This world and our metaphors do not coexist by "mirroring" each other. We would do better to imagine metaphors as configurational sweeps through the world through which it is possible—in the best moments—to grasp dimensions of these soils we call earth. Some metaphors devour the earth, others reveal the world less antagonistically, even as they contain dimensions of encroachment. For centuries a lot of Western civilization has painted nature in a singular hue as that which is trying to conquer us, that which we should try to civilize and conquer. Our metaphors are tightly entwined with a process that has brought us to the brink of global destruction, and it is clearly time—if there is time—to consider a profound change.

Christianity (along with its secularized legacy) has been profoundly antiecotone. Lopez writes:

> The Christian Church was historically embattled from the beginning. Without an enemy to fight, it had no identity. Until the time of the Christian emperors the enemy was the state. Then it was the paganism of northern Europe. Then came the Crusades and the war against the infidel. After . . . Charlemagne, the enemy was increasingly heresy. . . . Behind the heretic, like a puppet master, is the Devil. A wolf in sheepfold.[51]

In recent, more secularized, centuries the enemy has been wilderness, the Third World, the Native American, the poor, the sexual deviant, the Jew, the black, the woman, the wolf. We need another set of metaphors. We need to go beyond the obsession with singularity, be it the totality or the individual self, by which we have been seized for so long. We need a perspective that deviates from the terrain Hegel sketched two hundred years ago but could not himself avoid.

Adorno and Lopez in their different ways sketch the beginnings of an alternative terrain, or at least an alternative way of inhabiting our terrains, in which self and that which lies beyond are seen to belong together most profoundly not because they are part of one great happy harmonious system (though many of the interrelationships within the global ecosystem do seem to indicate a greater degree of this than is commonly recognized), but rather because the agonistic dialogical intermingling of their nonidentities is the wellspring of what intelligence, freedom, and fertility we can live and impart to the living earth around us from our bizarre position of awesome potential power. To begin to narrate the earth by way of the ecotone is to begin to proliferate emblems that call our attention both to that richness of the wild being called earth and to our deepest and highest possibilities for living here.

Perhaps—as we consider these steps—we are not too far from one impulse of Christianity after all. At the end of a sublime chapter called "Ice and Light," Lopez evokes the early Christian "agape" (love) to get at the kinds of thoughts I have been exploring in this essay. He has in mind here not the insidious love—dripping with pity—that Nietzsche disclosed as a twisted will to power, but rather "an expression of intense spiritual affinity with the mystery that is 'to be sharing life with other life' . . . a humble, impassioned embrace of something outside the self." [52] Less poetically, Adorno referred to a "mimetic impulse" that might animate our difficult relationships—our thought, our art—a "nonconceptual affinity" with the "unposited other." [53] Metaphorically, Lopez describes it thus: "Austere. Implacable. Harsh but not antagonistic. Creatures of pale light. I looked out at the icebergs. They were so beautiful they also made you afraid." [54]

I take this juxtaposition of beauty and fear to be central to Lopez's reading of "agape," for the "intense spiritual affinity" of which he writes is not a return to a notion of easy harmonious attraction, but an attraction born of austerity, fear, implacability, radical alterity, and distance, as well as of similarity, comfort, beauty, and proximity. Agape is an embrace at a distance of all the complexity of coexistence. If it remains just an emotion, it weathers and fades quickly. Instead, it must frequently seek its imperfect articulations in complex conceptual textures that both anchor us and return us to the profound mystery of being alive on this earth.

## A Parting Thought

Through Adorno and Lopez I have tried to explore an agonistic sensibility and thought entwined with an agonistic agape, both of which are crucial dimensions of an environmental ethic—an ecological judgment. The development of such thinking will require thought and science of unprecedented openness and rigor. Yet the home of both, I think, is in a wild enjoyment of life, this earth. Such enjoyment is often not easy in a world as tragic as ours. We need both an ethics and concrete practices that encourage its appearance. I have drawn heavily upon the conceptual fertility of Lopez's work, yet as important as any of this is that he simply tells great stories. He warns us against an insistent conceptuality that might squeeze out the space for the dialogical ethos that emerges in his texts. Describing and opposing those Euro-Americans who want to reduce every "coyote tale" to a message, he writes: "The reasoning was that you had to have a purpose in telling the story—and simple enjoyment or tribal identity wasn't reason enough." [55] I have a strong hunch that making better sense is inseparable from this thought, that the Lopez who presents such a conceptually textured understanding of wolves, the Arctic, metaphor, is inseparable from the Lopez who loves coyote stories, the Lopez who weaves *Desert Notes: Reflections in the Eye of a Raven* with such lines as "One morning as I stood watching the sun rise, washing out the blue black, watching the white crystalline stars fade, my bare legs quivering in the cool air, I noticed my hands had begun to crack and turn to dust." [56] A wild imagination welling out of a wild pleasure is integral to a patient conceptual labor with a world that exceeds our concepts.

Adorno gestured toward a world more free, fertile, enjoyable, yet one senses there was very little he himself was able to enjoy. God knows we cannot blame him for this. We owe it to him to fashion and let be a world in which he might have found a greater capacity to enjoy.

### Notes

1. G. W. F. Hegel, *Phenomenology of Spirit*, trans. A. V. Miller (Oxford: Oxford University Press, 1977), 294–355. See also Jane Bennett, *Unthinking Faith and Enlightenment: Nature and the State in a Post-Hegelian Era* (New York: New York University Press, 1987).

2. William Ophuls, *Ecology and the Politics of Scarcity: Prologue to a Political Theory of the Steady State* (San Francisco: W. H. Freeman, 1977).

3. Richard A. Watson, "A Critique of Anti-Anthropocentric Biocentrism," *Environmental Ethics* (Fall 1983): 256.

4. Bill Devall and George Sessions, *Deep Ecology: Living as if Nature Mattered* (Salt Lake City: Peregrin Smith, 1985), 67. The totalizing holism also reveals itself in a frequent insistence upon achieving "consensus." See also Arne Naess, "A Defence of the Deep Ecology Movement," *Environmental Ethics* (Fall 1984).

5. Devall and Sessions, *Deep Ecology*, ix.

6. See John S. Dryzek, "Green Reason: Communicative Ethics for the Biosphere," *Environmental Ethics* (Fall 1990).

7. Compare John Tallmadge, "Saying You to the Land," *Environmental Ethics* (Fall 1981): 354, 360–61, and Martin Buber, *I and Thou*, trans. W. Kaufmann (New York: Charles Scribner's

Sons, 1970), 57–58, 62.

8. John Kultgen's critique of Tallmadge in "Saving 'You' for Real People," *Environmental Ethics* (Fall 1982), has some moments of insight regarding Buberian mysticism, but is itself too firmly within the anthropocentric enlightenment position.

9. Maurice Merleau-Ponty, *Signs*, trans. R. C. McCleary (Evanston: Northwestern University Press, 1964), 180.

10. David Abram, "Merleau-Ponty and the Voice of the Earth," *Environmental Ethics* (Fall 1988): 117.

11. Abram, "Merleau-Ponty," 119.

12. Merleau-Ponty, *Signs*, 167.

13. The distance Merleau-Ponty describes gains another dimension when one considers his understanding of language as that which wells out of our social relations, hierarchies, technologies—many of which have an ecocidal bent—as well as our bodily presence to wind, crickets, forests, animals. A basic task humans always have before them is trying to sort out these dense and often antagonistic relationships in which we have access to nothing like an unproblematic "Eco-logos."

14. Maurice Merleau-Ponty, *Phenomenology of Perception*, trans. C. Smith (London: Routledge & Kegan Paul, 1962), xx, 361.

15. Maurice Merleau-Ponty, *The Visible and the Invisible*, trans. A. Lingus (Evanston: Northwestern University Press, 1968), 218.

16. Herbert Marcuse, *One Dimensional Man* (Boston: Beacon, 1964), 238.

17. Jürgen Habermas, "A Reply to My Critics," in *Habermas: Critical Debates*, ed. J. B. Thompson and D. Held (Cambridge: MIT Press, 1982), 243–45. John Dryzek, in "Green Reason," attempts to salvage Habermas's project for environmental ethics. While this essay is very insightful at times, I think that if one carefully explores the underpinnings of Habermas's thought, its universalism, consensualism, transcendentalism, and philosophy of identity, the project of doing eco-ethics near this terrain is, as Habermas rightly recognizes, next to impossible. I fully embrace Dryzek's general project of a communicative ecological ethic, but I think it should be approached through a more thorough consideration of the nature of this dialogue itself—one markedly different from Habermas's.

18. Theodor Adorno, *Negative Dialectics*, trans. E. B. Ashton (New York: Continuum, 1973), 193.

19. Theodor Adorno and Max Horkheimer, *Dialectic of Enlightenment*, trans. J. Cumming (New York: Continuum, 1972), 54.

20. Adorno, *Negative Dialectics*, 162.

21. Ibid., 5.

22. Ibid.

23. Ibid., 6.

24. See Jürgen Habermas, *The Philosophical Discourse of Modernity*, trans. T. McCarthy (Cambridge: MIT Press, 1987), chap. 5.

25. For example, Richard Rorty, *Contingency, Irony, Solidarity* (Cambridge: Cambridge University Press, 1989); and Stanley Fish, *Doing What Comes Naturally* (Durham, N.C.: Duke University Press, 1989), 436–37.

26. Ibid., 15.

27. Adorno and Horkheimer, *Dialectic of Enlightenment*, 15.

28. Ibid., 16.

29. Adorno, *Negative Dialectics*, 13.

30. Theodor Adorno, *Minima Moralia: Reflections from a Damaged Life*, trans. E. F. N. Jephcott (London: Verso, 1974), 43.

31. Adorno and Horkheimer, *Dialectic of Enlightenment*, 23.

32. Theodor Adorno, *Aesthetic Theory*, trans. C. Lenhardt (London: Routledge & Kegan Paul, 1983), 161.

33. Adorno, *Minima Moralia*, 73–74.

34. Adorno, *Negative Dialectics*, 27–28.

35. Adorno, *Aesthetic Theory*, 104–5, 115, 104, 114.

36. Friedrich Nietzsche, *The Gay Science*, trans. W. Kaufmann (New York: Vintage, 1974), 32.

37. Adorno, *Negative Dialectics*, 33.

38. Barry Lopez, *Crossing Open Ground* (New York: Vintage, 1989), 71.

39. Adorno, *Minima Moralia*, 28.

40. Lopez, *Crossing Open Ground*, 198.

41. Barry Lopez, *Arctic Dreams: Imagination and Desire in a Northern Landscape* (New York: Bantam, 1986), 12, xxvi.

42. This is not entirely true; see, for example, his rich engagement with Hegel in *Negative Dialectics*.

43. Barry Lopez, *Of Wolves and Men* (New York: Charles Scribner's Sons, 1978), 3, 4, 55, 63, 93.

44. Ibid., 97.

45. Ibid., 284.

46. Ibid., 3.

47. Lopez, *Arctic Dreams*, 109–10.

48. Ibid., 12.

49. Ibid., 110.

50. Ibid., 124.

51. Lopez, *Of Wolves and Men*, 238.

52. Lopez, *Arctic Dreams*, 224.

53. Adorno, *Aesthetic Theory*, 80.

54. Lopez, *Arctic Dreams*, 225.

55. Barry Lopez, *Giving Birth to Thunder, Sleeping with His Daughter: Coyote Builds North America* (New York: Avon, 1977), xx.

56. Barry Lopez, *Desert Notes: Reflections in the Eye of a Raven* (New York: Avon, 1976), xiii.

Chapter 12

# Primate Visions and Alter-Tales

Jane Bennett

In *Primate Visions* Donna Haraway offers a reading of primatology—its texts and textbooks, its *National Geographic* documentaries, its graduate programs—as a contemporary cultural tale about the natural and the human. She exposes the imprimatur of the myth of Eden on the scientific study of apes. This reading, like any other, proceeds by way of a set of political affirmations, moral priorities, and hopes for the future. Haraway not only unearths the myth within primatology, she crafts an alternative to it. This alter-tale is concerned not with sin but with "the nature and meaning of difference," not with salvation but with "the prospects of survival for nuclear humanity that also face[s] deep ecological crisis." [1]

Her widely read "A Manifesto for Cyborgs" is an early presentation of this alter-tale; the cyborg myth reappears in *Primate Visions*, albeit mostly between the lines.[2] A rich mosaic of biography, bibliography, photography, historical chronicle, biblical interpretation, and feminist criticism, *Primate Visions* is highly successful in bringing out the sheer volume and complexity of primatological discourse. Perhaps the submersion of the alter-tale in *Primate Visions* is a function of this success.[3]

What I would like to do, however, is raise the alter-tale up in order to explore a possibility suggested by *Primate Visions*—the possibility of a feminism that is itself an environmentalism, and vice versa. Or, to state it more boldly: the possible eclipse of "feminism" and "environmentalism" by an orientation of care for earthly life and for difference.[4] Such an exercise in utopian imagination would combine dreams of naturalists and ideals of feminists; it would work toward improving "the prospects for primate survival, including ... human survival" while promoting "differentiated meanings, material abundance, and comprehensive equality."[5]

I would like in this essay to think with and against Haraway's work. I present that work first as a representative of a new strain of nature discourse, and then as an exemplar of a particular kind of rhetoric, one that seeks to combine social critique, antiessentialism, and methodological self-consciousness with *myth*. I wish, through Haraway, to explore the political potential of this kind of rhetoric. After excavating Haraway's alter-tale, I shall turn, then, to the question of narrative strategy, to the poetics of the alter-tale.

## The Origin Story

*So Yahweh expelled him from the garden of Eden, to till the soil from which he had been taken. He banished the man, and in front of the Garden of Eden he posted the cherubs, and the flame of a flashing sword, to guard the way to the tree of life.*

Genesis 2:5–7

Haraway's alter-tale issues from a critical confrontation with the "origin stories" of environmentalist, feminist, and primatological discourses. The story of Eden is, of course, their prototype. It begins with a place of sensory splendor, perfect harmony amidst exceedingly rich diversity, plenty without toil, joyful wonder at existence that does not fade with maturity, maturity without death. It ends with land that is posted: for reasons not entirely clear but somehow just, we are no longer allowed in. The Book of Genesis invokes feelings of happiness and longing and remorse, and it links each of these emotions to another on the list, producing a sort of associational cascade. The appeal of the story lies partly in the bittersweet experience of going down this falls: sweet is the thought of purity and perfection, bitter is the regret at having brought forth the banishment; sweet is the knowledge that the garden grows even in our absence, bitter is the taste of homesickness; but, still, sweet is the thought of purity and perfection, and so on.

Euro-Americans tell and retell this story in a variety of contexts. Haraway discerns its presence, for example, in documentaries about African primates. These films often depict women scientists hugging or romping with apes in the wild. Through video technology and mystical womanhood, we are able to glimpse nature-without-human-toil (the jungle is not a garden, but at least there is no agriculture) and touch hands with humanoid creatures as innocent as Adam-before-the-Fall. In the background of these shots are the natives, agents of recent independence movements. Their presence is vaguely disturbing—will they once again restrict our access, turning the wild into a commercial or agricultural resource? Joy at reunion gives way to a familiar longing and then to remorse for our geopolitical miscalculations and their ecological shortsightedness.[6]

Many narratives are described in *Primate Visions* as "origin stories," although the reasons given for this designation vary. It seems, however, that what makes an "origin story" is the presence of an interlocking network of assumptions about the human condition. "Origin stories" develop not only according to the logic of a cascade of emotions (happiness/longing/ remorse), but also according to a linked set of ontological claims. I would like now to delineate this second cascade.

Origin tales begin with what one might term the Original Happiness Assumption: the authentic state of being is free from conflict and contradiction even though its sheer diversity pleasures the eye and delights the imagination. This leads to the Pitiful Creature Assumption: because we are exiled from this variegated yet harmonious land, homesickness is our fate, and human being is best characterized by the terms *degeneration, sinfulness, failure, alienation*. Linked to these assumptions is another, the positing of a Prediscursive Source: although we are barred from experiencing it, Nature endures independently, in tranquility and unity; Nature, lying beyond or behind our semiotic constructions, does not require a web of discourses to sustain it but is the "raw material" of culture.[7] Inside *that* view lies the Moral Source Assumption: the prediscursive source, because it is both original and structured in a way (at least partly) intelligible to humans, ought to be the blueprint for a social order; Nature provides a morally privileged complex of rankings, divisions, affinities, and antinomies. Alongside each of these assumptions—helping to prop them up—is, finally, the Assumption of the Loving Father. Men are agents of action. Adam speaks for Eve. God the father creates and presides for all eternity over the Garden.

Haraway's wariness of origin stories stems from her rejection of these assumptions, each dangerous because it anticipates, issues from, or is embedded within the others. To posit a prediscursive moral source, to view agency as essentially male, to lament paradise lost, and to assign oneself the status of exile is to depoliticize the responsibility humans currently bear for the precarious state of earthly affairs and to downplay the presence of power in practices of gender, health, science, philosophy.[8] It is to restrict the scope of politicoethical vision to the cultural "uses" to which

Nature is put. Haraway approvingly quotes Susan Leigh Star: "What we must begin to give voice to as scientists and feminists is that there is no such thing, or place, as underneath it all. Literally, empirically, physiologically, anatomically, neurologically." [9]

Haraway's alter-tale must somehow "give voice" to this skepticism. The poetics of this task is yet to be considered, but surely it will be alert to the *fungibility* of "something underneath it all." Even those like Foucault whose careers were devoted to excising this ground have been found to rely upon it.[10] Perhaps less surprising is its pervasive place in contemporary American environmentalist discourse (which has included post-Nietzschean voices only recently).[11] I turn briefly to this discourse in order to address its relationship to the alter-tale.

## Holists, Technocrats, and Cyborgs

Environmental discourse of the last thirty years might be characterized as a debate between holistic and technocratic positions. The presence of foundational claims in the first camp, which includes forms of ecofeminism,[12] is overt and unapologetic. High technology, and the quest to master and humanize the earth, is rejected in favor of small-scale tools and agricultural, medicinal, social, and spiritual practices attuned to the murmur of being or respectful of earth conceived as mother.[13]

The second approach repudiates holist faith in nature, speaking instead of environmental management, land-use strategies, and resource maximization.[14] But its focus on reason, science, and technology reproduces another version of the Prediscursive Source Assumption:[15] ecotechnical models of geological change, rational-economic choice, and resource-stress capacities make most sense in the presence of an independently structured Nature existing prior to science. On the computer screen, as on the organic farm, the environmentalist seeks a glimpse of the "primitive and original heart of the world."[16] Technocrats, those "patriarchal, monotheistic children of the father-God [who] learned to read the Book of Nature written in the ciphers of numbers in the founding times of the Scientific Revolution," transform "salvation history into natural history" and then construct biology, anthropology, economics, and policy analysis on its stage.[17] Thus speaks Haraway.

Traces of the Garden of Eden can also be found in the environmental managers' responses to radical ecological proposals. Their angry refusal to rethink consumption and production priorities and to consider structural changes in late corporate capitalism may disclose resentment against exile—a resentment that, if made explicit, might go something like this: Nature has (chosen to) shut us out, why should we change to suit it?[18]

In Haraway's alter-tale, the term *nature* rarely makes an appearance. She prefers "to translate . . . 'facticity' and 'the organic' into a cumbersome entity called a 'material-semiotic actor.' " [19] This translation presents a picture of the physical world as always already implicated in human projections of meaning. Her alter-tale tells not of a man standing as namer of animals and then falling into toil and the need to create machines, but of cyborgs and of the permeability of boundaries between human/animal/machine. The cyborg reworks/is a reworking of nature and culture in such a way that "the one can no longer be the resource for appropriation or incorporation by the other." [20]

Cyborgs are contemporary selves bored by the current environmentalist debate, tired of the same old story. They are sympathetic to the holist protest against the technocratic orientation to the world: they too refuse to translate the world into a "problem of coding"; they too reject the quest for "a common language in which all resistance to instrumental control disappears and all heterogeneity can be submitted to disassembly, reassembly, investment, and exchange." [21] But cyborgs can never be accused of technophobia: "Taking responsibility for the social relations of science and technology means refusing an anti-science metaphysics, a demonology of technology." [22] Cyborgs are thus also skeptical of holists, in particular of their assumption of harmony. The earth surely contains a profusion of forms, species, personalities, and propensities, but why think that this diversity was once (or will ever be) a coherent whole, without productive tensions or fruitful contradictions? As antiessentialist feminists, cyborgs also steer clear of conceptualizations of earth as primordial mother.

Neither mother earth nor natural resources have a part in the alter-tale, only a "coyote," another material-semiotic actor: "Perhaps the world resists being reduced to mere resource because it is—not mother/matter/mutter—but coyote, a figure of the always problematic, always potent tie between meaning and bodies." [23] Coyote is a transfiguration of "nature," but it is not simply a figure of speech. Haraway rejects the "radical 'reduction' " of nature to "a blank page for social inscription," to "the ephemera of discursive production and social construction." [24] She describes the coyote as a "witty agent" in order to make the point that even socially constructed entities confound human attempts to render them productive and interfere with human attempts to discover meaning within them. The coyote (like our fallen nature in the Edenic tale) surprises and resists. It refuses to be tamed, and thus reveals the limits of both the literary and the technological imagination.

The coyote embodies what Henry Thoreau called "wildness." [25] Wildness is the unexplored potential—of the outdoors or the self—always left over from even the most reflective or relentless exploration. It is the remainder or excess that always escapes Thoreau's taxonomies of flora and fauna or inventories of his character or conscience; it is the difference of the woods that remains no matter how many times he walks them, the distance never bridged between two friends, no matter how familiar and intimate. The wildness of anything consists in its ability, on the one hand, to inspire fresh experience, startling metaphors, and unheralded associations, and, on the other hand, to challenge familiar experience, beautiful metaphors, and associational cascades.

But in Haraway's alter-tale it is not only the coyote that is wild: each cyborg-self is too, for to be (with) cyborg is to come into contact with a dynamic compound of forces and to experience an irreducible element of opacity that can, like Nature in origin tales, stimulate curiosity and creative speculations as well as frighten and harm. Other high-tech devices, which break from their roots in human intentions themselves not transparent, also have this ability to awe, challenge, thwart, provoke. With computers and things such as E-mail, for example, we are rethinking what counts as freedom, autonomy, authority, and community. Wildness—that which inspires *and* frustrates, a power assigned by Thoreau primarily to the woods—is in Haraway's alter-tale located in a variety of new sites.

The coyote, like the cyborg, is a real construction drawn from a finite range of imaginative materials, materials provided in part *by* the Edenic tale. As with P. T. Barnum's mermaid, if one examines the cyborg and the coyote critically, one finds them to be made of ordinary and familiar parts. But, also like Barnum's hoaxes, exposure to Haraway's dares the audience to rethink the relation between nature and culture:

> Hoax was a popular nineteenth-century form of entertainment that tested the intelligence of the audience; it was less a form of deception than a form of interrogation and an invitation to find the flaw in an apparent natural truth. Hoax assumed greater confidence in the active intelligence of the audience than did the more reverent television nature special. . . . the practice of hoax . . . resists the closures of those hegemonic discourses on nature in which each being finds its ordained place. [26]

## Techniques of the Cyborg-Self

The cyborg is presented by Haraway as one among many possible ways to pronounce a self. And like other definitions of self, it is experienced both as cultural imposition and as one's own. It is easy enough to see the cyborg as an effect of domination, as the ultimate realization of militarist/capitalist projects of dehumanization, objectification, utility-maximization. But cyborgs, by making "imaginative apprehension" of their condition, see in it also an opportunity to subvert these projects.[27] As a hybridized species, cyborgs have an enlarged repertoire of powers: the ethical concern of sentient beings, the stubborn stamina of genetic material, the momentum and inertia of machines, the survival instinct of animate creatures, the reflexivity of intelligent beings. These forces can be harnessed, temporarily and uneasily, to a feminist environmentalism of cautious play with the coyote, of respectful acknowledgment of wildness in the self and in the landscape.

Cyborg might be, then, an identity one actively seeks to foster. Techniques for doing so include exposing and excising the influence of the Edenic tale upon political and ethical thinking, and developing an eye for sites of categorical and boundary breakdown (e.g., biotic body-parts, signing chimps, artificial intelligence). This overt consciousness of "complex hybridization with other communication devices" allows cyborghood to be experienced lightly.[28] Cyborgs, unafraid of their "joint kinship with animals and machines ... and of permanently partial identities and contradictory standpoints," are less individuals than coalitional creatures.[29]

Cyborgs also cultivate a distinctive attitude toward marginality. According to Edenic geography, all inhabitable land is, alas, peripheral, for at the center lies the forbidden Garden. All roads in the land of exile lead toward the center, though they end abruptly before it. In contrast, on the map of the alter-tale, every locale appears as simultaneously center and margin—center from the perspective of some set of indignations, priorities, and concerns, marginal from those of others. Cyborgs appreciate the multivision this offers them; they playfully and sometimes painfully switch perspectives. They move, for example, from the Edenic tale, whose ideal of self (as not-animal, not-object, not-multiple) makes cyborgs into monsters, to their own tale, where cyborgs appear as the only selves in touch with the technoreality of the late twentieth century.[30] In both stories, cyborgs are powerful creatures.

Cyborgs are edified by the Edenic tale; they draw upon it in order to alter it, but they also affirm the marginal status assigned to them in the original version. Marginality is for them a political opportunity; it puts the cyborg in a critical position, a position to recognize and expose the exclusions and reductions inherent in any given story.[31] From the margins of the origin story, for example, cyborgs can display themselves as soft evidence of the nonuniversality and nonintegrity of the hard categories "man," "woman," "nature," "culture," "Western identity." Cyborg politics compromise distinctions presented as natural in favor of those requiring explicit political defense and periodic relegitimation or rejection. Haraway's dream is that alertness to the myriad ways in which we make, unmake, and remake "nature" and "human nature" will foster a greater sense of responsibility toward it.

## Identification

Cyborg techniques of self function as reminders of the relational and contingent character of any gendered or national identity and of the need to destabilize fundamental, organic, or pure ideals and practices.[32] Haraway's texts do just this: the interpretations offered in *Primate Visions*, for example, consistently disturb settled understandings about human (i.e., nonanimal) identity, about woman, about science, about nature. But this disruptive skepticism coexists in the text with another voice, one deeply committed to a set of political claims. These affirmations are repeated as a kind of litany, a cyborg profession of faith, if you will, and it goes something like this: to idealize perfection and unity is to suppress anomaly and multiplicity; to define beauty as harmony is to elevate fear of difference into an aesthetic imperative; to dream of an original order is to depoliticize the current one; to be homesick for the Father's land is to be tempted to assign the status of Truth to the ways of one's own.

Haraway explicitly acknowledges the need for stabilizing practices such as this litany; the boundary-blasting cyborg, she says, must nevertheless carefully *preserve* the "permanent and fruitful" tension between problematization and identification.[33] The sculptor Marisol seems to me to have accomplished what Haraway has in mind. In her "Heads of State" series, Marisol reimagines Charles de Gaulle: a large, rectangular box-body, with a painted-on but impressive uniform; atop it, an official-looking bust of de Gaulle carved in wood; beneath it, supporting its full weight, a delicate carriage; next to his head, like a bird alighted on his shoulder, a small hand in a ta-ta gesture. The piece, with its combination of the grand and the ridiculous, functions to destabilize the authority of de Gaulle. Museum curators note, however, that de Gaulle's hand is cast from Marisol's own. Her relation to de Gaulle might be characterized, then, as ambivalent attachment: she was born in France (de Gaulle has a hand in her) but she is an artist of the *1960s* (she puts a hand on de Gaulle). The cyborg's relations to itself and to others ought to be like Marisol's relation to de Gaulle, one that negotiates the "paradoxical relation" of identification and destabilization.[34]

But why Haraway's interest in "identification"? Why, in other words, is destabilization of established identities and nature-tales insufficient for the cyborg project?[35] This is not a question that Haraway addresses directly; she does hint that destabilization alone cannot sustain a cyborg politics: "Destabilization is a collective undertaking," she says, implying that even a subversive politics requires coalitions, compromises, allegiances.[36] These will be shifting and uneasy, but insofar as they exist they imply some kind of affective link among cyborgs.

But what makes these links "identification"? Again, Haraway does not say, but is it not, at least in part, their ability to induce momentary amnesia? Don't cyborgs, through political identification with others, necessarily *forget while acting* that they are artificialities not grounded in any prediscursive source? This moment of forgetting is something "destabilization" cannot achieve, for destabilization is suspended in it.

If "identification" is integral to cyborg politics in the way I have suggested, it is also required, I contend, for the cyborg tale to succeed as a *tale*. If the story of coyote, cyborg, and political engagement is to compete with the older tale of snake, apple, and Adam and Eve, it must do more than question identities and blur boundaries, it must also affirm values that in some way resonate with the hearer; it must evoke sentiments, dreams, and convictions that are in some way familiar; it must somehow inspire.

*Primate Visions* tells a story on behalf of a particular ontological-ethical-political vision: cyborgs wish to speak a word for "heterogeneous earthly survival." For this message to be heard, "identification" must take place not only between cyborg and cyborg in the public realm, but also between reader and text. And again, for this to happen, the rhetoric of the alter-tale must allow readers to lose themselves in the story, to get carried away in it, at least temporarily.

Let's take a closer look, then, at the mechanism of cyborg identification. In her discussion of the relationship between feminism and cyborgs, Haraway says that cyborgs are to "identify" with the patterns in the lives of females, but not in a way that appeals to a prediscursive source—not, that is, by saying, "As a woman, I identify with the woman in other women and therefore claim privileged access to certain kinds of knowledge." [37] Cyborgs must "identify" in a way that "takes responsibility" for defending the chosen objects of identification:

> I ... try to show how woman/female get constructed and sustained
> in discourse, including science and politics. My unpacking of
> semiotic and other practices necessary to construct these objects
> aims to destabilize ... any moves I or you might make to claim
> authority based on "natural" identification. In my sense,
> deconstruction does not forbid identification; rather, *it displays
> what kind of move it is and forces responsibility for making it.*[38]

But I wonder about this explicitly self-responsible mode of "identification" [39]—can it induce narrative forgetfulness and political bonding? Or does an "identification" that *continually* defends itself become another, different cyborg practice, one that Haraway calls "foregrounding"? A favorite metaphor in *Primate Visions*, to foreground is to focus on an object while cognizant of the fact that it is not really a singular, meaningful entity, but a fragment elevated to the status of object by a willed, temporary, and highly contingent act of human perception or projection, which is *understood as such*. Self-forgetting is unlikely here.

I am more convinced than Haraway that tales persuade and inspire partly by inducing forgetfulness; that while the length and intensity of suspension varies from reader to reader, if suspension is not achieved, the imagination will be unable to rouse the will to *act* upon the vision endorsed. The alter-tale has a tough row to hoe: in order to see cyborgs and coyotes instead of man and nature you have to suspend ordinary understandings of inner and outer worlds; in order to criticize those understandings you need to be highly self-conscious about them.

Haraway herself addresses this as the "paradox" of identification/destabilization, but I think her poetics makes her response less successful than it might be. The dominant rhetorical effect of Haraway's alter-tale is to do to origin stories what they fail to do themselves—challenge their assumptions, expose their participation in oppressions, reveal their contestable status. Cyborgs must be critical practices "for recognizing our own 'semiotic technologies' for making meanings." [40] Haraway treats her own story in the same way: she constantly reminds readers that "cyborg" and "coyote" are strategic constructions, that she presents "an argument for the cyborg *as a fiction* mapping our social and bodily reality and *as an imaginative resource* suggesting some very fruitful couplings." [41] But an alter-tale needs to be more wary, I think, of metatheory; "identification" requires a rhetorical sleight of hand.

## Rhetoric and Political Ethics

I would like to conclude by considering the role of forgetting in ethical and political life, and even defending a kind of nostalgia for foundations that Haraway works so hard to expunge from herself and her readers. Can there be a mode of identification that eschews *both* the essentialism of Genesis and the relentless "foregrounding" of the alter-tale? Is there a rhetoric that acknowledges the constructed character of affirmative ideals without making *that* the issue?

Cyborgs might learn something here from the poetics of another mythmaker, Henry Thoreau. As I read him, Thoreau is not the bearer of a naive faith in "Nature," but pronounces the world as Nature because not all his experiences contradict this image and because such an artifice supports the identity he seeks to sustain.[42] A mountain in Maine, some wetlands in Massachusetts, some rabbits at Walden, become, via Thoreau, "Ktaadn," "the Swamp," "Winter Animals." Thoreau is cognizant of this process, but he acknowledges that "Nature" is a work of art in a way that seeks also to foster reader "identification" with it. Consider the following section from "Walking":

> I wish to speak a word for Nature, for absolute freedom and wildness, as contrasted with a freedom and culture merely civil,—to regard man as an inhabitant, or a part and parcel of nature, rather than a member of society. I wish to make an extreme statement, if so I may make an emphatic one.[43]

At one, important level, Thoreau asserts a radical alterity between free, wild Nature and enslaved, social "man." But read with an emphasis on the first phrase—"I wish to speak a word for Nature"—the passage also takes on another sense:

"I Thoreau wish to *speak a word for* 'Nature': Here is *my* case for thinking of the world as wild and other, as Nature, Source of Non-Conformist Energies. I would like to speak of a prediscursive source, and so I shall."

"I wish to speak a *word* for Nature: I will substitute words for that which is not reducible to an act of linguistic constitution. I shall translate the world as 'freedom' and 'wildness' while acknowledging it to be my translation. In writing Nature I generate an image that can never get to a thing-in-itself or even assert what it would be like to do so. I note my participation in my tale but I refuse to engage further or more explicitly in debates about epistemology or ontology."

Thoreau's linguistic contribution to "Nature" and to the resistance it faces ("wildness") is not "foregrounded." Instead, it is slipped into the background of a tale of nonconformity, individuality, civil disobedience. He experiences the very act of writing as an erasure of the boundary between nature and culture that he nonetheless finds quite useful to posit. The notion of an independent Nature is useful to him insofar as it denotes the wild, the inexplicable or alien dimensions of earthly life. Thoreau seeks to spot and then accentuate these dimensions, for they provide an antidote to what is for him the greatest danger: submersion in the world of the "they." A self-conscious act of writing foregrounds *for Thoreau* the artificiality of the border lines he draws, but he does not wish his readers to have quite the same level of awareness, for he seeks to foster reader "identification" even as he destabilizes conventional views and herd impulses.

Thoreau does not advertise the fact that Nature is always something of a work of art; at best, he acknowledges it. And much of the time he distracts the reader from explicit focus on the status of his words. If his detailed naturalist accounts are to do the work of jarring one out of the they-world, one must, for a while, in some way give oneself over to them, free from explicit consciousness of his and one's own interpretive effect upon them. One of Thoreau's best moments at Walden was, he said, when "at length one [chickadee] alighted on an armful of wood I was carrying [and] the squirrels . . . occasionally stepped on my shoe, when that was the nearest way." [44] At *that* moment, Thoreau had become "part and parcel of Nature." He had succeeded in worming his way into a partnership with Nature—a fanciful relationship with real, albeit temporary, effects. Thoreau snuck his body, camouflaged as a perch for birds and a twig in the path of squirrels, into Walden pond. He insinuated himself into Nature so subtly, so quietly, that, for a moment, he didn't notice a human presence there. He tries to translate the reader into that moment too; he strives for the same gentle and surreptitious slipping in of self when he writes. Thoreau's words must not only allow the world to make itself present as Nature, it must do so in a way that makes it possible to forget his contribution to this process. Thoreau practices a delicate and deliberate art of forgetting.

There are good reasons for cyborgs to be wary of Thoreau's rhetorical strategy of indirection, for his poetics could fail to preserve the fragile tension between identification and destabilization by failing to *retrieve* the self sunk in myth. (Haraway and I agree that most of the time in contemporary politics, the problem is too much forgetting.) Moreover, Thoreau's tale expresses nostalgia for a time when Nature was an article of faith, a transcendental ground. And nostalgia is often a sign of reluctance to "take responsibility" for one's identifications. Nostalgia is also treacherous: to consort with a prediscursive source is to risk falling into the origin story cascade.

But perhaps the elements of that cascade can be disaggregated; if, in particular, it is possible to speak of a source of wildness without attributing authenticity or moral certainty or prediscursivity or fathership to it,[45] then Thoreau's nostalgia is worth pondering. For the idea of a "source" whose status is at times forgotten fosters wonder that cyborgs might cultivate and draw upon; nostalgia for foundations has an ethical or transformative energy that could be put to cyborg use.[46] While forgetfulness (as the relaxation of self-consciousness) poses political dangers, it seems also that aesthetic power cannot be divorced completely from it. And if forgetfulness is unavoidable for certain stretches of time, then a cyborg politics of affirmation probably should find something positive in it. In other words, nostalgia is more complex and ambiguous than Haraway may credit.

Nostalgia for foundations is a longing for something solid, fixed, final and true, morally certain, and fatherly. As such, it leads to patriarchal laws, imperialistic claims, religious or scientific dogmatisms, or normalizing constructions presented as inevitabilities. But nostalgia for foundations can also become a kind of will to wildness, an ache for that which is extra-ordinary, different, perhaps improved. As a contrast model, it is one of the ways Euro-Americans create conceptual space for ways of life not yet in social and political place. It is a source of ethical energy and political imagination in that the experiences nostalgia makes possible can overshadow the very motives that inspire them.

Genesis, for example, tells of a harmonious place guaranteed by a creator, but it also speaks of a counterworld where diversity is not considered a threat but a provocation of wonder. It is this dimension of nostalgic tales that cyborgs might turn into a joyful attachment to heterogeneous earthly survival, into care for material-semiotic actors who always exceed expectations, institutions, theories, and stories. Nietzsche complains, in *Twilight of the Idols*, that Christianity seeks to "extirpate," to "exterminate" irrational desires, when the thing to do is "spiritualize, beautify, deify" them.[47] Cyborgs might "beautify" the longing for the Garden.

However, the contestable status of the tale that evokes this (ambivalent) attachment probably cannot itself be one's constant focus. One can also be critical of one's appeal to a wild "source" gently, ambiguously, indirectly. Haraway's cyborgs wield critical swords against the Edenic tale to remove its undue influence—that is, to cut out that portion of the story's power deriving from its claim to extrahuman authorship or inspiration. Whatever influence their alter-tale might have will, on the other hand, be *earned*, for *it* is up front about *its* origin. The crux of my argument with Haraway, however, is that because she "is not innocent of the intent to have effects, . . . to shift reading and writing practices,"[48] the demystifying sword must occasionally be dropped, lest she extirpate what one might call, following Foucault, the "productive power" of the cyborg myth.

A tale that valorizes the role of self-forgetting in (political-ethical) identifications courts the danger that we will be seduced too well, losing sight of ourselves long enough to slide into sentimentalism or dogmatism or unambiguous foundationalism. But the zeal to expose false harmonies and to denaturalize identifications also entails a risk—the risk of becoming prosaic, of forfeiting politically indispensable identifications and the ethical imagination inspired by wonder. Haraway's cyborg tale provides a superb countermyth through which to engage prevailing interpretations. If it needs adjustment, it is, I think, in the balances it achieves between forgetfulness and the problematization of itself.

## Notes

1. Donna Haraway, *Primate Visions* (New York: Routledge, 1989), 372, 371.

2. Donna Haraway, "A Manifesto for Cyborgs: Science, Technology, and Socialist Feminism in the 1980s," *Socialist Review* 15, no. 2 (1985): 64–107. The definition of *cyborg* in *Webster's Ninth New Collegiate Dictionary* reads this way: "[*cyber*netic + *org*anism] (ca. 1962): a human being who is linked (as for temporary adaptation to a hostile space environment) to one or more mechanical devices upon which some of his vital physiological functions depend."

3. Haraway chooses in *Primate Visions* to focus attention more upon the primatological

voice(s) than upon the alter-tale. I've come to think of *Primate Visions* as a maze with long, smooth corridors and also cul-de-sacs; sometimes I ran straight ahead, sometimes I had to double back. But there was a free space in the center, and there stood the cyborg, Haraway's wonderful imaging of a self ambivalently attached to modernist discourses of woman, nature, science.

4. Donna J. Haraway, "In the Beginning Was the Word: The Genesis of Biological Theory," *Signs* 6 (1981): 469–81, notes George Wald's immodest insistence that "a scientist should not just study nature but should take care of humanity, life, and our planet" (p. 475). The care that I am claiming is part of the passion of *Primate Visions* is *not* Wald's care, which is infused with a (deliberate) innocence about power. Care and difference do coexist uneasily, but part of care, as I use the term, is recognition of the resilience of the tension, good management of it, and the will to maintain it alive.

5. Haraway, *Primate Visions*, 372, 366.

6. See Haraway, *Primate Visions*, chap. 7. Sociobiology is another site for the origin story. It "promises more than knowledge of the self; it also promises, like all humanisms, human unity, a real togetherness of nature beneath the merely verbal icing of culture. The lonely hero, the true child, will take us back to the garden of ourselves." Haraway, "In the Beginning," 473.

7. Haraway, *Primate Visions*, 280.

8. To be sure, the origin story assigns plenty of *moral* responsibility, but because the human condition is essentially failure, moral responsibility does not carry with it much incentive for political change.

9. Haraway, "In the Beginning," 476.

10. Judith Butler, for example, discerns in the logic of Foucault's genealogy a use of "the body" as a prediscursive site for cultural inscription. See "Foucault and the Paradox of Bodily Inscriptions," *Journal of Philosophy* 86 (November 1989): 601–7. I will argue that the alter-tale too cannot proceed as a tale without some notion of a "source" for its political-ethical vision. Everything depends, then, on how one presents this "source," on what status is assigned to it, and how that status is revealed rhetorically.

11. The essays in this volume are examples of this new voice.

12. For an excellent discussion of this perspective, see Kathy Ferguson, "Cosmic Feminism," in *The Man Question in Feminist Theory: Reversal and Its Discontents* (Berkeley: University of California Press, 1993).

13. See, for example, John Compton, "Re-inventing a Philosophy of Nature," *Review of Metaphysics* 33 (September 1979); Erazim Kohak, *The Embers and the Stars* (Chicago: University of Chicago Press, 1984); E. F. Schumacher, *Small Is Beautiful* (New York: Harper & Row, 1975).

14. Examples here include publications by the Brookings Institution and much of the environmentalist work done by economists and political scientists.

15. I have developed this argument in Jane Bennett, *Unthinking Faith and Enlightenment* (New York: New York University Press, 1987), chap. 2.

16. Haraway, *Primate Visions*, 264.

17. Ibid., 288.

18. I read this resentment as an attribution of *agency* to Nature.

19. Donna Haraway, "Situated Knowledges: The Science Question in Feminism and the Privilege of Partial Perspective," *Feminist Studies* 14 (1988): 595.

20. Haraway, "A Manifesto for Cyborgs," 67.

21. Ibid., 83. For another critique of the enframing orientation to the world, see Martin Heidegger, *The Question Concerning Technology*, trans. William Lovitt (New York: Harper, 1977), and the Sikorski essay in this volume.

22. Haraway, "A Manifesto for Cyborgs," 100. The recurrent emphasis in Haraway's writings on *responsibility* even in the absence of full *agency* (cyborgs are both victims and authors of high-tech selves) reveals a link between the alter- and the Edenic tale. I have addressed the issue of invocations of responsibility under nonideal conditions of agency in "Deceptive Comfort: The Power of Kafka's Stories," *Political Theory* (February 1991). How the notion of responsibility might be recast in a cyborg world is, I think, a question worth pursuing.

23. Haraway, "Situated Knowledges," 596.

24. Ibid., 591–92.

25. "Wildness" versus "domesticity" is the central contrast animating Thoreau's negotiation of the traffic between nature and culture. The wild in the woods and in the self constitutes much of the meaning of Thoreau's term "Nature." One might note that *coyote* is also a term for men who bring Mexicans across the border illegally. These coyotes surprise and perplex, often with violence and betrayal. Coyotelike figures also appear in the theophany of the Book of Job. That text, like the Southwest American Indian tales that Haraway invokes, makes the point that experience always exceeds conceptualization. Job's god, the voice of the whirlwind, is one representation of this excess; coyote and "the wild" are others. See William Connolly's "Voices from the Whirlwind," in this volume.

26. Haraway, *Primate Visions*, 279.

27. Haraway, "A Manifesto for Cyborgs," 66.

28. Ibid., 77.

29. Ibid., 72.

30. The Edenic tale is itself not as straightforward as an alter-tale tends to make it out to be. Even Adam and Eve did not quite live up to the ideal self described in Genesis. They were an impossible mixture of simplicity and agency, actors without the knowledge of good and evil that makes action possible. As simple agents, they were not quite *not*-animal, not quite unitary beings in harmony with themselves.

31. However, marginalization does not give the alter-tale a privileged moral or truth status—tellers of other tales have no such status by virtue of *their* exclusion from the cyborg story. Cyborgs may live in the margin at times, but they are never in "exile." Cyborgs are strong, resourceful, flexible, multiple, and have a real impact on their fate—they "refuse the ideological resources of victimization so as to have a real life." Haraway, "A Manifesto for Cyborgs," 96.

32. Jeanne Altmann, one of the primatologists described by Haraway in *Primate Visions*, issues such a reminder when she destabilizes the primatological categories of "female" and "rape" (p. 310). Altmann forbade herself as well the "resting place in a unitary female body grounding 'woman's' experience as nature grounds culture." She preferred to describe herself as a "strategic site," a "process" akin to "juggling—keeping several realities in precariously patterned motion and building strength to see the world that way" (p. 311).

33. Ibid., 342.

34. Ibid. Haraway first introduces the dynamic of destabilization and identification in her discussion of hoax. "Females," she says, "are not unlike . . . [the] mermaid composed of . . . a mummified monkey stitched to the tail of a large fish. Our problem will be to find the evidence of stitchery without ripping out the patterns in the lives of females" (p. 280). Expose the stitchery but don't rip out the pattern, a pattern that can be recycled, reused—retold and revised to create "new possibilities for the meanings of difference, reproduction, and survival for specifically located members of the primate order" (p. 377). The patterns formed by the origin story are worth salvaging also because the identities of even the postmodern feminist are woven into them. They play a role in even "permanently partial identities." I am grateful to Constance Bennett for introducing me to Marisol's work.

35. Haraway calls the tension between it and destabilization "necessary," and I take that to

mean that both processes are also necessary to (or at least important dimensions of) cyborg-selves.

36. Haraway, *Primate Visions*, 303.

37. Ibid., 417n.

38. Ibid., 417–18n.

39. This mode of identification is exemplified, for example, by Altmann, whose "deconstruction of identifications among women and between women and females in science . . . could be seen as a complex *kind* of identification." Ibid., 313.

40. Haraway, "Situated Knowledges," 579.

41. Haraway, "A Manifesto for Cyborgs," 66; emphasis added.

42. My reading of Thoreau has many similarities to the reading of Frazer in Marilyn Strathern, "Out of Context: The Persuasive Fictions of Anthropology," *Current Anthropology* 28 (June 1987): 251–70.

43. Henry David Thoreau, "Walking," in *The Natural History Essays* (New York: Peregrine Smith, 1980), 92.

44. Henry David Thoreau, *Walden* (New York: W. W. Norton, 1966), 182–83.

45. I am less confident of Thoreau's success in distancing his Nature from this last theme than I am about the others. But his failure would not imply that fathership must be part of a tale that distills ethical imagination out of nostalgia for foundations.

46. Haraway is appreciative of origin stories; *Primate Visions* does not seek to "prohibit" them and she is "edified" by them (p. 377). I don't think that her appreciation has to do with the transformative power of their rhetoric, however. Origin stories are interesting to her because they are a kind of raw material for new stories, for "new possibilities for the meanings of difference, reproduction, and survival" (p. 377).

47. Friedrich Nietzsche, *Twilight of the Idols* (New York: Penguin, 1968), 42.

48. Haraway, *Primate Visions*, 377.

# Contributors

**Jane Bennett** is associate professor of politics at Goucher College. Her works include *Unthinking Faith and Enlightenment* (New York University Press, 1987) and articles that explore the relationship between literary and theoretical portrayals of contemporary political issues. She is currently working on a book on Kafka.

**R. McGreggor Cawley** teaches environmental politics and public administration at the University of Wyoming. His research and publications focus on federal land policy. He is currently finishing a book on the Sagebrush Rebellion.

**William Chaloupka** teaches American politics and political theory at the University of Montana. He has written *Knowing Nukes: The Politics and Culture of the Atom* (University of Minnesota Press, 1992) and, with William Stearns, coedited *Jean Baudrillard: The Disappearance of Art and Politics*. He is currently working on a study of cynicism in American political culture.

**Romand Coles** is the author of *Self/Power/Other: Political Theory and Dialogical Ethics* (Cornell University Press, 1992), as well as numerous articles. He is currently writing a book on ethics of differential generosity that engages Kant, Hegel, Marx, Nietzsche, Habermas, and Adorno. On a less philosophical plane, he is working on issues of political economy and democratic theory as they relate to ecological problems.

**William E. Connolly** is professor of political science at The Johns Hopkins University, where he teaches political theory. He is the editor of *Contestations: Cornell Studies in Political Theory*. His two most recent works are *Political Theory and Modernity* (Basil Blackwell, 1988) and *Identity/Difference: Democratic Negotiations of Political Paradox* (Cornell University Press, 1991).

**Jan E. Dizard** teaches sociology and American studies at Amherst College, where he is Charles Hamilton Houston Professor of American Culture. His most recent book (written with Howard Gadlin) is *The Minimal Family* (University of Massachusetts Press, 1990). The issues he explores in "Going Wild" will be amplified and extended in a book by the same title to be published by the University of Massachusetts Press in 1993.

**Valerie Hartouni** is assistant professor of communication at the University of California, San Diego. She is currently completing a collection of essays that considers as a problem of discourse and culture the controversies surrounding the development and use of the new technologies of human genetics and reproduction.

**Bruce H. Jennings** is associate professor of environmental studies at the University of Montana at Missoula and the author of *Foundations of International Agricultural Research: Science and Politics in Mexican Agriculture* (Westview, 1988). He has taught international environmental policy and environmental legislation with the California State University at Sacramento and the U.C. Berkeley's conservation and resource studies program.

**Cheri Lucas Jennings** has been a professor of natural resource policy, women's and multicultural studies, and American politics at the University of Hawaii, Kauai College, and the California State University at Sacramento. She is currently a visiting professor of political theory and ethics at the University of Montana at Missoula. Among her recent works is *You Can't Get There from Here: Chicana Mobility in the Central Valley* (Sage Publications, 1993).

**Timothy W. Luke** is professor of political science at Virginia Polytechnic Institute and State University in Blacksburg, Virginia. His research focuses on the areas of political and social theory, international political economy, and comparative political systems.

**Shane Phelan** is assistant professor of political science at the University of New Mexico. She is the author of *Identity Politics: Lesbian Feminism and the Limits of Community* (Temple University Press, 1989) and of several articles on feminist theory and lesbian politics. Her second book, tentatively titled *Getting Specific*, is forthcoming from the University of Minnesota Press.

**John Rodman** is professor of political studies and environmental studies and director of the arboretum at Pitzer College, Claremont, California, as well as a member of the Exotic Pest Plant Council. His writings include "The Liberation of Nature?" (*Inquiry*, Spring 1977), "Four Forms of Ecological Consciousness Reconsidered," in *Ethics and the Environment*, ed. Thomas Attig and Donald Scherer (Prentice-Hall, 1983), and "Reflections on Tamarisk-Bashing," in *Restoration '89: The New Management Challenge* (Society for Ecological Restoration, Madison, Wisconsin, 1990).

**Michael J. Shapiro** is professor of political science at the University of Hawaii. Among his recent publications are *Reading the Postmodern Polity: Political Theory as Textual Practice* (University of Minnesota Press, 1992) and

*Reading "Adam Smith": Desire, History, and Value* (Sage Publications, 1993).

**Wade Sikorski** is the author of *Modernity and Technology: Harnessing the Earth to the Slavery of Man* (University of Alabama Press, 1993). He is writing a book on health, "dis-ease," and politics and is also active in a community movement to stop construction of a hazardous waste incinerator.

# INDEX

Abbey, Edward, 14-18
Abram, David, 229
absence, 101, 242
Adam and Eve, 258
Adorno, Theodor, 228-47; on
    encroachment, 234; on language, 229-
    32, 235-38; theory of judgment, 237
agency, 52, 264 n. 22 and 30
agonism, 228, 233-39, 242
agriculture, 26, 30, 173-78, 181-84, 187-92;
    organic, 178, 181
Alar (daminozide), 178
Alexina (Herculine Barbin), 198, 209-22
alienation, 74
alterity, xii, 24, 242, 260
Altieri, Miguel, 181
Altmann, Jeanne, 264 n. 32, 265 n. 39
ambiguity, 24, 31, 39, 44, 48-52, 203
ambivalence, 48, 81, 202
anarchy, 29, 31, 39
androids, 68, 69
animality, 67-70
animals, viii, ix, xi, 47, 65-73, 80, 256, 257;
    animal-as-sign, 69; animal-human
    boundary, 66, 70-73, 74; animal nature,
    67; rights of, 119, 135 n. 12
animism, 45
anthropocentricism, 206, 245
anxiety, 201, 214
Aristotle, 58
artificial, the, xi, 100, 215
Audubon Society, 115, 118
Augustinianism, 208
Auschwitz, 240
author, the, 223 n. 2
authority, 5, 20, 24, 255
autonomy, 255

Baby M, 87, 89
Barbin, Herculine. *See* Alexina
Barnum, P. T., 255
Bataille, Georges, 69-71, 80

Baudrillard, Jean, 3, 4, 15, 16; objective
    irony, 15
Bayles, Michael, 100
being, 226, 228
Bennett, Jane, 22 n. 22
Bernauer, James W., 16, 21-22 n. 11
Berry, Wendell, 169
Bill of Rights, 106
Bird, Elizabeth Ann R., 21 n. 5
*Blade Runner*, 65, 73-83; heteroglot speech
    in, 78
Blake, Robert, 76, 81
Bloom, Allan, 60 n. 9 and 25
body, the, viii, 15, 86, 90, 213, 225 n. 9, 227,
    229, 264 n. 32
borders, 72, 74, 80, 243
Borlaug, Norman, 181
Buber, Martin, 228
Burroughs, Edgar Rice, 70, 71
bush lupine, 141, 142, 144
Butler, Judith, 223 n. 7, 225 n. 9, 263 n. 10;
    critique of Foucault, 223-24 n. 7

California Certified Organic Farmers, 178
capitalism, 154, 159, 165-70, 253
cartography, 8, 87
Chase, Alston, 134 n. 6
Chavez, Cesar 177, 193 n. 7
children, 87
choice, 101, 106
Christianity, 10, 49, 51-53, 245, 246
cinema, 8, 12
civil disobedience, 260
civilization, 14, 29, 45, 49, 52, 111, 112
coastal zone, 145
Columbus, Christopher, 6, 180
community, 197, 255
compassion, 47, 52
Connolly, William E., 43 n. 40, 48
consciousness, 48, 231
conservatism, 45, 46
Constitution, U.S., 105, 106
consumerism, 154-59, 162, 170